China, the West and the Myth of New Public Management

In the West, innovations in New Public Management (NPM) have been regarded as part of the neoliberal project, whereas, in China, these reforms have emerged from a very different economic and social landscape. Despite these differences, however, similar measures to those introduced in the West have been adopted by the Chinese state, which has largely abandoned the planned economy and adopted market mechanisms in the pursuit of improved economic efficiency and growth.

Evaluating the results of these reforms in both China and the West between 1978 and 2011, this book shows that despite substantial improvements in economic efficiency in both cases under consideration, there have been considerable negative impacts on the distribution of wealth, access to public services, levels of poverty and the incidence of crime. Further, this book explores the different results of NPM in China and the West and the conclusions Paolo Urio draws have timely significance, as he suggests that China has been able to change its policies more rapidly and thus more effectively respond to the challenges posed by the current economic crisis.

Drawing on both Western and Chinese sources, this innovative book compares the consequences of their public management reforms, taking into account the impact on both the economy and society. As such, this book will be of great interest to students and scholars working in the fields of Chinese studies, Asian studies, business, economics, strategic public management and comparative studies in capitalism and socialism.

Paolo Urio is Professor Emeritus at the Faculty of Economics and Social Sciences, University of Geneva, Switzerland. Professor Urio has undertaken research on China's reforms since 1997 and has published *Reconciling State, Market and Society in China* (Routledge, 2010) on the subject. Between 1998 and 2003 he organized and directed a programme that trained in public management more than 400 senior Chinese civil servants and senior Party cadres.

Routledge Contemporary China Series

1 Nationalism, Democracy and National Integration in China
Leong Liew and Wang Shaoguang

2 Hong Kong's Tortuous Democratization
A comparative analysis
Ming Sing

3 China's Business Reforms
Institutional challenges in a globalised economy
Edited by Russell Smyth, On Kit Tam, Malcolm Warner and Cherrie Zhu

4 Challenges for China's Development
An enterprise perspective
Edited by David H. Brown and Alasdair MacBean

5 New Crime in China
Public order and human rights
Ron Keith and Zhiqiu Lin

6 Non-governmental Organizations in Contemporary China
Paving the way to civil society?
Qiusha Ma

7 Globalization and the Chinese City
Fulong Wu

8 The Politics of China's Accession to the World Trade Organization
The dragon goes global
Hui Feng

9 Narrating China
Jia Pingwa and his fictional world
Yiyan Wang

10 Sex, Science and Morality in China
Joanne McMillan

11 Politics in China since 1949
Legitimizing authoritarian rule
Robert Weatherley

12 International Human Resource Management in Chinese Multinationals
Jie Shen and Vincent Edwards

13 Unemployment in China
Economy, human resources and labour markets
Edited by Grace Lee and Malcolm Warner

14 China and Africa
Engagement and compromise
Ian Taylor

15 Gender and Education in China
Gender discourses and women's schooling in the early twentieth century
Paul J. Bailey

16 SARS
Reception and interpretation in three Chinese cities
Edited by Deborah Davis and Helen Siu

17 Human Security and the Chinese State
Historical transformations and the modern quest for sovereignty
Robert E. Bedeski

18 Gender and Work in Urban China
Women workers of the unlucky generation
Liu Jieyu

19 China's State Enterprise Reform
From Marx to the market
John Hassard, Jackie Sheehan, Meixiang Zhou, Jane Terpstra-Tong and Jonathan Morris

20 Cultural Heritage Management in China
Preserving the cities of the Pearl River Delta
Edited by Hilary du Cros and Yok-shiu F. Lee

21 Paying for Progress
Public finance, human welfare and inequality in China
Edited by Vivienne Shue and Christine Wong

22 China's Foreign Trade Policy
The new constituencies
Edited by Ka Zeng

23 Hong Kong, China
Learning to belong to a nation
Gordon Mathews, Tai-lok Lui, and Eric Kit-wai Ma

24 China Turns to Multilateralism
Foreign policy and regional security
Edited by Guoguang Wu and Helen Lansdowne

25 Tourism and Tibetan Culture in Transition
A place called Shangrila
Åshild Kolås

26 China's Emerging Cities
The making of new urbanism
Edited by Fulong Wu

27 China–US Relations Transformed
Perceptions and strategic interactions
Edited by Suisheng Zhao

28 The Chinese Party-State in the 21st Century
Adaptation and the reinvention of legitimacy
Edited by André Laliberté and Marc Lanteigne

29 Political Change in Macao
Sonny Shiu-Hing Lo

30 China's Energy Geopolitics
The Shanghai Cooperation Organization and Central Asia
Thrassy N. Marketos

31 Regime Legitimacy in Contemporary China
Institutional change and stability
Edited by Thomas Heberer and Gunter Schubert

32 U.S.–China Relations
China policy on Capitol Hill
Tao Xie

33 Chinese Kinship
Contemporary anthropological perspectives
Edited by Susanne Brandtstädter and Gonçalo D. Santos

34 **Politics and Government in Hong Kong**
Crisis under Chinese sovereignty
Edited by Ming Sing

35 **Rethinking Chinese Popular Culture**
Cannibalizations of the canon
Edited by Carlos Rojas and Eileen Cheng-yin Chow

36 **Institutional Balancing in the Asia Pacific**
Economic interdependence and China's rise
Kai He

37 **Rent Seeking in China**
Edited by Tak-Wing Ngo and Yongping Wu

38 **China, Xinjiang and Central Asia**
History, transition and crossborder interaction into the 21st century
Edited by Colin Mackerras and Michael Clarke

39 **Intellectual Property Rights in China**
Politics of piracy, trade and protection
Gordon Cheung

40 **Developing China**
Land, politics and social conditions
George C.S. Lin

41 **State and Society Responses to Social Welfare Needs in China**
Serving the people
Edited by Jonathan Schwartz and Shawn Shieh

42 **Gay and Lesbian Subculture in Urban China**
Loretta Wing Wah Ho

43 **The Politics of Heritage Tourism in China**
A view from lijiang
Xiaobo Su and Peggy Teo

44 **Suicide and Justice**
A Chinese perspective
Wu Fei

45 **Management Training and Development in China**
Educating managers in a globalized economy
Edited by Malcolm Warner and Keith Goodall

46 Patron–Client Politics and Elections in Hong Kong
Bruce Kam-kwan Kwong

47 Chinese Family Business and the Equal Inheritance System
Unravelling the myth
Victor Zheng

48 Reconciling State, Market and Civil Society in China
The long march towards prosperity
Paolo Urio

49 Innovation in China
The Chinese software industry
Shang-Ling Jui

50 Mobility, Migration and the Chinese Scientific Research System
Koen Jonkers

51 Chinese Film Stars
Edited by Mary Farquhar and Yingjin Zhang

52 Chinese Male Homosexualities
Memba, *Tongzhi* and Golden Boy
Travis S.K. Kong

53 Industrialisation and Rural Livelihoods in China
Agricultural processing in Sichuan
Susanne Lingohr-Wolf

54 Law, Policy and Practice on China's Periphery
Selective adaptation and institutional capacity
Pitman B. Potter

55 China–Africa Development Relations
Edited by Christopher M. Dent

56 Neoliberalism and Culture in China and Hong Kong
The countdown of time
Hai Ren

57 China's Higher Education Reform and Internationalisation
Edited by Janette Ryan

58 **Law, Wealth and Power in China**
Commercial law reforms in context
Edited by John Garrick

59 **Religion in Contemporary China**
Revitalization and innovation
Edited by Adam Yuet Chau

60 **Consumer-Citizens of China**
The role of foreign brands in the imagined future China
Kelly Tian and Lily Dong

61 **The Chinese Communist Party and China's Capitalist Revolution**
The political impact of the market
Lance L.P. Gore

62 **China's Homeless Generation**
Voices from the veterans of the Chinese civil war, 1940s–1990s
Joshua Fan

63 **In Search of China's Development Model**
Beyond the Beijing consensus
Edited by S. Philip Hsu, Suisheng Zhao and Yu-Shan Wu

64 **Xinjiang and China's Rise in Central Asia, 1949–2009**
A history
Michael E. Clarke

65 **Trade Unions in China**
The challenge of labour unrest
Tim Pringle

66 **China's Changing Workplace**
Dynamism, diversity and disparity
Edited by Peter Sheldon, Sunghoon Kim, Yiqiong Li and Malcolm Warner

67 **Leisure and Power in Urban China**
Everyday life in a medium-sized Chinese city
Unn Målfrid H. Rolandsen

68 **China, Oil and Global Politics**
Philip Andrews-Speed and Roland Dannreuther

69 **Education Reform in China**
Edited by Janette Ryan

70 **Social Policy and Migration in China**
Lida Fan

71 **China's One Child Policy and Multiple Caregiving**
Raising little Suns in Xiamen
Esther C. L. Goh

72 **Politics and Markets in Rural China**
Edited by Björn Alpermann

73 **China's New Underclass**
Paid domestic labour
Xinying Hu

74 **Poverty and Development in China**
Alternative approaches to poverty assessment
Lu Caizhen

75 **International Governance and Regimes**
A Chinese perspective
Peter Kien-Hong Yu

76 **HIV/AIDS in China**
The economic and social determinants
Dylan Sutherland and Jennifer Y.J. Hsu

77 **Looking for Work in Post-Socialist China**
Governance, active job seekers and the new Chinese labor market
Feng Xu

78 **Sino-Latin American Relations**
Edited by K.C. Fung and Alicia Garcia-Herrero

79 **Mao's China and the Sino-Soviet Split**
Ideological dilemma
Mingjiang Li

80 **Law and Policy for China's Market Socialism**
Edited by John Garrick

81 **China–Taiwan Relations in a Global Context**
Taiwan's foreign policy and relations
Edited by C.X. George Wei

82 The Chinese Transformation of Corporate Culture
Colin S.C. Hawes

83 Mapping Media in China
Region, province and locality
Edited by Wanning Sun and Jenny Chio

84 China, the West and the Myth of New Public Management
Neoliberalism and its discontents
Paolo Urio

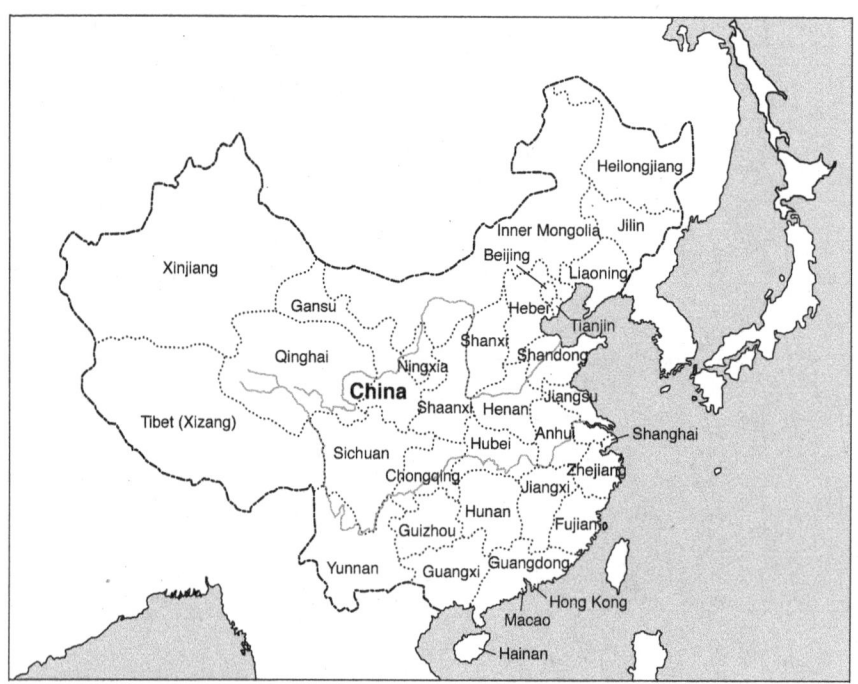

Map of China and its provinces.

China, the West and the Myth of New Public Management

Neoliberalism and its discontents

Paolo Urio

LONDON AND NEW YORK

First published 2012
by Routledge
2 Park Square, Milton Park, Abingdon, Oxfordshire OX14 4RN

Simultaneously published in the USA and Canada
by Routledge
711 Third Avenue, New York, NY 10017

Routledge is an imprint of the Taylor & Francis Group, an informa company

© 2012 Paolo Urio

The right of Paolo Urio to be identified as author of this work has been asserted by him in accordance with sections 77 and 78 of the Copyright, Designs and Patents Act 1988.

All rights reserved. No part of this book may be reprinted or reproduced or utilised in any form or by any electronic, mechanical, or other means, now known or hereafter invented, including photocopying and recording, or in any information storage or retrieval system, without permission in writing from the publishers.

Trademark notice: Product or corporate names may be trademarks or registered trademarks, and are used only for identification and explanation without intent to infringe.

British Library Cataloguing in Publication Data
A catalogue record for this book is available from the British Library

Library of Congress Cataloging in Publication Data
Urio, Paolo.
China, the West and the myth of new public management : neoliberalism and its discontents / Paolo Urio.
p. cm. – (Routledge contemporary China series)
Includes bibliographical references and index.
1. Public administration. 2. Economic policy. 3. Public administration—China. 4. China—Economic policy—2000– I. Title.
JF1351.U6275 2012
351–dc23
2011049157

ISBN 13: 978–0–415–69588–6 (hbk)
ISBN 13: 978–1–138–79052–0 (pbk)

Typeset in Times New Roman
by Prepress Projects Ltd, Perth, UK

Contents

List of figures	xv
List of tables	xvi
Acknowledgements	xviii
List of abbreviations	xx

Introduction   1

PART I
Analysing New Public Management in China and in the West   11

1   From public administration to New Public Management   13
2   Comparing New Public Management in China and in the West   26

PART II
The rise of New Public Management in the West and in China   65

3   The foundation of the Western experiment   67
4   The foundation of Chinese New Public Management   91

PART III
The crisis of New Public Management in the West and in China   107

5   The Western experiment   109
6   The Chinese experiment   145

Conclusion   199

Annex 1	211
Annex 2	214
Notes	219
Bibliography	276
Index	291

Figures

3.1	Real 'types' of NPM	73
5.1	Unemployment and invalidity benefits in the UK, 1979–1996	112
5.2	Income inequality in the UK, 1979–2008	116
5.3	Changes in Gini index in 14 Western countries, mid-1980s to 2009	117
5.4	Income inequality: Gini market income index vs. Gini disposable income index in 17 industrialized countries, *c*. 2000	120
5.5	Income inequality: international evidence, *c*. 2000	121
5.6	Relationship between low pay and non-elderly poverty rates in 11 industrialized countries, *c*. 2000	123
5.7	Relationship between cash social expenditures and non-elderly poverty rates in 11 industrialized countries, *c*. 2000	124
5.8	Child poverty rate before and after taxes and transfers, in 16 industrialized countries, 2000	128
5.9	Social expenditures versus child poverty in 17 industrialized countries, 2001	129
6.1	The ratio of China's urban nominal per capita annual disposable income to rural per capita net nominal income, 1978–2009	150
6.2	Income inequality and poverty in China, 1981–2000	160
6.3	Crime rates in China, 1978–2010	171

Tables

III.1	Major dimensions of reforms in China and in the West, 1978–2011	108
5.1	Unemployment rates for 17 Western countries, 1980–2011	113
5.2	Rise of GDP and income distribution in the USA, 1977–89	114
5.3	Income inequality for a choice of Western countries: overall trends	116
5.4	Gini index and ratio of richest 10% to poorest 10% in 20 Western countries and China, around 2005	119
5.5	Anti-poverty effect of government spending in 13 Western countries, c. 1990	125
5.6	Anti-poverty effect of government spending in 11 Western countries, c. 2000	126
5.7	Anti-poverty effect of government spending, 1990–2000	127
5.8	Relative poverty rates for vulnerable groups in 11 Western countries, c. 2000	127
5.9	HDI and ranking in 20 Western countries and China, 2007 and 2010	132
5.10	Crime rates in four Western countries, 1977–91	135
5.11	Number of prisoners per 100,000 population in 12 Western countries, 2000 and 2007–8	136
5.12	Major health indicators in 16 Western countries	138
5.13	Health expenditures in 16 Western countries	140
5.14	Self-perceived health status according to levels of job insecurity in Switzerland, 1997	141
6.1	Changes in employment and GDP of the three economic sectors in China, 1952–2009	146
6.2	China's main economic indicators, 2004–10	147
6.3	The proportion of China's GDP in the world total, 1820–2030	148
6.4	The proportion of exports in the world total (%, 1820–2030)	149

6.5	The proportion of China's industrial output in the world total, 1830–2009	150
6.6	China's urban per capita annual nominal disposable income and rural per capita net nominal income, 1978–2009	151
6.7	China's improvement measured by the 'old' HDI Index, 1980–2007	152
6.8	Provincial Human Development Index of China, 2008	156
6.9	Per capita annual income of urban and rural households in China, 2009	167
6.10	Health costs of economic transition and development in China	174
6.11	People with health insecurity in China, 2003 and 2008	175
6.12	Comparison of three kinds of medical insurance in China, 2008	175
6.13	Regional disparity in health: one China, four worlds, 2007–8	176
6.14	People insured by the major social insurances in Chinese urban areas, 2001–10	185
6.15	Reimbursement caps to patients from health insurances in China, 2010	188
6.16	The minimum living standard line in China, 2005 and 2010	190
6.17	From convergence to divergence and to reconvergence: population distribution of different GDP per capita groups in China (1980–2008)	194
6.18	From absolute poverty to well-off in China: population distribution of different Engel coefficient groups (1978–2007)	195
6.19	China's urban per capita nominal annual disposable income and rural per capita net nominal income and Engel coefficients in China, 1978–2009	196

Acknowledgements

Although I am fully responsible for the theoretical framework that guided the collection of the data presented in this book, as well as for the inevitable biases, errors and omissions that will accompany my comments and conclusions, I am very much indebted to those intellectuals who, even if not being always in tune with my own thinking, have stimulated the research and reflections upon which this book is based. Among the long list, let me at least mention two of the giants of the Western social science tradition, Max Weber and John Maynard Keynes and, amongst the contemporary, Joseph E. Stiglitz, Ha-Joon Chang, Fernand Braudel, Paul Bairoch and, in China, Hu Angang, Cui Zhiyuan, Wang Hui and many others who will be duly quoted in the following pages. One word of warning, however. By referring explicitly or implicitly to these, as well as to many other thinkers, I do not mean to follow their teaching completely, nor do I claim to interpret their writings faithfully. In referring to them while planning the structure of this book I did not aim to perform an exegesis exercise. Many outstanding colleagues have done so, especially for the great classics of the nineteenth century, and I am grateful to them for having done that very useful work. In referring to the authors just mentioned, my major interest was instead simpler: to find some suggestions for identifying the most pertinent facts related to the implementation of New Public Management in China and in the West, as well as some theoretical hints and frameworks that would help me in discovering and giving meaning to the facts collected in the process of my research. In any case, I am convinced that, by performing an exegesis of the writings of those thinkers I have just mentioned, one would run the risk of considering their work as a closed discourse, whereas a true academic discourse is never closed; only ideologies claim to have attained that final stage. The best illustration of this is certainly given by one of the major works of Max Weber, which is in fact a collection of writings on many themes such as power, state, legitimacy, law, economy, society, status groups and classes, households and enterprises, ethnic and religious groups, political communities, bureaucracy and many more (some of them in a preliminary stage of writing) that were put together after Weber's death, first by his widow, Marianne, and later by Johannes Winckelmann, and published under the title *Economy and Society*. Doubtless, Max Weber would have presented these themes in a different way, and would have developed, and probably changed, several paragraphs, if not entire chapters, had he had the chance to do so before his death.

To mention all those who helped me in the realization of this book would run the risk of forgetting some of them. However, let me at least mention first of all Hu Angang, founder and director of the Centre for China Studies at Tsinghua University in Beijing, who shared with me his views on the reforms strategy of his country during a relationship more than a decade long. Also at Tsinghua, Cui Zhiyuan, Wang Hui and Li Xiguang gave me some invaluable insights into the changing structure of Chinese society, and Yang Yongheng and his PhD student, Zhang Wankuan, took part in the international research on public–private partnerships for in-transition countries (including China) that I directed between 2005 and 2008. Hu Angang has also been so kind as to assign to me some of his best assistants to help in the collection of data and translations of Chinese books and articles: Zhao Li (2005, presently PhD student at Louvain-La-Neuve University in Belgium), Wei Xing (2005–7, presently Professor at the School of Public Policy & Management), Jie Lu (2009) and more recently Liang Jiaochen, Shen Ruomeng, Sophia Huang and Ma Ying Jun helped me collect the data that I use in Chapter 6 and in the conclusion. Between 2005 and 2010, my last assistant at the University of Geneva, Yuan Ying, was of great help in the collection of data and information and above all in giving me some important insights into the development of non-governmental organizations (NGOs) in China; my former student in Switzerland in 2007–8, Liu Dehao (presently teaching at Hainan University), helped me in updating the information given in Chapter 6 on the development of social security in China. A long-established cooperation with the School of Public Administration at Renmin University gave me the opportunity to benefit from the insights of Dong Keyong (the Dean of the School) and his colleagues, especially in the domain of social policies. Dong Keyong also supported a research on access to health care in Guangzhou, conducted by a team comprising Gianfranco Domenighetti (University of Lugano) and Hongbo Jia, presently teaching at the Public Administration School, Beijing University of Aeronautics and Astronautics, Beijing, who gave me some additional insights into the complex world of China's health system.

Last but not least, I thank my wife, Madeleine – a dual British and Swiss national – not only for her invaluable help in the difficult task of putting my English prose into a form readily understandable to an international reader, but also for her patience and understanding throughout the years necessary to bring this book to fruition.

Geneva, 22 November 2011

Abbreviations

$PPP	US dollars calculated in purchasing power parity
ACFTU	All-China Federation of Trade Unions
CAS	China Academy of Sciences
CIA	Central Intelligence Agency (Unites States of America)
CPC	Communist Party of China
CPPCC	Chinese People's Political Consultative Conference
EU	European Union
IMF	International Monetary Fund
GDP	gross domestic product
GNP	gross national product
HDI	Human Development Index
IFS	Institute of Fiscal Studies (London)
MPI	multidimensional poverty index of the OPHI (q.v.)
NBSC	National Bureau of Statistics (People's Republic of China)
NDRC	National Development and Reform Commission (People's Republic of China)
NPL	non-performing loans
NPM	New Public Management
NZI	New Zealand Institute
OECD	Organisation for Economic Co-operation and Development
OPHI	Oxford Poverty & Human Development Initiative (see MPI)
PPP	public–private partnership
PRC	People's Republic of China
R&D	research and development
RMB	currency of the People's Republic of China, also called yuan
UNDP	United Nations Development Programme
WB	World Bank
WHO	World Health Organization
WWF	World Wide Fund for Nature (formerly World Wildlife Fund)

Introduction

Let us start with three introductory remarks. First, this book deals not with public administration and operational management but with strategic public management, that is, with the 'upper' part of New Public Management (NPM), that part that Fernand Braudel would place at the upper layer of the hierarchy of production–consumption processes, namely within the capitalist layer in the West and at the state level in China.[1] For example, China's decision to abandon a planned economy and to introduce market mechanisms is clearly the first strategic decision orienting the subsequent Chinese strategic and operational decisions. Therefore, the reader will not find in this book a discussion of the operational elements of New Public Management such as analytical accounting, the techniques for successful privatization, risk evaluation, and laws and regulations for public–private partnerships (PPPs), and so on. Nor will the reader find an in-depth discussion about the differences in implementation of NPM or about the different 'empirical types' of NPM. These important aspects have been dealt with in the literature and they provide interesting insights into the world of NPM.[2] However, they say little about the typical elements of NPM: those that differentiate it from other types of public management; on the contrary, most of the time they have the consequence of concealing the essence of NPM. In the second chapter I will explain the rationale of this choice upon which this book is based.

Second, the major aim of the book is to tell the story of a long journey within the world of NPM and its impact on Chinese and Western societies. The book is based upon an NPM ideal-type, built following Max Weber's methodology, which has been used to generate four hypotheses that I will define hereafter. To do so, it has been necessary to identify the core characteristics of NPM, that is, to define NPM as a Weberian ideal-type, different from other types of public management, irrespective of the variations in reality. This ideal-type constitutes the basis upon which neoliberals have in practice oriented the definition and the implementation of both strategic goals (e.g. privatization) and operational devices (e.g. analytic accounting) in their attempt to reform public management.[3] Nevertheless, differences in the architecture of NPM among the countries concerned will not be neglected. On the contrary, and following Weberian methodology, the first major hypothesis of the book is that differences in the implementation of NPM will produce different outcomes. This will be done by defining two real types of Western capitalist countries (weak- and strong-NPM countries) and by taking China as a special case of NPM, not belonging to the general category of capitalist countries (however capitalism is defined). That China's reforms can be considered as a variant of NPM is attested by several scholars, for example by Ma Jun and Zhang Zhibin:

> The years since 1980 have witnessed a remarkable movement worldwide to reform public administration. For many . . . there is a striking international convergence of ideas among these administrative reforms, while others disagree . . . Despite these different stances, the international debate on administrative reforms has been overly influenced by the so-called New Public Management (NPM). In this context, the administrative reforms in China were also conceptualized as a variation of NPM with non-western characteristics.[4]

This is also my opinion in spite of the fact that, as I will show in this book, the Chinese leadership started to introduce, from the mid-1990s, several corrective policies to overcome the negative consequences of the Chinese NPM, and to sustain those who suffered from the process of marketization.[5] This trend has been further developed during the 2008–11 crisis, contrary to the strategy followed by Western countries, which preferred to save the core of contemporary capitalism, namely the financial system, as they have consistently done after all the major financial crises that appeared since the 1980s.[6] Starting from this difference between China and the West, I will develop several arguments to prove that, for the time being, China's system is not a variant of capitalism, but a 'socialist market economy with Chinese characteristics'.

From the preceding paragraph one can see that I will use two kinds of typologies: the Weberian ideal-typology and the empirical (or real) typology. The former defines the special, unique or typical elements of a phenomenon that differentiate it from other phenomena (e.g. New Public Management and traditional management); it is based upon a unilateral operation made by the researcher defining unambiguously the typical features of the phenomenon under research that will serve as a heuristic set of interrelated, unambiguously defined concepts, capable of orienting the process of research, by formulating hypotheses and orienting him or her in the search and identification of the most relevant elements in reality. The latter is based upon empirical observation and evidence that may identify differences in the implementation into the real world of the elements of the ideal-type, and therefore can lead to the appearance of empirically proved differences, and hence to several real-types (e.g. strong-NPM and weak-NPM).

Third, it is possible that by considering China as an NPM country we will surprise more than one reader. This idea is based upon the fact that NPM in the West and Chinese reforms introduced since the beginning of the 1980s have in common several core characteristics, namely privatization, contracting out, decentralization and deregulation, in spite of considerable differences in the structure of their culture, economy, polity and society. These similarities are also stressed by those who consider that China is in transition to a Western-type economy (and maybe also polity) and that the high degree of commonality is proved not only by the common trend that gives more space to the market economy by means of privatization, contracting out, decentralization and deregulation within countries, but also by the fact that this same trend was introduced into the global economy in all domains, including, and above all, financial global markets. At the end of this process, some people forecast that China would be fully integrated into the global capitalist system. These similarities are too important to ignore the high degree of commonality between the West and China, even if one can express some doubts about the probability that China will adopt a liberal democratic system in the foreseeable future. Thus, the second major hypothesis at the beginning of this research is that, in spite of the above-mentioned differences, similar public management strategies would produce similar outcomes. Nevertheless, differences in the structure of the political system and its relation to the economy (and, within the economy, in relation to the economic agents managing the economy) may have an impact on the capacity of these countries to react to the negative consequences of NPM implementation, and this would eventually lead to different policy answers, especially after the outbreak of the 2008–11 economic crisis. This is the third main hypothesis of this book. Finally, considering that it is not possible to maximize economic efficiency and social equity simultaneously, the fourth hypothesis is that if you give too much space to the market you will inevitably lose in equity, unless some social policies are implemented to counterbalance the negative outcomes of the expanded market.

Chapters 5 and 6 of Part 3 and the general conclusion provide some empirical evidence supporting our major hypotheses. However, already since the mid-1990s the most striking evidence, from data already available, was first of all that there were considerable differences among Western countries (first hypothesis). Second, in spite of considerable differences in their political, social and economic organizations, China and the West had produced similar results: economic development (measured by GDP), but also increasing disparities, increasing poverty rates and/or new forms of poverty, and considerable environmental damages (second hypothesis). Third, by giving more space to the market, China and the West have improved economic efficiency, but worsened the equitable distribution of wealth (fourth hypothesis). Finally, in spite of the similarities mentioned above, the two systems have implemented different policies for counterbalancing the negative outcomes deriving from the same innovations introduced in public management (third hypothesis). These differences have become even more evident after the onset of the 2008–11 economic crisis.

It is to be hoped that the comparison between Chinese and Western NPM will shed some light on the way our societies both in China and in the West are conceiving their future, their fundamental values and their political, social and economic organization, and, in a prescriptive perspective, how they should conceive them in order to set up (and this is of course a personal view) a more just society, respectful of human beings and their physical environment, and not at the service of ideologies that work to the advantage of only a small minority and harm so many ordinary people.

4 *Introduction*

This book is the result of a long journey within the world of public administration and management. It started in 1964 when I was engaged as an assistant with the task of undertaking some research at the newly created bureaucracy in Brussels, following the signature of the so-called Treaties of Rome (1957) instituting the Economic European Community and the Euratom, which along with the European Coal and Steel Community, created in 1952, were the predecessors of the present European Union. The creation of a supranational body not only instituted a new centre of power with its own political and administrative apparatus, but also meant the constitution of 'parliamentary groups' within the European Parliamentary Assembly (the predecessors of the European political parties within the European Parliament), and moreover attracted to Brussels a variety of pressure groups aware of the necessity of defending their interests not only at the traditional national level but also at the European one. Thanks to this fascinating experience, I was encouraged to embark upon the university research that led me to analyse the decision-making process of the European Communities, Switzerland, and more generally Western countries, the role of bureaucracies, the interface between state and market, and finally the different and evolving forms of public administration and management. Towards the end of the 1990s, I was invited to contribute to a collective book on neoliberalism with a critical chapter on the emergence of NPM in the West. Chapter 3 is an updated and expanded version of that chapter. At about the same time, opportunity and personal choice allowed me to develop a 10-year research project on the reforms process of China.[7] This opened several new perspectives that encouraged me to complete the collection of data necessary for writing this book.

At the moment of taking stock of what I had learned during this long journey, and taking advantage of the financial and economic crisis that broke out during the year 2008 and the different ways in which it has been faced by China and the West, I thought that the right time had come to bring to fruition the project, which I had envisaged for a long time, of comparing the results obtained by the reforms introduced in public management in these two systems, practically at the same time: between the end of the 1970s and the first decade of the twenty-first century. The most striking evidence from data already available towards the mid-1990s was that, in spite of considerable differences in their political, social and economic organizations, China and the West had produced fundamentally similar results: economic development (measured by GDP), but also increasing disparities, increasing poverty rates and/or new forms of poverty, and considerable environmental damage. In spite of those similarities, the two systems have been experimenting with quite different ways of trying to counterbalance these negative outcomes deriving from the same innovations introduced in public management: to give more space to the economy by means of privatization, contracting out and deregulation, not only within countries but also at the global level, and in all domains, including, above all, financial global markets.

Why do I propose to consider New Public Management as a myth? This term has its origins in ancient Greece and Rome, and is related to the Greco-Roman mythology. The famous Littré French dictionary, published between 1863 and

1873, gives the following meanings: (1) the first is the most general meaning, which considers myth as a specific characteristic of fable, of heroic narration or of fabulous times; (2) second, and more precisely, it is the narration of times or events that history does not explain, and comprises either a real event transformed into a religious belief or an invented event; (3) finally, in a figurative and familiar meaning, a myth is something that does not really exist. We can see that, already at the beginning of the second half of the nineteenth century, one of the more influential dictionaries of the French language points to some of the major characteristics of myths: narration of events that either do exist but are put in the form of a fable that may be transformed into religious beliefs (i.e. whose acceptance is based upon faith and not facts) or even on events that do not exist in reality. Even more interestingly, Littré chooses the domain of politics to give an example of myth – 'one can say that in politics justice and good faith constitute a kind of myth'[8] – thus suggesting that political discourse is obscured by ideological biases. It is remarkable that this example is given at a time when the two ideologies that were to dominate political discourse and politics for the decades to come were at their first stage of political struggle: on one hand economic liberalism, that is, the capitalist economy, was well established in the West, and political liberalism, that is, liberal democracy, was fast developing and progressing, and on the other hand socialism and Marxism were acquiring an increasing audience amongst the critics of liberalism.

Coming to the more recent interpretation of myth, and leaving largely aside the explanations of the term related to the Greco-Roman world, which is outside the scope of this book, I will retain the following interpretations that are more frequently presented by dictionaries of some of the European languages and are quite helpful for understanding how and why I consider that the NPM is a myth:[9]

1 The first meaning can be traced back to the idea of a narration about supernatural beings and their remarkable actions. Here, the examples quoted are generally linked to the Greco-Roman world, for example the myth of Prometheus, or the myth of Hercules, but can also be referred to the contemporary use of this meaning, for example when it is referred to charismatic political leaders such as John F. Kennedy, Charles de Gaulle, Maria Eva (Evita) Duarte de Peron, Silvio Berlusconi and others.
2 The representation of a person or a historical event that the popular imagination has made more beautiful and bigger than in reality so that he/she/it has assumed a legendary status, such as the myth of Joan of Arc (Jeanne d'Arc).
3 A construction of the mind that is not based upon reality, which is in fact synonymous with invention or lie, for example the myth of eternal youth.
4 A symbolic representation that influences social life and is synonymous with illusion, dream or utopia, such as the myth of progress.
5 An ideological representation of reality that is accepted almost as a faith by a people or by an era, such as the myth of progress or the myth of universal equality.

6 Stories or narrations that contribute to a cohesive social identity and thus of social cohesion, for example accounts of origins, explanations of values and taboos, and narrative legitimizations of authority.
7 A simplified representation of an event, a social phenomenon or a person, as is formed and accepted by a human group, such as the Italian myth of the 'Risorgimento', the myth of the British self-control. Moreover, the accepted representation may often be illusory, but because of the force with which it is expressed, and the consequent acceptance by people, it may bring about changes in behaviour within a human group, for example the myth of global disarmament, the myth of social success at all costs.
8 Finally, one can consider that the primary function of myths is to lend the appearance of universality to otherwise contingent cultural beliefs. In this respect, myth occupies much the same place as ideology and it secures consent for the status quo, for example the myths of liberal democracy and of a classless society.[10]

What can we retain from the above enumeration? In summary, a myth is (1) a simplified representation of event(s), social phenomenon (or phenomena) and/or person(s) that is based, at least in part, on elements that do not exist in reality, and therefore the myth is an illusion, a dream or a utopia, but (2) when it is expressed with force it may be accepted as true by members of a social group, or by the majority of a population or even by an entire population; (3) it thus may influence social life, individual and collective behaviour, contribute to social cohesion, and finally legitimize the existing authority and power; in this sense the myth can be considered as equivalent to or contributing to the dominant ideology, and thus it can secure consensus for the status quo; (4) finally, it may be expressed as a set of elements universally valid, and therefore those who believe in it, and who orient their behaviour accordingly, may be tempted to impose it on other groups, people or countries.

Now, in this book I will show that NPM possesses all the above-mentioned characteristics. New Public Management is the armed wing of neoliberalism when applied to developed countries, and is also the brother (or, I should say, the twin brother) of the 'Washington Consensus' through which neoliberalism has imposed its values on the developing countries since at least the beginning of the 1980s. Consequently, thanks to its brother, NPM is also inevitably linked to neoliberal globalization. Therefore, if NPM is a myth, so are also the 'Washington Consensus', neoliberal globalization (comprising the free market and free international trade) and the ideology that governs them all: neoliberalism. All these components together constitute a complex set of myths, linked to one another by their ultimate and fundamental ideological foundation, neoliberalism.[11]

The Italian philosopher Umberto Galimberti has summarized the complex set of myths of our time in an interesting volume published in 2009.[12] Galimberti's work goes well beyond the myths in which I am interested in writing this book, and subdivides them into two categories: the individual (such as the myths of eternal youth, of happiness etc.) and the collective ones. Among the latter we find some of those I will deal with in this book, namely the myths of the free market and of liberal globalization.[13] Although it is not possible to make an account of the very rich developments of Galimberti, it is nevertheless useful to take advantage of his preliminary remarks in the introduction of his book, which, I am convinced, shed some new light upon the definitions I have reported above. Galimberti commences by taking into consideration the 'simple ideas' that will, at the end of a complex socio-political-psychological process, constitute the core of myths. These simple ideas are so imbedded in our mind that they do not admit criticism or objections, not because we are rigid and dogmatic, but because we have never discussed them or looked at them closely. Contrary to ideas that we 'think', myths are ideas that possess us and govern us through means that are not logical, but psychological, and are deeply embedded in our souls, where the light of reason cannot reach. This is because myths are composed of simple ideas that we have transformed into myths, ideas that are comfortable, because they do not create problems for us by rendering our judgement easy, in a word because they reassure us by freeing us from any doubt about our vision of the world. In this way our conscience is no longer submitted to the destabilizing risk of the flood of questions and doubts and thus, in the end, our mind will be in a state in which our sincere adherence to the myths goes together with a very profound sleep. Galimberti ends his introduction by inviting us to revisit the myths of our time thanks to a critical approach; critique (in ancient Greek *krino*) means judgement, evaluation and interpretation. This will inevitably imply a crisis of the ideas that until now have regulated our life and that maybe are no more capable to help us in understanding the changes that are occurring in the world. This is certainly one of the aims of this book.[14]

This book comprises three parts, each one being subdivided into two chapters. The first part deals with the analysis of public management in China and the West and comprises two complementary chapters. As the perspective of this book is rather unusual, I thought that it was necessary to explain in Chapter 1 what had been the path (i.e. the 'journey') that led me to the idea of comparing the consequences of NPM in China and the West. This is done by presenting the first manifestations of my criticism of Western NPM, considering the data already available for the West in the mid-1990s pointing to the appearance of some negative outcomes of NPM. I also explain the difficulties in being heard by the ruling elite, as NPM was solidly embedded in the revival of liberalism, that is, neoliberalism, that had become during the 1980s the dominant ideology orienting public policies in the West. Then the 'discovery' of Chinese NPM at the end of 1997 strengthened my conviction that Chinese reforms had fundamentally the same logic as the Western NPM, namely to give more space to the market for the purpose of improving economic efficiency. Therefore, NPM should produce basically the same outcomes in China as well. However, at the same time the differences in political culture (ideology in the West and pragmatism in China) suggested that there would be some remarkable differences when the negative outcomes on NPM in both the West and China were recognized and would eventually demand the implementation of some corrective policies. How would China and the West react?

8 *Introduction*

In Chapter 2 I discuss the major theoretical and methodological issues upon which the book is constructed: first of all the concepts of market, free market, market mechanisms, capitalism and socialism, based upon the enlightening works of Fernand Braudel, as well as the academic debates on these concepts in the West and in China. Second, a discussion about the link between the ideological foundations of neoliberalism on one hand and of its two armed wings, the 'Washington Consensus' and New Public Management, on the other hand, is presented with the aim of showing the similarities between these two types of 'models' orienting public management in the West and in developing countries. Third, I will deal with the construction of empirical typologies of public management in Western states (based upon existing empirical typologies of capitalism and Welfare States) that will be used in the third part (Chapters 5 and 6) for evaluating the impact of empirical types of public management on economy and society, by correlating these types with a set of data. Fourth, the choice of the data is presented and discussed with the aim of showing the difficulties in measuring the phenomena concerned, for example income distribution and inequalities, poverty, crime and health. Finally, I will briefly say a few words about what I will actually compare between China and the West.

The aim of the second part is to explain how NPM has been implemented in China and in the West. What is its rationale in both cases, what are the similarities and the differences? The Western case will be presented first in Chapter 3, only for practical reasons, as the market economy (or, more precisely, capitalism) was historically conceived, implemented and developed in the West. The considerations presented in this section regarding the technical aspect of the market economy will be considered also valid for the Chinese case, presented in Chapter 4. In particular, it will be forecast that giving more space to the market may have some negative consequences for equity, especially as regards income distribution and access to public services. However, there will also be some remarkable differences. In fact, I will propose that Western NPM is ideologically the son of neoliberalism, and as such, like any other strong ideology, is not prone to accept any criticism. On the contrary Chinese NPM, based on Deng Xiaoping's development strategy, will be considered as a pragmatic response to the limits of the planned economy as a means of restoring China as a world power. The choice being not ideological, it is forecast that in case of negative outcomes the Chinese leadership will be able to change direction more easily than the Western leadership.

The aim of the third part is to propose an evaluation of the Western and Chinese New Public Managements (Chapters 5 and 6 respectively), by taking two types of indicators: first of all, the economic performance, measured by the increase in wealth and economic efficiency; second the impact on society, measured by indicators of employment, income distribution, poverty rates, crime rates and health. At the end of each of the two chapters, I will come back to the four hypotheses and evaluate to what extent they are confirmed by the empirical data.

In the general conclusion I will summarize the findings presented in the third part and, taking advantage of the fact that the 2008–11 crisis may have the consequence of further worsening the economy and increasing its negative impact on society, I will compare the policies that China and the West have implemented in order to overcome not only the economic crisis, but also, more generally, the negative consequences of market economy and, following again Fernand Braudel, its capitalistic developments. We shall see that it is in this respect that the strategies of China and the West show some remarkable differences.

In writing this book, I have tried to avoid a too technical approach. Although I will address the results of my research to an academic audience, I will present them in a form accessible to a wider public. In organizing the six chapters, I have tried to present them according to a sequence that should make the reading as easy as possible: (1) in Chapter 1 I start with the presentation of my personal journey through the world of public management and in Chapter 2 I explain the theoretical and methodological choices upon which the book is based; (2) in Chapters 3 and 4 I explain the rationale for the introduction of NPM in the West and in China; and (3) in Chapters 5 and 6 I evaluate the impact of NPM on economy and society in the West and in China. As all the dimensions dealt with in the six chapters are linked to each other within a kind of structural interdependency, there will be many cross-references that have made repetitions necessary. The academic experts in public management may find this way of presenting my argument rather tedious. My purpose in doing so was to facilitate the reading for laypeople, so that each chapter may stand on its own. Each chapter can be read independently of the others and, should the reader wish to find more detailed explanations, he or she may refer to the other chapters as suggested in the text.

Part I
Analysing New Public Management in China and in the West

Analysing and comparing public management in China and in the West is not an easy task and would require both an in-depth diachronic and a synchronic approach. Difficulties arise not only from the different pace at which the two areas have developed through history (differences that still persist today, as China has not yet caught up with the West) but also because they present today different ideologies, mind-sets and political and economic structures. Nevertheless, at the beginning of the 1980s, China started to introduce some of the same policies that were implemented at that same time in Western countries with the aim of replacing at least part of the planned economy with market mechanisms. At the level of strategic management, the main features of these new policies are privatization, contracting out, decentralization and deregulation. At the same time, these policies were pushing the Chinese leadership to also introduce some technical devices similar to the Western ones at the operational level, such as financial auditing and performance management. I will not go into too much detail in analysing the structure of Chinese New Public Management (hereafter NPM), as the above-mentioned features are sufficient to establish the similarities between Western and Chinese public management, in spite of important differences that appear when analysing their implementation within different cultural, political and legal structures. In fact, starting from those similarities, my interest consists in comparing the outcomes of NPM on economy and society in China and in the West, by formulating the hypothesis that similar strategic public management strategies will produce basically similar results, for example increasing economic performance but also increasing income disparities. The other hypothesis based upon the similarities of Western and Chinese public management, and on the impossibility of simultaneously maximizing economic efficiency and social equity, is that, by giving more space to the market, you will inevitably increase economic efficiency at the expense of equity. Differences will of course also appear. However, they will be, on one hand, of degree rather than of nature, as technically a market is a market within any type of society; and on the other hand, at the strategic level, if the choice of market is based upon pragmatic rather than on ideological considerations (as I will maintain to be the case of China), then the most important difference will be found in the capacity of China to change strategy if adverse consequences appear in the process of implementing privatization, contracting out, decentralization and deregulation. If this hypothesis is confirmed then we can conclude, contrary to the dominant thesis that there is a convergence between China and the West, that the Chinese economy is, for the time being, evolving not towards a capitalist system, but towards a socialist market economy with Chinese characteristics. As I will show in the second chapter, this is not only the thesis of the Chinese leadership, but also that of Chinese intellectuals put under the convenient umbrella of the Chinese New Left. Other Chinese intellectuals who are not in favour of socialism but demand a more radical modernization and liberalization of China nevertheless consider that China's modernization will and should present Chinese characteristics that will differentiate it from the West. Moreover, the 2008–11 economic crisis will be used in the general conclusion of this book as an indicator allowing us to compare the capacity of China and the West to overcome the negative consequences of the crisis.

In summary, the major hypotheses upon which this book is based are the following: (1) differences in the implementation of NPM produce different outcomes; (2) in spite of differences in the cultural, economic, legal and political structures, similar public management strategies produce similar outcomes; (3) differences in the structure of the political system and of its relation to the economy (and within the economy to the economic agents managing the economy) may have an impact on the capacity of the state to react to the negative consequences of NPM implementation, and this would eventually lead to different policy solutions, especially after the 2008–11 economic crisis; (4) as it is not possible to simultaneously maximize economic efficiency and social equity, if you give too much space to the market you will inevitably lose in equity, unless some social policies are implemented to counterbalance the negative outcomes of the expanded market.

To my knowledge, this approach comparing the consequence of reforms in public management in China and the West is quite new, as many scholars will sustain that NPM is typically a Western phenomenon and China's reforms cannot be compared to the Western NPM as they not only differ in content but also have been implemented within a different political and cultural environment. It is my conviction that this new way of analysing and comparing the consequences of public management reforms in China and the West needs to be explained in two complementary ways. First, in the first chapter, I will describe along what personal academic path I have come to develop this research project. I thought that I owed this explanation to the reader. Then, in the second chapter, I will deal with the major theoretical and methodological aspects of this project.

1 From public administration to New Public Management
An intellectual journey

Having employed the 12 years between 1983 and 1995 in the management of academic institutions, followed by a year-long sabbatical completing a research on organizational learning, publishing a book on the budgetary process in Switzerland[1] and catching up with the formidable task of reading the stack of books and articles that had accumulated on my shelves, I wondered what kind of new activity I might undertake for the concluding nine years of my appointment at the Department of Political Science of the University of Geneva. Managing academic institutions during that time was not a sinecure, as those were the years of serious budget cuts and of numerous renewals of tenure positions following the departure of those who were appointed at the end of the 1960s during the rapid and vast development of higher education in Switzerland and elsewhere in the West. Cutting budgets and replacing staff are rather difficult tasks to perform in an organizational environment where prima donnas abound and crimes of *lèse majesté* are too easily perpetrated. If you want to do this job well, the time left for other more rewarding activities is rather restricted. Not that I did not enjoy the job. On the contrary, I learned a lot about human nature, individual and collective strategies employed to advance private interests under the cover of the general good. Moreover, I developed a keen interest in that activity and was rewarded with great satisfaction in finding reasonable solutions to apparently insoluble problems. Probably my academic specialization in public administration and management helped me survive through this rather demanding and challenging period. Moreover, it gave me the opportunity to test, and to confirm in real and practical situations, the very academic results of my previous research on administrative behaviour.

Of course, by 1983 the diffusion of New Public Management (NPM) had already begun, and in fact one can pinpoint its birth a little earlier, to the time of the first elections of Margaret Thatcher (1979) and Ronald Reagan (1980).[2] I had been watching these developments with some perplexity and even, to be quite honest, with much concern that grew during my academic management years. Unfortunately, time did not allow me to put on paper a reasonable evaluation of NPM: one that would deal comprehensively not only with its ideological and theoretical foundation, but also with the practical consequences of its implementation, and especially its impact on people and society. Nevertheless, already during the 1980s I managed to devote enough time to introducing some criticism in my courses. This criticism found a more solid basis thanks to the reading done during my sabbatical year and thanks to the discussions I had with some colleagues in Europe and in the USA. I then became convinced of the very serious weaknesses of NPM that I will present in detail in the following pages. I also gave some conferences to civil servants, and occasionally to other audiences in Geneva, Lausanne and in the south of Switzerland, generally upon invitation by the Swiss trade union of civil servants, one of the rare institutions that expressed concern about the consequences of NPM on public services and public employment. This was indeed the time when Switzerland was at all levels of government starting to implement ('at last!' some people would say) or at least evaluate the possibility of implementing some of the NPM tools. A kind of 'Holy Alliance' had emerged amongst the political parties of the Right and the Social Democrats (whom I began to call 'the Managerial Left'), the majority of the mass media and the majority of intellectuals within and outside universities, some of them with the overt support of big multinationals and consulting companies.

Even more, amongst the few intellectuals who had at least dared to express some criticisms of NPM, some suddenly changed their mind when they discovered (in this, following one of the major features of NPM) that there was a market for their expertise, on the condition that they agree to embrace the 'NPM self-proclaimed new paradigm'. This should not come as a surprise, for at all times and places the majority of intellectuals have taken sides with the people in power. In fact this behaviour allowed these intellectuals to escape from the dull (at least according to the way they saw it) confinement to their ivory tower and come out into the limelight, without having to take the risk of being criticized or even scorned by the ruling elite. On the contrary, thanks to this attitude, they were publicly praised for their seriousness and their 'practical' (i.e. not ideological) approach to public management. Finally, this public recognition of their expertise had the positive result of considerably boosting their ego and, in many cases, even their bank account, or at least that of their institution. So, there was no reason to be surprised nor to feel offended, if you were so honest (some would say: so naïve) as to take the risk of not sharing the general and overwhelming enthusiasm for NPM and, consequently, of not being heard when publicly expressing the slightest criticism against it. What was nevertheless unbearable, at least to me, was the contemptuous and arrogant attitude of the defenders of NPM towards those who dared contest the validity of their new toy. This happened towards the end of 1997 when I read an article published at the beginning of October in the leading French-speaking Swiss newspaper *Le Journal de Genève* by one of the NPM intellectuals (whom I started to call 'NPM-ists'), in which he treated the few NPM critics as incompetent because they did not understand the true nature and goals of NPM; incompetent because they had not understood that NPM had no ideological biases, but was simply a box containing all sorts of practical and efficient management tools, whose laudable goal was simply to improve the management of the state and the delivery of public services in terms of efficiency, effectiveness and quality. In order to disqualify arguments that might reasonably have shed some light on the weaknesses of NPM, its promoters claimed that in any case globalization was inevitable, and as a consequence national states had to rationally adapt their management to the ineluctable development, opening up and deregulation of the global economy. How? By reducing the burden on the economy they had been damaging for years; privatizing, contracting out, deregulating and starting to treat their citizens as they deserved, like customers.[3]

That was much more than I could bear. I was given the opportunity to reply by the *Journal de Genève* in the 27 October 1997 issue (reproduced in English translation as Annex 1 below). In that article I expressed my surprise to learn that NPM had no ideological basis and I suggested that the most plausible reason for concealing its fatherhood was that its proponents wanted to please the Right as well as the Left (or at least the social-democratic Left). I maintained forcefully that NPM was clearly the legitimate son of the liberal revival (or neoliberalism) and of its outstanding pioneers such as Friedrich von Hayek and Milton Friedman, and therefore there was no reason to be ashamed and to conceal their paternity as if they had passed on an unavoidable disease.[4] To illustrate the practical weaknesses of NPM I referred to the empirical evidence already available at that time, showing that NPM countries had considerably increased income inequalities, rates of poverty and crime, and that their low rate of unemployment went hand in hand with an increase of low-paid, short-time and part-time jobs. I also mentioned a study published online in the *American Prospect* by Paul Krugman (the economist who 11 years later was to win the Nobel Prize). In this article Krugman showed that 70 per cent of the increase in gross domestic product (GDP) during the NPM–Reagan years went to the 1 per cent of the richest American taxpayers, whereas the first quintile (i.e. the lowest 20 per cent) experienced a decrease of 9 per cent. I also asked the inevitable question typical of detective stories, 'Who is profiting from NPM?', and I suggested that, apart from the rich, the main beneficiaries of NPM were politicians favourable to a reduction of the role of the state, high-ranking civil servants, most likely with a degree in business administration, and consultancy companies eager to expand their business in the public sector in addition to their traditional private enterprise domain. In case of difficulties in convincing the 'customers' of the state, they could easily use the argument of the 'inevitable globalization'.[5] I ended the article by asking the rhetorical question: 'is NPM by any chance the latest manifestation of some old private conservative interests?'

It was by that time clear to any reasonable observer of Western countries that NPM was urgently asking for, and in fact obtaining, a substantial departure from 'traditional' liberalism, as it had been developed since the Great Depression of the 1930s and even more in Europe after the end of the Second World War. Following the teaching of John Maynard Keynes, and considering the damage done to great numbers of people by unrestricted capitalism, state intervention had set up a whole range of public policies aimed at sustaining, regulating and controlling the economy, and at collectively helping those who were not able to contribute to the functioning of the economy because of illness, unemployment, old age or the like. That was a sort of compromise between capital and labour. Some people call this arrangement 'embedded liberalism'.[6] The new form of liberalism upon which NPM is based, that is, free-market liberalism or, more commonly, neoliberalism, had clearly the strategic goal of freeing the economy from the constraints of Keynesianism, and above all constraints on capital. Therefore, not only had management techniques to be transferred from the private to the public sector with the aim of improving public management on the assumption of the superior efficiency of the former, but the state should also retreat from all sorts of domains in which private entrepreneurship was supposed to provide better services at lower cost than what the state had been able to provide in the past. The road was then ideologically open to privatization, contracting out, public–private partnerships, and deregulation in all domains, including (and above all) the financial sector. In practice Western countries went a long way along this road. To what extent and with what consequences are the questions this book will try to answer. I should further remark that the proponents of embedded liberalism are now very keen, in face of the present financial and economic crisis, to claim their difference from neoliberalism, as if they would like to avoid bearing the responsibility for the crisis. Nevertheless, it must be remembered that, during the last three decades, the great majority of them have been the most faithful supporters of the neoliberal agenda, very likely because of their ideological proximity to the latter. Moreover, the present crisis has damaged not only the credibility of unfettered capitalism, but also millions of ordinary people who lost their homes, jobs and savings, not to mention their dignity.[7]

Whereas the trend set in motion by neoliberalism and its armed wing, NPM, was quite clear to independent scholars, there has been very little they have been able to do to contain, and even less to stop, the overwhelming wave of NPM. Several years later some people active in politics and in the public administration asked me: 'Where were intellectuals like you when we needed academic expertise to oppose the implementation of NPM?' The question is rather cruel and, I must admit, not ungrounded. Nevertheless, history shows that in similar circumstances, when a powerful and very large coalition exists, such as the one I mentioned above in favour of NPM, it is practically impossible to resist: quite simply one is not heard. After the publication of that article, I received only two letters of support. This is exactly what happened to the neoliberals during the years of the Welfare State, 1945–1975, what the French call *les trente glorieuses*: they were not heard either. In the preface to the second edition of his famous work *Capitalism and Freedom* Milton Freedman very bitterly complains about the ostracism liberal economists faced during that era:

> Those of us who were deeply concerned about the danger to freedom and prosperity from the growth of government, from the triumph of welfare-state and Keynesian ideas, were a small beleaguered minority regarded as eccentrics by the great majority of our fellow intellectuals.[8]

As I mentioned before, the critics of NPM were not even paid the compliment of being described as 'eccentrics' – which after all is not necessarily an offence – but were simply regarded as incompetent.

Nevertheless, after the publication of that newspaper article I was contacted by a colleague from the Geneva Graduate Institute of Developmental Studies who was editing a book on NPM and neoliberalism, asking me to contribute to it with a long article. I secured agreement that this article would bear the title 'Public Management at the Service of the Market'.[9] In my opinion, this was exactly what NPM had turned out to be. On the contrary, a conception of the role of the state in line with traditional democratic values would be that public management should be at the service of the people. You may say that this is too subtle a distinction and a distortion of what serious defenders of NPM really propose, as by serving the market (considered to be the best way of efficiently using and distributing resources) one is in fact serving the people. I am sorry to dissent, and I will prove it in this book, where in Chapter 5 I will update and expand the findings presented in that article. For the moment, it suffices to mention that the very serious World Bank expressed exactly that opinion when in 1997 it published a seven-volume evaluation of China's public management: 'the [Chinese] government must begin serving markets by building the legal, social, physical, and institutional infrastructure needed for their rapid growth.'[10] Luckily, as I will show later in this book, in the mid-1990s China stopped blindly serving the market, and later, since the beginning of the leadership of Hu Jintao in 2002, started to set up policies aimed at serving the people. By quoting this example, I do not mean that the government of any country should not support the market; I just want to say that the market alone, even if supported by the government, cannot satisfy all the people's needs, and that the first duty of any government is to serve its people, be it by supporting the market, by correcting the market, by substituting the market or even, if necessary, by opposing the market.[11]

In that article I provided (in a more detailed manner than for the newspaper article of 1997) the empirical evidence available at that time that showed that countries with strong NPM policies had increased inequality in the distribution of income, as well as the rate of poverty and crimes, and obtained a relatively low rate of unemployment but at the price of increasing the number of short-time, part-time and underpaid jobs. Moreover, all these features meant the exclusion from prosperity of large sectors of society. While admitting that the evidence provided at that time needed to be complemented by additional research, I concluded by saying that the available evidence already allowed us to prove not only the NPM's incapacity to solve those social problems, but that NPM was the cause of making them worse than ever. I suggested that another type of public management was needed, one that would be less oriented by economic rationality and the desire to serve the market, but more respectful of the democratic values that are the real foundations of a society of belonging and not of exclusion.[12] The reader will not be surprised to learn that the publication in 1999 of my article in the collective book by the renowned Presses Universitaires de France did not contribute to the diffusion of these ideas, and even less to their success.

In the meantime, at the beginning of 1999, when I had started writing that article, I was invited by one of my former assistants, who was at that time professor at the Institut de Hautes Etudes en Administration Publique (IDHEAP), to deliver a speech at an international congress organized at the University of Lausanne on the theme of 'The Administration in All Its Moods: Realizations and Consequences'.[13] The Congress was supposed to be a Grand Mass of NPM, and my former assistant, knowing my opinion on the matter, was clearly hoping to introduce some animation within the congress. I introduced my speech by saying, with a sense of humour that was not recognized as such by the majority of the participants, that I was quite at ease with addressing some criticism to NPM because I was not too far from retirement and in any case (for my last years of activity) I had just obtained two important mandates that would keep me busy until retirement.[14] In fact my presentation, entitled 'The role of the scientist in the definition of the strategies of reform', was a passionate, but well documented, critique of the proponents of NPM, and more specifically an attack on those intellectuals who first of all were betraying the scientific criteria of their academic training by promising miracles they obviously could not deliver (what I called 'the intellectual betrayal') and, second, by accepting to orient their expertise according to the policy goals of the public authorities who hired them, were violating the deontological criteria of their profession (what I called 'the professional betrayal'). In that speech I supported my personal conviction by quoting an American private consultant who, in the July–August 1997 issue of the very serious *Public Administration Review*, denounced the numerous attempts by American public administrations to corrupt individual consultants as well as consultancy companies by asking them to change the conclusions of their expert reports. He furthermore testified that freelance experts who would try to resist such pressure would run the risk of being put on a black list and not being hired any more in the future.[15] At the end of the conference several of my former students who were at that time working for international and national consulting companies that had become some of the most fervent suppliers of expertise for public administrations in line with NPM came to see me to confirm, in private, that the analysis I presented was correct.[16]

This was the only reaction I had after the conference, but by that time my academic activity had undergone a fundamental change as I had been entrusted with the direction of two international training programmes, in China and in Vietnam. Although both programmes have contributed to significantly improve my understanding of NPM, the Chinese programme has been by far the more inspiring, not because Vietnam was not an interesting case, but because of the different nature of the two programmes: the Chinese one was meant for the training of Chinese senior civil servants over a period of more than five years, whereas the Vietnam programme was meant for training professors of the National Academy of Public Administration in Hanoi and lasted only two years. It was at the beginning of 1997 that I was contacted by an official of the Swiss Ministry of Foreign Affairs asking me if by any chance I would be interested in managing the Chinese programme. I must confess that at the beginning I was rather cautious. My knowledge of China was based mainly on what I had learned as a student at the Geneva Graduate Institute of International Studies, where I had chosen China's nineteenth-century history, and on what I had learned, I suppose like any intellectual of my generation, by reading newspapers and a few academic books and articles. The Swiss were themselves quite cautious, as everybody in the West was waiting for what would happen after the death of Deng Xiaoping (who was very ill at that time) and, above all, to hear whether the Congress of the Chinese Communist Party programmed for the autumn of 1997 would confirm the reform process or not.

On the other hand, the proposal was tempting. I would have something new and stimulating for my last nine years at Geneva University, in addition to my 'traditional teaching' and hopefully a new research project on the countries I already knew, and very likely on Switzerland.[17] Moreover, China could turn out to be a good case for testing, in a fast-developing country that had introduced some market mechanisms, the hypotheses I had developed in the 1997 article. There was another important reason why China was an interesting case: in organizing its development strategy since the end of the 1970s China had clearly rejected the so-called 'Washington consensus', which in fact was the other armed arm of neoliberalism directed towards developing countries, whereas NPM was meant for the developed ones.[18] Therefore, the additional questions were: How would China resolve the apparent contradictions between its rejection of one aspect of neoliberalism (the 'Washington consensus') and the adoption of some of the neoliberal prescriptions (i.e. at least part of NPM)? How and to what extent did the 'Chinese NPM' succeed in modernizing (i.e. developing) the country's economy, whereas the majority (if not all) the developing countries that implemented (or were forced to implement) the 'Washington consensus' failed to do so?[19] Moreover, the framework of the training programme, already negotiated at the political level, very clearly indicated that the senior civil servants were to be trained in the modern management techniques, and thereby inevitably in NPM. In order to decide whether I would agree to manage the training programme, I started to do some more serious reading about China's reforms during the spring of 1997, hoping that the Swiss would take their decision after the Party Congress. However, suddenly during the month of May the Swiss informed me that they had decided to go on with the programme, and would I still be interested? I had to secure the hiring of a project manager and of at least one person of Chinese origin to work within the programme's team, this being a condition I posed to the Swiss for accepting the job. This caused me no difficulty because one of my former assistants, a private consultant, was available for a part-time job, and at Geneva University there were already at that time several well-educated students from mainland China. Moreover, according to the practice of the Swiss Development Agency, a so-called planning phase was to precede the signing of the contract, during which I had to go to China twice for the purpose of negotiating the actual and practical content of the programme with the Chinese partner in Beijing. This was quite reassuring for me, because, had I encountered some problems, or been presented by any other aspect I would not like, I could always refuse to sign. On the other hand, it was clear that the Chinese partner and the Swiss government could do the same. The deal was quite fair.

During the summer I did some more reading and finally I went to Beijing twice, with my 'potential' project manager, to negotiate the programme. The discussions, which lasted three weeks, went very smoothly and we were able to easily agree on a detailed programme, leaving some practical decisions for later, such as the actual choice of the individual experts and the training institutions. By then I was sure that China was an extraordinarily good example for testing, and very likely also for confirming, one of the main hypotheses implicit in the 1997 article: put very simply, that you cannot maximize economic efficiency and social equity simultaneously, and if you give too much space to the market you will inevitably lose in equity. To what extent and with exactly what kind of consequences for the Chinese people was something that I had to discover. Nevertheless, some indicators were already available at that time, showing that the introduction of market mechanisms had already increased unemployment to levels unknown in the past, and that, without the implementation of new safety nets to replace the social services provided in the past by the state-owned enterprises, this would inevitably favour the emergence of new forms of poverty. Moreover, the Party Congress that took place during my first visit to Beijing in September 1997 had decided to accelerate the reforms and to bring China into the World Trade Organization and the sooner the better: a clear sign that market mechanisms were going to acquire a greater momentum in China.

By now, knowing my very sharp criticism of NPM, the reader will imagine that I tried to avoid the hiring of training institutions that were most favourable to NPM. Well, I did not follow this strategy. On the contrary, I was by then convinced that the Chinese were knowledgeable and discerning enough to evaluate the suitability of NPM devices for their country. Moreover, not all the NPM tools were to be rejected as ideologically biased.[20] Finally, after discussion and agreement with the Chinese partner, we chose, among others, one of the training institutions most favourable to NPM: the British Civil Service College, which provided an outstanding contribution to the training; its experts (many of them senior civil servants) were highly appreciated by the Chinese participants.[21] Of course, we also hired the services of the French Ecole Nationale d'Administration (ENA), which also provided an outstanding contribution. Even if at that time the ENA was considered more traditional than the Civil Service College, the Chinese participants had been very much interested in the reforms introduced in France since the 1980s. In addition to this, as China was at that time privatizing state-owned enterprises (SOEs) and finding ways of improving the management of these enterprises, we also organized seminars not only in public administrations, but also in SOEs such as the SNCF (French Railways), privatized SOEs such as British Telecom, and private enterprises such as Nestlé, Thames Water, Alcatel and the major Swiss banks; and we did not hesitate to organize seminars with luxury companies such as LVMH and l'Oréal in Paris. Taking into consideration that the Chinese participants were mainly interested in the most practical and successful management tools used in the West, the only criterion for the selection was that these institutions should have outstanding expertise and practical experience in modern management strategies and techniques in both the private and the public sectors.

This programme has been my privileged entry into China. I have established contacts not only with senior officials of the Party-State at all levels of government, but also with intellectuals working in universities and think tanks. A book has been the product of this 10-year long endeavour.[22] How were the Chinese participants and their leaders approaching the management tools presented at the various seminars and conferences of the training programme? The following anecdote will allow me to avoid some too complicated explanations. In 2001 I was in Beijing to introduce the training programmes of the following year, discussing it with my Chinese partners and especially with the leaders of the delegations, all of them very senior officials within the Department of Organization, one of the most influential departments of the party organization under the Permanent Committee of the Politburo, the real government of China. One evening I was discussing the programme with the leader of one of the delegations in the convivial atmosphere of a traditional Chinese restaurant. Inevitably, the discussion revolved around the content of the programme, the topics to be dealt with, by whom, with what training technique and so on. The discussion went on more or less along the following lines.

'You see,' said the leader, 'we are interested in the practical aspects of management, how to do it, we want to know all the details . . .'

I said, 'Perfect, we can certainly deliver that, but would you be also interested to know something about the theoretical structure behind the practical aspects, what are the theories, the hypotheses upon which the practical aspects are based?'

'Well, this is certainly interesting,' replied the leader, 'but look at the decorations on the walls and ceiling of the restaurant! Look how beautiful they are, look at the details of the flowers and trees, the water of the rivers and lakes, the clothes of the people! We are interested in the details of management!'

I said, 'I understand, the details are really beautiful, but they could not exist without the architectural structure of the restaurant, they would collapse . . . The same is true for management!'

The leader waited a moment before answering in a tone that clearly was meant to put an end to the discussion: 'Yes, I understand, but you see, we have already got the structure!'

This conversation is quite revealing not only of how the Chinese were approaching the training programme, but more generally because it draws our attention to the fact that management tools (to use the terms of the proponents of NPM) are not simply practical devices, but they acquire their real significance only when they are considered within the general framework of the ideological and political structure that makes possible their adoption and orients the nature of the legal instruments upon which their implementation is based, as well as the delivery of the expected results that will be eventually submitted to political and/or scientific scrutiny. Tools are not neutral, since they are implemented within a teleological structure. A hammer can be used to drive nails or to kill somebody. Moreover tools may produce the intended or publicly proclaimed results, but also the unintended, unanticipated or hidden ones.[23] This is exactly what the defenders of NPM have not understood or, worse, what they have tried to conceal from the public. This is also what the traditional defenders of the interests of the less privileged people have not understood, by accepting the view of the promoters of NPM claiming that it was simply a set of practical tools with no ideological bias, aimed at improving the management of the state in terms of efficiency and quality. And who would be against this goal?

Of course, ideologies are indispensable and inevitable, as science cannot give all the answers and can seldom be helpful in choosing the fundamental values policies are expected to achieve.[24] Ideological premises, whether conscious or unconscious, are there and tend to orient the contending policy options, embedded as they are into the cultural structure that comprises the fundamental beliefs, values and behavioural rules.[25] Not taking into consideration these powerful elements that in fact constitute the foundation of the strategy of the contending parties is certainly a very serious 'strategic' mistake when appreciating the 'pragmatic' options presented by NPM.

In fact, even pragmatism cannot be considered as a reasonable alternative for ideology and eventually a substitute or a complement to science, as it is itself an ideology (i.e. a set of fundamental values, beliefs and behavioural norms); even worse, it may turn out to be an ideology of a more pernicious and vicious kind than clearly stated ideologies. In fact, pragmatism, as it is generally understood and implemented in the West, is too often used to mask the real ideological values that its proponents try to hide beneath proclaimed values such as moderation, propensity to compromise (or, to use a fashionable rhetoric, to negotiate win–win strategies and policies) and pragmatic adherence to the existing situation and to the actual possibilities of solving societal problems. Taking this last into consideration is certainly an excellent basis for designing successful policies, as China has shown during the process of reforms. However, Chinese pragmatism of the post-Mao era is quite different from the Western one. It is plausible that Chinese pragmatism appeared well before the post-Mao era. To my knowledge elements of pragmatism appeared at least in the mid-nineteenth century following the defeat of China by Western powers. Since then the Chinese leadership has not ceased to look for new institutional arrangements, wavering between the imitation of Western constitutionalism (during the last decades of the Empire), Western republicanisms (by the Nationalist Party), the Soviet model (during the Mao era) and a mixture of Western marketization and Chinese authoritarianism after 1978, not forgetting the more recent resurgence of elements of Confucianism (neo-Confucianism).[26] One could even dare say that in a sense Chinese pragmatism is pure pragmatism, without ideological bias. This may be a too radical statement. In fact some ideological features inherited from the imperial past are still active in China and orient the thinking and behaviour of Chinese people, including (and maybe above all) the Chinese leadership. These values are those of unity, harmony and stability that are necessary to realize the supreme goal of the Chinese government: restore China as a world power. The other choices (which may be interpreted as ideological ones) are mainly purely instrumental pragmatic ones, such as the choice of planned economy (1949–78), market mechanisms (since 1978) or modern social security (especially since the Hu Jintao leadership), as they are necessary for realizing the supreme goal.[27]

In the West we first define a model and postulate that, when implemented, it will produce some desired outcomes (e.g. market economy, liberalism) and then we try to change reality so that it corresponds to the model. The history of the implementation of NPM during the last 30 years shows, and even more so the debates going on since the outburst of the present economic crisis, that many policy options in the West have been based upon ideological considerations. On the contrary, the Chinese start from reality, see what aspects are favourable to the achievement of a fundamental goal (since the end of the nineteenth century: the restoration of Chinese power), and define some instrumental goals and policies aimed at realizing the fundamental goal (e.g. industrialization and modernization through planned economy 1949–78 or, since 1978, thanks to market mechanisms) taking into consideration what the French philosopher François Jullien has called 'the potential of the situation'.[28] Then the Chinese act upon some elements of reality that can be changed easily, this strategy being based upon the traditional motto 'the best victories are those that are achieved without fighting'. Finally, taking stock of the results obtained, the strategy is eventually changed if it has produced some consequences that may jeopardize the realization of the fundamental goal, for example the appearance of economic and social disparities both between and within regions, as was the case after the mid-1990s following the introduction of market mechanisms. Quite rationally, the fundamental goal (restoring Chinese power) is maintained, while some new instrumental goals and policies are designed and implemented (i.e. the setting up of policies aimed at rebalancing economy and society). Here the space for ideological choices is very limited; only during the Mao era were some very unsuccessful policies implemented upon purely ideological considerations such as the Great Leap Forward and the Cultural Revolution. However, since the end of the 1970s the Chinese leadership has systematically adopted the pragmatic way.

This does not mean that mistakes have been completely avoided. It is my opinion that market mechanisms have been introduced too rapidly since the beginning of the 1980s, and therefore the probable appearance of some unwanted consequences has not been clearly identified and forecast by the Chinese leadership. Nevertheless, when empirical evidence provided by rigorous applied research has pointed out the negative consequences of the implementation of market mechanisms, the Chinese leadership, freed from ideological considerations thanks to the adoption of the pragmatic way, has been able to easily change the pre-existing instrumental policies by adding the development of human capital, as measured by literacy, health and the availability of safety nets, to the development of the economy as measured by gross domestic product (GDP). Nor does this mean that ideological considerations have been completely absent from the decisions of reorienting China's public policies. It can be shown that the new policies set up by the Hu Jintao leadership to reduce inequalities and to 'put people first' have also been oriented by fundamental values such as equity, whereas, in the preceding period, economic efficiency was the fundamental value orienting public policies. However, it remains the case that, by reducing inequalities, the Chinese government is trying to avoid social and political unrest that will inevitably jeopardize the development of the economy and, consequently, the realization of the fundamental goal of restoring China as a world power.

In the discourse of the Western proponents of NPM, reality is generally a construct not corresponding to what exists in all circumstances, at least for some aspects (such as the inefficiency of the state and the superiority of the private sector). The aim of this construct is to support their policy choices in favour of privatization, contracting out, deregulation and, more generally, the reduction of the role of the state. This is exactly what the proponents of NPM have done during the last 30 years or so, both in China and in the West. For example, one of the arguments used in the West in favour of the reduction of the role of the state and consequently of its budget has been that taxation could not be increased, both for economic reasons (as excessive taxes run the risk of putting enterprises in a difficult position, especially in regard to international competition) and because of the opposition of the majority of taxpayers (what at the time was called 'the revolt of taxpayers'), which could not be overlooked in a democracy. In fact, there has been no clear proof of this. On the contrary, one can quote cases in which, as in Switzerland for the increase of the tax on petrol, citizens are ready to accept an increase in taxation on condition that the government can effectively provide good services in exchange for taxes. New Public Management claims in such circumstances that the services that the government would no longer be able to provide, following a reduction of taxation, will be provided at a lower cost and better quality by the private sector. This argument overlooks the fact that money must come from somewhere, and the private sector does not pay, but it invests and seeks profits from investment; so either the state covers part of the cost by subsidizing the private provider in order to reduce the selling price to its citizens (for example for transportation) and in this case the money comes from the taxpayers, or the private company sells its services at a price that covers its production cost, and in this case the money comes from the users. In this last case one can imagine the consequences in terms of access to the services, especially if it concerns vital services such as clean water, health care, education, housing and social insurance.

Moreover, NPM-ists accuse their critics of being the conservative nostalgic of a past that is completely outdated (generally referred to as 'socialist') that has clearly failed both as a radical experiment (the Communist-Soviet experiment that collapsed between 1989 and 1992) and as the more moderate social-democratic experiments of western Europe (1945–79). And globalization is the inescapable movement that has put an end to these experiments. In fact, if one is not prone to cheat with history, it is the NPM-ists who are the conservatives, and more precisely the reactionaries who have brought back to the nineteenth century the polity (by restricting some of its democratic features) and the economy by bringing back ideas and managerial habits of that brilliant past when workers were submitted to principles such as 'hire and fire', without any decent social security safety net. Taking into consideration the timing of the appearance of ideologies and theoretical models, it is clear that liberalism precedes socialism of any kind by at least several decades.[29] Today even the traditional defenders of capitalism recognize that Conservatism has overshot its limits.[30] However, what is at stake here is the conservatism of NPM's supporters, not of its critics.

In fact, one thing that has impressed me during the years of my research on

China's reforms (1978–2008) is that during exactly the same period, between 1978 and 2008, both China and the West have embarked upon a reform process with the aim of giving more space to the market. Of course the starting points were quite different, as were (and are still today) the cultural, political, legal and institutional environments in which these reforms are implemented. However, one of the major hypotheses at the origin of this research was, and I will confirm it in this book, that the logic of these reforms would inevitably present some striking similarities in spite of the differences mentioned above, namely that the improvement of economic efficiency would be realized at the cost of a deterioration in the equitable distribution of wealth. The similarities between China and the West became evident for me in April 2005 when I was invited to deliver a conference on the NPM in the West and its impact on state and society at the School of Public Policy and Management of Tsinghua University. After I presented both the positive and the negative consequences of NPM in the West, Professor Hu Angang took the floor and presented several Chinese data that exactly matched the Western ones: increasing difficulties for people in the labour market, increasing inequalities and criminal offences, increasing poverty rates, and impact of economic development on the environment and the health of people.

This was a short history of the journey that led me to the research presented in this book. In Chapter 2 I will come back in a more systematic way to the theoretical and methodological issues and difficulties that this research had to address: (1) the concepts of market, capitalism and socialism; (2) the nature of New Public Management and its origin in the 'Washington consensus' and neoliberalism; (3) the empirical typologies of public management and their link to typologies of capitalism and Welfare States; (4) the choice of indicators for testing the major hypotheses about the consequences of NPM and the difficulties in measuring them; and (5) what aspects the comparison between China and the West will deal with.

2 Comparing New Public Management in China and in the West

Some theoretical and methodological problems

In this chapter I will discuss several problems that are at the heart of the major goal of this book: to compare the consequences of New Public Management (NPM) in China and in the West. The first difficulty arises from the fact that in both areas market mechanisms are at work, and for some scholars China is practically evolving towards a capitalist economy (even if in the form of state capitalism). As this way of seeing the two areas is not, in my opinion, satisfactory, the first point to be discussed is what we mean by 'capitalism', 'market' and 'market economy'. Second, and closely linked to the first point, what is the relation between capitalism, neoliberalism and its armed wings: the 'Washington consensus' and NPM? This is an important point as the Chinese leadership, and a large part of the Chinese intelligentsia, has clearly refuted the idea that China should conform to the criteria of the 'Washington consensus' and, as a consequence, also to NPM. Third, it will be necessary to justify the typology that will be at the heart of the comparison made in the fifth chapter between several capitalist states. This typology comprises two types: strong NPM and weak NPM. Considering that practically all the countries that at the beginning of the 1980s were not NPM countries, but have become NPM countries (of either the strong or the weak variant) after 1980, I will also use the intermediary type of the in-transition-to-NPM countries. Fourth, I will have to discuss the choice of the dependent variables (employment, income, poverty, crimes and health) as well as the difficulties in measuring these variables, their reliability, and the lack of data in some cases. Finally, we will need some explanations about what I mean by comparison between China and Western countries.

Markets, free markets, market mechanisms, capitalism, and socialism

These concepts are closely linked to the Chinese strategy of development. It is here that the problems start when we try to understand this strategy, as evaluating China's development strategy is not an easy task, first of all because it has been implemented in a relatively short span of time involving practically all the dimensions of China's society. A mono-disciplinary approach would inevitably not only tell just one part of the story, but also very likely run the risk of misinterpreting the reform process, its official intentions and its objective outcomes. Moreover, approaching China from the West may be rather misleading as our models and theories have been built from within and during our historical experience, of which we are very proud, to the point that we tend to consider these models and theories as universal, whereas in fact they are, at least partially, different from the ways in which Chinese scholars have developed their own way of thinking and analysing China's reforms.[1] So, what is the best approach for understanding China: the Western one, considered by Westerners as possessing universal value, or the Chinese one, considered by Westerners as being parochial? Moreover, what about the different Western models and theories, that can, for the sake of simplicity, be subdivided into liberal (including neoliberal) and Marxist? Are there not also in today's China liberal, neoliberal and Marxist theoretical frameworks used by Chinese scholars? Of course, one could say that there is only one way of looking at China's reforms, and this is the scientific approach, which is, by definition, universal. This may be an objective that the academic community would like to constitute as a reality today, but, for the time being, it is far from being realized, as the different interpretations of China's reforms very well illustrate within the academic communities in China and the West. The same could be said of the interpretations of the 2008–11 financial and economic crises, which inevitably, as it is global, has an impact on China, the West and their economic and political relations. At the heart of the different ways of analysing these very complex phenomena lie concepts such as market, market economy, free market, capitalism, Marxism and socialism.

Experiments with a market economy did not start in China in 1978.[2] Already towards the end of the Empire China presented several features of an early capitalist society after centuries of societal development. The French sinologist Marie-Claire Bergère has described the changes of Chinese society as follows.[3] Before the nineteenth century China was not a stagnant society, as is too often described by Western observers. The remarkable dynamism between the sixth and the eleventh centuries was followed by the Mongol conquest and isolation that came to an end only under the Ming dynasty at the beginning of the sixteenth century. A new economic development then took place that continued under the Qing dynasty until the beginning of the nineteenth century. Moreover, China has been a pioneer in the development of science and technology since the tenth century.[4] At the point when Europe started its own scientific development (fifteenth to sixteenth century) China still possessed a considerable advance in science and technology over Europe.[5] The Chinese scientific innovations exerted a remarkable impact on the organization of economic production, as well as on social structures, including the appearance of forms of market economy that are still partially present today, and are therefore worth studying in order to understand the specific forms of the development of market mechanisms during the reform era; that is, after 1978.[6] An emerging entrepreneurial class was already active, especially in the coastal regions. Nor do I underestimate the economic and social development during the Mao era: industrialization and advances in education were considerable and improvements in public health were remarkable and overall more impressive than during the first two decades of the reform era (1978–98). However, it is the period after 1978 that interests us for the comparison of the consequences of NPM in China and the West. I will present this in Chapter 6, because it corresponds to the introduction of market mechanisms.

As already mentioned in Chapter 1 (note 11), I use the expression 'market mechanisms' instead of market economy to avoid frequent misunderstandings in Western literature, but often also in the writings of some Chinese authors. In the West, a market economy is often associated with the idea of freedom, hence the use of 'free market' to designate the Western economy. Moreover, it is considered that the Western economy is the only possible form of economy to deserve the qualification of 'market economy' or 'free market economy'; hence it acquires the status of 'THE market economy'. Starting from these premises, the majority of Western scholars and opinion leaders consider the Chinese expression 'socialist market economy' at best with some amazement, at worst with sarcasm. Why? First of all because, as suggested above, the only possible form of economy deserving the qualification of 'market economy' is the Western one. Now, if we look a little closer at the real meaning of 'free market' and 'market economy' in the West we discover that in reality what is meant by these expressions is 'capitalist market economy'.[7] If we accept this way of designating the form of economy that has prevailed in the West, the Chinese expression 'socialist market economy' becomes less strange. Nevertheless, and a second reason for not accepting the expression 'socialist market economy', many if not all the above-mentioned Western scholars and opinion leaders would continue to refuse the association of market with socialism, as they see in this association an indisputable and unacceptable contradiction in terms (and in reality): there cannot be a market economy with socialist characteristics, or, more precisely, there cannot be a socialist market economy.[8]

Fernand Braudel on market and capitalism

Economic history shows that there have been different forms of market economy, very likely since ancient times, and therefore capitalism cannot be considered as the only form of market economy. Many books have been written during the last decades on capitalism, its origins and main features.[9] Nevertheless, the works of Fernand Braudel remain for me the most interesting and stimulating analysis, as he has convincingly shown that there have been several stages in the historical process through which modern capitalism has emerged and, more disturbingly, for Braudel capitalism is not a form of market economy, but the upper layer of the hierarchical structure of human activities linked to production and consumption, which does not possess two of the major characteristics of a market: transparency and competition.[10] Braudel's analysis of the development of economic activities is based upon a historical analysis that goes back practically to the 'beginning of history'. In fact Braudel, whose approach contradicts many interpretations of the appearance and development of market economy and capitalism,[11] complains about the lack of historical perspective of too many analyses:

> Journalists, economists, and sociologists [and, I would add, political scientists] often fail to take historical dimensions and perspectives into account in their writings, and don't many historians do the same thing, as if the period they study existed in a vacuum, or was both a beginning and an end?[12]

In his historical analysis Braudel has chosen to deal with the long-term trends that led to the emergence of capitalism in different parts of the world:

> I chose to deal with long term equilibriums and disequilibriums. To my mind, the fundamental characteristic of the preindustrial economy is the coexistence of the inflexibility, inertia, and slow motion characteristic of an economy that was still primitive, alongside trends – limited and in the minority, yet active and powerful – that were characteristic of modern growth. On the one hand, peasants lived . . . in autarchy; on the other hand, a market-oriented economy and an expanding capitalism . . . gradually creating the very world in which we live . . .[13]

So, for Braudel there are three worlds that he treats not as three ideal-types (in the Weberian sense) but as real phenomena that have emerged through history: first, material life (in which markets do not exist, yet); second, markets; and, finally, capitalism. Moreover, the first world tends to persist after the appearance and the development of market economy and capitalism, and market economy tends to persist after the development of capitalism. Furthermore, these three worlds are organized within a hierarchy in which, at the end of the process, capitalism becomes the upper and dominating layer. In fact, Braudel shows through his historical analysis that elements of market economy were already present at the time when material life was by far the most frequent way of organizing production and consumption.[14] Similarly, elements of capitalism were already present when material life was in the process of being dominated, but not totally replaced, by market economy; only during the process of the industrial revolution capitalism becomes the dominant layer, even if elements of material life and market economy persist. Braudel is persuaded that his findings show an opposition between a 'normal economic activity' on one hand and a 'sophisticated, superior economy' on the other. Moreover, economic agents, actions and mind-sets are not the same within the three layers, and, even more interestingly, the laws of market economy, especially free competition as described by classical economics, operate more rarely within the upper layer, which is where calculations and speculation abound. Here there is a 'zone of shadow', and of insiders' activities; and this is what Braudel considers to be the root of the phenomena that can be covered by the word of 'capitalism' that are not the real, the true market economy, but so often its clear contradiction.[15] So for Braudel what characterizes capitalism is the lack of transparency and of competition. How far we are here from the dominant discourse of liberals and neoliberals in universities, mass media and political debates!

Let me end this short overview of Braudel's approach to market economy and capitalism by quoting his conclusion in his own words:

capitalism has always been monopolistic, and merchandise and capital have always circulated simultaneously, for capital and credit have always been the surest way of capturing and controlling a foreign market. Long before the twentieth century the exportation of capital was a fact of daily life, for Florence as early as the thirteenth century . . . Need I observe that all methods, dealings, and tricks ['ruses' in the French edition, p. 118] of the financial world were not born in 1900 or in 1914? Capitalism was familiar with them all, and, yesterday as today, its uniqueness and its strength lie in its ability to move from one trick to another, from one way of doing things to another, to change its plans ten times as the economic conjunctures dictate –, and as a result, to remain relatively faithful, consistent with itself.[16]

Even if we cannot interpret this assertion in the sense that capitalism is always totally monopolistic and that capitalist economic agents always behave in the absence of competition and transparency, it is evident that total transparency is never realized, and competition is at best limited to a small number of competitors, and at worse totally absent either because competitors conclude cartel agreements or because only one economic agent dominates the sector. The functioning of the capitalist economy tends to exclude transparency and competition in the search of increasing market shares and profits to the point that, in Braudel's analysis, markets do not exist any more in many important sectors. So, capitalism can be defined as an economic system in which private capital is invested for the purpose of making a profit; when capitalism becomes the upper and dominating layer within the production and consumption processes and succeeds in imposing its values and goals on the rest of society, including the polity, then we can consider that this society has become capitalist.

Braudel's approach to market and capitalism and the case of China

What is the interest of Braudel's approach for the study of Chinese economy, namely the discovery of the coexistence of three layers of economic activity: material life, market and capitalism? According to Braudel, only when one of the three layers acquires a dominant role can we use its name to describe the whole economic system: material economy before the advent of market economy, market economy before the advent of capitalism, capitalism when the upper layer succeeds in dominating the two subordinate layers. The difficulty arises when we have to decide at what point in time the characteristics of one layer have become so widespread and important that it has become the dominating layer. Many observers of China's economic development consider that the introduction of what I have called 'market mechanisms' is equivalent to the introduction of market economy. Moreover, as for them a market economy is equivalent to capitalism, they come to the conclusion that China's economy has become capitalist, even if they are compelled to qualify this statement by using the expression 'state capitalism'. It seems to me that this conclusion is a bit too rash and indeed quite superficial. Here another passage of Braudel's *Civilization and Capitalism* is very useful: the partial character of market economy may be due to the importance of material life, or to the state, which can take part of the production for its own use, or even more to the role of money that can artificially intervene in price formation in thousands of different ways; market economy can therefore be limited from below by material life, as well as from above by capitalism and/or by state intervention.[17] When in Chapters 5 and 6 I evaluate the consequences of NPM on economy and society in China and in the West, I label the analysis of the consequences on economy as 'a view from above', and the consequences on society as 'a view from below', thus following Braudel's approach because in the West NPM has been imposed 'from above' by neoliberals' capitalism, and in China by the Party-State, with the result of determining a number of societal changes 'below'.

Indeed, following Braudel's approach, it would be only partially correct to talk about the 'Chinese market economy'. It is true that China has introduced some market characteristics (i.e. competition and transparency) in parts of its economy. It is for this reason that the Chinese government has for a long time been asking the Western governments to recognize its economy as a market economy.[18] Nevertheless, the market economy covers only part of China's economic system. Indeed, it is also true that markets do not exist in other parts of China's economy, as they are in fact owned by, or under the monopolistic control of, the Party-State.[19] Moreover, it is also true that in some parts of China's economy some new capitalists are quite active and control pricing to a certain extent by using monopolistic or quasi-monopolistic strategies.[20] As mentioned before, some Western authors use this situation to describe the Chinese economy as a 'state capitalism'. This is not my opinion, as I will explain hereafter.

Using 'market economy' to describe the Chinese economy in Western academic and journalistic contexts would run the risk of giving the impression of considering that China's economy is similar to the Western one, or that it is at least moving in that direction. Indeed, it is the enlightening descriptions and analysis presented by Braudel that have suggested to me not to use 'market economy' when referring to the abandonment of the planned economy by China and the concomitant opening up of economic activities to private entrepreneurships and capital (both domestic and foreign), but to designate these innovations as the introduction of 'market mechanisms' instead of the adoption of a 'market economy'.[21] By this I mean that the form of economic organization that has emerged in China after 1978 is by no means a capitalist market economy, but a 'socialist market economy' very different from the 'capitalist market economy' of the West.

Many features of the new China system point in this direction. First, the freedom of the new Chinese capitalists mentioned above is limited by the Party-State: nothing can be done in the economic sphere without the explicit or implicit approval of the Party-State. One has also to remember that, contrary to what happened in the former Soviet bloc, economic reforms introducing market mechanisms have been decided, implemented, developed and controlled by the Communist Party-State for a period of more than 30 years with the success we know. There is evidence that the majority of Chinese capitalists have no reasons for opposing the Party, as it seems that the policies of the Party-State are the conditions of their economic and social success.[22] Second, land is still collective property in China and this constitutes a powerful instrument in the hands of the Party-State for orienting and controlling economic and social development.[23] Third, as I have already pointed out elsewhere, and as I shall further develop in Chapter 6 and in the conclusion, the Party-State has reoriented its public policies away from a strategy of 'economic development first' towards a strategy of 'putting people first', with a clear departure from the neoliberal policies implemented during the 1990s in strategic domains such as health and education, alongside the replacement of the social functions of the state-owned enterprises of the Mao era with a modern safety net.[24] Fourth, the banking system is still under the political control of the Party-State, in spite of several measures taken for improving its economic efficiency that have given to Western observers the impression that it was progressively reformed in order to make it compatible with capitalist criteria.[25]

This predominance of the Party-State is a very clear indicator that the Chinese economy is by no means a capitalist economy. It is therefore in the presence of elements of material life (i.e. of large sectors of the informal economy), of some important, but not dominant, capitalist economic agents, that market mechanisms have been introduced by a dominant Party-State that occupies a large sector of the economy and orients and controls the development of China's economic activities.[26] There are clearly several differences from what happens in the West, where economic agents of capitalism dictate in fact the essential items of the political agenda and the essential content of public policies, as the way the West is managing the 2008–11 crisis demonstrates very well.

The features of the present-day Chinese economic and political systems mentioned above are clear indicators of the progressive implementation of a 'socialist market economy', in which the economic side stands for the development of market mechanisms under the control of the Party-State (and not of a neoliberal elite), and the socialist side is represented by the policies that 'put people first'. Of course, this does not mean that there are no problems in the management and control of the interface between material life, informal economy, market mechanisms and capitalist elements of the Chinese economic system.[27] However, so far, the capitalist elements are not yet sufficiently widespread and important to qualify China's economic system as a capitalist economy, whatever the further qualifying adjective. In conclusion, for the time being, the difference between China and the West is therefore one of nature and the two systems cannot be considered as simple variations within the type of 'capitalist economy'.[28] This does not mean either that the Chinese system may not evolve towards a capitalist economy in the future; but for the time being many indicators point to the opposite direction.

The academic debate on the 'Chinese market' and the Western democratic model: the view from the West

The analysis presented in the preceding paragraphs contradicts both the opinion of Western mainstream scholars and opinion leaders on one hand, and that of Marxists or neo-Marxists on the other. The former applaud the Chinese reforms because they have transformed China's economy into a capitalist economy, which is for them a positive development, even if many in the West regret that Chinese capitalism is in fact a state capitalism in which the private sector has not (or not yet) been completely freed of state intervention.[29] On the other hand, Marxists regret the transformation of China's economy into a capitalist-state economic system that has abandoned the public property of some means of production, and is dominated by a Party that has betrayed the cause of the emancipation of the masses (which was for them one of the major goals and realizations – even if partial – of the Maoist system). Moreover, they fear that the political system is used by the CPC to further develop private property at the expense of the masses.[30] In my opinion, following Braudel once again, it is important to distinguish the market (or market mechanisms) from capitalism.

I am convinced that these opposed ways of interpreting the transformations of Chinese economy, polity and society are both hampered by two outdated theoretical frameworks of analysis, embedded in the old categories of Marxist and liberal analysis, namely the fundamental contradiction (and therefore impossible coexistence) between private property and public property, especially the property of the means of production.[31] In fact, the neoliberals regret not so much that public property persists in China, but that it is managed by the polity and within the polity by the Communist Party; consequently, they regret and condemn the fact that in China politics is in command and conditions and controls the development of private capital, whereas in the West capitalist organizations (right-wing political parties and owners' associations) dominate the political system and orient the production of public policies so that they do not contradict the 'laws of the free-market economy'. This interpretation of the neoliberal evaluation of the Chinese economy is clearly demonstrated by the fact that liberals and neoliberals accept public property in Western countries so long as the economic and political forces that sustain capital are in a position to dominate the political system and thereby decide what kind of freedom, space and function public property may possess within the capitalist economy.

In this context, the political mechanisms provided by liberal democracy (namely free elections, freedom of opinion, of speech and association) are used by these forces to maintain the dominance of capital over labour. There is in fact a symbiosis between economic, political and cultural elites (especially opinion leaders in the educational system and in the mass media) that sustain the fundamental values of economic and political liberalism and orient public policies in order to maintain the liberal order. Moreover, political forces that in the past have been the strong defenders of labour have little by little moved to the centre, thus inevitably moving also to the right, and this is a critique of the pretence of the 'third way' supported by some outstanding Western intellectuals such as Anthony Giddens.[32] Moreover, as at the same time the right-wing parties (of all persuasions) have further moved to the right, this has resulted in the left-wing forces accepting the 'market economy' as the best (and in fact the only) way of organizing production and consumption (and here Braudel is again useful), not understanding that by doing so they have in fact accepted not so much the market economy but the upper layer of the production–consumption hierarchy, namely capitalism. The surrender of the Left to the Right could not have been more complete. The door was then open to the acceptance of a series of policy options that have in fact increased the dominance of capital over labour.[33]

This is not to say that within the liberal system space was not given to social policies, but these are conceived by the dominant elites, voted on by parliaments (within which these elites have the majority) and implemented by the states' administrations only in so far as they do not jeopardize the essential characteristics of the liberal system: the freedom and dominance of capital. This is not a value judgement, but a simple observation of reality that moreover brings to light one of the fundamental contradictions of the liberal system: the polity is based upon democracy, in which every citizen possesses an equal weight (according to the maxim 'one man, one vote'), whereas in the economy only those who possess the economic and technical competence to run the economy are allowed to be in command. Hence the systematic opposition of the defenders of capitalism and liberal democracy to any form of co-decisional arrangements between capital and labour within enterprises, and more generally within the economy.[34] We can see this strategy in action when we consider the development of capitalism after the Great Depression of the 1930s. In order to save the system, social policies have been introduced (e.g. the American New Deal of President Franklin D. Roosevelt) and even more so after the end of the Second World War, when all the European countries implemented the set of social policies that have constituted the Welfare State. This trend was developed and improved until the mid-1970s when the difficulties experienced by Western countries in the management of the state and its relationship with the market led them to progressively diminish (some have said to dismantle) the Welfare State. Some have also said that in doing so they dismantled the democratic states as well.[35]

As I mentioned above, this has been possible thanks to the displacement of the axes of the political system to the centre, and hence to the right, following the collapse of the Soviet bloc and the alignment of the majority of the left-wing forces (and above all of the social-democratic parties) with the major themes of the liberal and neoliberal ideology, that is, the acceptance of the 'free market', in fact of capitalism. What remains of the old left political agenda is the attempt to limit the negative consequences of the implementation of the neoliberal project. I have briefly commented this trend in Chapter 1, and I have interpreted elsewhere the functioning of neoliberal democracy as follows:

> democracy as it is practiced today in Western countries is characterized by an inextricable symbiosis between the political elite that performs official public roles within the state's organs on one side and, on the other, the economic elite that dominates the market economy. It is within a complex game between economic, political and intellectual elites (including influential university professors and journalists) that policy options are examined, choices are made and then presented to the public. . . . Of course there exists a 'free press' that can monitor the work of the elites.
>
> Nevertheless, the majority of the mass media that have a large circulation within and amongst Western countries are under the control of powerful companies that themselves belong to the economic elite, with which they

share ideological values and economic interests. It is not likely that these mass media can exert an efficient and impartial control over the ruling elite . . . Moreover, some critics of Western democracy also consider that trade unions and left-wing parties that should defend the interests of the weakest sector of society have little by little, at least since the beginning of the 1980s, failed in this mission, and have embraced the major options of the liberal economic elite.[36]

We can see the last development of this trend after the outbreak of the 2008–11 crisis. Everything has been put into practice to save the essential component of the Western model, its financial system, which bears the main responsibility for the crisis, and very little has been done in favour of those who suffered and are still today suffering most from the collapse of the housing market, the increase of unemployment due to the contamination of the so-called 'real economy' and the consequent increase of the poverty rate.[37] Moreover, the crisis has accelerated the movement towards the reduction of the Welfare State. One of the most radical defenders of neoliberalism, the French writer Guy Sorman, has even published recently an article in the *Shanghai Daily* saying, with a badly (or hardly) concealed satisfaction, that the European Welfare State, which since the Second World War has provided Europeans with 'cradle-to-grave' social benefits, is at last coming to an end. His reasoning is that the Welfare State has been of benefit more to the middle class than to the poor. First globalization and more recently the 2008–11 crisis have put such pressure on European states (and also on the USA) that they 'have no choice but to reduce their expenditures, and targeting welfare benefits that represent, on average, half of European public spending is the easiest way to bring immediate fiscal relief.' At least Sorman concedes that 'the Welfare State will not vanish, but it is set to be scaled back – and focused on those who actually need help.'[38] These ideas are common for neoliberals, who place the main responsibility on the individual and are systematically opposed to the intervention of the state not only in the economy but also in the social domain; only the very poor need to be supported. However, if this is the case, how to explain the fact that the rate of poverty in these countries has not diminished over time and has even increased during the 2008–11 crisis, as has the number of working poor?[39] Not a word in Sorman's article on the responsibility for European and American unemployment, no reference to the enormous US military budget, no comment about the case for universal coverage . . . the only reason: it costs too much and the middle class does not need it. Really . . . ?

The academic debate on the 'Chinese market' and the Western democratic model: the view from China

Coming now to Chinese intellectuals, it is interesting to take into consideration their reaction to the situation that has emerged since the beginning of reforms, following the attempt by the Chinese leadership to combine public and private property without liberal democracy and without letting the new 'red Chinese capitalists' dominate the system. This experiment, whose aim is the attainment of economic efficiency and a fair distribution of wealth, has attracted criticism not only from neo-Marxist scholars, such as Li Minqi,[40] but also from the neoliberals (whom He Li calls 'new liberals') and from Chinese intellectuals who are generally in the West put under the label of 'The New Left'.[41] Let us note that most of the time the latter refuse the 'New Left' label as it introduces, according to them, the false idea that they are nostalgic dreamers of the Mao era; they would prefer the qualification of 'critical intellectuals'. According to one of the best specialists on China's intelligentsia, Arif Dirlik, the New Left label

> makes little sense within the context of a socialist society. Its use in contemporary China is one indication of unease that, in pursuit of national wealth and power as it appears through the lens of private interests, the country has strayed from the socialist goals of justice and equality, and national goals of autonomous development. . . . The term seemingly encompasses all those who have raised questions about post-1992 development and its social and environmental consequences. Some believe that there may be answers, if only as inspiration, in earlier revolutionary experiences, and invoke them in criticism of present-day problems.[42]

In my book on China's reforms I have already pointed to the difficulty of classifying Chinese intellectuals within the Western categories such as 'New Left', 'liberals' and 'neoliberals'.[43] To give an idea of the difficulty, it suffices to mention that authors have identified several Chinese 'schools': Reformers, Mainstream School, Non-Mainstream School, Liberals, Neoliberals, Liberal Left, Liberal Right, the Left; and, within the Chinese Left, authors distinguish subcategories such as Marxists, Stalinists, Anti-Imperialists, Statists, Social-Democrats and the New Left. Moreover, it sometimes happens that an intellectual is classified in different schools by different scholars.[44] Moreover, according to He Li only a few intellectuals 'openly embraced Neoliberalism or New Leftism.' And the resulting confusion that made the categorization so difficult is probably because 'being labelled as "against socialism, for capitalism" could spell the end of one's career.'[45] In fact, the major divide among Chinese intellectuals is between neoliberals and the New Left.[46] It is interesting to note that the authoritative *Foreign Policy*, in establishing in 2008 the list of the 100 top public intellectuals, included only two Chinese intellectuals: a new-leftist historian (Wang Hui) and a neoliberal economist (Fan Gang).[47]

Let us start with the position of a neo-Marxist scholar, who is also a Chinese expatriate living and teaching in the United States, Li Minqi.[48] Li considers that capitalism 'is a social system based on the production of profit and the endless accumulation of capital', based upon low environmental costs, low wages and low taxation; but these costs will mount in the long run, making capitalism no longer profitable.[49] In 1994 Li completed a book in which he refuted 'neoliberal economics and the myth that private property is indispensable for economic rationality' and 'discussed the inherent contradictions between democracy and capitalism.'[50] In his last book, Li develops the theme of the relationship between China's rise and the world capitalist system and concludes that:

the crisis of accumulation in the 1960s and 1970s marked the beginning of the structural crisis of the existing world-system.[51] The system's remaining 'strategic reserve' (China, India, and the earth's remaining resources and ecological space) were called upon to revive system-wide accumulation. By doing so, however, the system has exhausted its remaining space for self-regulation and restructuring.[52]

This is clearly the thesis shared by many neo-Marxists.[53] If it is true that we cannot exclude the possibility that capitalism will one day come to an end (as history shows that no one single system ever survived more than a few centuries) it is doubtful that Li's analysis will allow us to forecast the end of capitalism in the near future, as there are other 'spaces' that can still be integrated into the world-capitalist system, such as Africa and several other underdeveloped countries.

Li's analysis is similar to that of one of the most influential inspirers of the 'New Left', Immanuel Wallerstein, who has written recently:

> Some claim that the greatly improved economic position of Asia . . . will allow a resurgence of capitalist enterprise, through a simple shift of location. One more illusion! The relative rise of Asia is a reality, but one that undermines further the capitalist system by over-extending the distribution of surplus-value, thus reducing overall accumulation for individual capitals rather than increasing it. China's expansion accelerates the structural profit squeeze of the capitalist world-system.

Nevertheless, Wallerstein is careful in predicting what system will replace capitalism and he gives only a 50/50 chance to the victory of socialism.[54] In an interview given to the influential French newspaper *Le Monde* in October 2008, Wallerstein said that:

> the crisis we are living in corresponds to the end of a political cycle, the one of American hegemony that started in the 1970s. The USA will remain an important actor, but it will never again regain its dominant position in the face of the multiplication of the centres of power, with Western Europe, China, Brazil and India. A new hegemonic power, if we refer to the long time of Braudel, may take 50 years to impose itself. But I do not know which one.[55]

If we recall the quotation of Braudel mentioned above according to which the strength of capitalism lies

> in its ability to move from one trick to another, from one way of doing things to another, to change its plans ten times as the economic conjunctures dictate –, and as a result, to remain relatively faithful, consistent with itself,

it is not likely that the collapse of capitalism will occur in the near future, as the reactions of capitalist countries to the 2008–11 crisis demonstrate very well.

Nevertheless, it seems to me that, looking at the present situation of countries around the world, China is today capable of inventing for the future a system different from capitalism as well as from the failed historical examples of the Soviet Union and eastern Europe. This is exactly what some members of the 'New Left' are working on. Amongst the New Left Chinese intellectuals, Cui Zhiyuan has recently affirmed with force that there is not necessarily a contradiction between public and private property.[56] Moreover, Cui, who refers to John Stuart Mill, Henry George and Proudhon, is a serious advocate of 'petty bourgeois socialism' based upon the idea that after the Marxist revolution the proletariat cannot remain proletarian. By this Cui suggests that other social groups may constitute the social basis of Chinese socialism aimed at realizing a 'socialist market economy' and a 'relatively well off society', especially those left aside by the development strategy followed by Deng Xiaoping: peasants, laid-off workers, migrant workers, students, the emerging middle class and so forth. In fact, Cui considers that 'socialist market economy' contains a clear reference to 'petty bourgeois socialism'.[57] Referring more particularly to J.S. Mill, who mentions, in the last chapter of the third edition of *Principles of Political Economy*, examples of partnerships between workers and capitalists for running businesses in the USA, Cui mentions the 'joint-stock cooperative system' that has existed in rural China since the 1980s as an example of partnership.[58] Furthermore, Cui considers that the 'petty bourgeois socialism' is necessary for analysing the systemic innovation that emerged in China and that goes together with the concepts of a 'relatively well off society' and of 'socialist market economy' that are the main objectives of the Party-State. Finally, for Cui, 'petty bourgeois socialism' is not synonymous with social democracy, in which governments (and here Cui refers more particularly to Western countries) are promoting fairness focusing on the secondary distribution (i.e. on redistributive policies, after the market has operated the primary distribution of income), thus accepting the role of capitalism. A policy of balancing efficiency and fairness (or equity), as it was adopted by the Communist Party at the Congress of 2002, requires another theoretical framework, one that allows the combination of socialized assets with a market economy. In this sense the Chinese economy is in fact a 'socialist market economy'.

It is interesting to note that Cui complains about the fact that the West attributes China's economic success mainly to privatization and marketization:

> When interpreted in terms of bourgeois socialist thinking, however, the success obtained in China's economic reforms cannot be explained by marketization or privatization. I maintain that China's 'socialist market economy' must be taken seriously – that it is not a sort of political compromise. The essence of the 'socialist market economy' is the operation of socialized assets in a market economy, and this is precisely one of the systemic mechanisms for China's relative success.[59]

Moreover, Cui insists on institutional innovation, and for this purpose China should take advantage of both Western and Chinese experiments. Updating the references to J.S. Mill mentioned above, Cui refers to the changes operated since the 1980s by several states of the USA that have modified their corporate law requiring that management serve 'not only the shareholders, but the stakeholders as well. Such reform in American corporate law breaks through the seemingly axiomatic logic of private ownership, thus becoming the most significant event in recent US politics – and economy.'[60] This statement clearly dates from before the 2008–11 crisis. It is probable that Cui will no longer sustain this position today. In any case, in my opinion, the Braudel approach to market economy and capitalisms, presented above, should encourage great caution with this type of reforms at the local level (in this case, at the level of several member states of the USA) because what counts in a capitalist economy is the dominance of capital over the market, both national and international. On the other hand, Cui refers explicitly to experiments of the Mao era and considers that 'the failure of previous practice does not prevent its positive elements from being absorbed and transformed under new circumstances.'[61] Moreover, 'China also needs to look for lessons of experience in Mao Zedong's industrial practice since, to a great degree, it provides the most important modern form of industrial management, i.e. management through workers' participation.'[62]

But how to build a development strategy different from the Russian example? After having criticized the privatization strategy followed by Russia and eastern Europe that has produced huge income inequalities and social dissatisfaction and has thus jeopardized the development and consolidation of democratic regimes, Cui builds his alternative strategy for China starting from the works of the Nobel prizewinner J.E. Meade. This strategy will 'build wide public support by virtue of its efficiency as well as justice'; it 'aims to combine the best features of traditional capitalism and traditional socialism and has two main components: the labour–capital partnership and the social dividend.'[63] In short, labour and capital should share, on an equal basis, the benefits and risks involved in the management of a business: investors will hold capital shares, the workers labour shares; the two parties will elect an equal number of members of the boards of directors, and these will elect a chairman with a casting vote. This partnership is justified as follows:

> because shareholders have only limited liability, they do not bear the full cost of a firm's actions and therefore cannot claim to be full risk-bearers. Moreover, while outside shareholders can diversify their stock and reduce risk through a portfolio of shares in different companies, one worker cannot work for several companies at the same time. . . . Hence . . . workers should be partners with outside shareholders in sharing control rights and cash flow rights over corporate assets.

Finally, each citizen will receive a tax-free social dividend according to age and family status, meant to cover basic needs, especially in case of illness and unemployment.[64]

It is finally interesting to note that Cui has recently benefited from an opportunity to test his ideas in Chongqing. In fact, in 2007 Chongqing was designed by the Chinese government as an experimental zone for integrating rural and urban development. The local government has taken this opportunity to experiment with a whole range of policies that combine private and public investments with the aim of creating a harmonious development that should benefit all groups of citizens, especially the peasants and other groups that have not benefited, and in fact have suffered, from economic development so far.[65] Since the autumn of 2010 Cui has been seconded from Tsinghua University to the Chongqing municipality as assistant to the chairman of the State Assets Commission of Chongqing in charge of managing the public assets of the municipality. This experience has already allowed him to conclude that the 'Chongqing experience shows that public ownership of assets and private entrepreneurship are not necessarily contradictory and that they are not substitute for each other.'[66] I will come back to this interesting experience at the end of Chapter 6, when I will evaluate the capacity of China to rebalance its economy and society.

Taking a different, and probably also a more critical view, another 'New Left' intellectual also teaching at Tsinghua University, Wang Hui, recognizes that the Party-State has adopted several policies aimed at reducing the disparities within Chinese society, but unfortunately the results obtained are for the moment not sufficient.[67] In the preface (dated 23 October 2009) to his last book published in English (based upon articles written in the 1990s), Wang Hui very clearly reminds the reader that already in 1999 he had published with Professor Hui Pokeung a book that was a critique of:

> the rising trend of Neoliberalism and developmentalism. . . . Only by simultaneously presenting an analysis of growth that differs from the neoliberal one can their critiques [i.e. those of critical intellectuals] be truly persuasive. China's economic development has broken many predictions – a seemingly endless string of theories that China would collapse began to appear after 1989 [a clear reference to the crackdown of the protests on Tiananmen Square in June of that year] but then it wasn't China that collapsed but those theories themselves.[68]

For Wang Hui, in spite of the mistakes committed by the Party since the 1950s, what is important is that it succeeded in establishing the foundation of Chinese political sovereignty and independence, by continuously adjusting the policies of the state. 'These modifications were in essence self-modifications, carried out in response to the demands and problems of reality, rather than having been driven by external force or guidance.' The conclusion that he arrives at is that 'there are no ready-made models of reforms or policies, making the notion of "crossing the river by feeling the stones" correct'.[69] For Wang Hui, the lack of ready-made models has been a characteristic of the Chinese revolution as a whole. But then for him the question is: 'Without any basic value orientations, who knows where "crossing the river by feeling the stones" will lead us'. The values that oriented the Communist Party at the beginning of the twentieth century were to mobilize the peasants, and the Party was a party of the rural and worker's movements, which is, for Wang Hui, different from what happened in eastern Europe. Land reform in China was closely linked to village education, the development of literacy, of the capacity for self-organization and of technical skills. Wang Hui concludes: 'Compared to many socialist and post-socialist countries, the value of equality in China may have taken root to a greater degree in the popular consciousness than in other societies.'[70]

However, for Wang Hui, 'under conditions of marketization and globalization, discussions concerning the equal standing of peasants and migrant workers today will nonetheless differ drastically in content from discussions concerning how the standing of farmers changed in the early twentieth century.'[71] In the historical context prevailing before marketization and globalization, the role of the state was 'to represent the masses and the universal interests of the overwhelming majority, and this led to a break between the state or government and special interests.'[72] This is what Wang Hui considers to be the role and essence of a neutral state. However, marketization and globalization have shortened the distance between the state and special interest groups and this has posed a limit to socialist policies.[73] More significantly, globalization has transformed the traditional form of sovereignty. Wang Hui attributes this transformation first to the transnational movements of capital that have been directed to the Chinese coastal provinces, thus creating an increasing development gap between the coastal and the inland regions, as well as between rural and urban areas. The second factor is represented by the international regulatory mechanisms such as those implemented by the World Trade Organization (WTO), which have integrated China into the world economy after its accession at the end of 2001, so that 'a crisis elsewhere can quickly become China's own crisis.'[74] Furthermore, even if China has not suffered from 'shock therapy' like Russia and some eastern European countries, not having followed entirely the neoliberal path and not having privatized land, the Chinese state has not been quick enough to resolve the rural crisis, to set up a modern social security system, to assure the protection of the environment, to increase investment in education, to curb corruption and to abandon an export-led development and adopt a strategy based upon internal demand and needs. This has led to what Wang Hui calls a basic paradox:

> on the one hand China's ability to govern effectively has been widely acknowledged . . . but on the other, contradictions have appeared between officials and the people in certain areas. . . . The key issue is that such contradictions are often blown up into large-scale and widely debated legitimacy crises. . . . This issue is closely connected with democracy as the source of political legitimacy.[75]

But take care: for Wang Hui it is not a question of China's imitating Western democracy, as there is 'a universal democratic crisis, one closely connected to the conditions of marketization and globalization.'[76] This decline of Western democracy is explained by Wang Hui by four factors: (1) political parties are becoming less representative as their political values become obscured in the process of their search to attract votes; (2) globalization makes the solution of societal problems independent from the will and capacity of single states; (3) the development of oligarchical forms has produced a 'gradual disconnection of democracy as a political structure from the basic units of society'; and (4) 'the reliance of the election process on large amounts of money . . . has resulted in the existence of both legal and illegal forms of election fraud in many democratic countries, thus destroying public confidence in the election process.'[77]

In China as well, the role of the Party has undergone changes, as under market conditions there has been, as mentioned above, an 'intense permeation' of the state apparatuses by special interests. In the face of this loss of neutrality, what can be done? Wang Hui does not answer this question, but by posing three questions he indicates the road to follow: (1) given that the Chinese society has developed through history and retains today

> an acute sensitivity towards the demands of fairness and social equality . . . how should these values be translated into democratic demands under contemporary conditions . . .; (2) how can [the] party become more democratic and how can the state's ability to represent the universal interests be preserved, while the role of the party is being transformed; (3) how can a new political form be constructed upon the social base, granting greater political capacity to mass society and thereby overcoming the condition of 'depoliticization' created through Neoliberalism's marketization?[78]

The answers to these questions must be based on China's increased self-reliance, but not in the sense

> of nationalistic and ethnocentric tendencies, but as the reestablishment of values and politics along different lines – if anything, it is a new internationalism. The global significance of this exploration should be obvious, given the universal crisis of democracy and market.[79]

Given these analyses, it is not surprising that Wang Hui, who is a professor at Tsinghua University and has published articles and books in English outside China, has acquired an international and national fame that has recently caused him some problems. I am not in the position to establish a link between Wang Hui's criticisms of the present situation in China and these problems, but here are the facts: in 2007 Wang Hui was relieved of the direction of one of the most important Chinese academic literary journals (*Dushu*) and more recently he has been accused of plagiarism in one of his books.[80] In spite of these problems, he continues to teach at Tsinghua University and has received many manifestations of support from both China and abroad.[81]

Another New Left intellectual is the Tsinghua professor Hu Angang, who has a more pragmatic approach, and who has been involved for years in the orientation and reorientation of Chinese public policies, particularly for the Eleventh and Twelfth Five-Year Plans. He is more optimistic, probably based upon the impact he had in the past, and still has, on Chinese public policies.[82] From the writings of Hu Angang one can certainly see that he has a very marked sense of justice and equity. Moreover, while being very positive about the economic success of market-oriented reforms, he also is very much in favour of reforms aimed at correcting the main negative consequences of economic development such as disparities and pollution. Finally, he has put forward several proposals for developing democracy in China and his condemnation of corruption is definitely one of the most radical I know.[83] Hu, who is founder and director of one of the most influential think tanks, the Centre for China Study, continues to employ all his energy and research skills to provide empirical evidence to the Chinese leadership for orienting public policies towards a more balanced society, a more in-depth development of the human capital, thanks to public policies such as health, education and safety nets that should be made accessible to all Chinese people, and policies aimed at reshaping the Chinese production system so that it becomes respectful of the environment and parsimonious in using natural non-renewable resources.[84] Hu Angang is convinced that, by implementing such rebalancing policies while continuing to develop the economy at a reasonably steady pace, China will soon become a new world power.[85]

In the first handout for his students attending his Master's course on China's economic development, Hu explains that what he is concerned about is the problems of the common people, such as unemployment, social security, the income of peasants, the poverty in areas inhabited by minorities, inflation and other matters of public concern.[86] He focuses his research on the most important issues concerning the development and progress of the entire society instead of limiting it to a particular discipline or theoretical framework. He thinks that an outstanding scholar must lead the social tide instead of going with it. Finally he considers that only reforms that benefit the overwhelming majority of the people can be regarded as true reforms. Hu has oriented his research along three lines: first the understanding of China's national conditions; second the adoption of an incremental strategy towards reforms; third that China should ape neither the Western nor the Soviet model of development, but strive for a model of socialist modernization aimed at reducing the gaps between regions, between rural and urban areas, and between the rich and the poor. Hu's policy advice has very often been followed by the Chinese leadership. Hu explains this success by the fact that he has never adopted a strictly economic point of view, but has tried to analyse problems and issue proposals based on economic, social and political perspectives, having nevertheless a scientific approach, that is, based upon empirical evidence.

Finally, Wang Shaoguang,[87] who with Hu Angang already at the end of the 1980s and in the first part of the 1990s started to draw the attention of the Chinese leadership to the negative consequences of the economic development initiated in 1978 by Deng Xiaoping,[88] has recently affirmed with force that China will be socialist in the future, meaning by that, and this is certainly an opinion that all the 'New Left' intellectuals are ready to share, that public property will remain in command in China, thus orienting the development of the economic system. It is only by this means that the realization of a 'better and more just society' will be possible in China.[89] Let us note that Wang Shaoguang and Hu Angang, thanks to a 1993 *Report on China's State Capacity*, written when they were at Yale University, have been the first New Left intellectuals who have succeeded in persuading the Chinese leadership to reorient its public management towards fiscal centralization for the purpose of affording to the central government the financial means it needed to correct the negative consequences of the process of liberalization and privatization.[90]

Moreover, it is also very interesting to report how Wang Shaoguang has worked on the concept and practice of democracy. In an interview, given in 2009 to Emilie Frenkiel, Wang explains his changing understanding of democracy:

> My view of democracy has changed quite substantially. Originally, I grew up during the Cultural Revolution so my understanding of democracy was popular participation; mass participation meant democracy. But there were some chaotic years during the Cultural Revolution and I wasn't entirely satisfied with the situation, therefore my attention shifted to the West. . . . That's one of the reasons for which I chose to study in the United States, which for many Chinese intellectuals was seen as a model of democracy. . . . But then I lived in the US for almost twenty years and I became increasingly dissatisfied with this conception of democracy. I saw that elections could bring in and bring out politicians, but these politicians, once elected, were not necessarily responsive to the people's desires, demands and preferences.[91]

Wang then did a lot of reading on democracy going back to ancient Greece:

> while reading I realized that many people, in established democracies, have become dissatisfied – there have been talks about the 'democratic deficit' in the UK, in Canada, Australia, the US, and many parts of the world. And people have begun to invent a new way for ordinary people to participate in politics. . . . participation of ordinary people is important. Not just the elite, not just the indirect selection of a certain leader; more people should be involved in the whole process of decision-making . . . so that's how my understanding of democracy evolved in the last thirty years.[92]

Wang admits that he has not yet developed a theory of democracy, but he is moving in this direction. We find here the same orientation shared by many Chinese intellectuals both within and outside the New Left (see Wang Hui's position mentioned above), namely that Chinese democracy should not imitate the Western model, but should invent its own way, based upon its history, culture and conditions.

Finally, Wang Shaoguang has developed an analysis of China's transformation during the years of the People's Republic based upon the works of Karl Polanyi.[93] According to Polanyi:

> the idea of a self-adjusting market implied a stark utopia. Such institution could not exist for any length of time without annihilating the human and

natural substance of society; it would have physically destroyed man and transformed his surroundings into wilderness.

As a consequence, if one wants the market to produce its beneficial outcomes to society, one must embed it into society; more specifically it must be subordinated to the polity. Otherwise, a 'disembedded' market will produce such negative consequences that it will inevitably 'trigger a counter-movement aimed at protecting man, nature and production organization'.[94] On this basis, Wang interprets China's reforms as a sequence and interpenetration of two movements: on one hand, the introduction and expansion of the market and the consequent commodification of social activities outside the economy (such as health and education) with the negative consequences already described by Polanyi and, above all, the widening of inequalities; on the other hand a countermovement aimed at rebalancing society by re-establishing the supremacy of polity over economy (which existed during the Mao era) thanks to the implementation of a set of public policies that will reduce inequalities by redistributing wealth, will reduce insecurity by freeing the people from the market for the satisfaction of basic needs, and will protect the environment from economic activities that pollute the ecosystem and destroy non-renewable natural resources. Therefore, for Wang China's model of transition must be interpreted as a double movement combining market mechanisms that create wealth, and state policies that 'embed' the market within boundaries so that it does not harm the people and the environment. This is obtained thanks to a pragmatic orientation to policy-making and implementation that avoids a strict adherence to any ideologically based model.[95] Wang Shaoguang has provided empirical evidence that the policies implemented since 1999 for rebalancing Chinese society and economy have started to produce positive results. He share this view with other New Left intellectuals, especially with Hu Angang,[96] who is also interpreting China's development as a double movement and also provides empirical evidence sustaining this view. I will use this evidence in Chapter 6 when I evaluate the impact of NPM on China.[97]

But what has been the influence of the New Left on Chinese public policies? I quite agree with He Li, who says that the New Left gained influence over the Chinese leadership, especially since the 2002 Party Congress that led to the appointment of Hu Jintao as State President and Party Secretary General and Wen Jiabao as Prime Minister. A 2005 report speaks of Hu Jintao

> tacitly supporting the New Left and using it to attack former President Jiang Zemin and his Three Represents theory, which was widely blamed for many of the deep inequalities gripping China. . . . Meanwhile, ordinary peasants and laid-off workers had become natural allies of the New Left's struggle against prevalent neoliberal practices in the name of market efficiency and globalization.[98]

Nevertheless, one should not forget that in China neoliberals are still very active within both universities and governmental and non-governmental think tanks.[99] Neoliberals are easy to define, as they are quite similar to their Western colleagues: they believe in the power of the market as the best means to allocate resources and to manage production and distribution in the most efficient way. Moreover, the market is also the most equitable way to allocate resources as it sanctions the contribution of all the economic actors according to their contribution to the development of the economy. For the Chinese neoliberals, the government should push for further privatization and liberalization, thus reducing the government's scope and grip over economy and society. These intellectuals have been influenced by neoliberal thinking when they spent some time in Western universities and/or by reading liberal economics textbooks that have been translated into Chinese and are freely available in China's bookstores, including those of the 'founding fathers' of neoliberalism, Friedrich von Hayek and Milton Friedman.

In addition to reforms of the economy based upon the Western free market, many of the Chinese neoliberals also favour a process of democratization of the Chinese society similar to the Western model, the development of modern governance based upon the rule of law and the respect of human rights, of which 'private property rights are the most basic human rights in the world.'[100] Moreover, following Liu Junning, who according to the Singaporean professor Zhang Yongnian has established the philosophical basis of Chinese neoliberalism, Chinese neoliberals consider that:

> liberalism is universal, and it stresses universal rights and values such as representative democracy, indirect democracy, constitutionalism, rule of law, limited government, and basic human rights. While the state often deprives people of these rights, the market helps people to realize these rights.

As mentioned before, these values are considered to be universal, and therefore, 'individual freedoms resulting from market-oriented economic reforms and capitalist development cannot be regarded as a process of "westernization". . . . If China wants to be "civilized", it has to accept liberalism.'[101] And this is why, contrary to the New Left, Chinese neoliberals criticize the government for not pushing forward marketization, privatization and deregulation, and some of them are not opposed to the 'shock therapy' that has been used to manage the transition from the Soviet Union to Russia. However, this is not to say that the New Left intellectuals are not in favour of democracy, the rule of law and human rights. They nevertheless are convinced that the process of democratization will be a long one, for the sake of assuring social, economic and political stability, this being the *conditio sine qua non* for developing the economy; and, even more importantly, democratization should not be a simple imitation of the West, but should be based upon Chinese cultural characteristics.[102]

Coming now to international relations, Chinese neoliberals are convinced of the validity of the theory of comparative advantage and are therefore favourable to a complete integration of China into the world economy.[103] This, of course, would imply that the government would abandon completely the planned economy and as a very likely consequence (in my opinion) continue to stick to the export-led strategy of development. Given what we have said before about the analysis of the strategy China should follow according to the New Left intellectuals, it is not surprising that they are very strongly opposed to a complete abandonment of planning (even if it is nowadays very different from the planning of the Mao era) as, according to them, it is thanks to planning that the state can, on one hand, orient the economic development and on the other, correct the adverse outcomes of market mechanisms and thus implement the economic and social policies that should rebalance Chinese society.

Finally, we should not forget that some very powerful vested private interests, which have already benefited from the process of marketization, privatization and hence the freedom the Party-State has granted to the private sector, may try to further enlarge their space by trying to orient the economic (and eventually the political system) towards forms of organization not very dissimilar to the Western ones. Therefore the establishment, fulfilment and permanence of a socialist market economy are by no means assured. Much will depend on the decisions taken at the next Party Congress in the autumn of 2012. The new leadership will have the formidable task of deciding either to continue on the road defined by Hu Jintao and Wen Jabao, or to drive Chinese society closer to the dominant Western model. In the latter case, the integration of China into the capitalist world would then be completed and the dream of a 'socialist market economy' will have faded away for a very long time.[104]

New Public Management, capitalism, neoliberalism, and the 'Washington consensus'

We have also to deal with the international dimension of capitalism, which has been only marginally dealt with in the previous paragraphs. This will be done by linking NPM to neoliberalism and the 'Washington Consensus'. Let us start by recalling two important remarks about the major objectives of this book. First, the approach of the book does not deal with public administration and operational management but with strategic public management, in other words with the 'upper' part of NPM, the part that Fernand Braudel would place at the upper layer of the hierarchy of production–consumption processes, that is, within the capitalist layer in the West and at the state level in China. For example, China's decision to abandon the planned economy and to introduce market mechanisms is clearly the first strategic decision orienting all the subsequent Chinese strategic and operational decisions. Second, the aim of the book is not to analyse the operational aspects of NPM in China and the West (these aspects have already been developed, analysed and commented upon in the literature). The aim of the book is to show what the consequences of introducing NPM in China and the West have been.

Having said that, some scholars are right in saying that there are differences in the implementation of the NPM agenda in Western countries. I hesitated to deal in detail with the debates about these differences because they have already been analysed by several outstanding scholars. I quote some of them in Chapter 3, note 6. I will therefore limit this section to some general considerations that should further clarify the main purpose of this book. What I found interesting in these analyses is that they show that NPM has been implemented differently within Western countries. I have taken these findings into consideration by defining different varieties of NPM countries, especially weak- and strong-NPM countries, as I will explain in more detail in a later section.

Although this is of course an important finding, it nevertheless says little about the essence of NPM. It does not answer the question: is there a set of core principles common to all the different implementations? Now, this is exactly what I have been interested in: to find out if, in spite of the differences in implementation, there were a set of core principles at the level of the 'NPM model'. I will do this in Chapter 3 (pp. 71–75) by analysing four of the so-called 'models of NPM' and will show that, in spite of some differences, the core features of NPM are present in each of the four types. If there were in fact some core features within any 'NPM model', I thought that this was what a scholar should try to discover. Hence my list of ten NPM features presented in Chapter 3 (pp. 85–87). The most typical principles of NPM are privatization, contracting out, decentralization and deregulation, all these being dominated by the fundamental NPM principle of economic efficiency. These are clearly principles that have oriented strategic public management away from traditional management; the other NPM principles are simply the necessary consequences at the operational level.

Of course, the existence of a set of core principles does not mean that different implementations produce the same results. On the contrary, the typology of weak- and strong-NPM countries (which I will present hereafter) that corresponds to differences in the status and role of the state in Western countries has led me to forecast different consequences, that is to say in terms of income distribution, poverty rates and so on. For example, countries with a strong tradition of a generous Welfare State are not likely to implement NPM prescriptions fully or at least to reduce (for example) the outcome of the primary (i.e. market) distribution of income. This is clearly the case of weak-NPM countries compared with strong-NPM countries, as is confirmed by data presented in Chapter 5.[105]

To make my point clearer, I suggest a comparison with another domain.

For example, we can certainly agree that liberal democracy has been implemented differently in the various liberal countries (e.g. the USA, the UK, Switzerland, Italy, Sweden) but nevertheless we can also certainly agree that there is a set of core principles common to all the historical cases in which liberal democracy has been implemented. In the same way, the fact that NPM has been implemented differently in Western countries does not exclude the possibility that there is a set of core principles giving to NPM its special – in the Weberian sense, typical – profile that differentiates it from other types of public management.

I have been encouraged to explore this path for three reasons: first, because the proponents of NPM quite often claim that NPM principles can be implemented with good results (in terms of effectiveness and, especially, efficiency) in all circumstances in both developed and developing countries,[106] this being a clear case of the application of the general principle attributing 'universal value' to the

Western way of organizing society, economy and polity, including public management, and more particularly strategic public management; second, because these same proponents very often define the NPM's core principles when they compare them with those of traditional public management;[107] and third, because of the findings of the literature on globalization.

From the analyses provided by these three sources it appears that the 'Washington consensus' principles are very similar to those of NPM.[108] Scholars differ slightly in establishing their lists of principles, but these are basically the same.[109] There is a good reason for this; the 'Washington consensus' and NPM are the armed wings of the neoliberal political project and ideology.[110] There is a huge literature on the very negative impact of the 'structural adjustment' the 'Washington consensus' has imposed upon developing countries by means of the International Monetary Fund and the World Bank, in particular in Latin America and Africa.

What is striking in this literature is that both those who approve globalization and those who on the contrary contest it come to the same conclusion: that there is globally a convergence (either already or in the process of being realized) at least in the way the economy is organized and managed. Consequently, the majority of Western scholars forecast that countries such as China, which have adopted a market economy, will (or should) necessarily adopt a Western-style political system. Then the convergence will be complete. This is not my opinion and I will argue (in Chapter 6 dealing with China and in the conclusion dealing with the 2008–11 crisis) that China is on the way to succeeding in managing market mechanisms (or, if you prefer, a market economy) without introducing a liberal democracy, and that there is a chance that it will succeed in this endeavour.[111] Moreover, some of these scholars have defined other forms of 'consensus' that they oppose to the Washington one[112] and these 'consensuses' have been widely debated by Chinese scholars within universities and think tanks, as well as between Western and Chinese scholars. Finally, that the NPM and the 'Washington consensus' are the cause of the debacle of the 2008–11 crisis has been recognized even by knowledgeable people who are strong defenders of capitalism. Gideon Rachman, one of the leading journalists of the *Financial Times*, is a very good example.[113]

Coming now to China, it is also quite correct to claim that the context in which NPM has been implemented in China is different from the Western one. I have recognized this in my book on China's reforms.[114] However, it is indisputable that some of the same Western NPM core principles have also oriented China's reforms, namely privatization, contracting out, decentralization and deregulation.[115] These principles have been introduced within Chinese universities and think tanks by young scholars trained abroad in the orthodoxy of mainstream neoclassical economics and NPM.[116] These scholars gained a decisive influence on governmental policies in the 1980s and up to about the mid-1990s when scholars such as Wang Shaoguang and Hu Angang (and others, who in the West have been put under the convenient umbrella of the 'Chinese New Left') gained influence over the Chinese leadership, thus contributing (at least partially) to reorient Chinese public policies with the aim of 'putting people first'. Following this, I have formulated the hypothesis that the implementation of the NPM principles would produce basically the same outcomes in China as in the West in spite of different contextual characteristics. This is exactly one of the major hypotheses that are at the core of this book. I provide empirical evidence that this is the case in Part III.

As for the link between neoliberalism, the 'Washington Consensus' and NPM, I refer to what I have recently written in a collective book.[117] Since the beginning of the 1980s a vast movement of trade liberalization (the origins of which can be traced back to the immediate period after the Second World War) occurred at the international level, based upon the revival of liberalism (later labelled neoliberalism), of which the most operational consequences have been the 'Washington consensus' and NPM. Based upon neoclassical economy and public choice theory, this movement has favoured a total liberalization of the world economy (including liberalization and deregulation of financial markets), as well as the privatization or semi-privatization of large sectors of the national economies (including both hard and soft infrastructures).[118] This trend has been powerfully supported not only by the most advanced nations (led by the USA and later by the European Union) but also, and maybe more significantly, by global international organizations dominated by these countries, such as the World Bank, the International Monetary Fund, the World Trade Organization and the Organisation for Economic Co-operation and Development (OECD). Neoliberalism has thus become the admitted (and imposed) orthodoxy for organizing the global economy and for boosting economic and social development in both developing and in-transition countries. It is in this context that the latter have been forced to implement structural reforms based upon neoliberal orthodoxy in exchange for loans from the IMF and other organizations, international and national. This meant basically two sets of measures: (1) opening their national economy to the world, and (2) privatizing large segments of their economy, including both hard and soft infrastructures. This, of course, has reduced the choice of these countries about the better strategy for boosting their development. As the negative consequences of these events are well documented, it is necessary in the context of this book only to direct the reader to the scientific literature that has criticized the neoliberal movement on both its theoretical flaws and its material consequences, for both developed and in-transition countries.[119]

This permanent and, we must recognize, consistent faith of the international economic organizations in market mechanisms, even when markets very clearly do not exist, has been criticized by Joseph Stiglitz and associates in their book about capital market liberalization, addressed more particularly to the policies of the IMF: even if IMF experts recognize that capital market liberalization has not led to growth and efficiency, they persist in considering that it 'should', and describe as 'anomalous' the empirical findings that prove that liberalization does not bring the benefits promised. Stiglitz and associates conclude that 'the basic problem is that their "theory" (i.e. orthodox neoclassical theory) is predicated on perfect capital markets ... Yet it has long been recognized that such assumptions are also entirely unrealistic.'[120]

Capitalism, Welfare States, and empirical typologies of public management in the West

Quite briefly (and leaving aside the 'Washington consensus' as we deal here only with Western countries) the basic idea is the following: the ideological base of NPM is neoliberalism; neoliberalism determines a special type of capitalism (and consequently of Welfare State) different from other types of capitalism (and Welfare States); within the framework of 'neoliberal capitalism', public policies (including those constituting the Welfare State) are conceived and implemented through a special variety of public management, namely NPM. The public management of countries belonging to other types of capitalism present different characteristics from NPM. In other words the types of the typology of capitalisms (and of Welfare States) comprise basically the same countries as the typology of public management. There is a serious literature on types of capitalism and Welfare States that points to this conclusion.[121]

Let me recall what I have already said in the introduction. I will use two kinds of typologies: the Weberian ideal-typology and the empirical (or real) typology. The former defines the special, unique or typical elements of a phenomenon, independent from reality and its variations, that differentiate it from other phenomena; it is based upon a unilateral operation made by the researcher defining unambiguously the typical features of the phenomenon under research that will serve as a heuristic set of interrelated, unambiguously defined concepts capable of orienting the process of research, by formulating hypotheses, and orienting him or her in the search and identification of the most relevant elements in reality. I use this methodology for defining NPM. The major hypotheses suggested by the NPM ideal-type have been presented in the introduction and again at the beginning of Part I. By contrast, the real typology is based upon empirical observation and evidence that may identify differences in the implementation in the real world of the elements of the ideal-type, and therefore can lead to the appearance in real life of empirically proved differences, and hence to several real-types. I use this typology for defining different varieties of NPM that derive from the implementation of the principles of the NPM ideal-type (e.g. strong NPM and weak NPM). Three interesting empirical typologies have oriented this research: those of Gosta Esping-Andersen, of Peter Hall and David Soskice, and of Bruno Amable. Let us see how they comfort our typology of NPM countries.

The fundamental work of Gosta Esping-Andersen, published in 1990, presents three types (or varieties, or regime-types, in Esping-Andersen terminology). He sees 'the Welfare State as a principal institution in the construction of different models of post-war capitalism. Hence, the choice of [the title of the book]'.[122] The typology is based upon several dimensions: first, the extension of social rights as a means of 'de-commodification', that is, the degree to which social rights 'permit people to make their living standards independent of pure market forces'; second, social stratification; third, the nexus of market and state in the distribution system, based upon the idea that 'it is a myth to think that either markets or the state are more naturally equipped to develop welfare'; fourth, the link between labour-market structures and welfare-state regimes; and finally the impact of Welfare States on employment.

Based upon these dimensions, Esping-Andersen defines three types of welfare capitalism. The first is the liberal Welfare State:

> in which means-assistance, modest universal transfers, or modest social insurance plans predominates. Benefits cater mainly to a clientele of low-income, usually working-class, state dependents. . . . Entitlement rules are . . . strict and often associated with stigma; benefits are typically modest. Instead the state encourages the market, either passively – by guaranteeing only a minimum – or actively – subsidizing private welfare schemes.

The second type is the conservative corporatist-statist regime; here:

> the liberal obsession with market efficiency and commodification was never pre-eminent . . . What predominated was the preservation of status differentials; rights, therefore, were attached to class and status . . . private insurance and occupational fringe benefits play a truly marginal role. . . . the state's emphasis on upholding status differences means that its redistributive role is negligible.

The third type is the social-democratic model in which:

> the principles of universalism and de-commodification of social rights were extended also to the new middle classes. . . . The social-democrats pursued a Welfare State that would promote an equality of the highest standards, not an equality of minimal needs as was pursued elsewhere. This implied . . . that equality be furnished by guaranteeing workers full participation in the quality of rights enjoyed by the better-off.

Thus the social-democratic model presents a high degree of de-commodification and of universalism.[123]

By taking three levels of conservatism, liberalisms and socialism (which he calls strong, medium and low), Esping-Andersen is able to place Western countries within the three types. Of course, there are some clear cases where countries can be qualified as 'strong' or 'low', and some more problematic. Nevertheless, what is interesting for us is that, already at the end of the 1990s, Esping-Andersen's data show a consistent strong polarization between liberal countries such as the USA, the UK, Canada and New Zealand on one side and social-democratic Scandinavian countries on the other, the continental European countries being somewhere in between, some closer to the former on some dimensions (e.g. Switzerland for 'strong' liberalism) and some to the latter (e.g. Belgium and Austria for 'low' liberalism). Now, it does not come as a surprise that the liberal Welfare States are also those in which NPM has been most developed contrary to the Scandinavian states and also, in part, to the continental European ones.[124]

Eleven years later, Hall and Soskice adopted a strategy more closely related to the economic actors, especially the firm, and edited a collective book that proposed an alternative simpler typology, as it presents only two types. In their introductory chapter, they explain that their approach is based upon five dimensions: industrial relations, vocational training and education, corporate governance, interfirm relations, and coordination between firms and their employees. Based upon these dimensions, they restrict the field of capitalism to two types: liberal market economies, in which 'firms coordinate their activities primarily via hierarchies and competitive market arrangements', and coordinated market economies, in which 'firms depend more heavily on non-market relationships to coordinate their endeavour with other actors and to construct their core competencies.'[125] They further classify countries as follows: liberal market economies include the USA, the UK, Australia, Canada, New Zealand and Ireland; coordinated market economies include Germany, Japan, Switzerland, the Netherlands, Belgium, Sweden, Norway, Denmark, Finland and Austria; 'leaving six more ambiguous positions: France, Italy, Spain, Portugal, Greece and Turkey', which they suggest may represent another type of capitalism, the 'Mediterranean' type. Thus, these authors confirm the difficulty already present in Esping-Andersen regarding some intermediary cases.

In spite of this difficulty, and working with OECD data, the authors provide a number of analyses that comfort the choice of our typology of NPM countries. First, by taking employment protection and stock market capitalization they obtain two clusters of countries: on one side a group with relatively low capitalization and high employment protection, comprising continental European countries (France, Germany, Austria, Belgium, the Netherlands, Italy, Norway and Denmark) and, on the other side the USA, the UK, Canada and Australia. Next, looking at performance, they come to the conclusion that:

> in the liberal economies the adult population tends to be engaged more extensively in paid employment and levels of inequality [measured by the Gini index] are high. In coordinated market economies, working hours tend to be shorter for more of the population and income more equal.[126]

The first group comprises again the USA, the UK, Canada and Australia with the addition of New Zealand, and the second Sweden, Finland, Norway and Germany, whereas Spain, France and Italy are clearly outside these groups (low full-time equivalent and medium inequality). Finally, by taking unemployment protection and employment protection they obtain two clusters. The first, with low protection for both unemployment and employment, comprises the USA, the UK, New Zealand, Australia, Canada and Ireland; the second, with high protection for both, comprises continental and northern European countries.[127]

Taking a larger institutional perspective, Bruno Amable put forward in 2005 a third attempt to create a typology of capitalist states that defines more than two types. Based upon five dimensions – market of goods, industrial relations (including employment protection and employment policy), financial systems, social protection and education – Amable's typology comprises five types of capitalism: the market model (corresponding to the 'liberal market economy' of Hall and Soskice), the social-democratic, the continental European, the Mediterranean and the Asiatic.[128] By using factor analysis methodology the author is able to place the countries concerned on a two-dimensional space representing the two first axes; this is done progressively by integrating in the analysis the five dimensions mentioned above one after the other. The final result allows Amable to identify five or six groups of countries corresponding to the five types of capitalism.[129] The market model comprises the USA, the UK, Canada and Australia; France, Germany, Belgium and Austria belong to the continental European model; Japan and South Korea to the Asiatic model; Denmark, Finland and Sweden to the social-democratic one; Portugal, Spain, Italy and Greece to the Mediterranean. It is interesting to note that Ireland, the Netherlands and Switzerland are placed in between the market model and the continental European countries on both axes. Three interesting remarks can be made from Amable's analysis. First, this typology very clearly confirms those of Esping-Andersen and Hall/Soskice: there is a clear-cut difference between the liberal market countries (all belonging to English-speaking capitalism) and the continental and social-democratic European countries. Second, within the latter some countries are clearly regrouped together, whereas some others (the Netherlands, Switzerland and Ireland) occupy an intermediary position between the liberal market and the other European countries. Third, the countries of southern Europe can be regrouped together, in spite of the fact that they are closer to the European continental countries than to the other groups, on both axes. During the fourth year of the 2008–11 crisis, the identification of the 'Mediterranean type' has become more pertinent, as these countries present more serious difficulties than other countries in managing their public debt, and constitute an increasingly worrying threat to the stability of the Eurozone.

Starting from these typologies, I suggest two types of Western public management (strong NPM and weak NPM) corresponding to two types of capitalist countries (liberal market and European countries, both continental and northern social-democratic). In fact, when taking a diachronic perspective from about the beginning of the 1980s, three types are necessary when analysing NPM, as I do in Chapter 5. At the beginning of the 1980s we have three pioneers of NPM (the USA, the UK and New Zealand) that have very become quickly strong-NPM countries, while some other Western countries can be considered to belong to the non-NPM type (e.g. France, Germany and the Scandinavian countries).[130] Then, little by little, practically all the OECD countries started to implement some NPM prescriptions, some following the example of the pioneers and thus becoming strong-NPM latecomers (e.g. Ireland and Italy); as this process has taken several years, I will sometimes refer to these countries as 'countries in transition to NPM'. However, several other European continental countries (especially the northern ones) simply became weak-NPM countries, having adopted only a few NPM prescriptions and, moreover, in a limited way (e.g. privatization and deregulation) while maintaining, contrary to the strong-NPM countries, a relatively generous Welfare State.

If this is a good typology, then it will allow us to predict (or, if you prefer, to formulate the hypothesis) that different management types will produce different policy and management outcomes. This can be done by correlating capitalist countries and variables such as income distribution and poverty rates. The hypothesis is confirmed if (1) we obtain two groups of capitalist countries with different characteristics (e.g. in terms of income inequality and poverty rates), and (2) these two groups of capitalist countries correspond to the weak-NPM and strong-NPM countries. Of course, based upon the three typologies of capitalist states presented above, we can expect to have a clear-cut difference between the strong-NPM countries (which belong to the liberal market type of capitalism) and the other European countries, and among the latter some ambiguous cases. This is exactly what the data presented in Chapter 5 demonstrate. These results confirm those of Richard Wilkinson and Kate Pickett.[131] In Chapter 6, dealing with the consequences of China's reforms, which I qualify as the Chinese NPM, the comparison is made between the end of the Maoist and the reform eras, as well as with Western countries, using data collected in China in 2010 and 2011.

Measuring the impact of NPM in China and in the West

In addition to the information given above, I would like to add the following introductory remarks. Establishing clear evidence of causal mechanisms in the social sciences is much more difficult than in the experimental sciences, in which research performed in laboratories allows the researcher to isolate dependent and independent variables from the 'outside interference' of other variables. Nevertheless, even in this case, the established causal mechanisms may be considered as valid only until, in real life, some other variables interfere and destroy the previously established causal relations. This is the formidable challenge and fate of scientific modelling.

In the social sciences, in which experimentation in laboratories is generally impossible, we are most of the time limited to establishing correlations and, on this basis, extrapolating to causal relations. This is why many proponents of NPM contest the criticisms addressed to this type of public management (especially when the argument is based, as in my case, on correlations between NPM and variables such as income distribution and poverty rates) saying that it is not possible to establish such a causal link, suggesting that there may be other variables at work that explain income inequalities and the like. Nevertheless, this argument is not very plausible. First, it goes against the declared goal of NPM proponents: to improve public management thanks to privatization, contracting out, decentralization and deregulation. Second, this new way of organizing the role of the state and the market that is, according to NPM promoters, considerably different from traditional public management should improve the delivery of services (in terms of effectiveness, efficiency and quality) and, by liberating economic resources through a reduction of taxation both on households and enterprises, should also improve the efficiency of the economy to the benefit of everybody. So it would be surprising if NPM did not have an impact not only on economic variables (such as GDP) but also on socio-economic variables such as income distribution and poverty rates. Third, as the strong-NPM countries are also those with a less generous Welfare State (which may correct the negative consequences of primary income distribution, i.e. by the market), one can predict that strong-NPM countries will present a more unequal distribution of income and a higher rate of poverty. Chapter 5 is based upon many researches performed by several outstanding scholars specializing in this domain, such as Timothy Smeeding and Andrea Brandolini (working often with the Luxembourg Income Study [LIS] data).

Finally, I would add that in a very complex domain such as public management, and the related domain of economic development, one should not be too ambitious in trying to establish causal chains; this idea has been strongly put forward by one of the most influential founders (maybe the most influential) of neoliberalism, F.A. von Hayek: 'The creation of wealth is not simply a physical process and cannot be explained by a chain of cause and effect.'[132]

I propose to evaluate the 'health' of a society by taking the following data. First, employment and unemployment are used as indicators of the capacity of that society to offer to those of its members who do not own capital or land access to the labour market, the only source, for them, to gain some revenue. Second, the distribution of income is used as an indicator of the capacity of that society to offer to all its members a sufficient income to assure them a decent life. This second step will lead us to the third step: to discover if through that distribution of income that society is capable of avoiding the emergence of poverty (as it is determined by the labour market), and if, in case the distribution of income by the market (i.e. primary distribution) determines a certain level of poverty, to find out whether that society is capable of setting up some social policies capable of eradicating or at least of reducing poverty. Fourth, in case the distribution of income and the insufficiency of social policies are such that society is not capable of avoiding or eradicating poverty to find out if that situation leads to an increase of crimes, especially of petty crimes, those that are easily perpetrated by poor people when in a situation of economic and psychological distress. Finally, I will use data about the state of public health.

It is clear that the collection, the elaboration and the analysis of these data present a certain number of practical and methodological problems that must be at least mentioned before we go any further. First, not all the data are available for all countries. Second some data are not reliable; the more evident case is data about unemployment, as I will explain hereafter. Finally, the measurement of some of the phenomena concerned is subject to interpretation, arbitrary decisions and debates. It is some of these problems that I will now comment upon.

First, I will depend on available data, not being in a position, as a single researcher, to collect data and missing data on my own initiative and at my own expense. Moreover, as different countries do not necessarily collect, elaborate and present the data in the same way, a formidable problem faces the researcher who needs to use standardized, and thus comparable, data. Fortunately, this is done by international organizations. Moreover, when the data in which we are interested are not always elaborated and standardized by international organizations, we will use the data of the LIS, whose researchers have done an invaluable job of standardizing most of the data we will need and have published numerous research papers that present their analysis of much of the data we are interested in. Nevertheless, as the choice of countries is not always the same from one research to the other, this will make our demonstration more difficult. Moreover, the available research papers cover, most of the time, only the two first decades of NPM (from 1980 to 2000); this is particularly true for the measurement of poverty rates and the effect of anti-poverty policies. However, as the NPM deployed its effects especially during the 1980s for the pioneer countries, and the 1990s for the latecomers, this will not constitute a major obstacle to our demonstration. Finally, countries cannot be qualified as strong, weak or non-NPM once and for all. This will result in some 'intermediary cases' that are difficult to classify with a sufficient degree of confidence. In fact, as I will use a diachronic approach, some countries will start as non-NPM and may evolve towards a weak-NPM or strong-NPM type, as by the end of the 1990s practically all the OECD countries had introduced at least some NPM prescriptions. As we have seen, this difficulty has already appeared in the typologies of capitalist states presented above. However, the main countries that can be indisputably qualified as strong NPM and weak NPM are generally taken into consideration in these researches. Therefore, we are confident that our demonstration will be sufficiently robust, even if comparative researches based upon standardized data are not always available for the first decade of the twenty-first century. In this case we will provide the most recent data available from reputable sources.

Second, without entering into too much detail, the major, and indisputably, NPM countries are the USA, the UK, New Zealand (which can be considered as strong NPM countries) and to a lesser extent Canada and Australia. Weak-NPM countries are indisputably almost all of the northern European countries, together with France, Belgium and Germany. The major difference between weak- and strong-NPM countries is that the latter have used privatization, contracting out, deregulation and decentralization to a larger extent, have reduced the coverage of the welfare policies, and by this have considerably limited the role of the state, whereas the weak-NPM countries have been much more reluctant to do so and have maintained a strong state and efficient welfare policies. These differences have become more apparent during the 2008–11 crisis.[133] I will come back to this important point in the general conclusion of this book. As for the group of countries in transition to NPM, I will consider Ireland and Italy as in transition to strong-NPM newcomers, and Switzerland and Spain as cautious late newcomers to NPM. Except for the cases that fall indisputably within the categories of strong-NPM and weak-NPM countries, the classification of the other cases must be made with great care as the situation is moving all the time; nothing is definite and immutable. We must again insist that practically all the OECD countries have introduced some of the NPM prescriptions, but with some remarkable differences.

Third, some experts consider that NPM is the first generation of reforms introduced in the West at the beginning of the 1980s, and that the reforms proposed after the mid-1990s are of a quite different nature, which is generally put under the umbrella of 'Good Governance'. There are of course some differences, but these are most of the time over-emphasized. As a consequence, the periodization of Western reforms proposed by these experts has the consequence (very likely intentional) of giving to Good Governance a 'nice guy' role that it has still to prove. In fact, a quick glance over this literature shows that there is not only a considerable overlap between NPM and Good Governance, but also a common philosophy (or even a common ideology). Most of the time it is said that Good Governance integrates some NPM principles; Good Governance comprises public–private partnerships (PPPs) and NPM includes contracting out and PPPs; or even that Good Governance is an umbrella concept . . . and I would add: just like NPM.[134] In fact, the present 2008–11 crisis is a good indicator of the continuity of the philosophy of the reforms introduced (in the West and elsewhere) since the beginning of the 1980s. Considering that PPPs are a form of contracting out (incidentally, a practice that existed already in the eighteenth and nineteenth centuries in France and in the UK), one is particularly struck by the recent statement by one of the most neoliberal economic organizations, the European Union, in favour of a yet further development of PPPs, on which there is already a huge serious literature demonstrating the advantages but also the disadvantages of this way of providing public services.[135] After these introductory remarks I will now comment upon the five sets of data upon which Chapters 5 and 6 are based.

Data on employment

Official data on unemployment must be viewed with great care, and in some cases even with great suspicion. It is generally admitted that official data quite often underestimate the rate of unemployment. In some cases people working a very low percentage of the time are considered as employed even when their low rate of employment has not been voluntarily chosen. Second, it is common practice for the establishment of unemployment statistics not to record as unemployed those who are not registered as such. Third, statistics on unemployment do not consider as unemployed people who are not working because they are permanently or temporarily handicapped physically or mentally and therefore beneficiaries of invalidity insurance.[136] We will see hereafter that there are good reasons for believing that these persons (or at least a great many of them) are unemployable, that is, invalid for work, because the deregulated labour market has submitted them to such a high level of stress that they became temporarily or permanently ill. Moreover, statistics on unemployment say nothing about the impact of employment and unemployment on the distribution of income.

Data on income distribution and inequality

First, we are interested in comparison between 'strong-NPM' countries and 'weak-NPM' countries. Second, we need to take into consideration changes in time both for each of the countries concerned, and for the rank they occupy compared to other countries. This will in particular allow us to see if countries pass from one group to the other, especially from the non-NPM to the NPM countries. Third, we are interested in the level of inequality in income distribution and we will make the hypothesis of a positive correlation between income inequality and poverty. Finally, we will use different measures of income inequality, provided most of the time by the LIS working papers, based upon standardized data.[137]

Of course, one does not expect an equal distribution of wealth – an absurdity that has never been defended by reasonable people. Nevertheless, any reasonable person would probably be shocked if it could be proved that the increase of wealth (which may have occurred despite economic crises) had been distributed not only unevenly, but in such a way as to even further increase inequalities. That this may be the case was proven by the American economist Paul Krugman, in a study published already in 1992.[138] I will come back to this research in Chapter 5.

Measure of poverty and inequality

First of all, many people could assert that the inequality in revenue distribution is not necessarily a regrettable thing, as it is totally normal in a society where the weight of responsibilities is assumed by citizens in different ways; there is no reason to insist at all costs on a decrease in inequalities, thereby taking the risk of discouraging the most entrepreneurial ones. Everybody would suffer from this. I would be ready to accept this outlook, if those situated at the bottom of the unequal distribution of income could at least have a sufficient income to lead a decent life. However, we will see in Chapter 5 that this condition is not fulfilled. Not only is the increase in income distributed in a very unequal way, but this inequality has also the consequence of maintaining, and even increasing, the size of the population whose income is below the poverty line.

Second, the measurement of poverty is more difficult and controversial than the measurement of income inequality because one has to define a threshold under which a person is considered to be poor. This could entail decisions that may be considered as arbitrary. This is valid for the definitions of both absolute and relative poverty. The definition of the former entails the choice of the goods and services that within a community (a whole country or a subdivision of it such as province, department, member state if a federal state, or municipality) are necessary for being not poor. Then one calculates the money necessary for buying these goods and services and the total is considered as the threshold below which someone is considered as being poor.[139] The arbitrariness here is determined by the choice of goods and services (the household basket). The other method, the relative measure of poverty, entails the choice of a statistical reference against which the situation of a household is compared, hence the qualification of 'relative'. Generally, the statistical reference is a percentage of the mean or the median income of the community concerned; households below that line are considered as being poor. The arbitrariness here is constituted by the choice of the statistical reference and of its percentage.[140] Moreover countries use different standards and methodologies, but luckily, as mentioned before, the LIS provides a standardization of the relevant data for a choice of OECD countries, to which in-transition countries are constantly added. In spite of these difficulties, what is striking when one analyses the available data in a comparative manner is that most of the time the countries retain the same ranking, no matter the methodology. So, one could certainly contest the size of the poverty rate obtained by the method chosen by the researcher, but certainly not the fact that the rate of poverty is higher in some countries, and that these countries are almost always the same, no matter the methodology used. I will show that these countries are, with only a few exceptions, the strong-NPM countries and that for the countries in transition to the NPM the rate of poverty has increased over time. Of course, it will also be necessary to provide, in Chapter 5, some evidence showing the relation between income distribution and poverty, and between the level of social expenditures and the poverty rate.

However, there are some more important problems related to the measurement of poverty that have been addressed more recently in the literature. So far, we have suggested using economic indicators to measure both inequalities and poverty rates. Certainly, real GDP per capita ($PPP) may serve as a proxy for the resources needed for a decent standard of living. Nevertheless, this approach has attracted much criticism and has resulted in several alternative proposals for measuring these phenomena, especially poverty. Some of these new methods have already produced empirical results, whereas others are still at the beginning of the process. First, two of the most renowned experts on income inequalities and poverty have recently proposed a new way of taking into consideration not only income or expenditure when measuring poverty, but also the related financial assets of a household, thus integrating wealth into the analysis of poverty. In their article (written with another colleague) they propose some empirical evidence, but the exploratory character of their research and the rather narrow choice of countries make it impossible to use their findings for the purposes of this book.[141]

Second, the Oxford Poverty and Human Initiative has produced a new method for measuring and comparing poverty in 104 developing countries: the multidimensional poverty index (MPI), which has been integrated into the UNDP report since 2009 as a complement to the HDI (Human Development Index). The MPI is a measure of serious deprivations in the dimensions of health, education and living standards that combines the number of deprived and the intensity of their deprivation. These three dimensions are made up of 10 indicators: health (child mortality, nutrition), education (years of school education, child enrolment) and living standards (electricity, drinking water, sanitation, flooring, cooking fuel, assets).[142] Note that this index is used for developing countries only; it is not useful for our research, which covers mainly developed nations. Nevertheless, we will use the MPI when dealing with China.

Third, David Woodward takes the analysis of poverty measurement a step further by proposing a new method for measuring poverty based on the perspective of human rights.[143] After having criticized the other methods, the executive summary of his paper affirms:

> We therefore propose a new approach to the definition of poverty, which we call the Rights-Based Poverty Line (RBPL), based on . . . a country-specific outcomes-based approach. The RBPL approach is based on the estimated

statistical relation between income and indicators of well-being which correspond to different economic and social rights (health, nutrition, education, etc). By setting a single universal threshold level of the indicator concerned, and establishing the income at which that level is actually achieved in each country, we can in principle define a poverty line for each country which is at a different level of income, but gives rise to an equivalent standard of living in each country. This approach, we argue, both avoids the issues arising from 'input-based' approaches and resolves the problems inherent in any global poverty line defined in terms of incomes, while maintaining consistency between countries. We present estimates of RBPLs for six countries (Bolivia, Egypt, India (rural and urban), Nicaragua, Senegal and South Africa) using the infant mortality rate as an indicator of the right to child survival, based on four alternative threshold levels. This demonstrates the wide range of incomes required to achieve equivalent living standards in different countries.[144]

This approach is certainly the most promising in terms of a fair estimation of poverty corresponding to the actual situation of the countries concerned. Nevertheless, by linking poverty to the recognition of human rights this method is bound to attract serious criticism and opposition from political and economic circles hostile to such recognition. It is nevertheless to be hoped that research realized on this basis could be financed by think tanks and/or public institutions of higher learning.

In spite of the great interest of these new approaches to poverty, given the lack of research so far based upon the new methods mentioned above, I will limit the analysis of this important dimension of the impact of NPM to the findings of the Oxford Poverty and Human Initiative and to the United Nations HDI, which combines life expectancy at birth, education (measured by literacy) and GDP per capita. These three dimensions are then given equal weight and combined into a single indicator, the HDI. Since the 2009 Report the countries are classified into four categories: Very high, High, Medium and Low development. Before they were classified in three categories: High, Medium, and Low. Moreover, for the 2010 Report the methodology for calculating the HDI has been revised. The results obtained with the new methodology are presented in the 2010 Report. Here is the explanation given by the UNDP:

> As in past Human Development Reports, the HDI remains a composite index that measures progress in the three basic dimensions – health, knowledge and income. Under the previous HDI formula, health was measured by life expectancy at birth; education or 'knowledge' by a combination of the adult literacy rate and school enrolment rates (for primary through university years); and income or standard of living by GDP per capita adjusted for purchasing-power parity (PPP US$). For the new HDI, UNDP still measures health by life expectancy at birth, but it measures achievement in knowledge by combining the expected years of schooling for a school-age child in a country today with the mean years of prior schooling for adults aged 25 and older. The income

measurement, meanwhile, has changed from purchasing-power-adjusted per capita Gross Domestic Product (GDP) to purchasing-power-adjusted per capita Gross National Income (GNI); GNI includes remittances and foreign assistance income, for example, providing a more accurate economic picture of many developing countries.[145]

The changes introduced in the new methodology for calculating the HDI used for the 2010 Report has the result to generally lower the index compared to the old methodology. Consequently, diachronically comparisons must take into consideration this change. Nevertheless, the general picture (especially the ranking of the countries) remains fundamentally the same.

Finally, UNDP has produced several new indexes. The most interesting are those that are used to qualify the HDI. First, the Inequality-adjusted Index (IDHI)

> adjusts the Human Development Index (HDI) for inequality in distribution of each dimension across the population . . . The IHDI accounts for inequalities in HDI dimensions by 'discounting' each dimension's average value according to its level of inequality. The IHDI equals the HDI when there is no inequality across people but is less than the HDI as inequality rises. In this sense, the IHDI is the actual level of human development (accounting for this inequality), while the HDI can be viewed as an index of 'potential' human development (or the maximum level of HDI) that could be achieved if there were no inequality. The 'loss' in potential human development due to inequality is given by the difference between the HDI and the IHDI and can be expressed as a percentage . . . The inequality in distribution of the HDI dimensions is estimated for: life expectancy, years of schooling and household income (or consumption).[146]

Second, the Gender Inequality Index (GII) is a measure that captures the loss in achievements due to gender disparities in the dimensions of reproductive health, empowerment and labour force participation. Values range from 0 (perfect equality) to 1 (total inequality). Third, since 2009 the UNDP reports integrate the MPI mentioned above. In the third part we will present data from both the old and the new HDI.

Data on crime rates

Data on crimes will be taken from the Interpol website, consulted in 1999 when data were still available on the net. This is more than enough to show that in the West during the first 15 years of NPM there was a considerable increase of petty crimes in the beacon NPM countries (the USA, the UK and New Zealand) whereas in the benchmark country (Switzerland) that started to introduce NPM devices only around the mid-1990s, and therefore during that period could be considered as a non-NPM country, the crime rate remained unchanged. For China we will use the official data as well as calculations provided by Chinese scholars.

Data on public health

Evaluating the performance of a country in the domain of public health is a particularly difficult task, even more difficult than the assessment of income inequality and poverty rates. A vast literature, and several world-famous academic and professional journals, cover this complex domain. It is out of the question to cover exhaustively the interrelationships between NPM and public health. Moreover, data for China are not always available in spite of great efforts made in recent years by the Ministry of Health to collect reliable data useful for reforming the Chinese health system. Nevertheless, data are available, in particular thanks to the World Health Organization, which makes available the main health indicators allowing a comparison between Western strong- and weak-NPM countries and China.

What we will actually compare

The fifth point concerns the comparison between China and the West. It would be neither interesting nor fair to compare the present economic and social situation, as China and the West are at different stages of their development: the West has practically completed its economic modernization (some consider that it has entered into the post-modern era),[147] whereas China is still in the process of modernization. This comparison is interesting only from the perspective of China's strategy of catching up with the West, but this is not the main goal of the third part of this book. Nevertheless, I will also explore this perspective for the purpose of evaluating how well China has done at developing its economy since the end of the 1970s. However, I will devote more space to the main purpose of that part: to compare the consequences of the strategy of giving more space to the market in China and in the West. Therefore, I will proceed for China as I have done for the impact of NPM in the West, by examining, whenever data are available, employment, income distribution, poverty rates, crime rates and public health. By doing so, I will in fact compare China as it was at the end of the Mao era with China as it is at the beginning of the 2010s. Finally, in the general conclusion of this book, taking advantage of the fact that the 2008–11 crisis may have the consequence of further deteriorating the negative aspects of their economic development, I will compare the policies that China and the West have implemented in order to overcome not only the economic crisis, but also, more generally, the negative consequences of the market economy. We shall see that it is in this respect that the strategies of China and the West show some remarkable differences.

Part II
The rise of New Public Management in the West and in China

In this part I will analyse the rationale for the introduction of NPM in China and in the West, the similarities and the differences. Technically, the two historical experiments with NPM are the same: the further development in the West and the introduction of market mechanisms in China. however, the general strategy and fundamental orientation given for this experiment are quite different, the Western one being mainly oriented by ideological considerations in favour of a radical implementation of free-market economy, the Chinese one by practical choices aimed at restoring China as a world power. For the West the fundamental goal is to give more freedom in the economy and to reduce the role of the state, on the assumption that by doing so the economy will be made more efficient and the provision of public services will be both more effective and efficient. For China, the departure from a rigid implementation of planned economy and the consequent introduction of market mechanisms has the instrumental goal of developing a strong economy and society that will realize the fundamental goal of restoring China as a world power. As the choice in favour of market economy in all its forms has been first developed in the West, I will present the case of NPM in the West in Chapter 3 and then, in Chapter 4, I will deal with the Chinese NPM. As the analysis of the ideological, theoretical and technical problems of NPM presented in Chapter 3 dealing with the West is also valid for China, Chapter 4 will mainly deal with the peculiarities of the Chinese experiments with NPM. This will entail a theoretical evaluation of the validity of the choice of NPM in both cases. In other words we should be able to forecast what will be the consequences for society given the underlying causal links suggested by the theoretical foundations of NPM.

Whereas some criteria for evaluating both cases will be the same (namely the consequences that it is theoretically possible to forecast both the efficiency and the equity of society), part of this evaluation will have to take into consideration that two unique historical developments have produced two different political cultures in China and in the West. The West has developed a political culture that treasures freedom in the political and economic sphere as a means to achieve individual and collective goals, whereas China has developed a political culture that gives priority to harmony, unity and to social, economic and political stability. If we do not take into consideration these differences, we run the risk of evaluating China's NPM experiment from an ethnocentric point of view, thus misunderstanding the true nature of the Chinese experiment. Similarly, in evaluating the Western experience we will take into consideration whether NPM is in harmony with some fundamental features of the Western model, for example some legal principles such as the respect of legality and equal treatment, and the role of the citizen within the public sphere.

3 The foundation of the Western experiment

Neoliberalism, New Public Management and the 'Washington consensus'

Introduction

This chapter is a revised and enlarged version of the first part of a long article I prepared in 1998 for a collective book published in 1999 by PUF (Presses Universitaires de France) about neoliberalism and New Public Management.[1] The title of the article ('Public management at the service of the market') may have looked somewhat provocative at that time, when NPM and the 'Washington consensus' had acquired a status equivalent to the Ten Commandments of God.[2] But that was indeed my intention, and in retrospect I think that the chapter's title very well reflected the very essence of NPM. The World Bank itself had written in 1997, concerning China: 'the [Chinese] government must begin serving markets by building the legal, social, physical, and institutional infrastructure needed for their rapid growth.'[3]

In spite of the provocative character of the title and its first paragraphs, the article was an overall critique of NPM, including ideological, theoretical, methodological and empirical aspects. In particular I provided a good deal of the empirical evidence available at that time showing that countries that had implemented the devices of NPM to a large extent had simultaneously increased the inequality in the distribution of income, the rate of poverty and the crime rate. In Chapter 5 I will bring up to date the empirical findings I commented upon 13 years ago by placing them into the same theoretical framework of the 1999 article. The reason for this is quite simple. The financial and economic crisis that burst out at the end of 2008 has at least one positive outcome: the overall approach of the NPM, within which deregulation has been one of the major dimensions, has shown not only its limits but also its devastating consequences to the point that some of the defenders of neoliberalism, the 'Washington consensus' and NPM have recognized the mistakes made and now consider at least that the intervention of the state is not necessarily to be avoided at all costs and in all circumstances.[4]

Indisputably, during the past 30 years there has been a profound reinterpretation of the relationship between state and the market in most Western countries. It consequently became inevitable that new approaches towards public management be introduced and that universities, public management institutes, consulting companies (generally specialized in private company management), politicians and civil servants would propose something new in order to assure the management of the state–society interface.

The analysis of the characteristics and consequences of these new ideas is not an easy task, bearing in mind that the interests at stake are powerful, often resulting, within the discourse on the new ways of managing the public sector, in mixing up descriptions of reality, proposals for pragmatic reforms, scientific analysis and ideological biases. The works of the followers of the trend called NPM generally do not escape from this confusion. Certainly, the emergence of new approaches to public management claiming to replace the former ones and thus to constitute the new dominating paradigm is nothing new in the history of the development of ideas on the management of modern organizations. Nor is there anything new in the virulence of the critique aimed at former approaches.[5]

What was new during the wonderful years of NPM was the incapacity of most of its followers to accept criticism, to admit other solutions to the problems of the public sector, which is reflected in the totalitarian character of their attitude towards those who dared express any doubts as to the validity of the NPM. The critics were immediately and summarily disqualified: either they had understood nothing about NPM (which makes them out to be incompetents) or they were presented as defenders of a system of bureaucratic public management, undemocratic, wasteful, ineffective and inefficient, working mainly to the profit of a class of bureaucrats and of privileged individuals, beneficiaries of the generosities of the Welfare State. And who wanted to pay any attention to incompetents or to reactionaries?

Actually, this attitude is quite understandable: those who are certain of being the repositories of an absolute truth, and of being entrusted with a kind of divine mission, are almost inevitably bound to reject any opinion that differs even slightly from their own. To me, this attitude was nothing less than intolerable and deserved to be firmly denounced, and even exposed to polemic. This is what I did in the 1999 article, showing that, from a scientific point of view, there never existed a new paradigm of public management, inasmuch as the views presented under the pretence of NPM are so diverse, even contradictory, that they are incapable of supplanting, notwithstanding their triumphant and messianic language, a management of the public sector founded on a Weberian–Keynesian approach.[6]

However, obviously, all this was not sufficient. On one hand, one had to identify what constitutes a common denominator (for there is one) that gives coherence to all these differences and, on the other hand, one had to put pressure on the NPM followers, or at least the governments that were implementing it or intended to do so, to seriously evaluate the realizations of the NPM. This was the least one could demand from those who based an important part of their reform proposals on a negative evaluation of the performance of the Weberian–Keynesian management of the state. The common denominator, not surprisingly, is to be found not so much in the scientific (theoretical and empirical) foundations of NPM, but in its ideological and political foundations, as I have shown above (Chapter 2, pp. 47–50) when discussing the commonality of NPM and the 'Washington consensus', as they have been promoted worldwide by the 'unholy trinity' composed of the World Bank, the IMF and the WTO.[7]

There is no doubt that the attack on NPM has been a complete failure. People who dared criticize NPM were not heard. They were in fact in a similar position to the neoliberals who had practically no voice between 1945 and the mid-1970s, when the Western countries were reconstructing their economies after the Second World War and implementing the Welfare State thanks to huge state interventions.[8] It was only with the accumulation of annual deficits, the resulting increase in public debt and the concomitant dominant opinion that it was not possible to increase taxation that the voice of neoliberals came into the open in the public debate. The neoliberals were skilful enough to describe these real problems as a major crisis of the state, to explain that they were the consequence of the Weberian–Keynesian management, and to maintain that they had the medicine to cure those illnesses. Only then were their proposals (the NPM and the 'Washington consensus') seriously taken into consideration by politicians, intellectuals and even civil servants; not to mention big consultancy companies that have been very quick in seizing the new opportunities to develop their businesses, by proposing their competencies to public authorities. This was a natural move, as one of the major proposals of the NPM was precisely to take the management of the private sector as the model to which the state should conform, by privatizing or contracting out public services, or at least by introducing quasi-market mechanisms and corporate management techniques within the public sector.[9]

Before going any further, I would like to emphasize once and for all that I am, and have been for a very long time, deeply dedicated to the improvement of the action of the state, in terms of both effectiveness (to attain the goals fixed by policy and in legal instruments) and efficiency (to reach these goals at a minimum cost and without wasting the taxpayer's money). On the basis of what we know about the functioning of organizations, it is furthermore obvious that a permanent policy of evaluation and reform should constitute one of the fundamental concerns of the persons responsible for any organization, be it public or private. Thus, if it is true that the NPM cannot constitute an absolute truth, it is just as true to say that it poses the same fundamental and pertinent questions for the management of public bodies that have been dealt with by scholars and practitioners of public administration and management for at least 100 years. These questions concern the effectiveness and the efficiency of the action of the state. Of course, we still have to agree on the meaning of these words.[10] However, even in the narrow perspective adopted by most of the followers of NPM, the questions they ask deserve an answer, or at least the implementation of an organizational and research strategy enabling us to address them.

Nevertheless, it must be admitted that these questions are not new. Without going back too far, it can be said that the question of effectiveness and efficiency of the state action has been at the centre of the concerns of public authorities and researchers in public management for at least 100 years.[11] What is new is the context in which they have been posed since the mid-1970s and that the followers of NPM have adroitly used. First of all, it concerns the deficit of the public accounts stemming from a structural disequilibrium between revenues and expenditures. The latter are due mainly to society phenomena such as the ageing of the population, the explosion of health costs, but also of military expenditures, the emergence of long-term unemployment and/or the appearance (or reappearance) of the working poor.[12] Added to this are the costs of different forms of pollution,[13] not to mention the cost of infrastructure, financed by the states in the first instance, as well as other state subsidies in favour of the market economy. Then came the globalization of the economy. Finally, as mentioned before, preceding and supporting the solutions proposed in order to solve the problems resulting from the foregoing factors, is the renewal of liberal thinking: neoliberalism.

That these circumstances raised great problems of effectiveness and efficiency to the states and to international organizations, as the NPM followers claim, nobody denies. The problem with the NPM is not the questions it raised, but the answers it claimed to provide.

The New Public Management or the impossible new paradigm of public management

In a publication focusing on the current problems in managing the budget of the Swiss Confederation, I commented on the appearance of the NPM in Switzerland in the following terms:

> The appearance of New Public Management has engendered a very interesting debate in Switzerland, where the hopes of the Right and the Left converge (with the exception of the extreme left), to master the management of the public sector which seems to have escaped all control; the former probably seeing there the 'scientific' proof of the 'lean state thesis', the latter the last 'providential' chance of saving the Welfare-State.[14]

This convergence (a new consensus?) of the Right and the majority of the Left must have appeared somewhat surprising to the observer uninformed about the evolution of the discourse of what I call 'the managerial left' over recent years. However, knowing that it is the organ of the intelligentsia of 'the managerial left' that has spread the 'good news' of NPM in the French-speaking part of Switzerland, this convergence becomes less surprising.[15] Even so, the fact that NPM is highly prized by both the Right and the Left is the sign of the considerable – let us say – political and ideological proximity (to say the least) between the Right and the Left. The same could be said of Western countries in general.

Indeed, the first difficulty one encounters in trying to understand NPM consists in the fleeting, multiform and incomplete character of the definition provided by many of its followers. This characteristic takes many forms. Indeed, some authors commence by stating what the NPM is not, or at least they immediately qualify their definition of NPM with a declaration about what it is not. Thus, for example Jean-Daniel Delley, then editor-in-chief of one of the leading Swiss 'managerial left' journals, writes:

> The new public management proposes a combination of principles and methods . . . aiming at improving the efficiency of the state by better adapting

the offer of public services to the needs of the users. These principles and methods do not stem from a neoliberal ideology trying to impose the laws of the market on the public sphere. They rather result from experiences made in numerous local and national bodies. There is no prefabricated model here to be applied mechanically, but an approach to be put into concrete forms according to the individual needs of each public authority, its political culture and its institutions.[16]

Thus, here there is no ideological neoliberal filiation, but a combination of principles and of methods that can (and should) be applied to all sorts of realities.[17] Granted. However, what the people belonging to the managerial Left have not understood is that these 'principles and methods' have been used by the skilful hands of neoliberals and 'put into concrete forms according to the individual needs of each public authority, its political culture and its institutions' as they have been gradually but surely modelled by the neoliberals who succeeded in imposing the laws of the market in the public sphere; or we should say, more precisely, to impose the will of the private sector, as in reality most of the time we were far away from the idealized image of the market as it is presented by neoliberals.[18] The idea of considering a model for organizing the public sector on the basis of a set of tools is not bad in itself. Problems arise when the tools are not used for obtaining the proclaimed goals, or when the implementation of the tools obtains some of the proclaimed goals but at the same time creates problems.

However, as to the elasticity in defining NPM one could do even better. Thus, a collaborator of one of the big consulting companies specializing in NPM went so far as to write that 'the NPM as such does not exist! There is no unique model of NPM. It is rather a mixture of concepts and practices that have developed in different OECD countries . . . presenting a certain number of similarities.' He continues: 'It seems that several "hybrid" models of NPM exist, combining and balancing against each other the different orientations in a variety of manners.'[19] Furthermore, this author admits that 'the NPM draws its inspiration from economic neoclassical thinking and its preference for market mechanisms' but he thinks that it would be 'wrong to try to assimilate the NPM into an undifferentiated application of neoliberal precepts.' Thus, here too, there is a differentiated application, but the author at least admits that it is a question of implementing the precepts of neoliberalism.[20]

The New Public Management and the impossible typology of NPM variants

To my knowledge, the best attempt to define several 'models' of NPM has been done by Ferlie and colleagues, who propose four models of NPM, which they label (1) the efficiency drive, (2) downsizing and decentralization, (3) in search of excellence and (4) public service orientation.[21] They inform us that these 'models' are their 'initial attempt to build a typology of new public management ideal types' and they explicitly refer to Max Weber's ideal-type approach. They also recognize that 'typology construction requires careful thought . . . if the categories derived are to be meaningful, exhaustive and mutually exclusive.'[22] They are quite right in pointing to the key concepts guiding the construction of a typology. First, it must be meaningful; this means, for Max Weber, that it should allow the researcher to understand what is going on in reality. Weber suggests that, when a typology has ceased to realize this goal, then it must be changed.[23] Second, it must be exhaustive, that is, it must cover the totality of the domain it is supposed to cover. Third it must be exclusive, that is, there should be no overlapping between the different types. Unfortunately there are several problems with the Ferlie typology. According to Weberian methodology, each of the types that compose a typology must comprise the phenomena that are typical of that type, that is, that are not present in the other types. In their attempt to differentiate between the four types, Ferlie and colleagues are right to insist on presenting in detail the characteristics that should differentiate them from each other (see Figure 3.1).

Unfortunately, by doing so, on one hand they introduce a few, but important, elements that are present in several types (e.g. references to the market under different forms – market-mindedness, market-like experiments, quasi-market – and contracting out) and on the other hand they hide (or at least they leave aside) the fundamental element, the core dimension, that is common to all the four types, namely economic efficiency. Efficiency is used explicitly to define only the first type, but, paradoxically, very clearly efficiency is present in the other three types, as I will show hereafter. In short, Ferlie and colleagues are very useful for analysing the various NPM tools at the level of operational management, but are of little (or even no) help for understanding the fundamental NPM policy choices that have been taken at the level of strategic management. In other words, the four types are certainly useful for seeing and analysing the trees that compose the NPM at the different historical stages of its implementation, but have difficulties in helping us to see, and understand, the NPM forest: what is common to the four types. Very clearly, the typology does not respect the requirement of exclusivity, and this shortcoming jeopardizes, according to Weber's theory, the heuristic power of the typology. In fact, how is it possible to understand what happened from the early 1980s to nowadays, and especially since the outburst of the 2008–11 economic crisis if we do not very clearly (i.e., for Weber, unequivocally) identify the core features typical of NPM? I have already mentioned that even a strong defender of capitalism such as Gideon Rachman of the *Financial Times* has very clearly identified the causes of the crisis. Let us quote the main elements of his analysis:

> The current financial crisis can be traced to three of the central ideas of the Reagan–Thatcher era: the promotion of home ownership, financial deregulation and a fervent faith in the market. Each of these ideas did sterling service for 30 years, increasing prosperity and freedom. But pushed too far – and combined – they have created a disaster. . . . Investment bankers, the shock-troops of the Reagan–Thatcher revolution, were allowed to bet their banks on this new market, because regulators and politicians believed so firmly in the magical and self-regulating qualities of the market. The same process of

1. Efficiency drive

Making the public sector **more business-like**, i.e. focus on **efficiency** gains, more **market-mindedness,** financial controls,
value for money, getting more for less, more elaborate cost and information systems. Extension of audits (both financial and professional), standard setting and bench-marking, **monitoring of performance**. Increased stress on provider responsiveness to consumers; **a greater role for non-public sector providers**; **more customer orientation**; but no moves to fully fledged **quasi markets. Deregulation** of the labour market; more short-term contracts, **marginalization of elected representatives and trade-unionists**; move to a board of directors model; shift of power to the strategic apex of the org.,
shift of power from professionals to management

2. Downsizing & Decentralisation

Extension of market mindedness to **more elaborate quasi markets**, and **customer orientation.**
From management by hierarchy to **management by contract**;
Split between a small strategic core and a large operational periphery.
Market testing and contracting-out non-strategic functions.
Drastic **downsizing**; flatter organization structure. **Increased contracting-out.**
An increased role for network forms of organisation; stress on strategic alliances between organizations as a new form of coordination

3. In search of Excellence

Strong emphasis on the importance of organizational culture, role of values, rites and symbols.
Two types:
(a) « bottom-up », based upon the **learning organization** movement
(b) « top-down », attempts to **secure cultural change**, based upon a charismatic leadership; **more intensive corporate training programmes**, mission statements, explicit communication strategy

4. Public service orientation

Fusion of private and public sector management ideas, re-energizing public sector managers by outlining a distinct public sector service mission (Gaebler & Osborne, 1992). Major concern with **service quality**,
a value driven approach but based on a mission to **achieve excellence** in the public services; scepticism as to the role of markets in public services, reflection of users (rather than customers), concerns and values.
Stress on securing participation and accountability as legitimate concerns of management. Alongside a proclamation of difference, **however, lie attempts to adapt ideas generated in private sector contexts (e.g. total quality management, organizational learning) to public sector organizations.**

Figure 3.1 Real 'types' of NPM. Adapted from Ferlie *et al., The New Public Management in Action*, Oxford: Oxford University Press, 1996, pp. 10–15, emphasis added.

intellectual overshoot happened with other signature ideas of the Reagan–Thatcher era: privatisation, scepticism about environmentalism and democracy promotion.[24]

One cannot be clearer.

In conclusion, the Ferlie typology, as well as similar typologies of NPM, is at best a rational description of the different (and, most of the time, cumulative) operational forms through which NPM has been implemented in the West since the early 1980s. At the end of her research on the implementation of NPM in the health sector of Switzerland, using the first three Ferlie types, Iva Bolgiani concludes, 'The three models have been a fundamental tool for [my] research', but she is obliged to recognize that 'in reality everything, or almost everything, is reduced to the efficiency dimension.'[25] In my opinion, it is not possible to sustain the idea that NPM has fundamentally changed its logic since the early 1980s or, even worse, that today NPM is no more implemented in the West.

That the logic of NPM is still today on the agenda of its supporters is shown by a paper published by the authoritative *McKinsey Quarterly* that in the middle of the 2008–11 crisis still requires governments to reform, taking example from the private sector:

> few of them [i.e. governments] have an established track record of reputation for managerial excellence [and the reforms undertaken in the past] typically fall short: with few exceptions, they skim the surface, cover little ground, take too long, and leave much of the public sector relatively untouched. That's why we see a need for broader, deeper, and faster reforms.[26]

The goal of these reforms is clearly to improve the state's performance, which is certainly a laudable goal. However, the article insists on many occasions on just one aspect of performance management; that is, cutting costs by reverting to the traditional (NPM) promise to cut costs in the public sector prior to making an in-depth investigation. The article is not very explicit in what domains the 'deeper, broader, and faster' reforms should be implemented. However, the introductory paragraph gives a clear hint by enumerating the domains that constitute today, according to the authors, the major challenges for governments: health care, social security, education, national security, crime and critical infrastructure. The list is not very different from that at the end of Milton Friedman's second chapter of his famous book *Capitalism and Freedom*, which moreover, as noted by the author, 'is far from being comprehensive.'[27]

Let me show how the same fundamental logic of NPM is present in each of the four Ferlie 'types', or more correctly in the four historical phases through which NPM has been implemented in the UK. The first Ferlie model is based upon *economic efficiency*. If this is true, then the best way to introduce and improve efficiency in the public sector is by privatizing the state's activities, and if this is not possible at least to contract them out to the private sector.[28] The problem is that, at that historical moment (1975–1995), the majority of Western countries were experiencing some serious difficulties in the management of their budgets, because the growing cost of state activities, the resulting chronic annual deficits and the explosion of public debts could not be matched by an increase of taxation. Now, in theory, efficiency can be implemented in two alternative ways: either one fixes a level of performance or benefit (in terms of quantity and/or of quality) and then tries to minimize cost, or one fixes a level of cost and then tries to maximize performance or benefit. Unfortunately, in the historical situation when NPM was put forward by its promoters, and this was one reason why they did so, only the second way was practically and politically possible, that is, to fix the cost at a level considered affordable and then try to maximize the benefit. However, even that was not possible, as the NPM proponents, in their quest to reduce the scope of the state, put forward proposals aiming at 'doing more with less'.[29] The way was thus open to large-scale reductions of state expenses through privatization and contracting out and, coming to the second Ferlie type, to *downsizing and decentralization*. Then comes the third type, the *search for excellence*. However, even this type is closely related to efficiency and the logic of the market. In a market producers are in competition and therefore they are forced to be efficient, that is, to cut costs and, to do so, they promote excellence within their organizations for the purpose of being competitive in the market. This is of course linked to strategies of human resource management, motivation theories, learning organization theories and so on. However, these important elements cannot be dissociated from the logic of efficiency best promoted by the market.[30] Finally there comes the *public service orientation* type. Yet here again its features (a major concern with quality, reflection of user concerns etc.) are closely linked to the market model. In a market not only do producers have to cut costs in order to be competitive but, while doing so, they have also to put products of good quality on the market, otherwise, for the same price, consumers will buy from their competitors, provided their products are of better quality.

The problem with the NPM logic lies not so much in the fact that there are not several NPM models, but just one with different implementations, in the same way as we have one model of liberal democracy with different implementations. The problem lies rather in the claim to apply management techniques of the market to sectors in which the market very often at best is far from being perfect or, at worst, does not even exist, for example in the domains of water provision, health services, and more generally soft infrastructures providing basic needs, and social safety nets. Moreover, by having a tendency to cut state expenses and simultaneously to cut taxes, this double scissor movement is very likely to result in a new legitimacy crisis, when the state will no longer be able (as it was during the 30 years of the Keynesian era, 1945–75) to provide its population with the public services it needs. Many citizens, transformed by NPM into clients, may not have the financial means to buy the services they need. In Chapter 5 we will see that in the West the implementation of NPM has in fact produced this type of outcome, although with some remarkable differences between strong- and weak-NPM countries. We will see in Chapter 6, dealing with China, that the introduction of market mechanisms in sectors such as health and education, along with the deregulation of the labour market without the establishment of sufficient support for the unemployed, has led to new forms of poverty, in spite of the fact that the introduction of market mechanisms (in both agriculture and industry) has produced a spectacular increase of economic efficiency that has allowed the Chinese leadership to raise half a billion people out from traditional poverty.

The New Public Management and the doing away with of democratic values

We can conclude the preceding paragraphs by saying that, if the attempts to define NPM and to build a typology of NPM variants are quite surprising, they at least have the merit of displaying the recurrent references (even if one notes the contradictions between the authors): pragmatism with or without ideological reference, a large variety of conceptions and applications, a concern for effectiveness and especially efficiency, a better adaptation of the offer of public services to the needs of the population, transposition of management methods from the private to the public sector. This raises several comments.

First, I am convinced that to have recourse to an ideology is not a fault in itself. On the contrary, I consider that it is impossible to avoid assuming an ideological perspective, especially when principles, precepts or prescriptions of an apparently pragmatic or technical character are proposed in order to solve problems. These certainly entail managerial, financial, technical and administrative as well as other perspectives and the necessary competencies, but, what is equally important, their solutions have definitely an impact on individuals, groups, social classes and public authorities; in other words on humankind. In this context, it is understandable that the authors, notoriously situated on the left, hesitate or even refuse to recognize the obvious neoliberal filiation of NPM, for this would create disorder in their discourse. The same goes for consulting companies,[31] as for them it is a question of selling a product (expertise in public management) to potential public clients that are not necessarily open to ideological references, but are more easily inclined towards pragmatic approaches. It is, however, quite surprising that academics so easily make the same mistake. It is in fact well known in all disciplines of human sciences that the systems of values, beliefs, in short, of ideologies, constitute one of the most powerful foundations of individual and collective action and that they confer the real meaning of the implementation of principles, precepts or management techniques. There is no practice without ideology.

I also find it difficult to understand that those who propose to implement the teachings of such brilliant scholars as Friedrich von Hayek or Milton Friedman can deny this paternity, as if they wanted to avoid at all costs admitting that they had contracted a shameful disease by heredity (for the neoliberals) or by an unfortunate 'unprotected' intercourse (for the managerial left). It is undeniable that the revival of liberal thinking has strongly influenced the ideas of NPM followers. Whether one likes it or not, this is not a shameful illness. So, why not acknowledge one's forefathers? To please everybody? Both the Right and the Left? Or are we really here talking about Right and Left? Has the official Left been swallowed by the Right?[32]

But there is worse. No reference is made in most of the works of NPM followers to the fundamental democratic values of a Western society and to the conflict of values that this society is going through; the only values that are explicitly mentioned are those of the '3E' (economy, effectiveness, efficiency) typical of NPM.[33] Would the NPM followers consider that we have (at last?) reached the end of history? The end of ideologies?[34] More precisely, are the values of the 3E all that remain? Would those people think that the final goal of politics is thus reduced to the implementation of values of economy, effectiveness and efficiency? Without referring to fundamental democratic values (and non-instrumental ones as is the case for the 3E) how can one proceed to choose priorities, an undertaking that – as all those who have seriously tackled this problem are very well aware – cannot be settled by an approach founded solely on motives of economy, but also, and above all, requires political and indeed ideological considerations about human nature, the relations between the individual and the state, and so on. In addition, it is precisely on the choice of priorities in matters of both state expenditures and taxation that political debate focuses. The NPM is of no use whatsoever in helping politicians make these choices. However, the followers of NPM persist in telling us: adopt the NPM and everything will come out right as if by enchantment. Faith replaces a comprehensive and well-documented analysis of the country's situation and of its international position, of the needs and wants of its citizens.

The New Public Management, or when the citizen gives way to the customer

It must be mentioned, however, that even within mainstream liberalism some voices have arisen to temper the neoliberal euphoria. Limiting myself to Switzerland as an example, I cannot help welcoming the perspicacity of Jean-François Leuba (at that time an outstanding politician of the Right, member of the Liberal Party), who, in a remarkable article written when he was President of the Swiss National Council (one of the two chambers of the Swiss parliament), makes the distinction between economic liberalism and political liberalism:

> political liberalism, as we understand it in Switzerland . . . has always put the state at man's service, and not vice versa, which is the way of totalitarianism. Also, economy is at the service of man, and not the reverse, which is peculiar to wild capitalism. It has often been said that there are two sides of liberal thinking: the humanist dimension and the economic one. But both will doubtless join sides, to remind us that, even in the world of globalization, one cannot sacrifice man to profit alone.[35]

One can easily subscribe to such a statement. The truth is, unfortunately, that in practice the liberal movement has been dominated worldwide by the economic side and that NPM is its spearhead. It is in effect the market that, together with NPM, becomes the privileged sphere for social interactions, by considerably reducing the space for the political sphere and reducing the role of the state to that of guarantor of a market that has finally been freed from all state hindrances.[36] This necessarily called for a change in actors: the citizen (privileged actor of a political democratic system) gives way to the customer, actor 'king' of the market. How is this possible?

We have seen, in the definition by Jean-Daniel Delley given above, that NPM aims at 'improving the efficiency of the state by better adapting the offer of public services to the user needs.' In order to achieve this objective, NPM proposes one of its most surprising innovations in the field of relations between public bodies and individuals, by substituting the citizen for the customer. Thus, one reduces the role of the individual, member of a community, to that of a purchaser of products in a multitude of markets separated one from the other. One destroys in this way the democratic figure of the individual-citizen, bearer of a combination of rights and duties, attributed to him or her by the public authority (i.e. the citizens as a whole) through the political process. It is the participation of the citizens (equal to each other) in the activities of the state that is typical of the political activity in a democratic state, and not the capacity of acquiring goods and services in the market, this depending upon the purchasing power of each individual (different from one citizen to another, according to their positions in the economic sphere). By sweeping aside the concept of citizen and citizenship, the followers of NPM come to adopt one of the principles of neoliberalism, the deregulation and 'flexibilization' of work (which inevitably translates into the vulnerability of workers and employees), and forget, as Pierre de Senarclens fittingly reminds us already in 1997, that 'modern citizenship was built on the protection of the workers. It will not resist a world devoid of boundaries, where political powers must give way to the conditions of businesses and financial markets.'[37] How prophetic were these words, a decade before the financial and economic crisis of 2008 was to reveal to the world the despotism and the unbelievable greed of those who controlled the financial markets, freed as they have been by the irresponsible deregulation promoted by NPM and its followers!

The New Public Management or the 'inescapable' consequences of the globalization of the economy

In this context, it is rather pathetic to claim that the NPM brings the citizen-customer closer to power. This kind of assertion, coming from persons who use globalization of the economy to justify the adoption of the NPM, is surprising, when one knows (as rightly emphasized by the followers of NPM) that fundamental decisions guiding the living conditions of society today increasingly depend on the decisions taken by large multinational companies and economic international organizations over which the citizens and local bodies have practically no influence whatsoever. Why (re-)attribute power to the citizens of Alfriston (UK), Caltanisetta (Italy) or Chattanooga (USA) if the essential is being decided on a world scale? It is at this level (the level of the WTO, the World Bank, the IMF, the OECD) that one must re-attribute power to the citizen, and not only at a local level.[38]

This leads us quite naturally to appreciate the use of the argument for the globalization of the economy in order to impose the application of the NPM principles on public management. It is not a question of analysing here the debate on globalization. Already in the 1999 article I considered that:

> the term 'globalization of the capital' seems to us to correspond better to reality . . . In fact, the important factor that dominates the restructuring of the economy on a worldwide level is the deregulation of financial markets, which, in a drive towards profitability (generally on a short-term basis) urges investors to move capital to where labour is the least expensive (if the goal

is to invest in productive processes) and/or where the returns are the highest (where it is a question of purely speculative investments).[39]

It is not my aim in this chapter to determine the consequences, although they are well known, of these movements in both developing and developed countries. I will come back to these problems in Chapters 5 and 6 and in the general conclusion of this book when I take the 2008–11 crisis as an indicator of the negative consequences of neoliberalism, comparing the different ways adopted by China and the West to overcome the crisis. However, already in the 1999 article I thought it was important to emphasize that most of the NPM followers present globalization as a beneficial and ineluctable event and, above all, an event that states can do nothing about except to adapt to it – naturally, by adopting the precepts of the NPM. Nevertheless, the Asian crisis of 1997 had already sown doubts in the minds of some observers and decision-makers about the benefits of a wide and rapid liberalization of the world economy. In this context, it was noteworthy that the country which had best resisted that crisis was the one least integrated into the international economic system and the least deregulated in home affairs: the People's Republic of China.[40] I concluded that paragraph of the 1999 article by posing the question:

> Is there no other way but to adapt oneself to the demands of international finance? Could one not envisage, as some do, an 'empowerment' of politics on a worldwide basis that would restore democracy and the roles citizens are supposed to play within it, where the destinies of mankind are decided?[41]

Unfortunately the lessons of the 1997 crisis were not taken seriously by leading economic actors and politicians, nor by many economists. Deregulation of financial markets went on all the way to the more serious 2008–11 crisis. Are we now taking the necessary measures in order to avoid another and eventually even more dramatic crisis? The last and fatal one?

The New Public Management or the art of marketing in public management

Before going on to the essential nature of NPM, let us conclude this part by some comments on the terminology used by its followers. The past 30 years have witnessed what one can only term a flood of magical words, of which one wonders whether the majority of their users realize their full meaning or, which seems more likely, they use them because they are in the spirit of the times.[42] The very term 'New Public Management' hardly expresses anything about its contents. We have seen that some of its prophets even say that it does not exist as such and that it can assume different forms. Notwithstanding, the term 'NPM' conveys the magic idea of something new, very much in demand in a world where one must constantly innovate and improve quality and performance, at the risk of not being competitive. Note, in this respect, that one of the authors who has analysed the very essence of NPM, and does not hesitate to talk about the ideology of NPM, uses in place of the initials 'NPM' the initials 'DPM'. This is by far richer in information on the real nature of NPM, because D = deregulation, P = privatization and M = marketization.[43] Moreover, by using DPM instead of NPM one brings to light the real essence of New Public Management, and it becomes therefore difficult to claim that NPM can assume several forms fundamentally different from each other. I will come back to these considerations in the last part of this section. Moreover, the promoters of NPM use all sorts of shock terms, such as 'reinvent', 're-engineering', 'rethink', 'debureaucratize', 'deregulate', 'decentralize'. All six, but particularly the first three, illustrate very well the obsession of the followers of the NPM with novelty. The last three, in addition, illustrate just as many illusions that must be clarified.

Debureaucratization?

If to debureaucratize means to attenuate and correct the effects of the dysfunctions that inevitably appear in the functioning of bureaucracies, one can but agree. However, the effect of novelty is practically null as these problems have been dealt with since at least the 1930s.[44] Furthermore, since the 1960s, Michel Crozier has convincingly demonstrated that dysfunctions are a normal characteristic of bureaucracies. Moreover, he showed that bureaucracies try to correct their dysfunctions by reinforcing the bureaucratic features that produced them, in such a way that, inevitably, new dysfunctions will appear in the future. This process will repeat itself in what Crozier called a bureaucratic vicious circle.[45]

Furthermore, a century ago, Max Weber formulated the hypothesis, partially confirmed and never refuted, that bureaucracy can disappear only with the disappearance of the society that it supports.[46] Indeed, he proves in a convincing manner throughout a whole series of historical analyses that the quasi-bureaucratic organizations that have existed in such diverse societies as Imperial China and the Egypt of the Pharaohs have disappeared only with the disappearance of the corresponding society of which they were the indispensable support. The Weberian analysis is founded on the hypothesis that the different components of a society are inevitably linked to each other by a certain degree of coherence. Starting from this hypothesis, Weber demonstrated that bureaucracy is the typical form assumed by all organizations (public and private) in a society such as the Western one. This type of society is ruled by a process of rationalization that gives coherence to society as a whole: the existence of a rational economy (market or planned) based on the calculation and maximization of the predictability of behaviours, and thus on the reduction of uncertainty, requires a rational state and a rational public bureaucracy (i.e. whose behaviour is predictable), in charge of implementing a rational legal system (i.e. also predictable).[47] The radical challenging of bureaucracies would thus imply a radical challenging of the whole organization of Western society and not merely an academic exercise of organizational engineering at the nation-state level, in which most of the NPM followers indulge. In addition, as the hierarchical form of public bureaucracies is only a special case of a general principle operating throughout Western societies (i.e. concerning all organizations, including private companies), we are confronted here with an additional and formidable problem that a process of debureaucratization applied to the public sector alone would have difficulty in overcoming.

Finally, the Weberian analysis of power clarifies another fundamental point at the centre of the debate on the NPM. In the structure of the ideal type of legal-rational power,[48] in which the state endows itself with a bureaucratic-type administration, the latter is totally under the control of the political power. However, when Weber analyses – thanks to his typology – the reality of contemporary political systems of the legal-rational type, he discovers that the state bureaucracy has a tendency to escape political control thanks to its specialized knowledge, the strategic position it holds within the society and the practice of secrecy. Thus, bureaucracy could, in an extreme case, exercise the power itself. In this context, the only power capable of counterbalancing the power of the state bureaucracy – according to Weber – can come from other bureaucracies, and more particularly from bureaucracies in the private sector. In fact, they also function on the basis of formal and technical rules, being structured in hierarchical offices, hiring personnel with specialized know-how, practising secrecy, and holding a strategic position within society thanks to the provision of goods and services.

It now remains to be seen if the private bureaucracies occupy today a strategic position in our society and if, comparatively, the bureaucracies of the nation-states have lost their strategic position. The answer, based upon the analysis of the present situation prevailing at the moment of the present global economic crisis, is clearly yes.[49] Paradoxically, this is exactly what NPM logic demonstrates with the argument of globalization of the economy put forward for justifying the introduction of an NPM style of public management. However, in fact, what the NPM followers fail to account for is that NPM at the state level is nothing else but the projection at this level of the international 'agreement' known as the 'Washington consensus', based upon neoclassical economic theory (represented by the Chicago School), arrived at by the US Treasury, the International Monetary Fund and the World Bank.[50] The logic, and the policy agenda of this 'consensus', implemented at the global level since the beginning of the 1980s, have strongly oriented the rush towards NPM at the state level, first in the USA, the United Kingdom and New Zealand.[51] Then the partners of the 'Washington consensus' have imposed it on the rest of the world, in both the developed and the developing countries.[52] The loss of power of the nation-states has left free rein to the major economic actors (the financial elite, multinationals and international economic organizations), which act on a planetary scale, very adequately sheltered from democratic control, only recognizing the control of the 'free market' and urging the states to dispossess themselves of what little sovereignty they have left in the economic sphere.[53]

The conclusion is very clear. Contrary to the claim of the tenants of NPM who maintain that its adoption by the nation-States (in their attempt to adapt themselves to the 'beneficial' and 'ineluctable' process of globalization), will terminate the irresistible development and supremacy of bureaucracy, we note that the process of bureaucratization reaches today its apogee on the planetary scale. It is all the more entrenched in that it is reinforced by a particular application of the hierarchical principle that tends to subordinate politics to the economy and its rationality. It goes without saying that a society based essentially on the ideology according to which the accomplishment of man is attained above all by the possession of an increasing quantity of goods and services, optimally produced and distributed by a 'free market' (and the freer the better), constitutes a very favourable cultural environment for the establishment and the maintenance of the hegemony of the bureaucracies that have been constituted by the most powerful economic international agents.[54] It is difficult to see in this context how this process can be stopped if the states do not agree amongst themselves to give back the power to their citizens, by setting up a democratic system on a worldwide basis that would allow a real debate on the fundamental choices with which all citizens (and not only a small elite) are confronted today.

Deregulation?

Deregulation is a special case of debureaucratization, bearing in mind that, as already mentioned, a bureaucratic management necessarily abides by formal rules.[55] The meaning NPM followers give to this term must be related to the principle of freedom, the only principle capable of releasing the creative strengths of man, particularly in the economic sphere and, by transposition, in any other field of activity.[56] The same goes for the field of international trade, for the domestic market and also, by transposition, for the management of the public sector, particularly the functioning of the state. Further to our comments on debureaucratization, it will be sufficient here to emphasize three fundamental aspects of regulation.

First, the rules that determine the behaviour of public officials are generally meant to implement some important principles of constitutional law, of which I mention here only those of legality and equal treatment. Any too great latitude left to the official in the application of law to individual cases objectively leaves open the way to found a decision on subjective elements that may violate the above-mentioned principles.[57]

Furthermore, a large part of the legislation, particularly in the social field and in the field of environmental protection, has been set up in order to palliate market failures and faulty behaviours by economic actors that have been generally considered as irresponsible. Deregulation in these fields would be equivalent to leaving the way open to the resurgence of unacceptable behaviours, and to considering them admissible in the pure interests of economic profitability alone and/or in order to support the competitiveness of the economic actors concerned.

Finally, deregulation may, like any other organizational arrangement, provoke the appearance of dysfunctions that necessitate a return to the formerly abolished regulation, or the implementation of new regulations, which may be even more dense and bothersome than the former. The privatization of numerous public enterprises in the United Kingdom (gas, electricity, transports, telecommunications etc.) has necessitated the implementation of regulation and control agencies, as well as the definition of a number of indicators to measure the services rendered, procedures of which one wonders finally if they do not rather contribute to making the management of these sectors more difficult, less efficient and even more bureaucratic than it was when it was managed within the traditional hierarchical structures of the state.

Decentralization?

Just as in the case of deregulation, decentralization can be considered a special case of debureaucratization. Indeed, one of the characteristics of bureaucracy, the hierarchical character of its offices, involves the existence of numerous hierarchical tiers. The main consequences are, on one hand, that information circulates slowly, running the risk of being utilized within the framework of strategies by officials or offices who distort it and/or retain it according to their particular interests, and, on the other hand, that the subordinates who are too far distant from the centre of decision-making become demotivated. According to the analyses of Michel Crozier, the distancing from the centre of decision-making, which fulfils the function of reinforcing the impersonal nature of the norms and their implementation, may also give rise to the appearance of dysfunctions that endanger the organization's capacity to accomplish its missions in a satisfactory manner.[58] It is therefore not surprising that decentralization is also a part of the arsenal of NPM marketing.

Decentralization can take two forms. First, it can mean the delegation of public tasks to private organizations: it may then take the form of a pure and simple privatization (with or without state control), or contracting out (with or without competition), necessarily implying greater responsibility being given to the decentralized units, as well as control by the state. Second, it may be within the public sector itself, by relying on a service agreement concluded between the minister and a state agency, assigned with a clearly defined mission (with quantitative and qualitative standards that must be satisfied), wide autonomy and a budget frame. I will come back to the difficulties of such a management strategy. For the time being, it is enough to mention, as in the case of debureaucratization and deregulation, that decentralization will never be able to eradicate all traces of hierarchy and regulation, in other words, all bureaucratic aspects in the management of a public or private organization. A minimum of centralization is in fact needed for the management of bureaucratic-type organizations, which dominate all the fields of activity of our societies. On the other hand, excessive decentralization runs the risk of causing the appearance of new dysfunctions. Of these, it is sufficient to mention the increased difficulties in coordinating the different state activities, at present one of the most difficult tasks to tackle in the public sector. All one can do is to alleviate the negative aspects, the dysfunctions due to centralization. The best way of doing this is most likely not by designing an abstract organizational and managerial model and then by trying to squeeze reality within it, as we Westerners are accustomed to do, but by analysing the situation within the organization concerned and then trying to change the elements of the situation so that, in the long term, they conform to the objectives of the organization. This is what I suggested in Chapter 1 when I compared and contrasted the Chinese and Western ways of 'thinking and doing'.

In conclusion, claiming to revolutionize public management by debureaucratizing, deregulating and decentralizing is certainly a good strategy to use to sell a product on the market of management expertise, but, in the long run, it may prove an impossible mission, whose failure will be difficult to justify, considering the

NPM's wealth of messianic promises. In the end, after serious discussion with some of NPM followers, one realizes that it is a question of muddling through, no more and no less, trying to find partial, tentative and uncertain solutions to classical management problems, or introducing technical elements (such as analytical accounting) to speed up technical and operational management and/or to make it more transparent. All well and good! But then why talk in a bombastic language bulging with words bigger than the product that one is effectively capable of putting on the market?

If it were only a question of this, there would be no problems of mutual understanding between NPM followers and other observers of public management, who themselves are also concerned with considerations of efficiency, but also, and even more so, with respect for the rule of law, democracy and therefore the primacy of the citizens over any elitist group, however competent it may be. Unfortunately, for a majority of the NPM followers, it is, on the contrary, a question of implementing an entire programme based on a coherent and rational strategy, the full dimensions and consequences of which, it must be said, they are often only too careful not to define. The real essence and practical consequences of the NPM must therefore be made clear so that the reader may form his own opinion. I will do so in the last section of this chapter.

The New Public Management ideal-type

The tenets of the NPM generally proceed from an analysis of the dysfunctions of the state, an evaluation of the hindrances that the development of state intervention increasingly burdens the market with, as well as taking into consideration the consequences of globalization of the economy and especially of the financial markets. Globalization demands a rationalization of the activities of enterprises towards greater efficiency. Failing to do so, they will be confronted with bankruptcy, or they will be forced to transfer their activities to those countries where production costs of the same product are lower, in terms of salaries, employers' contributions to social insurances, income tax burden and so on. The consequence thereof would be in both cases a loss of jobs in the countries concerned. This is something one of the countries where the proponents of NPM have been the most vociferous, the USA, has experienced in recent years.[59]

Yet, the NPM argument goes on, what happens in developed countries? The efficiency of enterprises is jeopardized by the activity developed by states over the last century, but particularly since the Second World War. Three aspects of this policy are particularly evident: excessive regulations, inflation of the administrative system and immoderation and irrationality of the Welfare State.[60] The consequence of these three characteristics of the role of the state has been a considerable increase in the cost of the functioning of the state: on one hand salaries must be paid to a constantly increasing number of officials, and on the other hand social security allocations must be paid. In addition, the employer's contributions towards the financing of social security and the obligation to respect all sorts of regulations (e.g. for the environmental protection or public health) contribute to increasing production costs.

The result for society has been increased taxes hitting not only households but also and above all enterprises, which renders their situation in the market even more difficult. At the level of state financial management, this policy has shown its limits when it became impossible to increase the revenues to match the increase of expenditures. As the latter are very often listed in legislative instruments that can hardly be changed without the consent of the people or its representatives, an infernal vicious circle sets in of persistent annual deficits, resulting in an increase in the public debt. An increasing part of state expenditures is thus used no longer to accomplish public activities but to pay interest on the debt.

It is true that this analysis is not very far from reality. It is quite a correct description of what really existed during the last part of the 1970s. However, at this point, one could envisage several possible solutions. The NPM followers furnish only one reply: adapt to the market. This is what someone has called 'the dictatorship of no alternatives' and some others 'market fundamentalism'.[61] The proposed remedies are straightforward: deregulate and 'flexibilize' the labour market (as this is the only area where savings can still be made); decrease state expenditures by privatizing profitable activities,[62] for example social policies, thereby diminishing expenditures on social security and relative contributions, particularly those paid by enterprises; and decrease the unemployment insurance benefits (the amount of allocations and time of coverage) with the aim of pushing the unemployed to accept (any) jobs. There is nothing surprising in the foregoing, knowing that the fundamental principle of NPM is economic efficiency. We will see in the general conclusion that this same strategy has been imposed upon European countries, especially Greece, Portugal, Spain and Italy in 2011.

It is encouraging that several authors have carried out useful analyses, which help us directly or indirectly, to determine the real nature of NPM, that is, the NPM ideal-type.[63] The following is what I have retained from these analyses. I will first define the core principles of the NPM ideal-type and, if necessary for the sake of clarity, I will give some real-life examples of their implementation.

1 *The principle of economic efficiency* is the fundamental concept that gives coherence to the reform strategy of NPM and on which all other principles logically depend. It is based, on one hand, on the postulate of economic rationality used to explain the behaviour of the social actors in all spheres of activity, and, on the other hand, on the premise according to which the market is the best means to optimize production and wealth distribution. As we have already seen with Milton Friedman, the role of the state should be limited to maintaining the framework necessary for market functioning. The market, in turn, is based upon the concept of competition. If this is the case, the best way to improve the management of public affairs is to 'marketize' the state, in other words, to deregulate the markets and privatize state activities that have nothing to do (at least directly) with the state's functions aimed at sustaining the market (such as fiscal policy and anti-trust policy), which means that practically all the other state's activities could be privatized, including social policies.[64] Failing this, one should introduce, at least partially, market elements into the management of the public sector by means of contracting

out with private or public entities and/or by introducing competition.[65] The following principles serve in fact to reinforce and/or to facilitate the implementation of the economic efficiency principle.

2 The second principle is that of *separation between strategic and operational decisions*. Despite the novelty of this terminology in public management, this term, borrowed directly from enterprise management, is a mere resumption of the former theory of separation between politics and administration, brought forward by Woodrow Wilson in 1887 and reformulated in 1945 by Herbert Simon.[66] This principle reinforces the tendency towards privatization and contracting out by claiming that it is possible to manage in an optimal way the production of certain services, even if the privatization cannot be complete in case the state wishes to keep at least supervision or control over the production of services without actually producing the service itself. The result is an obvious saving in both cases. In the case of privatization of those sectors over which the state would like to keep control,[67] the economy would result from the decrease in the number of public officials as well as from the improved efficiency of private enterprises in charge of the service production concerned. In the case of contracting out, the benefit would result from the fact that the beneficiaries of the contract (public or private) would be forced to improve their efficiency. Indeed, in those cases where they are subject to competition in competitive tendering,[68] they would find themselves in a market situation and would thus be naturally driven to decrease production costs (at equal quantity and quality); in the case where the state addresses itself directly to a unique supplier, the improvement of efficiency would result from the fact that these entities would be liberated from the rigidity of bureaucratic management typical of public services, particularly of those concerning personnel management. Moreover, contracts are generally limited in time (from four to seven years), and are either renegotiated or put on tender again at the end of the contract period. According to NPM theory, this should put some additional pressure on the contract beneficiaries to manage it efficiently and according to the requirements of the public authority. However, the implementation of contracting out as a means to improve efficiency thanks to competition has some serious limits, especially when the duration of the contract is extended well beyond the four to seven years of the first wave of UK contracts. This is the case for schools, hospitals and prisons, for which durations of more than 20 years are the rule.[69] In any case there is competition to obtain the contract, but after that there is no competition at all.[70]

3 The principle of *decentralization* naturally reinforces the two foregoing principles, that is, it reinforces the tendency towards privatization and contracting out that can be considered as particular forms of decentralization. Moreover, if for any reason privatization and contracting out are not possible, one can give more autonomy to state sectors by instituting autonomous agencies as has been done, for example, in the UK with the so-called 'Next Step Agencies'.[71]

4 These first three principles are then supported by what the proponents of the NPM call the *orientation of state activity to results and therefore to customer*

satisfaction, rather than according to respect of procedures. The market, driving the service suppliers to produce at low costs and by satisfying the client's expectations of quality, is the guarantor of an optimal resource management. In this context, privatization, contracting out and decentralization seem to be management techniques bringing closer together the state and its customers, as in the case of private sector enterprises. It is thus the customer who becomes the privileged reference of NPM, and not the citizen.

5 However, as the implementation of this New Public Management happens within a particular context, as mentioned before, characterized by persistent deficits and the consequent increase of the public debt, as well as by the impossibility of increasing taxation, the implementation of the efficiency principle is necessarily biased by a new fact: the need to balance the state budget, a need that can be satisfied only by a *systematic policy of savings*. This is the core of the slogan of the American version of the NPM: the 'National Performance Review' was launched in 1993 under the slogan 'A Government that works better, and costs less'.[72] The implementation of this principle naturally leads to the following two principles:
6 *The primacy of financial control* and
7 *The generalization of audits and performance evaluations* (implementation of the slogan 'value for money'), which entails the definition of qualitative and quantitative standards.
8 Bearing in mind the foregoing three principles, it is inevitable, in the management of the public sector, to operate a *transfer of power in favour of the managers,* to the detriment of professionals (for example, to the detriment of doctors in hospitals).[73]
9 The rule of the market translates in a more dramatic way into one particular field, as here it directly concerns men and women: the *deregulation of the labour market.*
10 However, as the trade union organizations can present an obstacle to the implementation of the foregoing principle, this last must be supported by a tenth principle: the *marginalization of the trade unions*.[74]

In the next chapter I will examine the rationale of the Chinese NPM and will show to what extent it is also based upon the principles we have just presented above. Then, the question to which we must give an answer is: how do these principles translate into reality in China and in the West? This will be discussed in Chapters 5 and 6 on the basis of empirical data that will reveal the economic and societal consequences of NPM in Western countries and in China between the early 1980s and 2010. However, for the moment it is necessary to discuss the main technical difficulties of NPM. These do not constitute the main object of this book and therefore I will not come back to them in the following chapters, which will be focused on the main object of this book: the economic and social consequences of NPM. However, it is important to point out these difficulties because they are not easy to overcome, and should therefore be kept in mind for an overall evaluation of NPM.

The technical difficulties of NPM

The first technical difficulty lies in the fact that the market does not always exist. The failures of the market being well known,[75] let us just remember – together with Paul Krugman – that markets are not magic, and the end result of seeking at all costs to impose recourse to the market by a pure ideological choice may be less satisfactory than solutions found through traditional public management.[76] Of course, one may consider that in the case of contracting out it is possible to introduce some market competition by opening up a fair bidding procedure. Nevertheless, it remains that in this case competition exists for the market (i.e. for obtaining the contract) but not in the market once the contract has been assigned to one of the bidders. This is an even more serious limitation (in the perspective of the defenders of NPM) when the contract has a duration of several years, or even decades, as is the case for the construction of hospitals, prisons, bridges, roads, water plants and so on. This, of course, does not mean that recourse to the market may not be envisaged at all. The market, as it is generally presented by the liberals (old and new) is in fact an ideal-type, similar to the Weberian bureaucracy. In reality there is no perfect market, no more than there is a perfect bureaucracy. One must therefore, in any case, carefully weigh up the advantages and the disadvantages of these two types of public management, as well as their possible coexistence and collaboration, and then choose the solution that provides the best guarantees of efficiency and respect for the will of the citizens as a whole, in other words, of democratic values.[77]

The second technical difficulty resides in the separation between strategic and operational decisions. We have already pointed out that this dream is 100 years old at least, and has led to a long series of trials in the United States, all resulting in failures, the 'National Performance Review' being only one of the latest episodes.[78] The fundamental problem stems from the fact that public policy objectives are being constantly defined and redefined throughout the policy cycle, including in the operational phase of their implementation and that, because of this fact, the politicians would be well advised not to lose control of them. We have here a good example of the difficulties (and false promises) of transposing managerial techniques from the private sector to the state. In an enterprise, separating strategic and operational decisions may be relatively easy most of the time. In fact the objectives of an enterprise are generally quite simple and non-contradictory: increase market share and profits. This being true, it is for example possible for the management of a multinational to assign to the director of its subsidiary in another country the task of increasing the market share of a certain product by, say, 20 per cent in three years. The director is free to organize his business as he chooses, provided that he respects the organizational culture of his company and the local legislation. After the three years, or more likely every year throughout the assignment, the general management will evaluate the results and in case of failure it will very likely dismiss the director. Within the state sector, objectives that can be defined so clearly are rather rare, if not non-existent.

One could no doubt maintain that it is sufficient to implement control bodies such as envisaged for contracting out, or, in the case of privatized sectors or decentralized agencies, under the supervision of regulatory organs or control bodies. Here one could raise two objections. First, the British experience shows that it is difficult to control from outside the very complex and high-technology sectors that constitute most privatized sectors – to such an extent that some observers do not hesitate to report what they call the 'capture' of the controller by the controlled, the former, depending on the latter for information, being gradually induced to agree with the evaluation criteria of the latter.[79] Moreover, the present economic crisis is a clear example of the difficulties that arise for the control of financial institutions when the sector has been highly deregulated by putting it in tune with NPM prescriptions.[80]

Furthermore, the implementation of control bodies entails costs that do not exist in a classical hierarchical bureaucratic system, namely transaction costs. The drawing up of a contract, the control of services rendered and the eventual renegotiation of a part or the whole of the contract entail costs that must be taken into account when comparing NPM with traditional management.[81] This is seldom done by proponents of NPM. Moreover, a comparison ex-post between sectors previously managed by the state and subsequently privatized or contracted out is often made impossible because the collection of data has been discontinued or organized in ways that collect different data, thus rendering the comparison in terms of efficiency and quality practically impossible.[82]

Third, the techniques of NPM management cause serious problems regarding democratic responsibilities. The great autonomy given to the public managers, the difficulties of control already mentioned, and the deregulation of procedures with the aim of reinforcing the officials' sense of responsibility and of encouraging them to show initiative and take risks (as in private enterprises) brings the question of responsibility dramatically to light. First, as mentioned before, there is a high risk of violating some of the important principles of administrative law, such as those of legality and equal treatment. Then, as shown clearly by Ronald Moe, this could lead to a fragmentation of the state's action in a great number of agencies independent from one another, rendering the coordination of the state's activity difficult if not impossible, and would contribute to dangerously relaxing the responsibilities of politicians with regard to democratic instances and the citizens.[83] Moreover, the nature of the coordination and the management of contradictions between the various sectors of state activity are quite different from what is the case for private enterprises, even the biggest. The state must often implement policies aimed at satisfying contradictory legitimate demands from citizens or interest groups, such as economic development versus environmental protection. Fragmenting state activity by generalizing contractualization would render the coordination and the management of contradictions particularly difficult.[84] Contractualization would render it quite difficult to implement the famous formula: the government must be 'steering, not rowing'.[85] With the generalization of contractualization the state would have considerable difficulties in guiding when several teams are rowing in different directions.

One of the beacon and pioneer countries of NPM, the United Kingdom, has experienced the negative consequences of the fragmentation of the state's activities following the generalization of contractualization. For this reason, the government of Tony Blair decided in 2001 to entrust the central government with instruments that should allow it to guide the enormous system of contracts into which the UK government has been fragmented. After 20 years of decentralization the British Civil Service College (i.e. the British national school of administration) has been placed within the Cabinet Office alongside the Centre for Management and Policy Studies, with the aim of allowing the government to acquire a comprehensive view of public policies, their definition and evaluation.[86]

Finally, the generalization of contracting out (and of contracts in general) significantly increases the opportunities for corruption of officials. Thus, for instance, Nicholas Henry shows that during the NPM period of the Reagan Administration the cases of corruption within the US federal administration more than quadrupled compared with the preceding period.[87]

Thus, even at the simple level of management technique, a whole series of major difficulties emerge on the way to the implementation of the NPM. However, the real and most serious weaknesses of NPM clearly emerge when one considers its impact on the society concerned as a whole. One may certainly object that in addition to a management style or orientation, in our case NPM, there are other variables involved in determining the structure of society; but it would be surprising if the management of the public sector had no effect whatsoever on the social structures, especially as it is based upon the implementation of economic efficiency (and, in addition, biased by the 'necessity' to save money, particularly on social expenditures), as well as on deregulation, privatization, decentralization and contracting out, thanks to which NPM followers promise miracles. Indeed, it is possible today, and even much more so than was the case when I wrote the 1999 article,[88] to furnish significant evidence that the countries I describe as strong-NPM countries present, when compared with countries that have not implemented NPM to such an extent, unenviable characteristics, in particular a higher income inequality, as well as poverty and criminal rates significantly higher than countries with a more active social state. This will be demonstrated in Part III. Moreover, as we will see in the general conclusion, this trend has been further accelerated during the 2008–11 crisis. The followers of NPM should now explain how they can justify NPM policies that threaten the security of an increasing number of citizens by reducing employment, salaries and social benefits, for the sake of saving and supporting the financial sector, which is the entity mainly responsible for the crisis.

4 The foundation of Chinese New Public Management

Deng's reforms or the demise of the planned economy and the introduction of market mechanisms[1]

Whereas the content of part of the Chinese NPM introduced in China since 1978 is quite similar to the Western one, that is, it also entails decisions in favour of economic efficiency and the means of achieving it, namely privatization, contracting out, decentralization and deregulation,[2] the political culture and the spirit in which this strategy has been chosen and implemented are quite different. First of all, as already explained in the first chapter, the partial abandonment of the planned economy and the adoption of market mechanisms have been carried out on the basis of practical and not ideological considerations. Moreover, NPM has been adopted and implemented within the Chinese political culture, which has developed through centuries a specific set of values, such as harmony, unity and stability, instead of political rights and freedoms, which are typical of Western political culture.[3] It is of course possible to evaluate China's public management on the basis of our Western values, which is generally done by Western sinologists, but, as already mentioned, by doing so we will place ourselves at an ethnocentric point of view with little capacity to explain and evaluate the Chinese way. My task in the second part of this chapter will therefore be to explain the way by which the Chinese leadership has adopted and implemented NPM, and to find out, as I have done for the Western NPM, what consequences one can predict following its implementation. As for the Western NPM, the actual consequences of the Chinese NPM will be evaluated using empirical analysis in Chapter 6.

The Chinese NPM: the choice of market mechanisms

For the purpose of explaining the choice in favour of market mechanisms and the rationale for that choice, we have to examine two rather important, and maybe also controversial, aspects. First, we have to determine what fundamental goal the Chinese leadership is pursuing through that choice. I will argue that the fundamental goal is to restore China as a world power. Second, we have to determine through what kind of thinking that choice has been made. I will argue that China still thinks, at least in part, and an important part, according to the traditional way, of which Sun Tzu's seminal treaty of Chinese military strategy is one of the best examples.[4] The conclusion will be that the choice of market mechanisms is based mainly upon pragmatic considerations and much less on ideological ones.

Restoring China as a world power

According to the well-known motto of Deng Xiaoping, the Chinese leader who introduced market mechanisms into the Chinese economy, 'No matter if it is a white cat or a black cat; as long as it can catch mice, it is a good cat.' Comparing the brilliant results obtained in the West by the market economy with the poor results of the planned economy, the choice was quite straightforward. Moreover, because of the damages inflicted by the Cultural Revolution (1966–76) not only on the Chinese people but also on the reputation of the Communist Party, it was imperative to give the Chinese people the goods and services that would improve its living conditions, and this would simultaneously contribute to the realization of the fundamental goal of the Chinese leadership: to restore China to its position as a world power.[5] This statement may be viewed with some surprise by scholars who insist mainly on the economic dimensions of China's reforms, and therefore it needs to be explained in some detail. First of all, an overview of China's history since the first opium war shows very clearly that the capitulation to the Western powers, and above all to the UK, after centuries of China's self-sufficiency, literally traumatized the Chinese imperial leadership. The distance that China put between the West and itself was not only economic, but involved all the dimensions of its society, culture, polity, military and even arts. It is true that the emperors of the Qing Dynasty had developed a keen interest in Western culture, especially the arts, but this never developed into an integration of Western arts into China. Most of the time it was the Western people who assimilated some of the Chinese cultural traits.

Let us take just two examples from about the mid-1600s to the mid-1700s. In 1662 Emperor Kangxi published a decision authorizing Christian missionaries to preach in China. Unfortunately, on 19 May 1715 Pope Clement XI published a bull that condemned the Chinese rites, thus making them incompatible with the Catholic faith. Reading a Chinese translation of the bull, Emperor Kangxi is reported to having added a note saying:

> After reading this decision, I wonder how these uncivilized Western people can talk about the great philosophical and moral principles of China . . . Most of their words and arguments are ridiculous. In light of this decision, I finally found that their doctrine is of the same kind as the petty heresies of the Buddhist and Taoist monks. We have never seen such a nonsense. From now on I forbid Westerners to spread their doctrine in China. This will avoid much hassle.[6]

The second interesting example, in the domain of figurative arts, is also related to Emperor Kangxi and his successors. The Italian Jesuit painter, Giuseppe Castiglione, arrived in Beijing in December 1715, coming from Macao. Emperor Kangxi, who at that time was 62 years old, had developed a keen interest in Western science, technology and arts, and welcomed Castiglione at the imperial court to teach the Western technique of oil painting, which was unknown in China at that time. Two remarks related to the activities of Castiglione at the Chinese court: first, Castiglione adopted the Chinese technique, and has left to posterity a considerable number of paintings in the Chinese style;[7] second, it was under the reign of Kangxi's successors, Yangzheng (r. 1723–35) and Qianlong (r. 1736–95) that Castiglione established his reputation and fame in Beijing under the Chinese name of Lang Shining. Thanks to his work at the Emperor's court, Castiglione was appointed third-class mandarin by Emperor Qianlong and was given the honorary title of Director of the Imperial Parks. Castiglione died on 16 July 1766 and was buried in Beijing's oldest Catholic cemetery, Zhalan, outside Fuchengmen, the western door of Beijing, where the Jesuits have been buried ever since 1610. Emperor Qianlong allotted a considerable sum of money for the funeral (300 silver taels) and elevated Castiglione to the posthumous rank of *shilang* (vice-minister).[8] So it is the Westerner who became Chinese and not the reverse. It is interesting to note that Emperor Qianlong entrusted Castiglione with the grandiose task of designing several Western-style palaces in his summer park (Yuanmingyuan, Garden of Perfect Splendour); the buildings, to which Castiglione added several 'Chinese characteristics', were completed in 1759. The park and palaces were destroyed by the British–French army during the second opium war in 1860.[9]

It is generally admitted that the opium wars reduced China to a semi-colonial status. The British and the French obtained the right to do business in China and were able to establish their business bases in the concessions obtained from China, that is, in parts of the Chinese territory in which they enjoyed extra-territoriality, and therefore were not subject to Chinese rule. In the course of the second part of the nineteenth century practically all the other Western powers came to enjoy the same rights, even the latecomers to colonialism such as Italy and Germany. In 1894 the humiliation reached its nadir when the nearby Japanese 'cousins' defeated China in a quick war that completely destroyed the Chinese navy. An unbearable contradiction had thus developed between the faith of the Chinese elite (and certainly also of the majority of the Chinese people) in the superiority of their civilization on one hand, and the reality of the evident inferiority of China's political, economic and military power on the other hand. It is understandable that the will to re-establish the strength of a country, whose dignity and sovereignty would be respected by other nations, would require the development of organizational, scientific, technological and military competences and means apt to attain that goal. As the superiority of Western countries had very well demonstrated during the nineteenth-century wars of aggression, economic power alone would not suffice, unless it were used to develop a military force capable of freeing the country and dissuading further aggressions. Therefore, we can conclude that, since the last decades of the nineteenth century, that is, during the last decades of the Chinese Empire, the fundamental goal of the successive Chinese leaderships that took into their hands the destiny of the country was to restore China as a world power. This is true for the Empire, the first Republic and the People's Republic during both the Mao and the post-Mao eras. There is a huge literature that supports this statement.

In her authoritative history of China, Patricia Buckley Ebrey informs us that:

> the [Chinese court] authorized setting up factories and docklands to manufacture western-style weapons and warships.... In 1884–85 when China was drawn into a conflict with France over Vietnam, it took only an hour for the French to destroy the warships built at the Fuzhou dockyard.

The lesson of this defeat was learned by some of the highest officials at the imperial court: 'Li Hongzhang, in particular, became convinced that guns and ships were merely the surface manifestation of western powers' economic strength and therefore in order to compete, China had to modernize its economy.'[10] Bai Shouyi adds some additional insights for understanding the strategy of the Chinese leadership at the end of the nineteenth century.[11] Bai confirms that, for the purpose of resisting foreign aggression, some of the high officials of the Qing wanted China to learn from foreign countries and proposed to set up Western-style factories to 'make the country *rich and strong*'. Let us note that the combination of wealth and strength is a recurrent theme in the literature on China's desire to free itself from foreign domination. One of the most renowned Western scholars, Kenneth Lieberthal, provides another explanation referring to the strategy followed by Japan in the nineteenth century that the Chinese leadership certainly did not ignore at that time. Japan was the first Far Eastern country to import Western technology and:

> by the 1890s had become *stronger in warfare* than had their 'elder brother' civilization China.... Japan's decisive victory in the Sino-Japanese war of 1894–95 shocked China far more than anything the West had done to that point.... Both the revolutionaries and the Qing loyalists sought desperately to achieve the goal shared by all Chinese: to enable the country to enjoy *wealth and power* in an age of Western and emerging Japanese imperialism.[12]

This idea is confirmed by two other renowned Western sinologists, John King Fairbank and Merle Goldman, who refer to the 'dream of China's reformers since the late nineteenth century to make China *'rich and powerful'* and recapture its *traditional greatness.*'[13]

Coming now to the People's Republic of China, we can provide evidence that the restoration of China as a world power remains the fundamental goal of the new leadership. Kenneth Lieberthal again supports this statement:

> During the 1960s some Chinese began to understand how dangerous the Western challenge could become. They advocated both learning Western ideas about international relations as well as using Western conventions to protect China, where possible, and *mastering Western military technology in order to use it to ward off Western aggression.*[14]

Even more assertive is the opinion of Immanuel C.Y. Hsü, which is worth quoting in full:

Though deeply committed to international communism, Mao and his followers were national communists at heart aware of China's misfortunes of the past century. *Like Chinese of all persuasions they were fired with the burning desire to restore China's rightful position under the sun, to achieve the big-power status* denied it since the Opium War, and to revive the national confidence and self-respect that had been lost during a century of foreign humiliation. . . . If there was such a thing as a national consensus in China, it focused on the commitment to the Four Modernizations . . . *The avowed goal was to turn China into a leading modern state* by the year 2000.[15]

The history of the Communist Party of China written by the official historians of the Party, and published in 1994, confirms our statement:

China has built up a strong enough defense to safeguard its security. New China stands erect in the East as an independent and sovereign state, developing equal exchanges with the rest of the world and actively participating in world affairs. . . . *A backward society can be attacked*, insulted, and even reduced to the status of a semi-colonial dependency. In today's world, negative examples of this which constantly emerge present a disturbing sight. . . . *Concerted efforts must be pooled* to surmount all kinds of difficulties and hardships so as *to make China a strong and really great socialist country.*[16]

Moreover, even the process of modernization can be seen as a development leading towards the restoration of China's national wealth and power, as asserted by He Ping: 'Modernisation, signifying mainly *national wealth and power*, as well as a vision of a better society and human existence, again became [after the Cultural Revolution] a paramount social agenda.'[17] Finally, even the Chinese neoliberals and New Left intellectuals, in spite of their fundamental ideological and theoretical opposition (as we have seen in Chapter 2, pp. 35–46), share the same vision for the fundamental goal China should realize:

Despite ideological clashes and heated debates, the liberal and the New Left have pursued similar agenda: *to make China rich and strong.* . . . 'To build a modern state by learning from the West' continues as the aim of the reform-minded Chinese leaders.[18]

In his last book, Tsinghua professor Hu Angang explains how China has risen so rapidly to become an emerging superpower and analyses the challenges ahead that should be addressed if China wants to surpass the United States.[19] This book should be read and meditated on by all Westerners (academics and laymen), as it gives a vision of China's future different from what is generally written in Western media. Whereas Hu is confident that China will soon become a new superpower, he is also convinced that it will not become a hegemonic power, thus contradicting the theories of the 'China threat' as well those of the 'China collapse'. In the eighth and last chapter ('Assessing China's development and grand strategy') Hu explains how the three stages of the socialist development strategy proposed by

Deng in 1978 will attain their full development in the years to come: 'This decade (2010–2020) will be a crucial period for realizing the goals of the third stage – the first 50 years of the 21st century.' Then Hu reminds us of the three steps of Deng's strategy: (1) during the first step, from 1981 to 1990, China should double its GNP and basically solve the problem of food and clothing; (2) during the second step, by the end of the 20th century, China's GNP should reach $1 trillion, with a per capita income of $800–1,000; (3) finally, during the third step lasting up to 2050:

> China shall strive to approach the level of developed countries and basically realize our goal of modernization. This third stage represents a creative phase of the development of socialism with Chinese characteristics, as well as a strategic opportunity for an invigorated Chinese nation to rise and become a *strong and prosperous country*.[20]

Furthermore, Hu considers that in order to become a superpower China must surpass the United States in terms of economic power, human resources and human capital, science and technology, and climate change. Hu presents in the other chapters of the book data that show that China has been developing in this direction during the last 30 years. Although he admits that the completion of this development will take 'dozens of years', he nevertheless is confident that:

> between now and 2020, China will continue to increase its economic strength until it attains superpower status, thereby ending the era of American hegemony. The international balance of power, then, will shift from unipolarity to a multipolar world dominated by the United States, China and the European Union. In other words, the world seems, yet again, poised to enter an 'era of great powers'.[21]

How the Chinese think and define their strategies

In the preceding section I gave the first explanation of China's choice in favour of market mechanisms, the restoration of China as a world power. I turn now to the second explanation, which is directly related to the first one. The way China has abandoned the 'Soviet-style' planned economy and has introduced market mechanisms is an excellent illustration of the way the Chinese think and act in general, and more particularly in very complex situations. In Chapter 1 (pp. 22–23) I have pointed to the characteristic way the Chinese think and act. Let me briefly illustrate this by taking the three levels which one can adopt for analysing a country's strategy: first, the choice of some fundamental goal(s); second, the choice of institutional arrangement(s); and third, the choice of public policies adopted and implemented within these institutional arrangements for attaining the fundamental goal(s). Traditionally, the Chinese do not start by defining a model and then try to make reality correspond to that model as the Western people do.[21] They start by analysing the situation, identifying the elements favourable and unfavourable to the fundamental goal(s); then they act upon the elements that they have a reasonable chance to alter (including institutional arrangements and/or public policies) until the situation is structured so that the objectives are obtained without effort (or, in the military domain dealt with by the Chinese classic Sun Tzu, without fighting);[23] finally, in case of adverse outcomes, they change the institutional arrangement and/or revise the policies that led to the adverse outcomes. Nevertheless, as I said in Chapter 2, China has learned from the West, at least since the end of the nineteenth century, how to think and act through models, especially in the natural sciences. However, in complex situations, such as the transformation of a traditional society into a modern one, modelling is not necessarily the best way forward, or at least not the only one.

In fact, given the fundamental goal of restoring China as a world power, China has regularly abandoned the institutional choice made at a certain historical moment, thus following its traditional way of thinking. First after the communist victory of 1949 it introduced a Soviet-style planned economy. Then, at the end of the 1970s, when taking stock of the limited efficiency of the command economy and the more efficient functioning of Western economies, market mechanisms were introduced. Finally, taking stock of the negative consequences of an excessive use of market mechanisms (especially in the labour market, as well as for health and education) a new set of public policies was chosen that 'put people first' (from the mid-1990s, but more clearly since 2002).[24] What a remarkable difference from the West, where institutional choices were made once and for all between the end of the eighteenth century and the first half of the nineteenth, namely capitalism and liberal democracy. In fact, since then the West has consistently affirmed capitalism and liberal democracy, apart from a departure from liberal democracy in some Western countries during the first half of the twentieth century when it was abandoned in favour of rightist dictatorships that nevertheless retained the essential features of capitalism. Western countries only adjusted the relation between capital and labour according to the situation and the need to promote and preserve the dominance of capital: giving more space to labour by building the Welfare State after the economic crisis of the 1930s, and after the tragic events of the Second World War, until the end of the 1970s; but since the beginning of the 1980s several Western countries started to give more space to the market and to reduce the scope of the Welfare State; they thus reversed the trend by bringing the relations between capital and labour back to the situation that prevailed during the nineteenth century. In spite of these important changes, the institutional framework (capitalism and liberal democracy) remained fundamentally the same.

Of course, one could think that the Chinese way of thinking is limited to the political leadership and that, for example, within universities and think tanks, modelling is widely used. Nothing is more wrong. Of course, many Chinese scholars are using 'Western-style' modelling, especially those who have been trained in the West in economics and in business administration. However, many, probably more than not, still use the traditional way, especially when dealing with very complex problems, or at best they mix the traditional way with modelling. Let us take an example in the domain of public law, a domain where models abound. In an article written for a book edited by one of the best Western specialists of Chinese law, Randal Peerenboom, the dean of the Law School of Peking University, Professor Zhu Suli, very clearly rejects the Western model of constitutional law as a basis for organizing China's legal system in general, and in particular for assuring the independence of the Chinese judiciary, one of the most crucial aspects of the modernization of China's law system. Moreover, he sustains that 'no model' can be useful for realizing those goals. To find the solutions that best suit China's peculiar situation one should take into consideration the history of China's cultural, political and economic situation, and within it the actual role played by the Nationalist Party first and, after 1949, by the Communist Party, as well as the actual interferences of the Party within the courts and the consequent outcomes for the Chinese people (i.e. individuals as well as groups of citizens), which, according to Zhu, are not necessarily negative.[25]

Coming back to public policy choices, China's policy of joining the World Trade Organization (WTO) has been given by the Sino-French economic adviser André Chieng as an interesting example of how Chinese leaders use traditional thinking.[26] For many years since the mid-1980s the Chinese leadership had tried to improve the performance of state-owned enterprises (SOEs) by putting some direct pressure on their managers by restricting the credit that the commercial banks used to grant to the SOEs on the basis of political considerations. This strategy unfortunately produced very limited results, and this failure has been duly highlighted by Western scholars and international organizations that pointed to the huge non-performing loans Chinese commercial banks had granted to inefficient and therefore insolvent SOEs. However, after the Party Congress of September 1997, when it was decided to accelerate and further expand the marketization of Chinese economy, the Chinese Prime Minster, Zhu Rongji, instead of directly putting more pressure on SOEs' managers, simply accelerated the negotiations that led at the end of 2001 to China's accession to the WTO. Quite rightly Chieng suggests that Zhu Rongji's manipulation consisted in replacing the direct pressure through the banks with the indirect pressure though the accession to the WTO, which changed the economic environment of Chinese SOEs, thanks to the opening up of the Chinese economy to international competition.[27]

So, the choice in favour of market mechanisms is essentially a very practical one. It is not because a market economy is ideologically or theoretically superior to a planned economy, or because, as Milton Friedman has maintained, that the market economy (i.e. the 'free market') is the condition for assuring freedom in the political sphere, that this type of economy must be chosen.[28] It is a purely practical choice deriving from the greater efficiency of market mechanisms based upon empirical evidence. The point of departure is therefore completely different from the starting point of neoliberalism in the West. Nevertheless, as we will see in Part III, some consequences of the Western and Chinese choice in favour of giving more space to the market have produced some remarkably similar consequences. However, it can be predicted that, thanks to this pragmatic approach, it will be easier for the Chinese leadership to react to the negative consequences of this choice, and to reorient the economy away from market mechanisms and towards state intervention, should the available empirical evidence prove that negative consequences can be attributed to an excess of market mechanisms.

Of course, such a radical change from the Maoist past necessitated that it be presented as a continuation of Mao's thought, not only because Chinese culture does not tolerates too sharp criticism aimed at the leaders and thinkers of the past,[29] but also because the Maoist faction was still quite powerful within the Chinese Communist Party. Deng has been quite skilful in managing this transition by referring to Mao, and more particularly to his motto: 'we must seek truth from facts'. This allowed Deng to discard the theory of Mao's followers, the theory of the 'two whatevers', according to which all that Mao decided must remain valid; none of the instructions of Mao must be violated. This has been one of the elements that allowed Deng to consolidate his position within the Chinese leadership. This new trend in Chinese politics was confirmed at the Third Plenum of the Party of December 1978. From that moment on, Deng put into practice his new strategy. The fundamental goal is still the same as for Mao: restore China as a world power by modernizing the economy. Only the means are different. Market mechanisms are first introduced within the agriculture and then into the industrial sector.[30] This reform process must be directed and coordinated by the Party, which Deng and the leadership of the Party considered as the only existing force capable to direct the country on the road of modernization.

Fundamentals of China's strategy for implementing NPM: market mechanisms, economic development, freedom and its limits

Bearing in mind that the fundamental goal is to restore China as a world power, let me now summarize the main features of Deng's strategy as follows. The strategic level is divided into two complementary levels; that is, the ideological and the economic–military levels. At the ideological level Deng reaffirms four of the main features of the Party's ideology by defining the Four Cardinal Principles: to keep to the socialist road; to uphold the people's democratic dictatorship; to maintain the leadership by the Communist Party; Marxism–Leninism and Mao Zedong thought.

At the economic–military level, Deng defines the target of China's modernization by identifying four domains necessary for restoring China's strength both internally and internationally: agriculture, industry, science and technology, and national defence. At the operational level the main goal is to improve economic performance and the standard of living of the Chinese people. The means for realizing this goal is the introduction of market mechanisms and opening up to the global economy. The strategy/tactics orienting the day-to-day implementation of this vast policy objective can be defined as follows: (1) maintain the leadership of the Party and restore its legitimacy; (2) introduce reforms on an experimental basis; (3) reform gradually (not like Russia); (4) privatize gradually and partially, by keeping the strategic economic sectors in the hands of the state, and reinforcing the macro-economic policies of the state;[31] (5) maintain economic, social and political stability; (6) in case of difficulties, slow down or stop, and then restart.

This strategy inevitably entails the opening up of Chinese society in the economic sphere. More freedom is allotted to the Chinese citizens, as, for Deng, market mechanisms must release the productive forces of the nation. However, there are limits to freedom; each time the manifestation of freedom risks endangering the leadership of the Party, the Party-State restricts freedom, with violence if necessary.[32] Of course, this has been interpreted in the West as a manifestation of authoritarianism, or even totalitarianism, this being considered in the West a 'normal' reaction from a communist party whose fundamental aim is to retain power. There is certainly some truth in this judgement, but it tells only part of the story. As mentioned before, the Party and its leaders are profoundly convinced that they are the only force able to direct China on the way of modernization, while maintaining political, social and economic stability, this being the condition for maintaining a steady path towards development. This conviction became even stronger when China witnessed, between 1989 and 1992, the collapse of the Soviet Union and of the Communist regimes of western Europe, and the negative consequences that ensued for these countries, both their peoples and their leaderships.[33] From that time on, the Chinese leadership has always had in mind the fate of these countries, but especially of the Soviet Union/Russia, when dealing with the necessity of balancing on one side the freedom necessary for the development of the economy and on the other side the limitations of freedom (especially in the political sphere) that are necessary to manage the process of modernization within a stable society. Moreover, the events of June 1989 in Tiananmen Square, when thousands of people demonstrated in favour of more freedom and especially against the negative consequences of economic development (inflation, unemployment and corruption), contributed to persuade the Party-State that it was necessary to put some limit on freedom, especially when it manifested itself in the public domain; only the economy would be the place where the Party-State would tolerate, and even promote, individual freedom.

The importance of Chinese characteristics and the reference to socialism

Another aspect that differentiates the Chinese NPM from the Western one, and that increases the importance of the pragmatic way, is the insistence on the Chinese characteristics that the China's way of managing the process of modernization must present. This, together with the constant reference to socialism, gives to the Chinese experiment with the introduction of market mechanisms its distinctive profile. Of course, in the West expressions such as 'a socialist market economy with Chinese characteristics' have been welcomed at best with polite attention, at worst with some sarcasm.[34] I am convinced that it would be a mistake to consider that such expressions are simply means used by the Party to disguise its 180-degree turn away from socialism and towards the full acceptance of capitalism (even if in the form of state capitalism), for fear of not being understood by the Chinese population.

That socialism is still a serious reference is further apparent when we consider two additional characteristics of the Chinese NPM. The first one refers to the 'theory of the Three Represents' defined by the successor of Deng Xiaoping, Jiang Zemin, which has acquired within the guiding lines of the Party a status equal to Marxism–Leninism, Mao's thought and Deng's theory.[35] Although one can have some doubts whether this theory has in fact the same importance as the other guidelines, it is certain that it has contributed to help the Party to gain and maintain the support of the majority of the new private entrepreneurs. Contrary to the forecast expressed by many Western observers of modern China, the development of the Chinese private sector and the appearance of a new class of private entrepreneurs has not introduced an opposition or even a competition between the Party-State and the private entrepreneurs. On the contrary, the majority of the latter have joined the Party (thus positively replying to the invitation from Jiang Zemin) and some of them sit in several official bodies, such as the national parliament. In fact, it seems that they are satisfied with the economic environment the Party-State has been able to set up to favour the development of the private sector.[36]

The other characteristic that points to the seriousness of the persistence of the reference to socialism, not only in the discourse of China's leaders but also in public policies, is represented by the innovations introduced by Jiang Zemin's successor, Hu Jintao, since 2002. Hu persists in referring to Marxism–Leninism, and he insists, much more than his predecessor, on the need to develop the economy upon the basis of scientific theory and evidence (which is a further confirmation of the pragmatic way) and also on the necessity to promote equity and justice and that the Party-State should pay more attention to the redistribution of income.[37] We will see in Chapter 6 to what extent these ideas have been translated into public policies and with what results. Of course, paying attention to socialism, to equity and justice and to redistribution of income may be considered as parts of the Party's ideology. There is certainly some truth in this interpretation. Nevertheless, this new orientation of China's development strategy is also and above all another manifestation of the Chinese pragmatic way. Indeed, it is because disparities and environmental pollutions put in danger the realization of the fundamental goal of restoring Chinese power that they must be corrected. As I have argued elsewhere, developing the economy (measured by GDP) and serving the people (measured by the provision of a healthy environment and a fair distribution of income and public services) are the two interdependent means for restoring China as a world power.[38]

The opening up of the decision-making process

The implementation of China's vast reform project has necessitated some substantial changes in the organization of the decision-making process. In order to obtain the most pertinent and reliable information for orienting the choice of public policies, the Party-State has implemented several strategies. These sources are both internal and external to China: universities, intellectuals, businessmen for the former; developed countries (both Western and Eastern) and international organizations for the latter. The Party has opened up the decision-making process thanks to four types of measures: association, cooperation, consultation and appointment. First, it associated with the decision-making process researchers within universities, governmental- and non-governmental organizations, as well as within governmental and non-governmental think tanks, where one can find researchers studying the positive and negative consequences of economic development.[39]

In particular, some think tanks constitute places where influential university professors and researchers sit along with important politicians, top civil servants and businessmen, and provide therefore the opportunity for exchanges of opinions, experiences and discussions on policy options. Many of them are foreign-educated returnees (called *haigui* or 'sea turtles' in China) who can bring into the debates the experiences they acquired abroad. According to Cheng Li (a renowned expert on China within the Brookings Institution in Washington, DC) 'public intellectuals, especially well-known economists who received PhDs from the West [the great majority from the USA], have now become almost equal partners' within the think tank elite. Moreover, the old distinction between officials and scholars 'is now blurring as foreign-educated returnees become government leaders', and some of them 'have dual identities as both officials and scholars.' Furthermore, Cheng Li considers that, 'although most members of think tanks are more often interested in pursuing "reform from within" rather than "revolution from without", they often differ in their particular views, values, and visions.'[40] We find here another testimony of the differences among Chinese intellectuals we analysed in Chapter 2 (pp. 35–46), especially between neoliberals and the New Left. According to information gathered in China between 2005 and 2011, many of the returnees who acquired a PhD in economics abroad are generally in favour of more privatization and liberalization, as is the case in the already mentioned Faculty of the Centre for Economic Research at Peking University: in 2005 among its 24 professors 21 held a university degree from US universities, one from the UK, one from Belgium and one from Japan.[41] Moreover, the majority of Chinese economists active within think tanks dealing officially with economic matters are in favour of more privatization and liberalization. Their opinion is nevertheless counterbalanced by those who are more open to the development of social policies, because they are more concerned by the fate of poor people and/or because they are convinced of the danger the unequal distribution of wealth may cause to national cohesion by provoking social and political unrest. This situation allows the Chinese leadership to obtain interesting and generally well-documented policy options, based upon a wide range of analytical frameworks, and this makes it possible to choose the ones that are more in tune with the strategy chosen by the Party-State.

The second way the Party has used to opening up the decision-making process is through the establishment of cooperation with international organizations such as the World Bank and the Asian Development Bank. These organizations are mainly interested in the improvement of economic efficiency, but for the last few years also with equity.[42] Third, the Party-State started to consult non-communist experts either within the above-mentioned organizations or through bilateral cooperation projects. Finally, several non-communist top-level experts have been appointed within the administration, and more recently even at the top political level; I can quote the appointments of the Minister of Science and Technology, Wan Gang, appointed in April 2007, and the Minister of Health, Chen Zhu, appointed in May 2007, who are not members of the CPC. As a consequence, the structure of the decision-making process has become more open and this allows the Chinese leadership to acquire the scientific knowledge it needs for choosing the policy options that best fit its overall development strategy, not only for sustaining economic development, but also for adopting the policies necessary for rebalancing Chinese society.

The search for the knowledge useful for the decision-making process is further strengthened by training the top officials at all levels of the Party-State. First of all, the Party uses the Party Schools that exist at the central, provincial and local levels. In this domain, the most important one, the Central Party School in Beijing, which depends directly upon the Permanent Committee of the Politburo of the Communist Party (the real government of China), has retained its traditional role of ideological and policy training for the top leaders.[43] Nevertheless, for at least 10 years it has introduced a whole range of more technical training programmes in all domains of the state's activities, including New Public Management.[44] In addition, four Party Schools, also depending directly upon the Permanent Committee of the Politburo, have been set up recently by the CPC to complete the training organized traditionally within the Beijing Central Party School. Apart from the two schools in Yan'an and Jingganshan, devoted to the study of China's conditions and traditions, the school in Dalian trains the top managers of SOEs, and the one in Shanghai-Pudong the top leaders of central and provincial governments, in modern management techniques and public policies in the economic, social and legal domains.[45] Training by the Party Schools is further strengthened by organizing training abroad for cadres of all levels, especially for top leaders.

Furthermore, amongst the governmental think tanks, the National Development and Reform Commission (NDRC) assumes a paramount role. This commission, which some authors consider a 'super-ministry', has replaced the old Planning Commission set up in 1952 for the purpose of steering the planned economy. Reporting directly to the Prime Minister, and comprising a staff of almost 1,000 researchers and some 30 functional departments, bureaux and offices covering all the domains of state activity, the main functions of the NDRC today are to formulate and implement strategies for national economic and social development in all domains.[46]

The fourth way used by the Party to obtain expertise useful for basing the decision-making process on scientific evidence, especially during the last decade, was to resort to contributions from the major Chinese universities. These fulfil three major roles. The first is training young scholars who could later become civil servants or Party cadres, as well as adult education addressed to civil servants and Party cadres. Moreover, the government has financed study abroad for many professors and young advanced students, and has conferred on the best universities the organization of Masters' programmes in public administration. The second task of universities is the provision of expertise to the government, either from individual academics or, as we have seen above, from university think tanks. Regarding the third and final role, the universities constitute an intellectual open space where policy options are freely discussed amongst academics of all levels. Within the best universities a great deal of research has been developed dealing with several very delicate topics, such as corruption, income disparities between and within provinces and regions, the role of NGOs and issues of foreign policy, such as the relationship with the USA, the best way towards further economic development in the global economy, and social security reform.

Last but not least, during the reform process and the consequent limited but effective liberalization of citizens' activities, China has witnessed the emergence of several hundreds of NGOs. This movement could not have developed without the explicit support or, in many cases, the tacit consent of the Party-State. Chinese NGOs are active in many domains, but the most interesting ones emerged in the social and environmental sectors, for reasons linked to the major negative consequences of the development strategy adopted by the Party under the leadership of Deng Xiaoping. By putting the focus on economic development measured by GDP, this strategy neglected the impact on both the environment and the people. On one hand, the lack of regulations and control of the process of production in both agriculture and, above all, industry, has resulted in considerable levels of pollution of air, soil and water. In the domain of environmental protection many NGOs are active in China, such as Friends of Nature, Global Village of Beijing, the WWF and the Trust for Environment (which promotes the Environmental Education Television Project for China). On the other hand, the deregulation of the labour market and the concomitant demise of the social functions performed by the SOEs under the planned economy, combined with the failure to replace them with a modern welfare system, have produced an unprecedented development of social exclusion. Of course, the Party-State, alarmed by the political activities of foreign-funded NGOs in eastern Europe, has established all sorts of limits and controls to the development of NGOs in China. Nevertheless, once again with a pragmatic attitude, it has recognized that in many cases NGOs could not only provide expertise to the government, but also accomplish activities of public interest the Party-State was not willing and/or capable to accomplish. For example, in the social domain, NGOs seem to have more and more freedom from state control. The emergence of this new charitable social sector is particularly important given the rapid growth of China's vulnerable population and the appearance of the phenomenon of social exclusion. Although Chinese NGOs are still subject to a very strict legal framework, the Chinese government observes, tolerates and sometimes encourages the 'illegal' development of some charitable NGOs, provided they are useful to maintaining social peace. It goes without saying that this remarkable development of NGOs contributes not only to the emergence of a Chinese civil society, but also to the opening up of China's decision-making process.[47]

We may conclude that thanks to these various inputs, most of the time based upon scientific evidence, the Party has become a learning organization, and this constitutes an invaluable support to its pragmatic approach to designing, implementing and monitoring public policies.

This is not to say that thinking and acting in this way the Party has succeeded in avoiding mistakes or, at least in avoiding collateral negative consequences of the implemented policies. The hypothesis we have formulated in the first chapter about the probability of losing something on equity when implementing policies aimed primarily at developing the economy thanks to market mechanisms has been formulated for the West and for China as well. And its validity has been proved to be correct in both cases, as I will show in the Part III. It is interesting in this perspective to point to the fact that scientific evidence about the negative consequences of the economic strategy implemented since the beginning of the 1980s was already available to the Chinese leadership during 1988.[48] Several remarkable pieces of research pointed out the probable development of disparities between and within regions, as well as important environmental damages. It is unfortunate that the Chinese leadership has been rather slow in recognizing the validity and importance of these warnings. Of course, the alternative explanation is that at that time the opening up of the Chinese decision-making process was just at its beginning, and that the choice made by Deng Xiaoping in favour of market mechanisms was to restore China as a world power by developing the economy the sooner the better thanks to the introduction of market mechanisms, with little attention paid to the negative consequences of this strategy. This interpretation seems to be supported by Deng's motto 'let some people become rich first', referring to the fact that the coastal provinces were better equipped for rapid economic development than the inland and western regions. In this respect, the most probable hypothesis is that the Chinese NPM is bound to produce similar consequences to the Western NPM. However, if our analysis of the rationale for choosing market mechanisms in China and the West is correct, then the Western choice in favour of an NPM oriented by neoliberalism and the Chinese one oriented by pragmatic considerations will very likely present remarkable differences when the negative consequences are recognized in both the West and China, and the question whether it is necessary to correct them and by what means will be on the table of the decision-makers. This is what I will try to discover Part III and in the general conclusion.

Part III

The crisis of New Public Management in the West and in China

In this third and last part I will propose an evaluation of NPM in the West and in China from two perspectives, first that of the economy and second that of society. As I have already said in Chapter 2 following Braudel's analysis of capitalism, I will call the former 'a view from above' and the latter 'a view from below'. I consider that looking at NPM from the point of view of the economy inevitably leads to adopt a view from above. In the West, this strategy has been imposed upon all social groups and strata by a coalition comprising economic, political and cultural elites favourable, explicitly or implicitly, to the neoliberal ideology and political strategy aiming at establishing the dominance of economic efficiency, realized by freeing the leading economic factor, capital, from state intervention. In China, the introduction of market mechanisms has been imposed by the Party-State. In both cases, this has been achieved thanks to privatization, contracting out, decentralization and the deregulation of the various markets, with the consequent rolling back of the state. We will see that this strategy, which gives priority to economic efficiency over social equity, has had several negative impacts on society, at least upon the most vulnerable social groups and, moreover, increased in the West their absolute and relative size within the countries concerned, whereas in China it led to the appearance of new forms of poverty and exclusion, in spite of the fact that, thanks to this strategy, China has lifted half a billion people out of poverty.

In short, the main characteristics of NPM are closely related to, and aimed at further developing, the market economy in the West, and at introducing a market economy, or at least market mechanisms, in China. As this way of organizing economic activities was first developed, in theory and in practice, in the West, it seems logical, and also practical for the purpose of argumentation, to start with the Western experiment. This is not to say that the Chinese experiment with NPM is a trivial carbon copy of the Western one. On the contrary, I will show that, in spite of some remarkable similarities, the Chinese experiment differs from the Western one at least in one fundamental aspect. Whereas in the West NPM has been imposed for the sake of the economy and by those who believe in the supremacy of the economy over the polity, in China the NPM has been conceived, implemented and kept under control by the Chinese Party-State. I will show in the general conclusion of this book that this substantial difference explains the different ways in which China and the West have reacted to the 2008–11 financial and economic crisis. Table III.1 summarizes the major dimensions of reforms in China and in the West by underlining the general tendencies, and without taking into consideration the differences that exist amongst the Western countries. The major differences between Western countries will appear in the following pages.

Table III.1 Major dimensions of reforms in China and in the West, 1978–2011

Domain	China	Western countries
Institutional choice	In search of the Chinese 'model' for democracy and economy	Confirm liberal democracy, develop capitalist economy
Governance	Politics in command, rule by law, one-party system	Economy in command, rule of law, multi-party system
Structure of public administration	Streamline and reorganize	Streamline and reorganize
Number of civil servants	Reduce and/or redeploy	Reduce
Policy making	More open and transparent, but dominated by Party	Maintain elite politics supported by free elections
Taxation	Increase	Reduce
Expenditure	Increase	Reduce
Market economy	Introduce market mechanisms under the control of the Party-State	Further deregulate, under pressure from the economic elite
Labour market	Introduce with few regulations	Deregulate
Utilities and SOEs	Privatize, or contract out, or give more autonomy, but maintain strategic SOEs	Privatize, or contract-out or give more autonomy, in almost all domains
Banking system	Make more efficient and get rid of non-performing loans	Maintain and develop
Financial markets	Develop with care	Deregulate and introduce new instruments for increasing return on investment
Social security	Get rid of old safety nets, experiment, modernize and develop in the long run	Reduce and/or privatize or maintain (until the 2008 crisis)
Global economy	Promote deregulation, take advantage of global market, resort to protectionism if national interest is in danger	Promote deregulation, take advantage of global market, resort to protectionism if national interest is in danger

5 The Western experiment
Some positive economic achievements, many societal problems

In the first section of this chapter I will propose an evaluation of the Western NPM by considering first its impact on the economy, as this is the main reason NPM proponents have put forward for explaining its superiority over the traditional Weberian–Keynesian public management. Moreover, NPM's economic performance is well known and documented, and therefore it does not need to be developed in detail in this book. Nevertheless, our brief overview allows us to see right from the beginning that the economic performance has been achieved alongside some negative consequences on labour. Second, in a more detailed section I will evaluate the impact of NPM on society. This perspective is very important because, according to the NPM proponents, the economic performance will inevitably benefit everybody within the countries concerned. This constitutes for them the indisputable argument that explains its superiority over the traditional way of managing the public sector and its interface with the economy. This will be done, as already mentioned in Chapter 2, by taking into consideration the impact of NPM on employment, income distribution, poverty, crime and health. Some other indicators will also be given when necessary. Before we go any further, the reader should refer to the remarks at the end of Chapter 2 (pp. 55–63) regarding the difficulties in collecting and analysing these data as well as the analysis in Chapter 3 (pp. 87–90) of the technical difficulties that NPM must overcome.

The economic perspective: a view from above, or the development of economic power

For reasons explained before, I will limit this section to recognizing the main economic achievements of NPM and pointing out some of its negative consequences that will be developed in the following sections. It is generally admitted that NPM has improved the economic efficiency of the countries that have adopted NPM management principles. Gross domestic product has increased and national enterprises have gained strength in the global economy. In particular, privatization have improved labour productivity and returns to shareholders.[1] Capital investment has generally increased and salaries of top managers have also increased. In the annual reports issued by the UNDP on human development, Western countries are all within the upper group with 'very high human development' reflecting an HDI over 0.787. Amongst non-Western countries, only Japan, South Korea, Israel, Hong Kong, the United Arab Emirates, Brunei, Qatar, Bahrain and Barbados belong to this same group. The same remarks can be made for GDP, GDP per capita, military expenditure as a percentage of GDP, and research and development spend as a percentage of GDP.[2] Between 1970 and 2008, in spite of difficulties experienced during this period in increasing GDP and several financial crises, the GDP of Western countries (with few exceptions) has nevertheless increased at an annual average of between 1.6 per cent (Denmark) and 2.6 per cent (Norway). Even if this percentage is far from matching that of China (as we shall see in Chapter 6) the increase in GDP over a period of almost 40 years is quite remarkable, considering the high level these countries had already reached at the end of the exceptional economic development between 1945 and the mid-1970s.

Nevertheless, one of the consequences of this development, especially for countries that have introduced NPM devices since the beginning of the 1980s, has been the reduction of the number of employees that occurred as most of the time the management, in the search for reducing production costs, considered that the work could be done with fewer people, by having recourse to different forms of mechanization and reorganization and/or by increasing labour productivity. Moreover, the number of underpaid, short-term and part-time jobs has increased, and general working conditions have deteriorated. For the small consumers there has been practically no decrease in cost for purchasing the services of the privatized public utilities, and there are several cases in which, on the contrary, the cost has increased.[3] Finally, some privatized public enterprises have been put under the supervision of so-called regulators and, as I have already said in the third chapter, this of course represents a cost that must be taken into consideration. The same can be said of another favourite device of NPM, contracting out. Here, savings have been realized, for example for refuse collection, cleaning and maintenance services, but much less for other services.[4] For quality of services there is no clear evidence. However, as for privatization, the negative consequences have been the reduction in the number of employees, the deterioration in working conditions, no significant reduction in cost for small users, and the appearance of transaction costs.[5] Moreover, as in the case of the USA already mentioned, several cases of corruption during the bidding procedure have been reported.

The social perspective: a view from below, or the development of inequalities

A great number of publications are available today to compare the social structures of strong-NPM countries, such as the USA and the UK, with those countries that have not implemented NPM devices to a large extent, which I characterize as weak-NPM countries. I will begin by providing empirical evidence already available around 1990–5, that is, about 10 years after the beginning of NPM, showing that strong-NPM countries presented greater income disparities and higher poverty and crime rates than weak-NPM countries (or even non-NPM countries: those that by the end of the 1990s had not yet started to introduce NPM devices). Then I will provide some more recent data that will prove that the trend already evident at the beginning of the 1990s has been further developed (with some rare exceptions). Moreover, countries that during the previous period could be placed under the non-NPM or weak-NPM countries, and that during the following years have become NPM latecomers (e.g. Italy and Ireland), started to present basically the same characteristics as the NPM pioneers such as the USA and the UK.

New Public Management and unemployment

Let me remind the reader that data on unemployment must be taken with great care as too often official data do not describe the exact extent of unemployment (see the remarks in Chapter 2, p. 58). Having those remarks in mind, we can see that already towards the mid-1990s it no longer needed proving that in strong-NPM countries salary levels and general working conditions had declined, particularly the lower salary levels. The minimum salary per hour in the USA was less than $5 towards the end of the 1990s. In order to illustrate the degradation in the living conditions of the unqualified labourer, let us mention the case of a local British road-sweeper in the mid-1990s. Following the obligation to adapt to the system of 'compulsory competitive tendering' a British municipality concluded a service contract with a private enterprise: the salary of its former workman, hired by the enterprise, decreased from £183 to £147 (loss: 36 per cent); the annual leave went down from 20 to 15 days; and the weekly working hours increased from 35 to 40. More generally, a report by OECD recognizes that the number of jobs has been reduced and that salaries have decreased.[6]

Of course, it could be objected that in strong-NPM countries a considerable number of new jobs were created during the 1980s and the early 1990s, and that the unemployment rate had clearly dropped lower than in the weak-NPM countries. This situation lasted at least until the outburst of the 2008–11 crisis. Even though the official unemployment statistics confirm this assertion, at least until 2008, several studies show that these statistics do not take hidden unemployment into consideration. A poll carried out in the United Kingdom by the Centre for Regional Economic Research of the University of Sheffield draws the conclusion that real unemployment in January 1997 (i.e. at the beginning of the New Labour government of Tony Blair) covered 15 per cent of the active population instead of the 6.1 per cent certified by official statistics.[7] Furthermore, according to a British trades unions (TUC) poll, at the same time, a quarter of the active population worked part-time, 7 per cent were temporary personnel and 3 million earned less than £3 per hour.[8] Similar statistics exist for the United States and New Zealand, two other beacon countries of NPM.[9]

Other data show that when the labour market is highly deregulated people are forced to accept underpaid jobs (as we shall see in the next paragraph), and are put under such heavy pressure that there are negative consequences for their health. I will come back to this point later. For the moment it is interesting to note that long-term illness due to excessive pressure on the labour market has the consequence of increasing the size of long-term unemployment. This in turn put an increasing number of unemployed people in the 'unable to work population' entitled to the state's invalidity benefits. At the end of the process it is possible that the total number of people out of work tends to be the same as before, as the following data provided by the very serious London *Times* seems to prove already in 1997 (Figure 5.1).

Moreover, data available in many Western countries showed already towards the mid-1990s that there were an increasing number of people living under the poverty line in spite of the fact that they worked full time.[10] Even a latecomer to NPM such as Switzerland started to experience the same phenomenon: in 2003 the Federal Office of Statistics published data showing that, out of a total population of 7.3 million, 7.7 per cent, corresponding to 231,000 people (living in 137,000 households totalling 513,000 people), were experiencing this type of situation.[11]

Coming back to the rate of unemployment, the defenders of NPM could claim, until recently, that unemployment in NPM countries was lower than in non-NPM countries. In fact, the strong-NPM countries are not doing very well since the outbreak of the 2008–11 crisis. Table 5.1 should persuade NPM advocates to be less enthusiastic about the positive impact of NPM upon employment.

Table 5.1 shows that, up to 2007, strong-NPM countries were doing significantly better than weak-NPM countries, except for a group of small weak-NPM countries that did much better than anyone else (Switzerland, the Netherlands, Norway and Denmark). Taking the 2007 data, the situation of the countries in transition to NPM (Italy and Ireland) was as good as the strong-NPM countries, whereas among the southern European countries Greece and Portugal were doing about as poorly as the weak-NPM countries, and Spain was doing much worse. However, as soon as the 2008 crisis exploded, the strong-NPM countries (with the exception of New Zealand) were suddenly doing as badly as the weak-NPM countries (but much worse than the four small weak-NPM countries mentioned above), whereas those in transition did as badly as the strong-NPM countries (Italy) or significantly worse than both strong- and weak-NPM countries (Ireland). Southern European countries further worsened their situation. Taking the 2010 and 2011 data, one can see that the weak-NPM countries (with the exception of

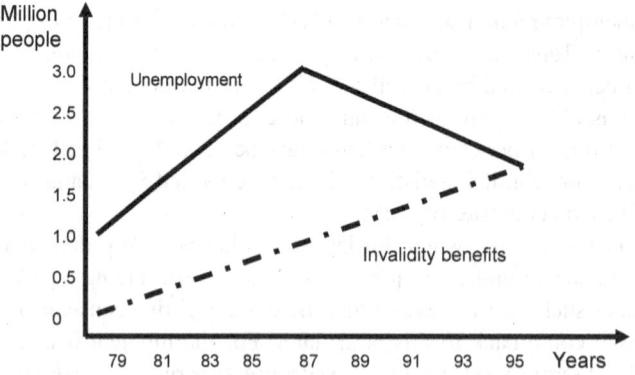

Figure 5.1 Unemployment and invalidity benefits in the UK, 1979–1996. Adapted from *The Times* (London), 29 April 1997, p. 14.

Table 5.1 Unemployment rates for 17 Western countries, 1980–2011

Country	1980	1990	2000	2005	2007	2009	2010	2011	Category
United States	7.1	5.2	5.6	5.0	4.6	9.2	9.7	9.0	Strong-NPM
United Kingdom	6.5	7.3	7.0	4.7	5.4	7.4	7.9	8.1	Strong-NPM
New Zealand	4.0	6.8	7.9	3.8	3.6	6.1	6.2	6.6	Strong-NPM
Germany	3.3	5.6	6.1	9.5	8.3	7.5	7.0	6.5	Weak-NPM
France	6.4	9.4	8.9	9.3	8.3	9.4	9.8	9.6	Weak-NPM
Belgium	8.3	6.6	6.9	8.5	7.5	7.7	8.6	6.8	Weak-NPM
Sweden	2.0	1.7	5.6	7.6	6.1	8.3	8.2	6.8	Weak-NPM
Finland	4.6	3.2	9.8	8.3	6.8	8.2	8.8	6.9	Weak-NPM
Switzerland	0.2	0.5	1.9	3.8	2.7	3.5	3.6	2.8	Weak-NPM
Netherlands	3.7	5.8	2.8	4.7	3.2	3.5	4.2	5.6	Weak-NPM
Norway	1.6	5.2	3.4	4.6	2.5	3.1	3.5	2.8	Weak-NPM
Denmark	7.1	8.6	4.8	5.1	2.7	3.6	4.2	4.2	Weak-NPM
Italy	7.3	9.6	8.7	7.7	6.1	7.8	8.7	8.3	In transition to NPM
Ireland	7.3	7.1	12.9	4.3	4.6	11.8	13.5	14.3	In transition to NPM
Spain	11.0	17.2	16.2	9.1	11.3	18.0	19.9	21.5	South European
Greece	2.6	6.8	11.3	9.9	8.3	9.3	11.7	16.3	South European
Portugal	7.8	4.2	4.0	7.4	8.1	9.6	10.7	12.1	South European

Source: IMF database; for estimates between second and third quarters of 2011, http://www.tradingeconomics.com/ (accessed 30 October 2011).

France) have improved their situation and are doing better than the USA and the UK, and as well as New Zealand, whereas southern European countries' situation has further deteriorated, thus confirming the existence of a 'Mediterranean type' identified by Hall, Soskice and Amable (see Chapter 2, pp. 53–54).

So the crisis has brought to light the apparent superiority of the strong-NPM countries regarding the limitation of unemployment to a rate between 3.6 and 5.4 per cent (2007 data), which many economists would consider as the natural rate of unemployment. However, as soon as the economic crisis creates serious difficulties, the rate of unemployment in the strong-NPM countries becomes as high as, or higher than, that of the weak-NPM countries. One probable cause of this situation is very likely to be found in the deregulation of their labour market, which, in the frantic search for savings, renders the laying off of employees easier than in weak-NPM countries. Moreover, as we have already mentioned, these countries have created many short-term, part-time and underpaid jobs, the holders of which are the easiest and the first to be laid off by enterprises that face serious economic problems. Moreover, these data only tell part of the story, as they do not take into consideration groups of people for which the unemployment rate is higher than the average, such as young people and women. Finally, knowing that these countries have reduced the benefits of their welfare policies, one can predict that the increase in the unemployment rate may have the consequences, first, of making the distribution of income more unequal and, second, of increasing the rate of poverty much more than in the weak-NPM countries that have retained an active Welfare State. We will verify these hypotheses in the following sections.

New Public Management, income distribution and inequality

The findings presented above on unemployment gain in significance when analysed jointly with available data on the distribution of income. Here again the reader should not forget the remarks presented in Chapter 2 about the problems related to the measure of income distribution. Of course, income distribution is important to determine if people for whom the unique, or main, source of income is the access to the labour market are sufficiently well off to enjoy a decent life.

Nevertheless, no reasonable people would expect, or require, an equal distribution of wealth – an absurdity that has never been defended by reasonable people. However, any reasonable person would probably be shocked if it could be proved that the increase of wealth (which may have occurred despite economic crises) had been distributed not only unevenly, but in such a way as to increase inequalities even further. This has been proven by the American economist Paul Krugman, in a study published as early as 1992.[12] Krugman shows that during the period from 1977 to 1989 (covering more or less the highly NPM years of President Reagan) 70 per cent of the increase in GDP was pocketed by the wealthiest 1 per cent of taxpayers (whose income increased by an average of 103 per cent) whereas 40 per cent of the Americans in the lower income bracket saw their income decrease. The complete figures presented by Krugman (Table 5.2) are the following: the

Table 5.2 Rise of GDP and income distribution in the USA, 1977–89

Percentile	% increase 1977–89
0–20	− 9
20–40	− 2
40–60	+ 4
60–80	+ 8
80–90	+ 13
90–95	+ 18
95–99	+ 24
100	+ 103

Source: adapted from Paul Krugman, 'The rich, the right and the facts', *American Prospect*, Fall 1992, no. 11, pp. 19–31.

least fortunate 20 per cent (in fact, the poorest) saw their income decrease by 9 per cent on average; the next 20 per cent lost 2 per cent; the next 20 per cent had an increase of 4 per cent; the next 20 per cent saw an increase of 8 per cent; the next 10 per cent an increase of 13 per cent; the next 5 per cent gained 18 per cent; the next 4 per cent gained 24 per cent; and the last 1 per cent gained 103 per cent. These last had an average income of $800,000 before tax. This trend, according to which the higher groups in the income distribution pocket a higher percentage of GDP increase, has been confirmed by a recent research by the Center on Budget and Policy Priorities.[13] The chart on p. 2 shows that between 1979 and 2007 the after-tax income of the top 1 per cent increased by an astonishing 281 per cent, that of the highest fifth by 95 per cent, that of the middle fifth by 25 per cent and that of the bottom fifth by only 16 per cent.

A series of studies carried out in the UK by the Institute of Fiscal Studies offer a similar picture of revenue distribution in this country. The curve is less spectacular than in the USA but the trend is basically the same: whilst 20 per cent of the less wealthy saw their income decrease between 1979 and 1992 (the Thatcher years), all other taxpayers benefited from an increase in income, which became increasingly and significantly higher as one climbs in the hierarchy of salaries.[14] Another study shows that the percentage of British families with incomes lower than half of the average doubled during the 1980s.[15] The papers of the Luxembourg Income Study suggest furthermore that inequality is increasing more rapidly in the strong-NPM countries than in others.[16]

A study by Timothy Smeeding provides some interesting insights into changes that may have occurred between the beginning of the implementation of NPM and the late 1990s (Table 5.3).[17]

We can see that between the mid-1970s and the late 1990s some countries only slightly increased inequality. Apart from Australia and Canada, these are Central (Belgium, France, Germany) and northern European countries (Finland, Norway, Sweden and Denmark). The champions are unsurprisingly the initiators of the NPM movement: the USA, the UK and New Zealand. In between, we have the latecomers to NPM – Italy and Ireland – and the Netherlands.

Of course the evaluation of changes in time depends very much on the time span taken into consideration. It would be easy to maintain for some strong-NPM countries that NPM has not contributed to an increase in income inequality. This could be done, for example, for the UK, where between 1990 and 2008 the level of inequality (measured by the Gini index) was kept rather stable, at worst with relatively small increases. Nevertheless, by taking the time span between 1979 and 2008, research by the London Institute of Fiscal Studies shows that, whereas it is true that between 1990 and 2008 the increase was only from about 0.34 to 0.36, between 1979 and 1990 (the Thatcher years) the increase in inequality was rather spectacular (from about 0.25 to 0.34), the subsequent Conservative (John Major) and New Labour (Tony Blair and Gordon Brown) governments just further increased the inequality to 0.36, i.e. less than one-third of the increase occurred under the Thatcher government (Figure 5.2).[18] The damage had been done before by Conservatives, and Labour did not repair it, but further slightly increased the inequality of income distribution in the UK.

Table 5.3 Income inequality for a choice of Western countries: overall trends

Countries	Mid-early 1970s to mid-late 1980s	OECD study late 1980s	Mid-late 1980s to mid-late 1990s
Denmark	n/a	n/a	–
Finland	–	0	+
France	–	0	+
Switzerland	n/a	n/a	+
Canada	–	0	+
Sweden	–	+	+
Germany	–	+	+
Belgium	0	+	+
Australia	0	+	+
Italy	––	–	++
Ireland	–	0	++
Norway	0	0	++
Netherlands	0	+	++
UK	++	+++	++
USA	++	++	++
New Zealand	0	+	+++

Source: adapted from Timothy Smeeding, *Globalisation, Inequality and the Rich Countries of the G-20: Evidence From The Luxembourg Income Study (LIS)*, July 2002, http://www.LIS.org.

Notes
+++, significant income inequality increase (more than 15%); ++, increase (7–15%); +, modest increase (1–6%); 0, no change (–1 to +1%); –, modest decrease (1–6%); ––, decrease (7–15%); –––, significant decrease (more than 15%); n/a, not available

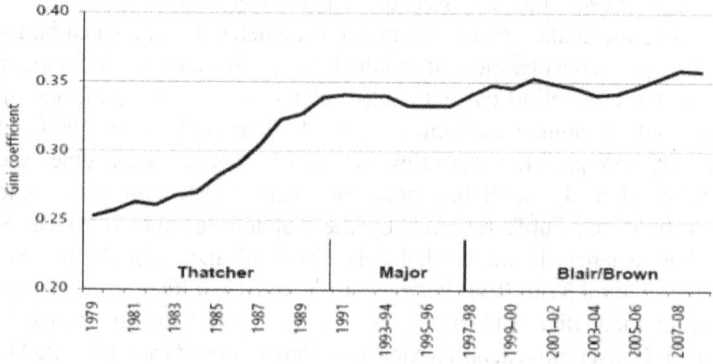

Figure 5.2 Income inequality in the UK, 1979–2008. Source: Robert Joyce, Alastair Muriel, David Phillips and Luke Sibieta, *Poverty and Inequality in the UK*, London, Institute of Fiscal Studies, 2010, p. 30.

With some exceptions, a similar pattern applies to other Western countries as we shall see hereafter.

If we take now the most recent data on inequality measured by the Gini index, we can see that strong-NPM countries present a more unequal distribution of income than weak-NPM countries (Figure 5.3). Let us note, before we go any further, that the Gini index can be calculated on the basis of different data (even if the method of calculation is the same) and this will give quite normally different levels of the index for the same country at the same date. We will not discuss here these differences, as we are mainly interested in the comparison between strong- and weak-NPM countries by taking into consideration their rank within the distribution of several strong- and weak-NPM countries.[19] I have already mentioned in Chapter 2 that different methods may produce different levels of inequality and poverty, but the ranking of the countries will be, with some rare exceptions, the same.

It has been difficult to obtain time series from 1979 to present from a single

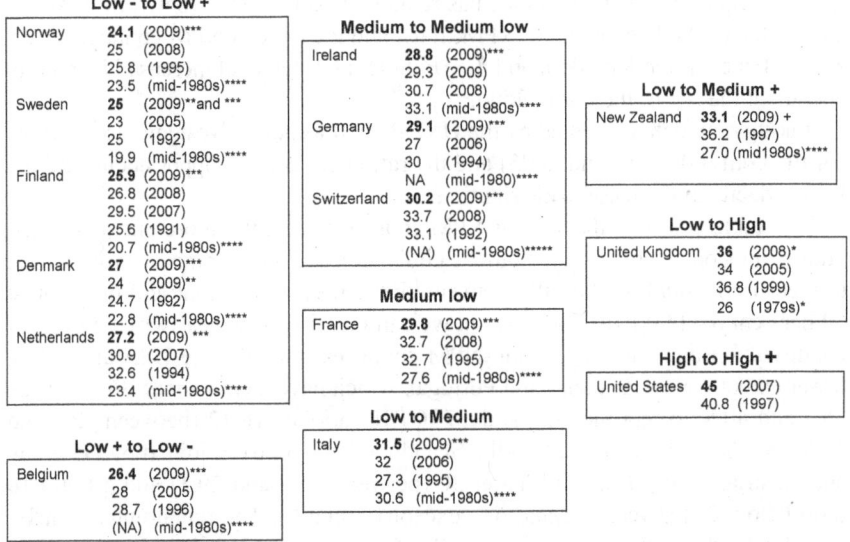

Figure 5.3 Changes in Gini index in 14 Western countries, mid-1980s to 2009. Legend: Low, 20–24; Low+, 24–28; Medium, 28–32; Medium+, 28–34; High, 34–40; High+, more than 40. Sources: all data from CIA Factbook 2010, US Government, available at https://www.cia.gov/library/publications/the-world-factbook/, accessed 7 March 2011, except * IFS 2010, London, available at http://www.ifs.org.uk/, accessed 10 March 2011, ** UNDP, *Human Development Report 2010*, available at http://www.beta.undp.org/undp/en/home.html, accessed 15 March 2011, *** Eurostat 2010, European Union, available at http://epp.eurostat.ec.europa.eu/portal/page/portal/eurostat/home/, accessed 7 March 2011, + NZI (New Zealand Institute) available at http://www.nzinstitute.org/, accessed 17 March 2011, **** OECD Stat Extracts, available at http://stats.oecd.org/Index.aspx, accessed 17 March 2011.

source. However, the data provided by OECD, UNDP, the CIA and other organizations or research centres show that the ranking of the countries is practically the same. Research by John Weeks working on OECD data for 17 OECD countries from the 1960s to the 1990s – in other words, also covering the first two decades of NPM – shows that during this period the only countries where the Gini index increased were Australia and the three beacon NPM countries: New Zealand, the UK and the USA.[20] In I have put together data from different sources between the mid-1980s and 2009 that very clearly show that strong-NPM countries, in particular the USA and the UK, have a Gini index well above the level of weak-NPM countries, such as the northern European ones, and central continental European countries such as Germany, France, Belgium and Switzerland. Even NPM latecomers, such as Italy and Ireland, have a Gini index lower than the USA and the UK. Moreover, even if the majority of the countries have increased income inequality between the mid-1980s and 2009, it is interesting to note that northern European countries and the Netherlands have managed to limit the deterioration so that they present a rather low Gini index (from 24.1 in Norway to 27.2 in the Netherlands). Belgium, Ireland, Germany and Switzerland have even managed to reduce inequality, whereas France has remained rather stable (between 27.6 and 29.8). One of the latecomers to NPM, Italy, and the beacon NPM countries, New Zealand, the United Kingdom and the United States, have all increased inequality and are at the top of the Gini raking.[23]

Taking now data presented by the UNDP 2010 Report,[24] we again use in Table 5.4 the Gini index (around 2005) and the ratio between the upper decile and the lowest decile in the income distribution.

This table confirms that strong-NPM countries present a more unequal distribution of income according to both the Gini index and another measure often used to measure inequality: the ratio between the richest 10 per cent and the poorest 10 per cent (or P90/P10). Here again, we can identify very clearly two groups of countries: on one hand the strong-NPM countries (the UK, the USA and – to a lesser extent – New Zealand) and Portugal, which have a Gini above 36 (between 36.2 and 40.8, except the UK) and a P90/P10 ratio above 12 (between 12.5 and 15.9); on the other hand we find the Scandinavian countries, joined by Germany and Austria, with a low Gini under 30 (between 26.9 and 29.1) and a P90/P10 ratio below 7 (between 5.6 and 6.9, except Denmark). The remaining countries can also be divided into two groups. Not far above the Scandinavian countries, we find a group of continental European countries and Canada with a medium Gini between 32.6 and 33.7 and a P90/P10 ratio between 8.2 and 9.4, whereas the last group, comprising Australia, two NPM latecomers (Italy and Ireland) and two southern European countries (Spain and Greece), presents a strong medium Gini (between 34.3 and 36) and a P90/P10 ratio equal to (Ireland) or above 9.4.[25]

It is further interesting to consider that the Gini index can be calculated both for market income and for disposable income, that is, after government taxes and social benefits. By doing this one can see the extent of the reduction in inequality attributable to the government and its redistribution policies. A study by Smeeding and Brandolini allows us to make this comparison (Figure 5.4).[26]

Table 5.4 Gini index and ratio of richest 10% to poorest 10% in 20 Western countries and China, around 2005

Country	Gini UNDP 2009	Rank	Richest 10% to poorest 10%	Rank
Finland	26.9	4	5.6	1
Norway	25.8	3	6.1	2
Sweden	25.0	2	6.2	3
Denmark	25.7	1	8.1	6
Germany	28.3	5	6.9	4
Austria	29.1	6	6.9	4
Belgium	33.0	10	8.2	7
Netherlands	30.9	7	9.2	10
France	32.7	9	9.1	9
Switzerland	33.7	11	9.0	8
Canada	32.6	8	9.4	11
Ireland	34.3	12	9.4	12
Greece	34.3	12	10.2	13
Spain	34.7	14	10.3	14
Australia	35.2	15	12.5	16
Italy	36.0	16	11.6	15
New Zealand	36.2	18	12.5	16
UK	36.0	16	13.8	19
Portugal	38.5	19	15.0	20
USA	40.8	20	15.9	21
China	41.5	21	13.2	18

Source: UNDP Human Development Report, 2009, pp. 195–196. Data *c.* mid-2000s.

This figure adds another confirmation of the divide between weak-NPM countries and the NPM beacon countries. In fact, there is not a clear difference between these countries as far as market income distribution is concerned: the Gini index is almost equally high for the USA (48) and the UK (51) on one hand, and for Germany (48) and Sweden (46) on the other. However, when one takes into consideration the disposable income (i.e. after taxes and social benefits) one again finds the now familiar pattern: the USA and the UK reduce the inequality determined by the market by only 23 and 33 per cent respectively, whereas countries such as Germany and Sweden reduce the disparity by 48 and 45 per cent respectively, thus reducing the Gini index to 28 and 25 respectively, against a much higher 37 (USA) and 34 (UK). The other continental European countries present a pattern similar to that of Germany and Sweden.

Other ways of measuring inequality produce practically the same results. This is the case for the ratio between the 10 per cent highest incomes and the 10 per cent lowest ones, or by representing the distance between the highest and the lowest incomes. This is done by taking the percentage of median income received

120 *The crisis of New Public Management in the West and in China*

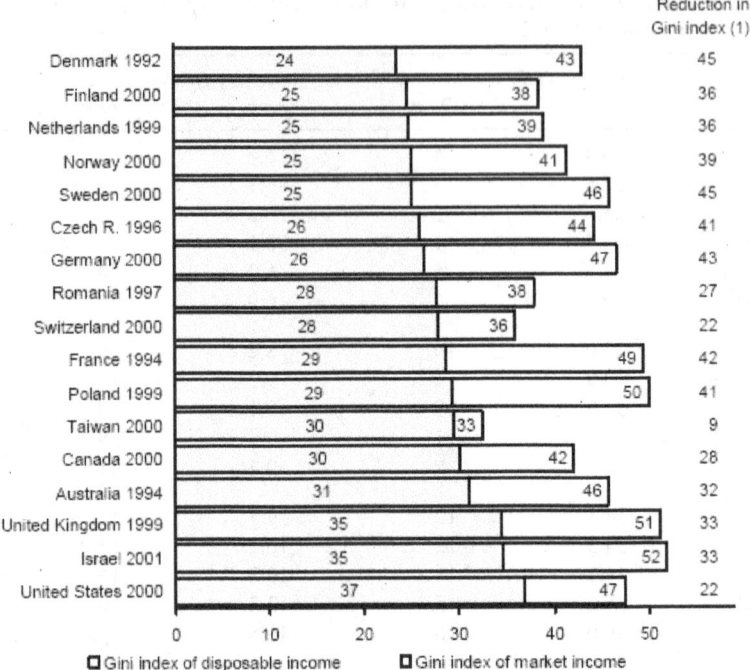

Figure 5.4 Income inequality: Gini market income index vs. Gini disposable income index in 17 industrialized countries, c. 2000. Source: Andrea Brandolini and Timothy M. Smeeding, 'Inequality patterns in western-type democracies: cross-country differences and time changes', LIS Working Paper No. 458, April 2007. Note (1): differences between the Gini index for market income and Gini index for disposable income, expressed as a percentage of the former. Authors' calculations from Luxembourg Income Study database, as of 15 February 2006. Both market and disposable income are adjusted for household size by the square-root equivalence scale.

by the lowest 10 per cent of incomes (P10) and the percentage of median income received by the highest 10 per cent of incomes (P90) and by then constructing bars of different lengths representing the distance between these two categories. For the sake of simplicity we will take a figure that simultaneously represent these methods as well and the Gini index, thanks to a paper by Brandolini and Smeeding (Figure 5.5).[27]

Figure 5.5, which presents income inequality using different methods, shows very clearly that, no matter what method used, the ranking of the countries is practically the same. Column P10 shows that the lowest 10 per cent of incomes in the beacon NPM countries are only 37 per cent of the median income in the USA and 47 per cent in the UK, whereas the poorest people in weak-NPM countries receive much more, for example 57 per cent in the northern European countries. At the other end of the income distribution, column P90 shows that the highest 10 per cent of incomes in the USA and the UK are more than 200 per cent of the

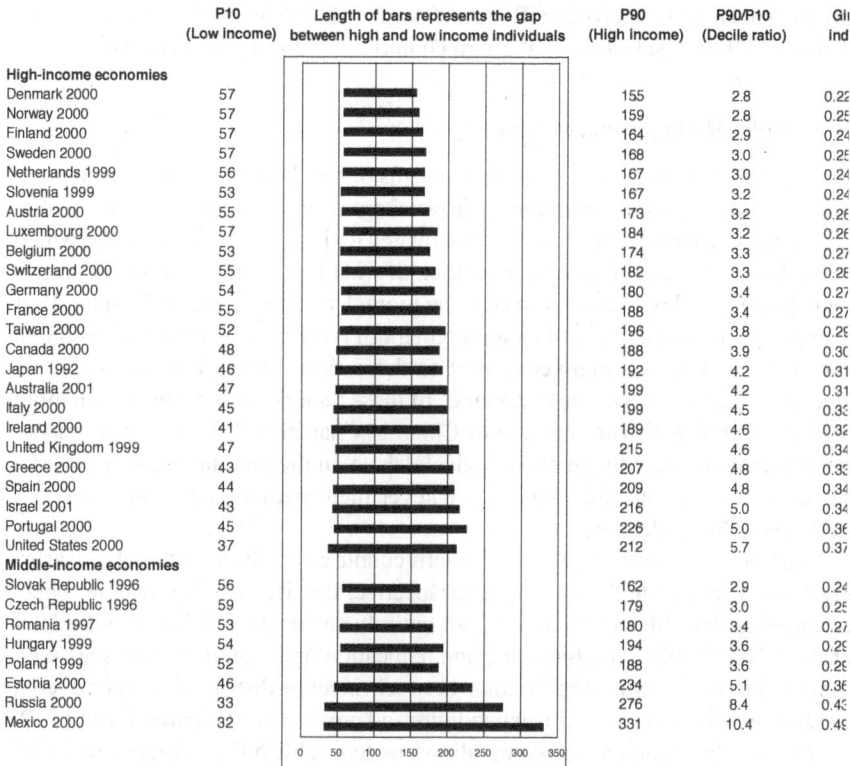

Figure 5.5 Income inequality: international evidence, *c*. 2000. Source: Andrea Brandolini and Timothy Seeding, 'Inequality patterns in western-type democracies: cross-country differences and time changes', Centre for Household, Income, Labour and Demographic Economics, Working Papers, ChilD no. 08/2007, p. 33, available at http://www.child-centre.it, accessed 20 February 2012. Also published as LIS (Luxembourg Income Study) Working Paper no. 458, April 2007.

median income, whereas in the northern European countries they receive between 155 and 168 per cent. Central continental European countries such as France and Germany are placed in between, with the received median income for P10 higher than 55, and lower than 188 for P90. By taking the ratio between P90 and P10, we find for northern European countries 2.8 to 3.0 and an astonishing 5.7 for the USA and 4.6 for the UK. Again, central continental European countries are placed somewhere in between with ratios ranging from 3.2 to 3.4. Finally the Gini index confirms the divide between strong- and weak-NPM countries, with the USA leading the distribution at the upper end with 0.37, and Denmark being placed at the lowest end with 0.225. Let us remark that the data used in this table are around the year 2000 and, as we have seen before in Figure 5.3, the distance between strong-NPM and other countries has increased since then, with the USA presenting a Gini index of 0.45 and the UK 0.37 (2008 data). Research using 2005 data presented as *The State of Working America, 2008*, based upon the percentage of

US median income received by P10 and P90, the Gini index and the ratio between P10 and P90 for a selection of Western countries, confirms this analysis.[28]

New Public Management and poverty

A reminder of my remarks about the problems of measuring poverty is even more necessary than for those mentioned above about unemployment and income distribution. Here most of the problems are related to the definition of poverty, which inevitably entails a subjective appreciation of what is accepted as 'poverty' in one society compared with another (see some more detailed remarks in Chapter 2). It is important to mention that the measurement of poverty is by no means a simple matter and that it is moreover subject to theoretical, methodological and even ideological controversy. The importance of these remarks will become even more evident when I deal with the case of China in Chapter 6. It is of course impossible to examine here the methodological debate on the measurement of poverty. Nevertheless, all consulted studies, whatever their methodology, fundamentally show the same tendencies.

In order to evaluate poverty in Western countries I will first use data measuring poverty by taking the economic perspective, that is, by using income. Then, considering that this perspective is not entirely satisfactory, I will use the HDI of the UNDP, which combines income, education and health. Let us start with some evidence showing the relation between income distribution and poverty, and between the level of social expenditure and poverty rate (Figures 5.6 and 5.7).

Research by Timothy Smeeding allows us to establish the existence of a correlation between income inequality and poverty.[29] By taking the percentage of full-time workers earning less than 65 per cent of median earnings as a measure of income inequality and the percentage of non-elderly who are poor (data around 2000) he arrives at a coefficient of correlation as high as 0.8532. Once again the strong-NPM countries such as the USA and the UK are among those that have at the same time a high percentage of workers earning less than 65 per cent of the median income (between about 20 and 25 per cent) and a high percentage of non-elderly poor (between about 11 and 16 per cent). New Public Management latecomers such as Italy and Ireland present the same pattern. In contrast, Sweden, Belgium and Finland present the lowest percentage of workers earning below the 65 per cent line (between about 5 and 7 per cent) and the lowest percentage of non-elderly poor (between about 5 and 6.3 per cent), while Germany, Austria and the Netherlands occupy a place in between, but closer to the latter countries than to the former.

The same research allows us to establish the existence of a correlation between social expenditure and poverty, by taking non-elderly and cash and near-cash social expenditure levels (as percentage of GDP) and the percentage of non-elderly who are poor. The correlation index is 0.6069. Once again the USA stands out as presenting the highest percentage of poor (16 per cent) and the lowest percentage of GDP invested in social policies (about 4 per cent). At the other end of the distribution we find countries such as Sweden, Finland, Belgium and the Netherlands, with poverty rates between 4.5 and 8 per cent, and social expenditures between

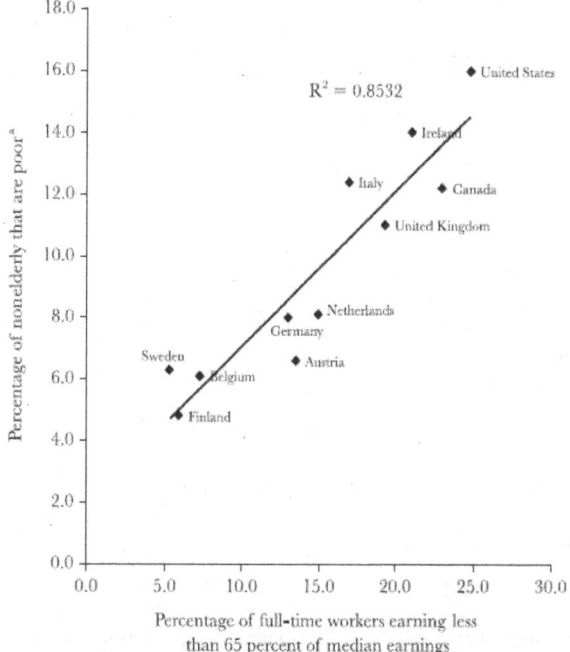

Figure 5.6 Relationship between low pay and non-elderly poverty rates in 11 industrialized countries, c. 2000. Note a: Percentage of persons below 65 in poor households. Source: Timothy Smeeding, 'Poor people in rich nations: the United States in comparative perspective', *Journal of Economics Perspectives*, winter 2006, vol. 20, no. 1, p. 86.

about 11 and 14 per cent of GDP. In between, but close to the USA, we find two latecomers to NPM (Ireland and Italy) and also, but closer to the second group, Germany and Austria. The UK is better placed in this analysis with the poverty rate as high as 11 per cent and social expenditures equal to about 10 per cent of GDP. It is also interesting to note that with about the same percentage of GDP for social expenditure (between 6.5 and 8.5 per cent) Germany and Austria with a poverty percentage of 6.5 to 8.0 per cent do much better than the two NPM latecomers (Italy and Ireland), which present a poverty rate of 12.3 to 14 per cent.

A research paper of the Luxembourg Income Study covering about 20 countries around the year 2000 allows us to further explore the impact of the state's social policies (Table 5.5).[30] In this study (based upon data around 1990, i.e. after the first 10 years of NPM) the poverty ratio is defined as the percentage of households the income of which is less than 50 per cent of the average income, before and after direct tax and social benefits.

The first column of this figure shows the poverty rate determined by the market. We can see that there is no clear pattern, if we take our typology of strong- and weak-NPM states. The USA and the UK do about the same as continental Europe, Sweden being even well above the US and UK level. Things change very radically when social security is taken into consideration, and allow us to separate the distribution

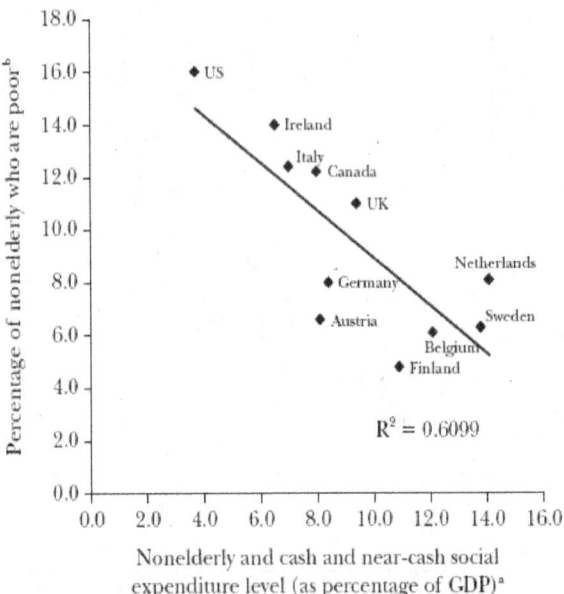

Figure 5.7 Relationship between cash social expenditures and non-elderly poverty rates in 11 industrialized countries, c. 2000. Notes: a: Cash and non-cash expenditures exclude health, education and social services, but include all forms of cash benefits and near-cash housing subsidies, active labour market programmes subsidies and other contingent cash and other near-cash benefits. Non-elderly benefits include only those accruing to household head under age 65. b: Percentage of persons below 65 in poor households. Source: Smeeding, 'Poor people in rich nations', p. 83.

into two groups: those with poverty rates between 23.5 per cent (the USA) and 15.5 per cent (Canada) and those below 9.6 per cent (Finland). In the latter group we find seven continental European countries. We have added the ranking from 1 (the USA) to 13 (Belgium). The third column shows that after taxes and social benefits the poverty percentage in the USA (23.5 per cent) and in the UK (23.0 per cent) is clearly higher than that of western continental European countries, where it is situated between 7 and 10 per cent, with the exception of Germany (17.5 per cent) and Spain (16.0 per cent). Let us note that Germany had just been reunified in 1990 and therefore its data reflect the impact of the former East Germany, which had a poverty rate considerably higher than that of West Germany. For Spain the high poverty rate can probably be explained by its late accession to the European Union in 1986. If we now calculate the percentage of poverty reduction due to social state policies, we find exactly the reverse ranking, from 13 (the USA) to 1 (Belgium). The first group presents a reduction between 31.1 per cent (the USA) and 52.7 per cent (Canada) whereas the second group reduces the poverty rate by more than 60 per cent: between 61 per cent (Finland) and 81.5 per cent (Belgium). We have already explained the cases of Germany and Spain.

Let us note that New Zealand was not included in the research. However, Jane

Table 5.5 Anti-poverty effect of government spending in 13 Western countries, c. 1990

Country	% of households with pretransfer equivalent income below 50% average	Rank	% of households with income below 50% of average after social security and direct taxation	Rank	% of poverty reduction	Rank
USA	34.1	5	23.5	1	31.1	13
UK	38.1	3	23.0	2	39.6	12
Australia	33.0	7	19.7	3	40.3	11
Germany	32.7	8	17.5	4	46.5	10
Spain	33.1	6	16.0	5	51.3	9
Canada	31.9	10	15.5	6	52.7	8
Finland	24.6	12	9.6	7	61.0	7
Italy	27.2	11	9.6	8	64.7	6
Netherlands	33.0	6	9.3	9	71.8	5
Sweden	41.4	1	9.1	10	78.0	2
Denmark	36.9	4	8.2	11	77.8	3
Norway	32.4	9	8.2	12	74.7	4
Belgium	38.3	2	7.1	13	81.5	1

Source: adapted from J. Bradshaw and J.-R. Chen, 'Poverty in the UK: a comparison with nineteen other countries', LIS Working Paper No. 147, 1996, http://www.lisproject.org.

Note: percentage of all people poor.

Kelsey mentions the economist Brian Easton, according to whom the number of persons living in poverty increased by 35 per cent between 1989 and 1993, to place the poverty proportion at 1:6. More recent data elaborated by the New Zealand Poverty Measurement Project (using a different methodology) show that 18.5 per cent of households, 20.5 per cent of individuals and one child in three live below the poverty level.[31]

Another research by Timothy Smeeding shows the situation about 10 years later, taking the poverty line as the percentage of households the income of which is less than 50 per cent of the median income (Table 5.6). Although the countries taken into consideration are slightly different and the methodologies are based upon two different measures of poverty the pattern of the ranking of strong- and weak-NPM countries is practically the same as 10 years earlier, but with some remarkable and interesting differences (see Table 5.7, comparing the 1990 and 2000 data).[32]

The USA (rank 1) and the UK (rank 4) are still among the group with the highest poverty rate both before and after taxes and social policies, and the continental European states present the lowest poverty rates both before and after taxes and social policies. Moreover, as in 1990, the percentage of poverty reduction is considerably higher for the latter than for strong-NPM countries. It is interesting to see that, 10 years after reunification, Germany has succeeded in reducing the poverty rate so that it is now within the group of continental European countries with the lowest rate. On the contrary, Italy, a latecomer to NPM, has left the group

Table 5.6 Anti-poverty effect of government spending in 11 Western countries, c. 2000

	Poverty rate after market income below 50% of median	Poverty rate after social insurance, taxes and social assistance	Rank	% poverty reduction after social insurance, taxes and social assistance	Rank
USA	23.1	17.0	1	26.4	11
Ireland	29.5	16.5	2	44.1	10
Canada	21.1	11.4	5	46.0	9
Italy	30.0	12.7	3	57.7	8
UK	31.1	12.4	4	60.1	7
Netherlands	21.0	7.3	9	65.2	6
Finland	17.8	5.4	11	69.7	5
Germany	28.1	8.3	6	70.5	4
Austria	31.8	7.7	8	75.8	3
Belgium	34.6	8.0	7	76.9	2
Sweden	28.8	6.5	10	77.4	1

Source: adapted from Timothy Smeeding, 'Poor people in rich nations', *Journal of Economics Perspectives*, Winter 2006, vol. 20, no. 1, p. 79.

Note: percentage of all persons poor.

with the lowest rate to join the USA and UK with a poverty rate, after taxes and social policies, similar to the UK and, with rank 3, is placed just before the UK. Unfortunately, Ireland, another latecomer to NPM, was not included in the 1990 study and therefore we cannot compare its 1990 and 2000 ranks. Nevertheless, by 2000 Ireland is clearly within the group with the highest poverty rate both before and after taxes and social benefits and, at rank 2, it is placed just after the USA. This new position for Ireland will be confirmed when we consider poverty rates for vulnerable groups in the next paragraph.

Some other indicators concerning vulnerable groups, such as child poverty before and after taxes and transfers, child mortality, social expenditures versus child poverty, and relative poverty rates for children, one-parent families with children, and elders over 65, allow us to complete the comparison between strong- and weak-NPM countries. In fact, the willingness of a society to fight against poverty can be further evaluated by taking into consideration the impact of state policies on the situation of some of the most vulnerable groups. Let us start with children, one-parent families and elders over 65. This is done by commenting on Table 5.8 presented by Timothy Smeeding in an already quoted study.[33]

This figure presents under the first column the same data as Table 5.6 based upon data around 2000. When taking into consideration the poverty rate of vulnerable groups after social policies and taxes, we see that the general pattern is confirmed, but with some exceptions. The five countries with the highest poverty rates – the two beacon NPM countries (USA and UK) and the two NPM

Table 5.7 Anti-poverty effect of government spending, 1990–2000

Country	Poverty rate (circa 1990) after social security and direct taxation below 50% of mean	Rank	Poverty rate (circa 2000) after social security, taxes and social assistance below 50% of median	Rank	Country
USA	23.5	1	17.0	1	USA
UK	23.0	2	16.5	2	Ireland
Australia	19.7	3	12.7	3	Italy
Germany	17.5	4	12.4	4	UK
Spain	16.0	5	11.4	5	Canada
Canada	15.5	6			
Finland	9.6	7	8.9	6	Belgium
Italy	9.6	8	8.3	7	Germany
Netherlands	9.3	9	7.7	8	Austria
Sweden	9.1	10	7.3	9	Netherlands
Denmark	8.2	11	6.5	10	Sweden
Norway	8.2	12	5.4	11	Finland
Belgium	7.1	13			

Sources: adapted from Bradshaw and Chen, 'Poverty in the UK', for 1990, and Smeeding, 'Poor people in rich nations', for 2000.

Table 5.8 Relative poverty rates for vulnerable groups in 11 Western countries, c. 2000

Country	Overall (% poor)	Rank	Children (% poor)	Rank	Children with one parent (% poor)	Rank	Elders over 65 (% poor)	Rank
USA	17.0	1	18.8	1	41.4	2	28.4	2
Ireland	16.5	2	15.0	3	45.8	1	48.3	1
Italy	12.7	3	15.4	2	20.1	8	14.4	6
UK	12.4	4	13.2	4	30.5	6	23.9	3
Canada	11.4	5	13.2	5	32.0	4	6.3	10
Germany	8.3	6	7.6	7	33.2	3	11.2	7
Belgium	8.0	7	6.0	9	21.8	7	17.2	5
Austria	7.7	8	6.4	8	17.9	9	17.4	4
Netherlands	7.3	9	9.0	6	30.7	5	2.0	11
Sweden	6.5	10	3.8	10	11.3	10	8.3	9
Finland	5.4	11	2.9	11	7.3	11	10.1	8

Source: adapted from Smeeding, 'Poor people in rich nations', p. 74.

Note: percentage below 50 per cent median adjusted disposable income, after social security, taxes and social assistance.

latecomers (Italy and Ireland) joined by Canada – present also the highest poverty rate for children. However, for one-parent families, Italy (rank 8) and to a lesser extent the UK (rank 6) should be placed in the group with the lowest rate, whereas the Netherlands (rank 5) and especially Germany (rank 3) should be placed in the group with the highest rate. Similarly, for elders over 65, Italy (rank 6) and especially Canada (rank 10) should be placed in the group with the lowest poverty rate. In contrast to Italy, the other NPM latecomer, Ireland, confirms its strong NPM profile by obtaining rank 1 for both one-parent families (poverty rate 45.8) and elders over 65 (poverty rate 48.3). These exceptions show that when we subdivide an entire population into subgroups (in this case into vulnerable groups) some countries may present poverty rates that are not necessarily similar to the data concerning the whole population. Specific cultural traits as well as specific social policies targeting some vulnerable groups may explain these differences, for instance in the case of Italy, a latecomer to NPM, but with a long-established tradition of care for children, families and the elderly.

Some other indicators allow us to complete and confirm the comparison between strong- and weak-NPM countries. In Figure 5.8 the authors of *The State of Working America* present data around 2000 concerning child poverty rates before and after taxes and social benefits.[34] I have added a horizontal line between Austria and Canada marking the divide between countries that considerably reduce child poverty and the others. The figure clearly shows once more that the poverty reduction attained by the beacon NPM countries (the USA, the UK, New Zealand) and one of the NPM latecomers (Ireland) joined by Canada and Portugal (a late member of the European Union) is considerably smaller than

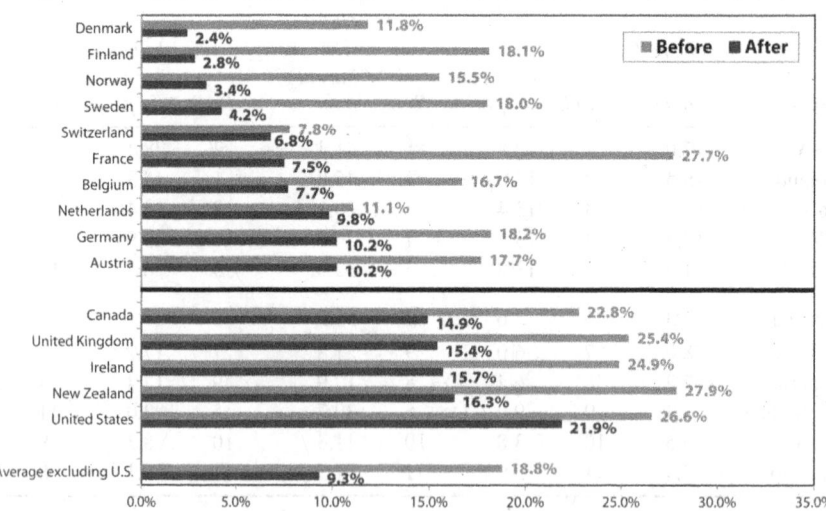

Figure 5.8 Child poverty rate before and after taxes and transfers, in 16 industrialized countries, 2000. Source: Economic Policy Institute, *The State of Working America 2006–7*, Washington, DC, http://epinet.org.

for continental European countries, especially the northern ones. For northern European countries the child poverty rate after taxes and social benefits ranges from 2.4 per cent for Denmark to 4.2 per cent for Sweden, and for central continental European countries between 6.8 per cent for Switzerland and 10.2 per cent for Austria, whereas for the strong-NPM countries the range is much higher, from 14.9 per cent for Canada to 21.9 per cent for the USA. Moreover, *The State of Working America* presents the correlation between social expenditures as percentage of GDP and child poverty, which can explain the difference in the reduction of child poverty rates mentioned above (see Figure 5.9).[35] It appears very clearly that in the USA social expenditures of about 2.5 per cent of GDP go together with a child poverty rate of 21.9 per cent. The northern European countries (Sweden, Norway, Denmark and Finland) constitute a group placed at the other end of the distribution with social expenditures between about 11.5 per cent (Finland) and 16 per cent (Denmark) with a low child poverty rate between about 3 and 9 per cent. Italy, the UK, Ireland and Canada are grouped together in between the USA and the northern European group, but closer to the USA, whereas the group constituted by Germany, France, the Netherlands and Switzerland is placed in between at about equal distance from USA and the northern European group.[36]

So far we have used economic indicators to measure both inequalities and poverty rates. As I have already mentioned in Chapter 2, this approach has attracted much criticism and has resulted in several alternative proposals for measuring these phenomena, especially poverty.

Given the empirical limits of some of the new methods mentioned above (Chapter 2, pp. 59–62), I will limit the rest of this section to the findings of the United Nations Development Programme (UNDP). I will use both the old Human

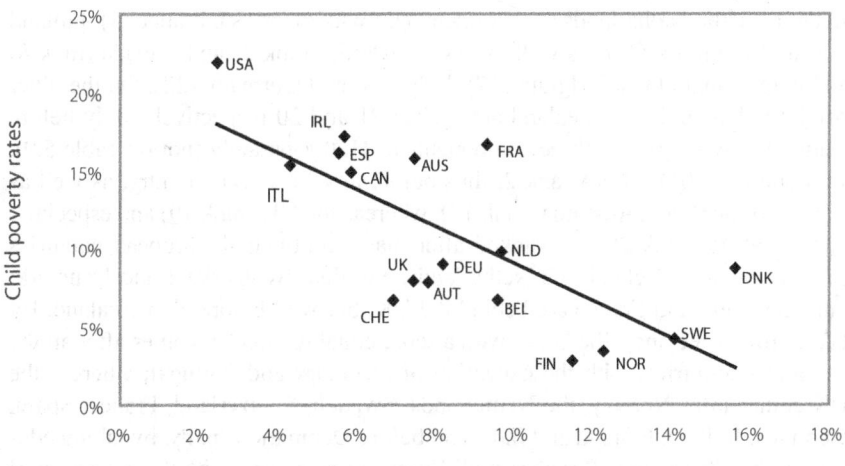

Figure 5.9 Social expenditures versus child poverty in 17 industrialized countries, 2001.
Source: Economic Policy Institute, *The State of Working America 2006–7*.

Development Index (HDI) and then the new HDI introduced in 2010, as well as a few new indices presented in the UNDP 2010 Report. The 'old' HDI, whose statistics were compiled from data on life expectancy, education and per-capita GDP (as an indicator of standard of living), has attracted a variety of criticisms, among which it is enough to mention (1) the failure to include any ecological considerations, (2) looking at development only from the national performance perspective, neglecting a global approach to development, (3) redundancy compared with the information given by its three components and (4) the focus on material development while completely neglecting moral development measures. Nevertheless, the HDI is today extensively used, maybe in the expectation of some of the results obtained by the new methods mentioned above. It has been useful for classifying countries according to their level of development in three categories until 2008 (high, medium and low) and four categories since 2009: very high, high, medium and low human development, the countries in the last group being certainly those in which the rate of poverty is the highest.[37] Yet it remains that for the purpose of comparing levels of income inequalities and poverty rates within the first group, which is in fact the purpose of the this chapter, the usefulness of the HDI is certainly inferior to the measures we have used so far. In particular, all the Western countries are ranked, with a few exceptions, at the top of the group with the highest development index, and the differences amongst them are rather narrow, as measured by the HDI index as well as by its three components. Nevertheless, even the HDI allows for seeing some clear cleavages amongst the Western developed countries.

By taking the old HDI for the latest data available, 2007 (first two columns of Table 5.9),[38] and taking into consideration for continental Europe only central and northern countries plus Italy, Spain and Greece[39] one can see that the USA is ranked 13, after several European countries such as Norway (rank 1), Ireland (5), the Netherlands (6), Sweden (7), Switzerland (9), France (8), Finland (12) and Denmark (16), as well as after Australia (rank 2) and Canada (rank 8) and before Spain (15), Belgium (17), Italy (18) and Germany (22). On the other hand, the UK and New Zealand are ranked 21 and 20 respectively, only before Germany. By taking the three components of HDI separately (not on Table 5.9), we obtain for GDP: USA rank 2, thus before any European country, as well as Canada (rank 9) and Australia (rank 12), whereas the UK (rank 10) and especially New Zealand (rank 20) are ranked after many continental European countries such as Norway, Ireland, the Netherlands, Sweden, Switzerland and Denmark; only Germany and France are behind the UK, but well before New Zealand. By taking life expectancy, the USA (with a score equal to Greece) comes after all the European countries, with the exception of Denmark and Portugal; whereas the UK comes after Norway, the Netherlands, Sweden, Switzerland, France, Spain, Germany, Ireland, Finland and Italy, and before Denmark. Finally, by taking education, the USA come after almost all European countries, with the exception of Switzerland, Germany, Italy, Austria and Portugal; whereas New Zealand occupies an astonishing first rank shared with Belgium and Finland and Australia; the UK comes before only Switzerland, Germany, and Portugal. One can see that the construction of the HDI composite index very clearly favours the countries with the highest income per capita. The USA is doing very well on this count, and very largely compensates for its weaknesses measured by the two other dimensions.

Let us now look again at Table 5.9, which presents data for the old HDI (2007) and the new HDI (2010) as well as the new inequality-adjusted index and the gender inequality index.[40] Taking now the new HDI, we can see that, whereas the English-speaking strong-NPM countries (with the exception of the UK, rank 26) do slightly better than the European countries on the HDI index (with the exception of Norway, rank 1), as soon as we adjust the HDI with inequality, and especially gender inequality, European countries (and more particularly the weak-NPM Scandinavian countries) do much better than the English-speaking ones. France, Italy and Austria are somewhat in between, and seem to suffer from their recent trends in favour of some neoliberal public policies. Only the European countries of southern Europe (Spain, Greece and Portugal) are clearly behind the others on practically all the indices. This seems to confirm, as we have seen in Chapter 2 (pp. 53–54), the results of the research by Peter Hall and David Soskice, and by Bruno Amable, that regroup southern European countries into a special type.[41]

We know that the per capita income obscures income distribution and we have seen in the preceding paragraphs that the USA has one of the more unequal distributions of income and a higher rate of poverty than European countries, with the exception of the UK. Moreover, by taking into consideration other indicators such as health, we see below that the US situation is overall considerably worse than the European ones also in this respect.

Poverty, income distribution and intergenerational mobility

We have already seen that the trend of all the major Western countries is towards a greater inequality of income distribution, as is suggested by Timothy Smeeding's research.[42] One could object that in countries such the United States and the United Kingdom, where competition is very keen, opportunities to improve one's financial situation over time should be greater than in other countries. Therefore the probability of escaping from poverty from childhood to adulthood should be greater in the USA and the UK. Contrary to this hypothesis, research by M. Jäntti and S. Danziger available already in 1993 shows exactly the opposite.[43] The relationship between the poverty rate and the escape rate is the reverse: the countries in which a greater percentage of poor families exit from poverty are the countries with the lower poverty rates. More recent research conducted by Jo Blanden and colleagues confirms these findings.[44] First, intergenerational mobility in the UK is of the same order of magnitude as in the USA, but these countries are substantially less mobile than Canada and the Nordic European countries.[45] Second, 'the US is seen by some as a place with particularly high social mobility . . . the idea of the US as "the land of opportunity" persists; and clearly seems misplaced.'[46] Third, intergenerational mobility has declined in Britain at a time of rising income inequality. Finally, income inequality has risen at the same time

Table 5.9 HDI and ranking in 20 Western countries and China, 2007 and 2010

Countries	Old HDI 2007	Old HDI rank	New HDI 2010	New HDI rank	Inequality adjusted HDI	Inequality adjusted HDI rank[a]	Gender inequality index	Gender inequality rank
Norway	0.971	1	0.938	1	0.876	1	0.234	5
Australia	0.970	2	0.937	2	0.864	2	0.296	18
New Zealand	0.950	20	0.907	3	NA	NA	0.320	25
USA	0.956	13	0.902	4	0.799	10	0.400	37
Ireland	0.965	5	0.895	5	NA	NA	0.344	29
Netherlands	0.964	6	0.888	7	0.818	4	0.174	1
Canada	0.966	4	0.888	8	0.812	7	0.289	16
Sweden	0.963	7	0.885	9	0.824	3	0.212	3
Germany	0.947	22	0.885	10	0.814	5	0.240	7
Switzerland	0.960	9	0.874	13	0.813	6	0.228	4
France	0.961	8	0.872	14	0.792	12	0.260	11
Finland	0.959	12	0.871	16	0.806	9	0.248	8
Belgium	0.953	17	0.867	18	0.794	11	0.236	6
Denmark	0.955	16	0.866	19	0.810	8	0.209	2

Spain	0.955	15	0.863	20	0.779	14	0.280	14
Greece	0.942	25	0.855	22	0.768	15	0.317	23
Italy	0.951	18	0.854	23	0.752	17	0.251	9
Austria	0.955	14	0.851	25	0.787	13	0.300	19
United Kingdom	0.947	21	0.849	26	0.766	16	0.355	32
Portugal	0.909	34	0.795	40	0.700	18	NA	NA
China	0.772	92	0.663	89	0.511	82	0.405	38

Sources: United Nations Development Programme (UNDP), *Human Development Report 2009*, New York, Palgrave Macmillan, 2009, pp. 195–198, and *Human Development Report 2010*, New York, Palgrave Macmillan, 2010, pp. 143–146 and 2002–2009.

Notes

a Calculated by author.

Not included: Liechtenstein, Iceland, Luxembourg, and Malta (all in the very High development group), as well as the eastern European countries in the very high development group (i.e. the Czech Republic, Slovenia, Estonia, Hungary and Poland; new HDI between 0.841 and 0.795); all the other European countries are in the high development group (new HDI between 0.783 and 0.701).

The *inequality adjusted HDI* takes into consideration (1) long and healthy life, (2) knowledge (mean years of schooling, expected years of schooling) and (3) a decent standard of living (GNI per capita in PPP US$)

The *gender inequality index* measures achievements using the same indicators as the HDI but captures inequalities in achievement between women and men. It is simply the HDI adjusted downwards for gender inequality. It takes into consideration (1) health (maternal mortality ratio, adolescent fertility rate), (2) empowerment (female and male population with at least secondary education, female and male shares of parliamentary seats) and (3) labour market (female and male labour force participation rates). The greater the gender disparity in basic human development, the lower is the adjusted HDI for gender inequality.

as the gap between the educational attainments of the richest and the poorest has grown.[47]

Conclusion from the increasing income inequality and poverty rates

Given the difference in income distribution and in poverty rates between strong- and weak-NPM countries, one can put forward the hypothesis that a society where a large part of the population is excluded from the economy, or is insufficiently inserted into it, will not fail to present other particularly negative aspects, which must be accounted for in a comprehensive evaluation of New Public Management. Following this idea, my first hypothesis is that of a positive correlation between poverty and petty crimes, that is, crimes that are most likely to be perpetrated by people in a very difficult financial situation at the limit of despair, such as theft.[48] The second and third hypotheses are related to public health and will be dealt with in the following section. The second hypothesis establishes a link between the level of income inequality and poverty on one hand and the most frequently used health indicators on the other hand: it is predicted that the strong-NPM countries with higher rates for income inequality and poverty will present a less healthy population than weak-NPM countries, with the likely exception of the UK, which has maintained an active public health system in spite of a very strong trend towards NPM initiated by the Conservative government of Margaret Thatcher.[49] The third hypothesis is that of a negative correlation between the pressures that a deregulated market exerts on people in an insecure employment situation and their health.

New Public Management and crime rates

These considerations prompted me first to consult the statistics on the development of criminality.[50] I have taken Switzerland as a non-NPM country during the 1980s and up to the beginning of the 1990s,[51] and I have compared the development of everyday crimes (thefts) in Switzerland with those in the three beacon NPM countries: the United States, the United Kingdom and New Zealand.[52] What we find (see Table 5.10) is an astonishing difference between Switzerland and the strong-NPM countries: the level of this type of criminality practically remained unchanged in Switzerland from 1977 to 1991, whilst it practically doubled in the UK and the USA during the same period. The case of New Zealand is particularly revealing, as this country had, prior to the NPM experiment, a very generous and equitable set of social policies aimed at sustaining the peasants and the ethnic minorities in particular. The introduction of NPM since 1984 has completely changed the relation between the government and the most vulnerable social groups, which lost a large part of governmental support. This change in policy constitutes very likely the most important factor that explains why in this country the level of petty criminality has more than doubled.[53]

Some commentators point out the decrease in crime rates in recent years in the USA as well as in some other Western countries. Different reasons are put forward

Table 5.10 Crime rates in four Western countries, 1977–91

Country	1977		1985		1990		1991	
	Total number of thefts	Crimes per 100,000 population	Total number of thefts	Crimes per 100,000 population	Total number of thefts	Crimes per 100,000 population	Total number of thefts	Crimes per 100,000 population
UK	2,105,329	4,286	2,782,793	5,592	3,417,417	6,758	4,025,906	7,937
USA	5,905,700	2,729	11,600,470	4,859	13,294,770	5,345	13,648,830	5,412
New Zealand	127,367	4,055	263,010	7,991	303,310	8,830	311,038	9,035
Switzerland	305,157	4,740	296,284	4,567	309,852	4,590	331,913	4,858

Source: data from Interpol website, http://www.interpol.int/.

to explain this reduction, such as a more liberal Welfare State or the fact that the new poor are not as skilled as the old ones. Contrary to these explanations I formulate the hypothesis that this is due mainly to an increase in the rate of imprisonment in recent years following a more repressive policy in several countries including the USA. In fact there is evidence of a more repressive policy towards crime, but this does not by any means constitute proof that the causes of crime have been addressed.[54] The data in Table 5.11 show the great difference between European countries and the USA in this respect.[55] The fact that more people are put in prison may of course be considered as the consequence of a political will to fight against crime, but it is certainly not the indicator of a healthy society.

One can see that between 2000 and 2007–8 the USA and Russia maintain their positions well above the level of the European countries, with a small increase for the USA (from 702 to 756) and a substantial increase for Russia (from 456 to 629). England and Wales and Scotland maintain their ranks, but with an important increase that remains nevertheless well below the rates of the USA and Russia. Amongst the other European countries only Spain presents an important increase, which places it just above England and Wales. In contrast, the other countries, including Northern Ireland, maintain their low level, with some minor changes. It seems therefore that one of the beacon NPM countries, the USA, exhibits with Russia the image of a rather violent society where crime is fought mainly by repressive means. Within Europe the other beacon NPM country, the UK, presents prisoner rates higher than those of continental Europe, with the exception of Spain. Let us note that New Zealand, the other beacon NPM country, which was not included in the 2000 research, presents in 2008 a prisoner rate of 185, higher than the UK and third only to the USA and Russia. Amongst the British

Table 5.11 Number of prisoners per 100,000 population in 12 Western countries, 2000 and 2007–8

Country	N (2000)	Rank	N (2007–8)	Rank
USA	702	1	756	1
Russia	465	2	629	2
Portugal	127	3	104	6
England and Wales	124	4	153	4
Scotland	115	5	152	5
Spain	114	6	160	3
Germany	97	7	89	10
Italy	94	8	92	9
France	89	9	96	8
Netherlands	87	10	100	7
Sweden	64	11	74	12
Northern Ireland	60	12	88	11

Sources: adapted from I. Irvine, and K. Xu, 'Crime, punishment and the measurement of poverty in the United States, 1979–1997', LIS Working Paper No. 333, November 2002, and Roy Walmsley, *World Prison Population List*, 8th edition, London, King's College, 2008.

Isles, only Northern Ireland has a prisoner rate comparable to that of continental Europe. If the case of Spain can very likely be interpreted as the consequence of the high rate of unemployment (see Table 5.1) and the outbreak of the violent secessionist movements, the high rates for England and Wales and Scotland can very likely be attributed to the NPM policies that have reduced the Welfare State.[56] Nevertheless, we will see in the following section that the UK has succeeded so far in maintaining an efficient public heath system that, in spite of the introduction of some market or quasi-market mechanisms, has maintained a high level of health indicators.

New Public Management and health

Evaluating the performance of a country in the domain of public health is a particularly difficult task, even more difficult than the assessment of income inequality and poverty rates. A vast literature, including several world-famous academic and professional journals, cover this complex domain. It is out of the question to cover exhaustively the interrelationships between NPM and public health. Nevertheless, data are available that allow us to propose a comparison between strong- and weak-NPM countries. As we have already mentioned, the UK, clearly a strong-NPM country, offers in the domain of health a profile closer to continental Europe than to the USA, thanks to the institution of the National Health Service (NHS). Even the Conservative and neoliberal government of Margaret Thatcher did not dare dismantle an institution on which the British population largely relies, and it has survived in spite of several attempts to introduce market or quasi-market mechanisms within the funding and functioning of the NHS and new market-oriented measures announced by the new British coalition government.[57] Moreover, we should also take into consideration that the other beacon NPM country, New Zealand, has a health system similar to the British one and therefore New Zealand has a public health profile closer to Europe than to the USA.[58] As for the choice of European countries, I have tried to have a sample of countries with a similar level of development, and therefore I did not include the latecomers into the European Union: eastern Europe, Greece and Portugal. By using the data provided by the World Health Organization (WHO) we can assess the performance of a choice of 16 developed countries (see Table 5.12).

One can see that the USA does not do as well as any of the other countries on all the indicators presented in Table 5.12. Life expectancy is two to four years shorter (except for Denmark, compared with which the USA is only one year shorter). More interestingly, healthy life expectancy at birth is also two to four years shorter, and rates for neonatal mortality, maternal mortality, infant mortality by age one and by age five, and adult mortality are worse than in any of the other 15 developed countries. Moreover, the adult mortality rate, measured by the probability of dying between 15 and 60, reaches an astonishing 107 per 1,000 population in the USA, whereas it is contained between 60 (Switzerland) and 94 (Finland) for the other 15 countries, and is as low as between 60 and 75 for nine countries. Finally, an indicator of a healthy and mature society is certainly the rate

Table 5.12 Major health indicators in 16 Western countries

Country	Life expectancy at birth, both sexes, 1990–2008	Healthy life expectancy at birth, both sexes, 2008	Neonatal mortality rate per 1,000 births, both sexes, 2008	Infant mortality rate by age 1 per 1,000 births, both sexes, 2008	Under-five mortality rate per 1,000 births, both sexes, 2008	Adult mortality rate: probability of dying between 15 and 60 per 1,000 population, both sexes, 2008	Maternal mortality rate per million live births, 2005	Adolescent fertility per 1,000 girls aged 15–19, latest data since 2000
Austria	76–80	72	3	4	4	75	4	12
Belgium	76–80	72	2	4	5	86	8	10
Denmark	75–79	72	3	4	4	90	3	6
Finland	75–80	72	2	3	3	94	7	9
France	77–81	73	2	3	4	87	8	8
Germany	75–80	73	3	4	4	78	4	10
Ireland	75–80	73	3	4	5	73	1	17
Italy	77–82	74	2	3	4	61	3	7
Netherlands	77–80	73	3	4	5	68	6	4
New Zealand	75–81	73	4	5	6	72	9	29
Norway	77–81	73	2	3	3	67	7	9
Spain	77–81	74	2	4	4	72	4	12
Sweden	78–81	74	2	2	3	62	3	6
Switzerland	77–82	75	3	4	5	60	5	4
United Kingdom	76–80	72	3	5	6	78	8	26
United States	75–78	70	4	7	8	107	11	41

Source: World Health Organization, *World Health Statistics, 2010*, http://www.who.int/whosis/whostat/EN_WHS10_Full.pdf, accessed 20 April 2011, pp. 25, 29 and 48–55. It also gives data by sexes.

of adolescent fertility. Here again, the USA shows an astonishing 41 per 1,000, whereas for 12 countries this rate is contained between four (Switzerland and the Netherlands) and 12 (Austria and Spain); only Ireland (17), the UK (26) and New Zealand (29) have rates higher than 16, but they are still considerably lower than the US rate. Let us note that the adolescent fertility rate does not account for either unwanted births or abortions. A study by the Guttmacher Institute published in January 2010 informs us that, whereas the US teenage pregnancy rate per 1,000 women aged 15–19 was 71.5 in 2006, the birth rate was 41.9 and the abortion rate 19.3, this figure being 56 per cent lower than its peak in 1998, but 1 per cent higher than the 2005 rate.[59]

It is also interesting to look at the money that it has been necessary to put into the health systems of the 16 countries in order to attain the above-mentioned health results. This is done in Table 5.13.

Looking at the data presented in Table 5.13 one is immediately struck by the remarkable difference between the USA and the other countries. In 2007 the USA spent 15.7 per cent of GDP on health, whereas the other countries spent between 7.7 per cent (Ireland) and 11 per cent (France). In other words the USA spent between 43 and 50 per cent of GDP more than any other country to obtain less impressive health results. This translates into a per capita expense of $PPP 7,285 whereas 13 countries spent between $PPP 2,487 (New Zealand) and $PPP 3,763 (Austria), only two countries being above $PPP 4,000 (Switzerland with $PPP 4,441 and Norway with $PPP 4,763). Thus the USA is also the only country that relies less on public expenditure for financing health (45.5 per cent) and consequently more on private money (54.5 per cent). All the other countries rely more heavily on public money: between 71.8 per cent (Spain) and 84.5 (Denmark). The only exception is Switzerland, which has adopted a hybrid system that resorts to private insurance companies (generally funded by premiums paid by citizens), the subscription to a health insurance having been made compulsory in 1985, in contrast to the USA, which has have only recently introduced this obligation.[60] So it seems that the data provided above point to the ineffectiveness, as measured by the results obtained presented in Table 5.12, and inefficiency of the US health system, as measured by the relationships between the results in Table 5.12 and the spending on health presented in Table 5.13. Also it seems that the Swiss system, although more effective and efficient than the US one, is less efficient than the UK system financed by taxation and offering universal coverage. This conclusion should be of some interest to the Chinese policy-makers. Finally, the data presented above are useful not only for shedding some light on the differences in performance between the USA and the other countries of Tables 5.12 and 5.13, but also because they show that two strong-NPM countries, the UK and New Zealand, can perform very well when they do not fully follow the prescriptions of NPM.

Let us now turn to the impact of the deregulation of labour markets on health. There is a vast and serious literature on this topic that unfortunately has been given insufficient attention in the mass media, where the dominant words accompanying the general acceptance of the present globalization have been, and still are today, adaptability and flexibility demanded of those who are looking for a

Table 5.13 Health expenditures in 16 Western countries

Country	Total expenditure on health as % of GDP, 2000–2007	General government expenditure on health as % of total expenditure on health, 2007	Private expenditures on health as % of total expenditure on health, 2007	General government expenditure on health as % of government expenditures, 2007	Out-of-pocket expenditure as % of private expenditure on health, 2007	Per capita total expenditure on health (PPP international $), 2007	Per capita government expenditure on health (PPP international $), 2007
Austria	9.9–10.1	76.4	23.6	15.9	65.2	3,763	2,875
Belgium	9.1–9.4	74.1	25.9	14.4	76.4	3,323	2,468
Denmark	8.3–9.8	84.5	15.5	16.2	89.0	3,513	2,961
Finland	7.2–8.2	74.6	25.4	12.9	74.3	2,840	2,120
France	10.1–11.0	79.0	21.0	16.6	32.5	3,709	2,930
Germany	10.3–10.4	76.9	23.1	18.2	56.6	3,588	2,758
Ireland	6.3–7.6	80.7	19.3	17.1	51.2	3,424	2,762
Italy	8.1–8.7	76.5	23.5	13.9	85.9	2,686	2,056
Netherlands	8.0–8.9	82.0	18.0	16.2	33.5	3,509	2,878
New Zealand	7.7–9.0	78.9	21.1	18.0	71.7	2,497	1,971
Norway	8.4–8.9	84.1	15.9	18.3	95.1	4,763	4,005
Spain	7.2–8.5	71.8	28.2	15.6	74.6	2,671	1,917
Sweden	8.2–9.1	81.7	18.3	14.1	87.0	3,323	2,716
Switzerland	10.2–10.8	59.3	40.7	19.8	75.0	4,417	2,618
United Kingdom	7.0–8.4	81.7	18.3	15.6	62.7	2,992	2,446
United States	13.4–15.7	45.5	54.5	19.5	22.6	7,285	3,317

Source: World Health Organization, *World Health Statistics, 2010*, pp. 130–137.

job.[61] The present crisis has considerably worsened the situation and will certainly increase inequalities within countries as a consequence of the deterioration of employment conditions. A group of experts in this domain has just published a short article in the *British Medical Journal* expressing their concern:

> the current economic recession has caused striking levels of unemployment, underemployment and job insecurity globally . . . the impact . . . is likely to increase the number of working poor . . . will increase global inequalities between social classes within countries. . . . In rich regions, such as the European Union, long established hazards at work – for example exposure to chemical products, . . . have remained stable or slightly decreased in the past decade. Studies, however, report the increase of other hazards, such as work intensification and non-standard employment, and the strong links between these different hazards and health inequalities.[62]

They support their argument by referring to a number of scientific findings establishing a link between employment conditions and health, especially unemployment, precarious employment, informal work, child labourers and bonded and slave labourers. They refer to research that shows that welfare regimes may help reduce health gaps and that 'wealthy countries with strong labour institutions, such as Sweden, tend to have the least harmful forms of employment relations, whereas equally wealthy but less labour friendly countries, such as the US, have higher occupational fatality rates.'[63] Of course heavy pressure on workers harmful to their health occurs even in the absence of economic crises. Table 5.14 presents the results of research conducted in 1997 in a country with a reputation for fair

Table 5.14 Self-perceived health status according to levels of job insecurity in Switzerland, 1997

Self-reported status	% difference between people with low fear and people with high fear of losing job
Not being in good health	+ 60
High perceived level of stress	+ 60
Low self-esteem	+ 190
Sleeplessness (regularly and often)	+ 60
Tranquillizers (daily or weekly consumption)	+ 110
Lower back pain (regularly)	+ 100
Smoking (regularly)	+ 60
Alcohol consumption (regularly)	+ 30
Have avoided medical consultation for fear of missing work (and losing job)	+ 240

Source: adapted from Gian-Franco Domenighetti *et al.*, *Health Effects of Job Insecurity*, Lausanne, HEC, 1999.

labour working conditions, Switzerland, but which has somehow deregulated the labour market, thereby very well illustrating this point: people in a working situation characterized by a high level of stress, resulting from the deregulation of the labour market, experience a far worse perceived health situation than people in a more stable working situation.[64] The difference in percentage between people with low fear and high fear of losing jobs is very high, and varies from 60 per cent for the self-perception of not being in good health to 240 per cent for not consulting the doctor for fear of losing the job.

Conclusion

The data presented in this chapter confirm to a large extent the four hypotheses upon which we have based this book. First, differences in the implementation of NPM have in fact produced different outcomes, as the opposition between, for example, Scandinavian countries on one hand, and the beacon NPM countries (UK and USA) on the other have shown on almost every count. In this respect it is interesting to note that even within the group of strong-NPM countries differences in the implementation of NPM devices can bring about different outcomes, as the example of the good performance of the British NHS compared with the US health system demonstrates.

Second, the data presented above also confirm that, in spite of differences in the cultural, economic, legal and political structures, similar public management strategies produce similar results. Similar, of course, does not mean identical. Indeed, even if there are important differences between strong- and weak-NPM countries, all the OECD countries have shown a common trend, for example an increase of income inequality and of the rate of poverty, even if with different magnitudes, as we have discovered in the process of verifying the first hypothesis. A more recent analysis summarizing three complementary research studies confirms that, in spite of differences amongst Western countries, the general trend is towards an increase in income inequalities, even if one leaves aside the USA and the UK, the strongest-NPM countries.[65] Moreover, in the general conclusion to this book I will take into consideration the impact of the 2008–11 crisis on Western countries. As 27 European countries are members of one of the most neoliberal organizations in the West, the European Union (17 of which are members of the Eurozone), it will be interesting to see to what extent the strategy implemented by these countries has contributed to overcoming the crisis, and what are the consequences for the inequalities, and more particularly for the poverty rates I have presented in this chapter. Finally, it will be interesting to verify this second hypothesis in Chapter 6, when dealing with China, a country that presents some remarkable differences from Western countries in the cultural, legal, economic and political structures.

The third hypothesis, that it is impossible to maximize economic efficiency and social equity simultaneously, has also been proven to correspond to the reality of Western countries. Practically all these countries have given more space to the market and have thus succeeded in improving economic efficiency; but the cost of doing so was the deterioration (to various degrees – according to the strong- and weak-NPM countries) of the equitable distribution of wealth.

The fourth hypothesis will be tested at the end of Chapter 6 dealing with China and in the conclusion: differences in the structure of the political system and of its relation to the economy (and within the economy to the economic agents managing the economy) may have an impact on the capacity of the state to react to the negative consequences of NPM implementation, and this would eventually lead to different policy answers, especially during the 2008–11 economic crisis.

At the end of our journey within the negative social consequences of NPM in the West, I am pleased to note that other researchers have embarked on a similar endeavour. Let me then finish this section by quoting the remarkable research by Richard Wilkinson and Kate Pickett.[66] Their research is based upon World Bank data of 2002 concerning a choice of developed countries comprising western Europe (i.e. Austria, Belgium, Denmark, Finland, France, Germany, Greece, Ireland, Italy, the Netherlands, Norway, Portugal, Spain, Sweden, Switzerland and the United Kingdom) as well as Australia, Israel, New Zealand, Singapore, Japan and the United States. Furthermore, the authors have built an Index of Health and Social Problems (IHSP) which is based upon 10 indicators: level of trust, mental illness, life expectancy, infant mortality, obesity, children's educational performance, teenage births, homicides, imprisonment rates and social mobility. Then they correlate these indicators with income inequality. The general index, comprising all dimensions, shows very clearly that the more unequal countries – the NPM beacon countries (the USA, the UK and to a lesser extent New Zealand) joined by Portugal – do very badly, whereas the northern European countries (Finland, Norway, Denmark and Sweden) joined by Belgium and especially Japan are the best performers, the other countries being placed somewhere in between. On the single dimensions, a similar pattern is reproduced, with some minor exceptions, for trust, mental illness, drug use and obesity, whereas the other dimensions, life expectancy, infant mortality, teenage births, crimes and imprisonment rates, education and social mobility, confirm my own analysis presented above.[67]

The conclusions of the authors are worth mentioning. First, 'the most important health and social problems of the rich world are more common in more unequal societies' and 'the relation is too strong to be dismissed as chance findings.' Second, 'the differences between more and less equal societies are large (from three to ten times).' Third:

> these differences are not differences between high- and low-risk groups within populations which might apply only to a small proportion of the population, or just to the poor. Rather, they are differences between the prevalence of different problems which apply to whole populations.

Fourth, it is possible

> to predict a country's performance on one outcome from knowledge of others. If – for instance – a country does badly on health, you can predict with some

confidence that it will also imprison a larger proportion of its population, have more teenage pregnancies . . . and so on. Finally, at the one end of the distribution we always seem to find the Scandinavian countries and Japan. At the opposite end, suffering high rates of most of the health and social problems, are usually the US, Portugal and the UK.

It is also interesting to note that the authors point to the different strategies Japan and Sweden resort to, to get greater equality within their societies: 'Sweden does it through redistributive taxes and benefits . . . Japan gets its high degree of equality not so much from redistribution as from greater equality of market incomes, of earnings before taxes and benefits.'[68] This interesting suggestion is that greater equality can be achieved through different strategies and policies, and this will be of some interest when we deal with the case of China in the next and last chapter. However, the research of Richard Wilkinson and Kate Pickett confirms that a healthy society is more likely to be realized when a more equal distribution of income prevails and that NPM is very unlikely to help us towards this goal.

6 The Chinese experiment
Many success stories, considerable disparities and environmental damages, but also an astonishing capacity for reversing past policies

As I have done for the West in Chapter 5, I will first present the economic performance of China's reforms since 1978, what I have called China's New Public Management. Then I will present the negative economic and social consequences of these reforms.[1] In the second section I will also devote some space to the analysis of the consequences of the new policies that 'put people first' on the rebalancing of Chinese society. I will propose an answer to the question: have these policies succeeded in reversing the trend towards increased inequalities and environmental damages that appeared since the beginning of reforms in the1980s?

The economic perspective: a view from above, or catching up with the West

In this part, by presenting the economic results obtained thanks to the reforms implemented under the leadership of Deng Xiaoping and Jiang Zemin, I will also try to evaluate to what extent China has succeeded in catching up with the West, and above all with the United States.

The positive outcomes of marketization

Since the beginning of reforms some spectacular results have been obtained. First, by taking the distribution of manpower in the three economic sectors as well as their contribution to GDP as a measure of economic modernization, we see that the contribution to labour by agriculture has decreased from 83.5 per cent in 1952 to 38.1 per cent in 2009, whereas during the same time the contribution of industry has increased from 7.4 to 27.8 per cent and that of services from 9.1 to 34.1 per cent (see Table 6.1). Even more spectacular has been the decline of the contribution of agriculture to GDP: during the same period it has decreased from 50.5 to 4.53 per cent, while the contribution of industry increased from 20.9 to 52.52 per cent, and that of services from 8.6 to 42.95 per cent.

In its 1997 report on China (i.e. before the reform trend was confirmed and accelerated by the September 1997 Congress of the CPC) the World Bank compared the time needed for doubling the GDP by several countries: the United Kingdom needed 58 years (1780–1838), the USA 47 (1839–86), Japan 34

Table 6.1 Changes in employment and GDP of the three economic sectors in China, 1952–2009 (%)

	Employment					Gross domestic product (GDP)				
	1952	1978	2003	2006	2009	1952	1978	2003	2006	2009
Agriculture	83.5	70.5	49.1	48.6	38.1	50.5	28.1	14.6	4.78	4.53
Industry	7.4	17.3	21.6	25.2	27.8	20.9	48.2	52.3	50.04	52.52
Services	9.1	12.2	29.3	32.2	34.1	8.6	23.7	33.1	45.18	42.95

Source: calculated by Professor Hu Angang, Tsinghua University, Beijing, from official data, National Bureau of Statistics of China (NBSC).

(1885–1919), South Korea 11 (1966–77) and China only nine (1978–87), not only once but twice (the second time from 1987 to 1996) and, even more impressively, during two consecutive periods of about 10 years.[2] We know that during the following decade (2000–10) China again doubled its GDP. Even the 2008–11 crisis has not stopped China's GDP rise: 9.0 per cent in 2008, 8.7 in 2009 and 10 per cent in 2010.[3] Other data confirm the spectacular development of the Chinese economy and the related domains: (1) the general standard of living has considerably improved (even though, as we shall see, it is counterbalanced by the increasing disparities between regions, provinces and individuals within provinces), (2) extreme poverty has been eradicated, (3) housing has been improved, especially in the coastal regions, (4) communication infrastructure has been improved (railways, roads, telecommunication) and (5) the education system has been improved at all levels; illiteracy has almost completely disappeared.

More recently, the World Bank has considered that China either has achieved most of the Millennium Development Goals of the United Nations or is well on the way to achieving them, and that between 1981 and 2004 the fraction of the population consuming less than a dollar per day fell from 65 to 10 per cent, and more than half a billion people were lifted out of poverty. Even if the rate of poverty is higher when measured by the new international poverty standard of $1.25 per person per day (using 2005 purchasing power parity for China), the decrease since 1981 is no less impressive: from 85 in 1981 to 27 per cent in 2004.[4]

Table 6.2 presents the most recent data for the main indicators of China's economy between 2004 and 2010. Taking into consideration the performance up to the third quarter of 2010, the World Bank comments as follows on China's economic performance: GDP growth declined from 10.6 per cent in the first half of 2010 to 'a still surprisingly strong 9.6 percent (year on year) in the third quarter', and the WB forecast a GDP growth of 10 per cent for 2010; exports are strong again (after the slowdown of 2008–9), while imports are slowing after the surge of the first quarter of 2010 so that net external trade has contributed significantly to growth and the external surplus is rising again; China's rapid growth during the global crisis reflected large-scale stimulus and strong underlying growth drivers; the energy intensity (i.e. energy consumption per unit of GDP) has been reduced and the World Bank recognizes that China has made impressive achievements

Table 6.2 China's main economic indicators, 2004–10

	2004	2005	2006	2007	2008	2009	2010
Population (million)	1,300	1,308	1,314	1,321	1,327	1,335	1,338
Real GDP growth (%)	10.1	10.4	11.6	11.9	9.0	8.7	10.3
Nominal GDP (US$ billion)	1,936	2,203	2,774	3,242	4,401	4,909	5,878
GDP per head (US$ at PPP)	3,068	4,186	4,793	5,478	5,962	6,914	7,536
Consumer inflation (%)	2.3	1.7	2.8	6.7	5.8	0.7	3.3
Current account balance (US$ billion)	68.7	160.8	249.9	371.8	440.0	297.1	305.4
Foreign exchange reserves (US$bn)	618.6	825.6	1,072.6	1,534.4	1,951.0	2,399.1	2,913.7
Exchange rate (RMB–US$)	8.28	8.07	7.81	7.31	6.82	6.8279	6.7703

Sources: elaborated by author from Economist Intelligence Unit, Country Report, June 2008; IMF Data Bank 2009; World Bank's China Quarterly Update, March 2009 and March 2011; Bulletin on National Population and Birth Control, 2009 for 2009 data; World Bank, 2010 for nominal GDP 2009; Asian Development Bank, 2010 for GDP per head US$ at PPP; NBSC, 21 January 2010 for 2009 data; http://www.chinability.com/CurrentAccount.htm for 2009 current account; People's Bank of China, December 2009, http://www.pbc.gov.cn/publish/html/2009s08.htm, for 2009 data. All data for 2010 from World Bank.

in energy conservation and renewable energy during the Eleventh Five-Year Plan; labour productivity has grown; China's terms of trade were unfavourable in the first half of 2010 but are turning around; consumer price inflation has risen above 3 per cent and is unlikely to escalate, but the World Bank warns that it could increase under pressure from commodity prices and increase in wages; and China's fiscal position remains sound, which helps to provide policy space.[5]

This remarkable economic situation goes together with the improvement of the relative position of China in the world economy.[6] It must be said, before we go any further, that most of the time the data presented to evaluate China's position in the world economy take into consideration not the European Union (EU) but its member-states. Of course the EU is not a state in the legal sense of the term. Nevertheless, talking about the economy, one must recognize that the EU is a 'common market' with a customs union and an internal market with a high degree of liberalization for goods, services, capital and labour. Moreover, 17 member-states of the Union have renounced their national currencies and constituted the so-called Eurozone, establishing a common currency, the euro, which, in spite of several difficulties and the forecast put forward by many experts about its (imminent) collapse, has established itself as an international currency, second only to the US dollar.[7] And this in spite of the serious crisis the Euro is experiencing at the end of 2011, at the moment of completing the manuscript of this book. It would therefore be more accurate, when making international comparison, to take into account the EU and the Eurozone. What is, for example, the purpose of talking about Germany's exports? It is the exports of the EU that matter. Only if one would like to evaluate the vigour of German firms in the global market compared with those of, say, Romania would that make sense. Similarly, when evaluating the contribution of the USA to global exports, it would not make sense to compare the contribution of California and, say, New England. The EU is an economic zone comprising 27 member-states, with almost half a billion people, with the highest GDP in the world, a standard of living amongst the highest in the world (in spite of the inclusion of several weak national economies from eastern and southern Europe) a highly qualified workforce, a strong technology in many domains and, last but not least, one of the most efficient welfare systems, in spite of the limits posed to it by the attacks from the neoliberal policies we have examined in Chapter 5. For example, according to the latest estimates of the CIA's Factbook[8] for GDP in purchasing power parity, in 2010 the European Union was in first place with $14,900 billion, the USA second with $14,720 billion and China third with $9,872 billion.

Bearing that in mind, in the following paragraphs I will follow the most frequently used way of presenting comparative data and will present China's position in the world economy without introducing data on the EU. First of all, let us look at China's share in the world GDP as shown in Table 6.3. In 2010 China's share was nearly 4.6 times what it was in 1950. Measured at purchasing power parity, it approaches that of the world's rich countries, and it has overtaken Germany and Japan to become the world's next biggest economy after the USA. Whereas China's GDP was just under one-third of world GDP in 1820 (i.e. before its decline during the Qing Dynasty), it dramatically dropped to 17.05 per cent a

Table 6.3 The proportion of China's GDP in the world total, 1820–2030

	1820	1870	1913	1929	1950	1973	2000	2010	2020	2030
China	32.88	17.05	8.83	7.37	4.50	4.62	11.23	20.70	28.90	33.40
USA	1.80	8.84	18.94	22.70	27.32	22.07	20.96	18.40	16.70	15.10
USA/China	0.05	0.52	2.14	3.08	6.07	4.78	1.87	0.89	0.57	0.45
Japan	2.98	2.28	2.62	3.45	3.02	7.76	6.87	5.40	4.40	3.20
UK	5.21	9.00	8.22	6.76	6.53	4.22	3.40	2.80	?	?
Germany	3.86	6.48	8.69	7.06	4.98	5.90	4.33	3.40	?	?
Russia	5.42	7.52	8.50	6.42	9.57	9.44	4.77	2.40	2.70	3.00
India	16.02	12.12	7.48	6.52	4.17	3.09	4.76	8.00	12.20	18.60

Sources: data for 1820–2000 are based on Angus Maddison, *The World Economy: A Millennial Perspective*, Chinese edition, translated by Wu Xiaoying, Beijing, Beijing University Press, 2003, pp. 178, 208. Data for 2010–2030 are estimated by Hu Angang, *China by 2030: A Changing World towards Common Prosperity* (in Chinese), place, Renmin University Press, 2011, p. 30. Table kindly provided by Professor Hu Angang.

Note: percentages calculated using purchasing power parity and 1990 international dollar by Professor Hu Angang, Tsinghua University.

few years after the second opium war (1870) and continued to drop until 1973 (i.e. about seven years before the beginning of the reform era), to reach 4.62 per cent. However, 20 years after the beginning of reforms, by the year 2000, it was already 11.23 per cent, and it even reached 20.70 per cent in 2010. Its ratio to American GDP decreased from 6.07 in 1950 to 0.89 in 2010.

Also, China's position has dramatically increased in the global economy if we take the share of exports (Table 6.4). In 1870 China had only a 2.49 per cent share of the world's exports, when the UK dominated international trade with a 21.76 per cent share. However, in 2010 China's share surged to 10.4 per cent, surpassing all the major players.

Finally, Table 6.5 shows the same pattern if we take China's share in world industrial output. In 1953 China's share had dropped to 2.3 per cent from a high near 30 per cent in 1830, when the USA (44.7 per cent), Russia (10.7) and the UK (8.4) dominated the world's industrial output. However, in 2009 China's industrial output rose to 15.29, second only to the USA (17.43).

So far, we have seen the overall performance of economic development measured by GDP and China's share in the world GDP, exports and industrial output. How does this development translate into the lives of Chinese people? Table 6.6 and Figure 6.1 provide some answers. For urban areas, the annual disposable nominal income has increased from a very low 343 RMB per year in 1978, at the beginning of reforms, to a fairly high 17,174.7 RMB in 2009, which is 50 times more. The improvement in the rural areas has been less impressive, but nevertheless, for net per capita nominal income, it increased 38.6 times from a very low 133.6 RMB per year in 1978 to 5,153.2 RMB in 2009. Of course, the data provided in Table 6.6 and also inform us of the income disparities between rural and urban areas. I will come back to this important aspect of China's development. What is interesting to note for the moment is that, in spite of significant

Table 6.4 The proportion of exports in the world total (%, 1820–2030)

	1820	1870	1913	1929	1950	1973	1998	2008	2009	2010	2020	2030
UK	15.51	21.76	16.65	9.57	10.47	5.27	4.77	2.8	2.90	?	?	?
Germany	–	12.02	16.16	10.49	3.51	10.80	9.75	9.1	9.80	?	?	?
US	3.46	4.44	8.12	9.08	11.47	9.71	12.81	8.1	8.21	8.4	10.0	9.0
Russia	na	na	2.82	1.02	1.72	3.23	2.06	2.9	2.44	2.5	2.7	3.5
China	na	2.49	1.78	1.87	1.69	0.65	3.27	8.9	9.86	10.4	18.0	24.0
Japan	na	0.09	0.71	1.30	0.94	5.29	5.95	4.9	4.3	5.1	5.0	4.0
India	na	6.16	4.01	2.45	1.46	0.54	0.70	1.1	1.28	1.4	2.4	5.0

Sources: Angus Maddison, *The World Economy: A Millennial Perspective*, Chinese edition, translated by Wu Xiaoying, Beijing, Beijing University Press, 2003 edition, p. 358; World Bank (2009) *World Development Indicators 2009*, Washington, DC; WTO (2009) *World Trade Report 2009*, Geneva; CIA (Central Intelligence Agency) *Factbook 2009*, US Government, https://www.cia.gov/library/publications/the-world-factbook/ (accessed 19 March 2012). Data for 2010–2030 are estimated by Professor Hu Angang, *China by 2030 A Changing World towards Common Prosperity*, Renmin University Press, Beijing, 2011, p. 34. Table kindly provided by Professor Hu Angang.

150 *The crisis of New Public Management in the West and in China*

Table 6.5 The proportion of China's industrial output in the world total, 1830–2009

	1830	1900	1953	1973	1980	1990	2004	2007	2008	2009
UK	9.5	18.5	8.4	4.9	5.24	4.58	4.36	3.8	3.19	2.73
Germany	3.5	13.2	5.9	5.9	8.65	8.52	6.60	5.75	5.73	5.21
USA	2.4	23.6	44.7	33.0	21.75	21.84	21.80	20.4	16.89	17.43
Russia	5.6	8.8	10.7	14.4	n/a	3.40	1.65	2.39	3.03	2.34
China	29.8	6.2	2.3	3.9	2.31	2.16	8.15	9.63	12.73	15.29
Japan	2.8	2.4	2.9	8.8	10.93	17.43	12.58	9.78	8.07	n/a
India	17.6	1.7	1.7	2.1	1.02	1.15	1.59	1.83	1.92	2.31

Sources: data for 1830–2007 are based on Paul Bairoch, 'International industrialization levels from 1750 to 1980', *Journal of European Economic History*, Fall 1982, vol. 11, nos. 1 & 2. Data for 2008–9 are based on World Bank, World Bank Indicators, 2011, http://data.worldbank.org/data-catalog/world-development-indicators/wdi-2010. Table kindly provided by Professor Hu Angang, Tsinghua University.

Note: percentages calculated by Professor Hu Angang, Tsinghua University.

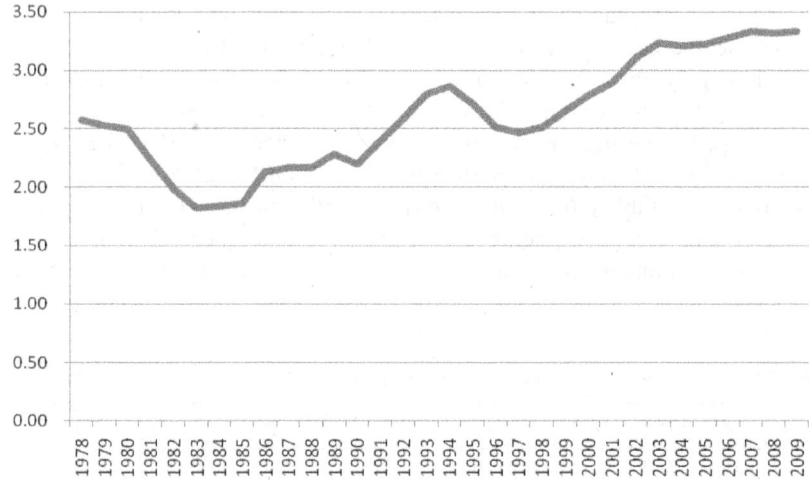

Figure 6.1 The ratio of China's urban nominal per capita annual disposable income to rural per capita net nominal income, 1978–2009. Sources: 1978–2008 data from *China Compendium of Statistics 1949–2008*, compiled by the Department of Comprehensive Statistics of the National Bureau Statistics, Beijing, China Statistics Press, 2010, p. 25; 2009 data from the National Bureau of Statistics of China, *China Statistical Abstract 2010* (in Chinese), Beijing, China Statistics Press, 2010, pp. 113, 115 and 119.

disparities between urban and rural personal incomes, both have increased since the beginning of reforms.[9]

Nevertheless, in international comparison, the improvement of the situation of Chinese people is far less spectacular than what appears from the overall economic indicators. Indeed, China's situation is much less favourable if we take into

Table 6.6 China's urban per capita annual nominal disposable income and rural per capita net nominal income, 1978–2009

	Ratio [1]/[2]	Urban per capita disposable annual nominal income (yuan) [1]	Rural per capita net annual nominal income (yuan) [2]
1978	2.57	343.4	133.6
1979	2.53	405.0	160.2
1980	2.50	477.6	191.3
1981	2.24	500.4	223.4
1982	1.98	535.3	270.1
1983	1.82	564.6	309.8
1984	1.84	652.1	355.3
1985	1.86	739.1	397.6
1986	2.13	900.9	423.8
1987	2.17	1,002.1	462.6
1988	2.17	1,180.2	544.9
1989	2.28	1,373.9	601.5
1990	2.20	1,510.2	686.3
1991	2.40	1,700.6	708.6
1992	2.58	2,026.6	784.0
1993	2.80	2,577.4	921.6
1994	2.86	3,496.2	1,221.0
1995	2.71	4,283.0	1,577.7
1996	2.51	4,838.9	1,926.1
1997	2.47	5,160.3	2,090.1
1998	2.51	5,425.1	2,162.0
1999	2.65	5,854.0	2,210.3
2000	2.79	6,280.0	2,253.4
2001	2.90	6,859.6	2,366.4
2002	3.11	7,702.8	2,475.6
2003	3.23	8,472.2	2,622.2
2004	3.21	9,421.6	2,936.4
2005	3.22	10,493.0	3,254.9
2006	3.28	11,759.5	3,587.0
2007	3.33	13,785.8	4,140.4
2008	3.31	15,780.8	4,760.6
2009	3.33	17,174.7	5,153.2

Sources: 1978–2008 data from *China Compendium of Statistics 1949–2008*, compiled by the Department of Comprehensive Statistics of the National Bureau Statistics, Beijing, China Statistics Press, 2010, p. 25; 2009 data from the National Bureau of Statistics of China, *China Statistical Abstract 2010* (in Chinese), Beijing, China Statistics Press, 2010, pp. 113, 115 and 119.

consideration GDP per capita: it is now estimated to be between $PPP6,000 and $PPP7,400 (according to the CIA's Factbook, 2010); and this ranks China at 127 out of 233 countries.[10] For example (taking the most recent data from the CIA's Factbook), China's GDP per capita in purchasing power party in US dollars is 7.7 times less than that of Norway (rank 5 in the world), 6.4 times less than that of the USA (rank 10), 5.8 than that of Switzerland (rank 16), 4.8 than that of Germany (rank 31), 4.7 than that of the UK (rank 36) and 4.4 than that of the European Union. Notwithstanding the above, there is no doubt that per capita revenue has been sustained by the growth of GDP, even if the newly created wealth has been very unevenly distributed amongst Chinese people, as I will consider in more detail later in this chapter. It is also plausible that in the future the evolution of per capita income will be more than proportionally linked to GDP growth, as the Chinese leadership has fully understood the danger of the inequalities that have dramatically increased since the 1990s, and is taking serious measures to rebalance the economy, especially after the adoption of the Eleventh Five-Year Plan in 2005 and the decisions announced by President Hu Jintao at the November 2007 Party Congress, more particularly in the domain of social policies.

It is of course possible to argue that monetary income is important for people living in a country where the main source of personal income is determined by one's position in the labour market. In fact, it is thanks to salaries earned in the labour market that one is able to purchase the goods and services one needs. Nevertheless, as I have already pointed out in Chapter 2, monetary income tells only part of the story. This gap is filled, at least partially, by the Human Development Index (HDI) developed by the United Nations Development Programme (UNDP), which combines life expectancy at birth, education (measured by literacy) and GDP per capita.[11] Table 6.7 shows that in 1980 China's HDI index was the same as Sudan's in 2007, and in 2007 China had the same HDI as the Dominican Republic in the same year. Taking the UNDP data for 1975, when China's HDI was 0.527, we can see that between 1975 and 1980 (i.e. during the Mao era) there was only a very small improvement (+0.033), whereas in the reform era, from 1980 on, the improvement is constant and impressive. According to UNDP calculations, between 1980 and 2006 China improved its HDI by 0.226, second only to Egypt (+0.233) and

Table 6.7 China's improvement measured by the 'old' HDI Index, 1980–2007

Year	1980	1985	1990	1995	2000	2006	2007
China's rank	131	128	125	117	101	94	92
China's HDI	0.529	0.596	0.628	0.685	0.730	0.762	0.772
Comparable country in 2007	Sudan	Cambodia	India	Namibia	Indonesia	Paraguay	Dominican Republic

Source: United Nations Development Programme (UNDP), *Human Development Reports*, New York, published by UNDP for 2004 and 2005, and by Palgrave Macmillan for UNDP since 2006.

before Nepal (+0.222), Iran (+0.218) and Indonesia (+0.205), while all the other countries in the UNDP statistics increased their HDI by less than 0.200.[12] At that time, the UNDP subdivided countries into three categories: High (HDI above 0.8), Medium (HDI between 0.5 and 0.8) and Low human development (HDI under 0.5). In 2007, ranked at number 92, China was in the upper part of the Medium HDI (0.772) with good prospects of reaching the High development group in a not too distant future. The 2010 Human Development Report, introducing the new HDI, does not present the progress of countries by rank. Nevertheless, in the 2010 report the UNDP provides evidence showing that China's new HDI progressed from 0.338 in 1980 to 0.663 in 2010, and that between 1980 and 2010 China's average annual HDI growth rate was 1.83 per cent, the highest for all countries belonging to the Medium development group.[13]

As I have already said in Chapter 2 (pp. 59–62), since the 2009 Report the UNDP countries are classified into four categories: Very high, High, Medium and Low development. The 2010 Report introduced a new methodology for calculating the HDI. The new HDI places China within the Medium development group at the 89th rank, in second position (with the Dominican Republic, with HDI 0.663), after Fiji and Turkmenistan (both with HDI 0.669). All the Western countries are in the Very high development group with scores between 0.701 (former Yugoslavia) and 0.938 (Norway).

Please refer to Table 5.9, which shows the ranking with the old HDI for 2007 and the new one for 2010 for a choice of the Western countries we have taken into consideration in Chapter 5; China has been added in the last row. We can see that, in spite of the considerable progress realized since the beginning of reforms, China is still far away from the Western countries. Nevertheless, when we take the inequality-adjusted index we see that China does slightly better and jumps to rank 82 from rank 89. Even more impressive is its achievement when we take the gender inequality index: at rank 38 China is just behind the USA (rank 37), even if this achievement must be qualified, as the USA is by far the worst Western country on this count. Here again, as we have already seen in Chapter 5, whereas the English-speaking strong-NPM countries (with the exception of the UK) do slightly better than the continental European countries on the HDI index (and especially with the new HDI), as soon as we adjust the new HDI for inequality, and especially gender inequality, continental European countries (and more particularly the weak-NPM Scandinavian countries) do much better than the English-speaking ones. France, Italy and Austria are somewhere in between, and seem to suffer from their recent trends in favour of more liberal public policies. Only the countries of southern Europe (Spain, Greece and Portugal) are clearly behind the others on practically all the indices.

I am convinced that these results, and especially the causes that explain them, should encourage the Chinese leadership to sustain and develop the new policies that it has developed in recent years aiming at correcting the disparities that have developed within China as a consequence of the reform process that has privileged economic development over human development. In commenting the results presented in its 2010 Report, the UNDP writes:

The economy grew at a phenomenal 8 percent a year for three decades, and monetary poverty measures fell more than 80 percent between 1981 and 2005. Yet this success was not matched by performance in other dimensions of human development. China ranks first in economic growth since 1970, but 79th of 135 countries in improving education and health. In fact, China is 1 of only 10 countries in the 135 country sample to have a lower gross enrolment ratio now than in the 1970s. Slow progress was associated with decentralizing the financing of basic services without providing adequate national support or increasing the fees levied on families. Public social services deteriorated and in some places even collapsed. The costs of single-minded pursuit of economic growth also became apparent in other dimensions [i.e. environmental pollution of land, water and air]. Income inequalities worsened. By 2008 per capita household consumption in the coastal region of Guangdong was more than four times that of Tibet.

However, at the end of this comment UNDP recognizes that 'Reducing social imbalances is now a priority in the five-year plan. China has also recently launched major new policy initiatives aiming to develop a low-carbon economy and expand adoption of climate-friendly technologies'.[14] We will come back to this important issue. For the moment it is interesting to take into consideration the progress made by the provinces, an important angle from which to tackle China's development, given the size of the country and the differences that exist within it.

China is a very complicated country. It is common in Western comments about China to reproduce the Chinese slogan 'one country, two systems' referring to the special administrative and political arrangement concerning Hong Kong and Macao. The Tsinghua professor Hu Angang has put forward another more interesting slogan: 'one China four worlds – one China four societies', referring to 'different systems of identity, education, employment, public service, and financial transfer for the inhabitants in rural and urban areas. "Four worlds" refers to the reflection of China's unbalanced development in different regions'.[15] Moreover, according to Hu, China can be subdivided into four societies: farming, manufacturing, services and knowledge.[16] We will see in the following paragraphs to what extent this diversity constitutes a negative outcome of the strategy of development giving priority to economy development over human development. For the moment, it is interesting to show that this diversity presents also some positive aspects.

Let us start with the HDI referred to the Chinese provinces as presented in Table 6.8.

Because the new HDI does not provide all the data needed for the following analysis, we will deal with the old HDI, for which UNDP provides data for 2008 for the Chinese provinces and for 2007 for the 182 countries considered by UNDP reports. For this reason, the analysis is a little distorted, but given the general trend (provided by UNDP) over a period of 20 years, and the small changes from one year to the next, the distortion is certainly negligible. Nevertheless, we will also refer to the new HDI whenever possible and necessary. Recall that the old HDI places countries within three groups, high, medium and low human development. What can be said from the data in Table 6.8? Apart from the very unequal level of development of the Chinese provinces (which I will deal with later) we can first of all remark that 14 provinces are placed within the 'high development group' above the 85th rank (equal to Ukraine), between the 34th rank (Shanghai, equal to Portugal) and the 83rd rank (Shanxi, equal to Lebanon) out of a total of 182 countries. All the remaining provinces are placed within the 'medium development group' between the 86th rank (Henan, equal to Azerbaijan) and the 133rd rank (Tibet, equal to Laos). Therefore, there are no provinces in the 'low human development' group. Also, if we take the classification of countries into four categories provided by UNDP since the 2009 report presenting the new HDI, there would be only one province (Shanghai) within the 'Very high development' group. So the first conclusion is that in spite of considerable differences the Chinese provinces present an overall profile that reflects the considerable improvement in the Chinese economy since the beginning of reforms in the early 1980s.

The second conclusion, taking again the old HDI, is that the Chinese provinces do much better for one component of the HDI, the education index, than for the GDP per capita and life expectancy indexes. For the HDI we have already seen that only Shanghai (rank 1 in China, with HDI 0.908) can match one of the countries (i.e. Portugal) placed within the upper part of the 'high development' group of the old HDI, i.e. above rank 38, defining the limit above which countries belong to the 'Very high human development' group of the new HDI. Beijing (rank 2 in China) had an HDI equal to Bahrain (0.891, ranked 39th in the world) and slightly superior to Poland (rank 41 with 0.880). Tianjin (rank 3 in China) had an HDI equal to Chile (rank 44 with 0.875) and slightly inferior to Poland. After Tianjin, the next province, Guangdong, is placed at rank 58 with an HDI equal to 0.844, followed by Zhejiang at rank 61 (0.841), Jiangsu at rank 63 (0.837), Liaoning at rank 65 (0.835) and Shandong at rank 66 (0.828). All the other provinces are placed after rank 72 (equal to Macedonia).

Almost the same pattern can be observed for the life expectancy index. Only Shanghai has an index equal to one of the countries in the Very high development group: Denmark, which, however, has one of the lowest indices within this group, that is, above rank 38. Amongst the other provinces, only nine have an index above 0.800. The other provinces, with indices between 0.656 (Tibet) and 0.799 (Hainan), can only match countries such as Laos, Pakistan and Bolivia; the only European countries with an index below, albeit very close to, 0.800 are Estonia (0.799), Romania (0792), Latvia (0.788) and Lithuania (0.780).

The situation of China's provinces is even worse if we take the GDP per capita index. This is not surprising, after what I have said above on the country's per capita GDP, which in 2010 placed China in 127th place out of 233 countries.[17] Whereas all the countries placed in the Very high development group present a GDP index above 0.900, only three Chinese provinces approach this level: Shanghai (0.879, equal to Hungary), Beijing (0.854, equal to Poland) and Tianjin (0.833, equal to Russia). All the other provinces have an index below 0.800: seven between 0.700 and 0.800 (where we find countries such as Colombia, Thailand,

Table 6.8 Provincial Human Development Index (HDI) of China, 2008

Province	HDI rank in China	HDI	Equivalent country in 2007 (rank)	Life expectancy index	Life expectancy equivalent in 2007	Education index	Education index equivalent in 2007	GDP per capita index	GDP per capita equivalent in 2007
Beijing	2	0.891	Bahrain (39)	0.852	Croatia	0.968	USA	0.854	Poland
Tianjin	3	0.875	Chile (44)	0.832	Slovakia	0.962	Austria	0.833	Russia
Hebei	10	0.810	Brazil (75)	0.792	Romania	0.951	Poland	0.687	Jamaica
Shanxi	14	0.800	Lebanon (83)	0.778	Turkey	0.958	UK	0.666	Nicaragua
Inner Mongolia	13	0.803	Kazakhstan (82)	0.748	Azerbaijan	0.920	Croatia	0.742	Colombia
Liaoning	7	0.835	Montenegro (65)	0.806	Bulgaria	0.964	Austria	0.737	Thailand
Jilin	9	0.815	Dominica (73)	0.802	Hungary	0.955	Germany	0.689	Jamaica
Heilongjiang	11	0.808	Colombia (77)	0.790	Romania	0.958	UK	0.676	Armenia
Shanghai	1	0.908	Portugal (34)	0.886	Denmark	0.960	Hungary	0.879	Hungary
Jiangsu	6	0.837	Romania (63)	0.815	Serbia	0.921	Venezuela	0.776	Serbia
Zhejiang	5	0.841	Bulgaria (61)	0.828	Slovakia	0.907	Cyprus	0.787	Bulgaria
Anhui	26	0.750	Philippines (105)	0.781	Lithuania	0.860	Slovenia	0.608	Indonesia
Fujian	12	0.807	Brazil (75)	0.793	Romania	0.898	Bahrain	0.731	Peru
Jiangxi	25	0.760	Paraguay (101)	0.733	Belarus	0.936	Switzerland	0.612	Honduras
Shandong	8	0.828	Malaysia (66)	0.815	Vietnam	0.921	Venezuela	0.746	Colombia
Henan	15	0.787	Azerbaijan (86)	0.776	Turkey	0.927	Slovakia	0.659	Maldives

Hubei	16	0.784	Thailand (87)	0.768	Iran	0.923	Venezuela	0.661	Maldives
Hunan	19	0.781	Iran (88)	0.761	Iran	0.942	Argentina	0.640	Guatemala
Guangdong	4	0.844	Venezuela (58)	0.805	Bulgaria	0.960	Austria	0.768	Brazil
Guangxi	20	0.776	Dominican R. (89)	0.772	Turkey	0.944	Argentina	0.614	Honduras
Hainan	17	0.784	Thailand (87)	0.799	Bulgaria	0.916	Croatia	0.637	Thailand
Chongqing	18	0.783	Thailand (87)	0.779	Turkey	0.924	Slovakia	0.645	Georgia
Sichuan	24	0.763	Paraguay (101)	0.770	Turkey	0.899	Bahrain	0.618	Sri Lanka
Guizhou	30	0.690	Tajikistan (127)	0.683	Lithuania	0.860	Trinidad	0.526	Pakistan
Yunnan	28	0.710	Uzbekistan (120)	0.675	Bolivia	0.871	Kuwait	0.585	Philippines
Tibet	31	0.630	Laos (133)	0.656	Laos	0.634	Cameroon	0.601	Tonga
Shaanxi	22	0.773	Belize (93)	0.751	Egypt	0.919	Chile	0.647	Georgia
Gansu	29	0.705	Guatemala (122)	0.708	Kyrgyzstan	0.829	Saudi Arabia	0.579	El Salvador
Qinghai	27	0.720	Moldova (117)	0.684	Pakistan	0.838	Dominican R.	0.639	Paraguay
Ningxia	23	0.766	Jamaica (100)	0.753	Indonesia	0.903	Cyprus	0.644	Georgia
Xinjiang	21	0.774	Belize (93)	0.707	Kyrgyzstan	0.953	Germany	0.661	Maldives
National average		0.793	Ukraine (85)	0.773	Turkey	0.923	Portugal	0.683	Kazakhstan

Sources: Countries were introduced by author taking the indices closest to the Chinese provinces and, in case of equal or near to equal values, giving priority to Western developed countries. Data for Chinese provinces, for 2008, are taken from UNDP: *China Human Development Report 2009/2010*. Data for countries, for 2007, are taken from *UNDP Human Development Report*, 2009. There are no comparable data for 2008 for both Chinese provinces and foreign countries.

Serbia, Bulgaria, Peru and Brazil); 18 between 0.600 and 0.700 (alongside countries such as Jamaica, Armenia, Indonesia, Honduras, Guatemala, Georgia, Sri Lanka and Paraguay); and three between 0.500 and 0.600 (with countries such as Pakistan, Philippines and El Salvador).

The situation of Chinese provinces looks much better if we take the education index. Here 23 Chinese provinces have an index above 0.900 that places them within the upper part of the ranking, matching Western countries such as the USA, as well as European countries, such as Austria, Germany and Switzerland. This is a very interesting finding because a good education index is the proof that China has devoted much attention to the building of human capital, one of the most important factors for sustaining economic and social development. Moreover, education 'is one of the key paths out of poverty . . . and an important source of inequality.'[18] This finding must be appreciated in the framework of the overall strategy of improving human capital.[19]

First of all, from about 1980 to about 2008 the average educational years have increased from 4.6 to 8.8. Second, China has increased the number of people at the different levels of the education system, especially at university level. Third, the government has invested heavily in higher education, not only in infrastructure facilities, but also in the training of researchers and professors, many of whom have spent some time (in some cases several years) abroad. The salaries of university personnel have been increased accordingly. In 2008, 98.3 million people had received higher education.[20]

The second dimension of human capital, professional training and development, has also been improved. In 2008 China had about 98 million people with professional training, 9.2 per cent of whom had received higher education; and programmes of continued education have been set up. Moreover, concerning science and technology, the number of scientific papers presented by Chinese scientists has grown from 20,000 in 1998 to 112,000 in 2008, compared with 265,000 to 340,000 in the USA for the same years. Moreover, the percentage of China's patent application in the world total has increased from 0.7 to 12.3 per cent in 2006 (compared with 34.9 and 22.3 per cent for Japan and the USA respectively). Finally, research and development expenditures have increased from 2.1 per cent of the world total (in PPP) in 1980 to 7 per cent in 2007 (compared with 10 and 23.8 per cent in Japan and the USA respectively). Of course, the most frequent objection put to these data is that quantity does not necessarily lead to quality. This is of course true, but only up to a certain point. To take just one example, university colleagues know from experience that in a class of 100 undergraduate students there may be just one who becomes an excellent PhD student. However, with 1,000 undergraduates we will have 10 excellent PhD students, with 10,000 we will have 100, and so on. Of course, quantity may lead to quality only if the increase in the number of students goes together with an improvement of the curricula and of the teaching capacity of professors, and if there is efficient and fair control of the performance of both professors and students. This is just what is going on in China in the domains mentioned above. According to the influential *South China Morning Post*:

China has replaced Japan as the world's second leading producer of scientific research and is on course to overtake the United States in two years' time, a top British academy says. The report released by the Royal Society in London is based on the publication data of scientific research papers published in recognised international journals between 1999–03 and 2004–08.[21]

The third dimension of human capital is public health. An efficient and fair health system is necessary for sustaining the technical and professional capacities of the population concerned. It is perhaps here that China's strategy has shown its limits, especially since the mid-1990s. Before 1949 the health of the Chinese people was rather poor by international comparison. It is to the credit of the Mao era that China has succeeded in almost totally eradicating serious infectious and parasitic diseases, thanks to a medical system for workers and peasants, and especially for poor people. Mortality rates dropped significantly both for young and adult people; life expectancy at birth increased from about age 37 in 1950 to almost 66 in 1980. Moreover, this system assured fair access to health care to all Chinese people. In view of this achievement, Hu Angang can say:

> in spite of the fact that there was a huge gap between rural and urban areas, as far as health is concerned, even for those who were very poor, the living conditions were still better than their counterparts in most developing countries.[22]

Unfortunately, since 1978 less attention has been devoted to health, when the implementation of several neoliberal ideas requiring that people pay for health services out of their own pocket had the consequence of excluding from health care a huge percentage of the population in both rural and urban areas. The same can be said for education. I will come back to this point in the next section.

In concluding this section, we are nevertheless forced to admit that the data of Table 6.8 show considerable differences amongst the Chinese provinces, and this brings me to the next section analysing the negative consequences of economic development.

The social perspective: a view from below, or the development of inequalities

Introduction

Let us start right from the beginning with some interesting data from a study published by the World Bank already in 2003, presented in Figure 6.2, which is a good summary of the evolution of the Gini index and the number of poor people in China between the beginning of reforms (early 1980s) and the end of the twentieth century.[23] The analysis of the World Bank's data in this figure constitutes a good introduction to the problems posed to the Chinese leadership by the strategy of economic development chosen at the end of the Mao era. Looking at the general trend of the two indicators we see that at the end of the Mao era

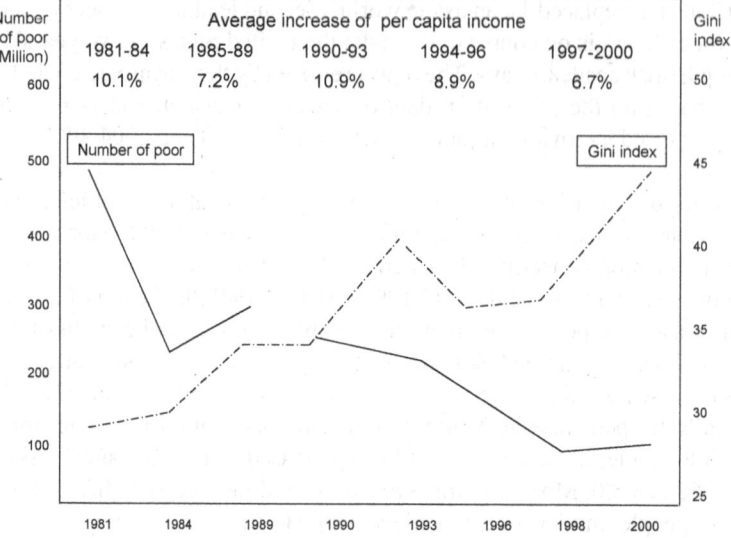

Figure 6.2 Income inequality and poverty in China, 1981–2000. Source: adapted by author from World Bank, *China: Promoting Growth with Equity*, p. 10. Data on number of poor were missing between 1989 and 1990 in the WB report.

the distribution of income was quite fair (low Gini index, just above 20) whereas the number of poor people was quite high, about 500 million. However, as soon as market mechanisms are introduced, economic efficiency is boosted, and the two indicators present a divergent evolution: poverty decreases dramatically while, at the same time, the Gini index increases showing that income distribution becomes more and more unequal (Gini index above 40 in 2000).[24] Looking at the details of the evolution of the two indicators, we see that, after a sharp decrease of poverty between 1981 and 1984 and a concomitant small increase of income inequality, there is a very sharp increase of both poverty and inequality between 1984 and 1989. This is due to the very liberal economic and social policies implemented by the Chinese government in the urban and industrial areas, that is, liberalization (especially of the labour market) with the consequent appearance of unemployment. This new situation (compared which what existed in the Mao era when SOEs were in charge of social policies in addition to their economic functions) is aggravated by the demise of the social functions of the SOEs and the failure to replace them with a modern welfare system. As a result, unemployed people fell inevitably into poverty. This situation clearly points to one of the major causes (maybe the major cause) of the protest movements that burst out in the spring of 1989 and led to the events on Tiananmen Square at the beginning of June of that same year. There was certainly also protest against corruption and a demand for more freedom, but one cannot interpret these events as a demand for a radical change of the regime along the Western model of liberal democracy.[25]

After reforms were further accelerated at the beginning of the 1990s there was again a divergent evolution of the two indicators: the number of poor people diminished while the index of inequality increased to about 40. Then, after a decrease between 1993 and 1996 and a small increase between 1996 and 1998, and following the Party Congress of September 1997 (which confirmed and even accelerated the reform process) the Gini index suddenly increased dramatically to about 45 whereas, contrary to the general trend since the 1980s, the number of poor people started increasing again. Some more recent data confirm this new trend, which very likely corresponds to the appearance of new forms of poverty (both in the rural and urban areas) linked to the development of market mechanisms, as is the case for Western countries, as we have seen in Chapter 5. The appearance of unemployment, in conjunction with the one-child policy and the consequent destructuring of the traditional solidarity, clearly needs to be compensated for by the setting up of an important social policy: unemployment insurance.

Other sources of poverty manifested themselves during the 1990s as a result of some new public policies, clearly of neoliberal inspiration, when the government decided to request users to pay out of their own pocket for health care and education. These policies, which further widened the scope of the marketization and commodification of the Chinese economy, worsened the living conditions of the Chinese people, and above all those at the lowest end of the income distribution. This situation very clearly demands the setting up of two additional social policies: public education and public health available to everybody. We must recognize that the Chinese government has been quite slow in replacing the social functions of the SOEs of the Mao era, with the consequence of creating the conditions for the appearance of new forms of poverty. These uncertainties that hit a large part of the Chinese population explain the high level of savings of the Chinese families and the consequent limitation to households' spending. This has a negative impact on the level of domestic demand, and may constitute a handicap in case of international economic crises that will inevitably decrease the international demand for Chinese goods. The government has understood this problem and has started to reorient the development strategy by giving more space to the household's domestic demands by starting to set up (in addition to other measures) a modern welfare system comprising free public education (at least at the level of compulsory education), a new public health system, unemployment insurance and old age insurance. I will come back to these new policies later in this chapter. After having put forward in our analysis of China's development strategy the dilemma between economic efficiency and equity, thanks to the World Bank 2003 report, it is now necessary to start with unemployment, as I have done for the West in Chapter 5.

New Public Management and unemployment

Evaluating the actual size of unemployment in China is not an easy task, in part for the same reasons as I have mentioned for Western countries but also because of the way China has managed the appearance, first, and then the rapid and important surge of unemployment that followed the introduction of competition and the deregulation of the labour market. The number of people laid off by SOEs and state bureaucracies at all levels of government is estimated at several million people, or even several tens of millions. The difficulty of estimating the total number of people out of work is mainly because many of the laid-off people were recorded not as unemployed but under the name of *xiagang*. These people were not working, but were still on the payroll of public enterprises and bureaucracies benefiting from only very small allowances. This system was progressively abandoned between 2001 and 2005 when the *xiagang* workers were integrated into the unemployment insurance. However, even then, the number of unemployed and underemployed people is quite difficult to estimate, especially in the rural areas. In spite of these difficulties in obtaining reliable data, it is possible to formulate the following remarks. First, it was inevitable that some unemployment would appear as a consequence of the liberalizing of the economy, the introduction of competition among enterprises, the deregulation of the labour market and the streamlining of public bureaucracies. The question is how much unemployment, what the government would do, and what would be the situation of the unemployed.

If we look at the official statistics for urban areas, the registered unemployment rate was 5.3 per cent in 1978 and declined to 1.8 per cent in 1985 when it started to constantly increase (with some minor variations) to 2.6 in 1989 (at the moment of the June events on Tiananmen Square) and stabilized between 4 and 4.2 per cent between 2003 and 2008. According to an estimate in the CIA Factbook 2010, in September 2009 the unemployment rate was 4.3 per cent in urban areas. It is true that following the 2008 global financial crisis an estimated number of 20 million migrant workers lost their jobs in the urban areas, and this was announced by many Western commentators as a clear sign that the crisis had also had a very negative impact on China, whose fantastic economic development was generally attributed to the increase of exports (i.e. China's export-led development strategy).[26] However, leaving aside the examination of the validity of this interpretation of China's economic development, it remains the fact that these migrant workers returned to their villages, where they found opportunities to earn enough money to overcome the crisis. Many have been reported as having refused the offer of urban employers to work for less than 700 RMB per month. Even by earning less than that in their home villages in the rural areas they have been able to make their living, very likely in a more socially friendly environment than in the urban areas where they had found more remunerative jobs, but also very difficult living conditions. Moreover, the catastrophic forecast by many Western commentators announcing the end of the two-digit annual GDP increase have been contradicted by the astonishing capacity of China to rebound rapidly and to restart its long march towards prosperity. The World Bank, as mentioned above, forecast a 10 per cent increase of GDP for 2010, while the CIA estimated, in its 2010 Factbook, an increase of 10.3 per cent. Overall, this looks quite an excellent performance compared with Western countries. It is expected that this robust economic development will create new jobs that will reduce at least part of the existing unemployment, and offer job opportunities to the several million job seekers who every year enter the labour market.

Nevertheless, one cannot be satisfied with the unemployment official figures. Already in 2005 the Tsinghua University professor Hu Angang produced estimates showing that between 1987 and 1997 the unemployment rate for urban areas increased from 4.5 to 9.6 per cent, and then declined a little to 8 per cent in 2003.[27] These data suggest that in urban areas unemployment is about twice that shown in official data, at levels similar to some Western continental European countries at the same time, as well as to the UK and the USA after the outbreak of the 2008–11 crisis. However, it is generally recognized that actual unemployment is higher than that. In the presence of contradictory estimates, let us propose an approximate rate of about 10 per cent in the urban areas, and much more in the countryside, where there is also a considerable amount of underemployment.[28] Moreover, the cost of unemployment may be considered as a very negative consequence of economic development not only because of its economic cost, but also because it affects many people who are not responsible for their predicament, which put them very low down the social structure, and for many even below the poverty line. Hu Angang has measured the cost of unemployment between 1997 and 2000 as being between 5.2 and 7.4 per cent of GDP.[29]

Finally, the most disturbing fact about Chinese unemployment (whatever its rate) is, in my opinion, that until recently the support provided to the unemployed has been very limited. The first regulations dealing with unemployment in urban areas were introduced in 1986.[30] At the beginning, the Chinese government was reluctant to recognize that there existed unemployment in a socialist country and created the terminology of the 'layoff system' (*xiagang* in Chinese), which was presented as being different from unemployment. As mentioned before, under this system, although *xiagang* workers had in fact lost their jobs, they still kept a legal link with their enterprises. As the reform of SOEs was progressing at a very rapid pace, a huge number of workers were laid off, many of whom became permanently jobless owing to poor education and lack of professional skills, flexibility and adaptability to the new labour market conditions. In 1998, in view of the increased pressure on SOEs to reposition their redundant personnel, and the inadequate coverage of the unemployment insurance, the Chinese government created the basic livelihood guarantee system for people laid off by SOEs. The main function of this system was the distribution of living allowances, payments for pension insurance and medical insurance, offering training and providing re-employment services and information for the *xiagang* workers. Since then, the Chinese government has taken several measures to improve the unemployment insurance system, as we shall see in the last section of this chapter.

As for the situation in rural areas, let us remark that data on unemployment insurance in rural areas are not available and, more generally, that the social security system in rural areas of China lags far behind the urban system. The Chinese government is taking some measures to promote a social security system for persons living in rural areas, especially by establishing a new rural cooperative medical system and extending the coverage of the minimum living standard system to the rural areas.³¹ Finally, the exact unemployment insurance benefits vary in different provinces; it usually ranges from 500–600 RMB per month.

New Public Management, income distribution, and inequality

By referring to Figure 5.3 and Table 5.4 we may form a first idea about income inequality in China, measured by the Gini index. Compared with Western countries, China has today the highest Gini index (41.5 according to the UNDP Human Development Report 2009), second only to the USA (45 according to the CIA Factbook 2010). Nevertheless, one must be careful with these data, as US data are for the year 2007, whereas China's data, from the UNDP Human Development Report 2009, refer to an unspecified 'mid-2000s' year. In 2003, a World Bank's report estimated that China's Gini index was already around 45 at the end of the twentieth century.³² In a more recent working paper published by the World Bank in August 2008, Xubei Luo and Nong Zhu calculated that the Gini coefficient has increased from around 30 to 45 between 1978 and 2004.³³ In its report on China's anti-poverty strategy, published in 2009, the World Bank estimates China's Gini index for the year 2003 at 45.3 (for income inequality) and at 47.4 (for consumption inequality).³⁴ Official data reported by the NBSC in 2010 place the Gini index at 48 for 2009; but, interestingly enough, the index has not increased since 2007, when it reached the peak of 48. Moreover, by taking the ratio between the 10 per cent richest and the 10 per cent poorest of Table 5.4, we see that China, with a 13.2 ratio, takes its place within the group with the highest ratio, that is, between New Zealand (12.5), the UK (13.8), Portugal (15.0) and the USA (15.9) and far from the countries of the lowest group with a ratio between 5.6 (Norway) and Denmark (8.1).

Finally, let us take into consideration the latest estimates by renowned Chinese scholars, as reported in May 2010 by the official *China Daily*, which help us to update the data presented in the previous paragraph, and moreover add some insights into the causes of China's increasing income inequality. First, according to Chang Xiuze, a researcher from the Academy of Microeconomic Research of the National Development and Reform Commission (NDRC), China's Gini was 47 in May 2010, 'overtaking the recognized warning level of 40.'³⁵ The newspaper further says that 'the Gini coefficient has been continuously rising after it reached the alarming 40 level ten years ago.'³⁶ Furthermore, the *China Daily* quotes Li Shi, professor at the Beijing Normal University, who said that 'the income of the top 10 percent of the richest Chinese was 23 times that of the bottom 10 percent in the country, compared with 1998, when the gap was only 7.3 times.' Finally, the newspaper quotes Su Nanhai, director of the Labour and Wage Institute under the Ministry of Human Resources and Social Security, according to whom the 'income of senior executives in some SOEs is about 128 times that of the average social income . . . and the gap is 18:1 between senior managers and common workers in the same listed SOEs.' It is interesting to note that the article also reports that, according to Chinese experts, 'the widening wealth gap is partially the result of large amounts of "illegal income" resulting from corruption.'

Furthermore, the article mentions that, according to Wang Xiaolu, deputy director of the National Economic Research Institute under the China Reform Foundation, about 4.8 trillion RMB ($703 billion) of urban income evaded tax, and 75 per cent of that 'hidden income' belonged to the high-income category. Finally, experts attribute the 'unreasonable high incomes [to] monopoly trades of electronic information, oil, finance and tobacco, and profiteering trades of real estate, coal mine exploration, and securities.'[37]

From the evidence provided so far, we can conclude that China's situation concerning income inequality is worse than in the majority of Western countries, but some similarities appear as well, namely the impact of the widening scope of market mechanisms that has resulted in the appearance of some forms of China's economic agents' behaviour, as well as some structural features of the Chinese economy, which are not without recalling the features Fernand Braudel has attributed to capitalism: the lack of transparency and the tendency to create monopolies (see Chapter 2, pp. 29–30). It remains to be seen, first, if the Party, which in my opinion, as I have argued in Chapter 4 (pp. 100–101), still dominates the political system and is still capable of orienting the economic development, is aware of these phenomena and, second, if it has started to introduce public policies aimed at reducing inequalities and contributing to rebalancing the Chinese economy and society. However, before we come to this important point, we have to go into more depth within the world of inequalities in China, as the Gini coefficient tells only part of the story.

The unequal distribution of wealth in China manifests itself between provinces and regions, between rural and urban areas, between rural areas, and inside provinces, regions, urban and rural areas. Official data for the Gini index we have presented above are available for the country as a whole, but not for provinces or regions.[38] Therefore we have to resort to other measures of inequality. The inequalities mentioned above are very well documented, so I will refer the reader to some references, and will use some more recent data to evaluate the scope of inequality in China.[39] Already published works demonstrate that the coastal provinces and three of the four municipalities under the supervision of the central government (i.e. Shanghai, Beijing and Tianjin) are generally much more developed than the inner and western provinces, especially Tibet, Guizhou, Qinghai, Gansu and Ningxia, on practically every dimension, including economic development, regional development, productivity and research and development (R&D), human development, education, social equity, public services, social security, infrastructure, environmental protection, and natural resources and geographical location.[40] Even by taking the HDI and its three components (education, health and GDP per capita) the overall pattern does not change.[41] Of course, as Yang Yongheng and Hu Angang show, there has been, with some exceptions, an improvement in practically all the provinces on practically all the indicators. However, their most interesting conclusions are the following. First, the reform strategy giving priority to economic development has brought a more rapid development in the economy than in education and health. Second, a 'coordinated development of education, health, and economy is a prerequisite to a more balanced development';

in this respect, they observe that all the provinces are now heading towards a 'Coordinated Human Development' as defined by UNDP. Third, the reforms 'have brought about increasingly serious regional economic disparities, and have made economic disparities the most predominant cross-regional gap'. Finally, they draw our attention to the fact that they use the provinces as the basic unit for their analysis, whereas 'the disparities within provinces, especially between urban and rural areas, can be extremely huge'.[42] I will come back to this important point, but let us start with some more recent data on inequality between provinces.

Let us go back to Table 6.8, on which I have already commented when evaluating the performance of China's development in international comparison. By now looking at the same data, we can see that there are considerable disparities between provinces that confirm the results of the researches mentioned above: the coastal provinces have a per capita GDP index significantly higher than those of the other provinces. The situation is more varied and balanced when the other two components of HDI (life expectancy and education) are taken into consideration, but the comprehensive HDI puts the coastal provinces and three of the four municipalities under the direct supervision of the central government (Beijing, Shanghai and Tianjin) at the top of the rankings, above 0.800, joined only by Inner Mongolia (0.803), whereas all the other provinces are below the national average (0.793), with the exception of Shanxi (0.800).

Following now the conclusion of Yang Yongheng and Hu Angang mentioned above, we go back to data showing the disparities, within the provinces, between rural and urban areas. Table 6.6 shows that the ratio between urban and rural per capita annual disposable income has always been, since the beginning of the reform era in 1978, 1.82 to 3.3 times higher than the rural per capita net income. The ratio first decreased from 2.57 in 1978 to 1.82 in 1983, very likely thanks to the reforms introduced in the rural areas that boosted rural incomes. However, subsequently the ratio has almost constantly increased to overtake the limit of 3 in 2002 (3.11) to finally stabilizing between 3.21 in 2004 and 3.33 in 2009. This relative flattening of the line, as shown in Figure 6.1 is quite an interesting finding, which we will consider when analysing the effectiveness of the rebalancing policies set up by the Chinese leadership.

In my book on China's reforms I had calculated the ratio between the rural and urban areas for the Chinese provinces, using official 2006 data, for the purpose of finding out whether there were differences between provinces.[43] Here I update those findings using data of 2009, and I will briefly comment on the changes that have intervened since (see Table 6.9). First, the national ratio slightly deteriorated from 3.28 in 2006 to 3.33 in 2009. Second, generally the changes between 2006 and 2009 within the provinces were not very high, with the exception of Chongqing (–0.5, from 4.02 to 3.52) and Guangxi (+0.78, from 3.10 to 3.88). The ratio has deteriorated in nine provinces, most of the them those with the highest HDI (Tianjin +0.15, Shanxi +0.15, Inner Mongolia +0.11, Liaoning +0.12, Shanghai +0.5, Jiangsu +0.15, Fujian +0.11, Shandong +0.12 and Guangdong +0.3) but also four other provinces with HDI below the national average (Hebei +0.15, Guangxi +0.78, Guizhou +0.31 and Gansu +0.18). Among the provinces

Table 6.9 Per capita annual income (RMB) of urban and rural households in China, 2009

Ratio [3]/[2]		Urban areas			Rural areas	
2009	2006	Region	Disposable income [3]	Total income [1]	Region	Net income [2]
3.33	3.28	National average	17174.7	18858.1	National average	5153.2
2.29	2.41	Beijing	26738.5	30673.7	Beijing	11668.6
2.46	2.29	Tianjin	21402.0	23565.7	Tianjin	8687.6
2.86	2.71	Hebei	14718.0	15675.8	Hebei	5149.7
3.30	3.15	Shanxi	13996.6	14983.2	Shanxi	4244.1
3.21	3.10	Inner Mongolia	15849.2	16951.4	Inner Mongolia	4937.8
2.65	2.53	Liaoning	15761.4	17757.7	Liaoning	5958.0
2.66	2.68	Jilin	14006.3	15155.2	Jilin	5265.9
2.41	2.58	Heilongjiang	12566.0	13689.9	Heilongjiang	5206.8
2.31	2.26	Shanghai	28837.8	32403.0	Shanghai	12482.9
2.57	2.42	Jiangsu	20551.7	22494.9	Jiangsu	8003.5
2.46	2.49	Zhejiang	24610.8	27119.3	Zhejiang	10007.3
3.13	3.29	Anhui	14085.7	15691.9	Anhui	4504.3
2.93	2.84	Fujian	19576.8	21692.4	Fujian	6680.2
2.76	2.76	Jiangxi	14021.5	15047.2	Jiangxi	5075.0
2.91	2.79	Shandong	17811.0	19336.9	Shandong	6118.8
2.99	3.01	Henan	14371.6	15408.0	Henan	4807.0
2.85	2.86	Hubei	14367.5	15698.1	Hubei	5035.3
3.07	3.09	Hunan	15084.3	16078.1	Hunan	4909.0
3.12	3.15	Guangdong	21574.7	24116.5	Guangdong	6906.9
3.88	3.10	Guangxi	15451.5	17032.9	Guangxi	3980.4
2.90	2.88	Hainan	13750.9	14909.3	Hainan	4744.4
3.52	4.02	Chongqing	15748.7	16990.3	Chongqing	4478.4
3.10	3.11	Sichuan	13839.4	15323.8	Sichuan	4462.1
4.28	4.59	Guizhou	12862.5	13793.4	Guizhou	3005.4
4.28	4.47	Yunnan	14423.9	15680.3	Yunnan	3369.3
3.84	3.67	Tibet	13544.4	14979.0	Tibet	3531.7
4.11	4.10	Shaanxi	14128.8	15311.3	Shaanxi	3437.6
4.00	4.18	Gansu	11929.8	12918.0	Gansu	2980.1
3.79	3.81	Qinghai	12691.9	14150.3	Qinghai	3346.2
3.46	3.32	Ningxia	14024.7	15550.8	Ningxia	4048.3
3.16	3.24	Xinjiang	12257.5	13602.2	Xinjiang	3883.1

Source: National Bureau of Statistics of China: *China Statistical Abstract 2010* (in Chinese), Beijing, China Statistics Press, 2010, pp. 113, 115, 119.

with HDI above the national average, only Beijing (–0.12) and Zhejiang (–0.3) have reduced the urban/rural ratio. The other provinces with HDI below the national average that present the most remarkable reduction are Ningxia –0.14, Tibet –0.17, Yunnan –0.19, Anhui –0.16, and Chongqing –0.50. For the other provinces the changes do not exceed ±0.02.

Table 6.9 shows very clearly that the increases of the ratio occurred mainly within the provinces with a high HDI, but a convincing overall interpretation would require a more in-depth analysis of the situation of these provinces. Nevertheless, the very interesting finding that these data suggest (and in this respect the differences between 2006 and 2009 do not constitute a contradiction), is that the lowest urban/rural ratio (i.e. below 3) is to be found in the fourteen provinces ranked in the top position of the HDI ranking, with the exception of Shanxi and Inner Mongolia (see Table 6.8). All the other provinces (i.e. with an HDI under or close to the national average) present an urban/rural ratio above 3, with the exception of Jiangxi (2.76), Hubei (2.71) and Hainan 2.88), and several of them have a ratio above 3.50 (Chongqing 3.52, Guangxi 3.88, Qinghai 3.79, Tibet 3.84, Gansu 4.00, Shaanxi 4.11, Yunnan and Guizhou 4.28). So, in spite of the small deterioration of the ratio in several high ranking provinces, it still remains, as in 2006, that the most developed provinces have the lowest income urban/rural ratio, which confirms results presented by other researchers.[44]

New Public Management and poverty

We have already seen that the number of poor has declined in China since the beginning of reforms, and this has been recognized by international organizations such as the UNDP, the OECD and the World Bank. Evaluations vary according to the authors, organizations and databases, but the general picture is basically the same. Let us take the assessment by the OECD, which is a good summary of the various evaluations:

> No matter which definition is adopted, be it the Chinese or the World Bank one, the trend is clear. According to the World Bank definition (income USD 1 per person per day at PPP), the number of people living in poverty in China fell from around 530 million (both in rural and urban areas) in 1981 to 129 million in 2004 and poverty incidence from 53 percent to 9.9 percent, respectively. The vast majority of those below the poverty line live in rural areas as indicated by a poverty incidence at 12.5 percent for rural China compared to 0.5 percent for urban China in 2001. Moreover, despite the progress made so far, a large part of Chinese population still lives just above the absolute poverty line as shown by the share at 34.9 percent of those who lived below USD 2 per person per day in 2004.[45]

Using more recent data, the World Bank in its 2009 report says that poverty declined from 65 per cent in 1981 to 4 per cent in 2007, and that from 2001 (the year of China's accession to the WTO) poverty declined from 16 per cent to 4 per cent.[46]

Nevertheless, Chinese scholars often consider that since the mid-1990s poverty has also arisen in urban areas, especially under the forms of new poverty, owing to the weakness of the social security system, the very strong competition in the labour market, the policy of reducing cost of both enterprises (public and private) and public administrations by laying off employees and workers, and the requirements for citizens to pay out of their own pocket for education and health. However, before dealing with these problems and the policies implemented by the Party-State to overcome these difficulties, let us take the data presented by the Oxford Poverty & Human Development Initiative's (OPHI) multidimensional poverty index (MPI), based upon a survey of 2003. I remind the reader that this index is composed of three dimensions that are made up of 10 indicators: health (child mortality, nutrition), education (years of school education, child enrolment) and living standards (electricity, drinking water, sanitation, flooring, cooking fuel, assets).[47]

First, the OPHI compares different measures of poverty taking 2003 data: the OPHI's MPI index puts Chinese poverty at 12 per cent, equal to 160 million people, whereas the World Bank indicators put poverty at 16 per cent (for the US$1.25 a day line, equal to 124 million people) and 36 per cent (for the US$2 a day line, equal to 481 million people). Moreover the OPHI compares these measures with the official national poverty line, which puts poverty in China at only 3 per cent. These different criteria for measuring poverty very clearly correspond to different appreciations of what are considered to be 'poor living conditions', as I mentioned in Chapter 2 (pp. 59–62). Very clearly, by putting the poverty line well below the World Bank and OPHI criteria, the Chinese government takes into consideration the very low living conditions that existed in China at the beginning of reforms. Its more urgent goal was to lift as many people as possible out of extreme poverty as fast as possible; and this is what it succeeded in accomplishing.

Second, by taking the components of the MPI as indicators of deprivation, the OPHI shows the average percentages of Chinese people who are deprived according to each indicator as follows: schooling 10, enrolment 0.0, nutrition 3.2, child mortality 0.0, electricity 0.0, sanitation 7.7, drinking water 3, flooring 3.2, cooking fuel 9.1 and assets 2.4. From this it appears that the indicator that contributes most to the overall MPI is schooling, followed by cooking fuel, nutrition and sanitation. Third, the OPHI confirms the differences that exist between urban and rural areas. Finally the OPHI provides comparative data between the 104 developing countries: China has a relative low percentage of poor, measured both by the MPI (12 per cent) and by the US$1.25 (16 per cent) criteria, compared with other developing countries, of which 41 have an MPI over 40 per cent, 34 over 50 per cent and 26 over 60 per cent.

To conclude this section on poverty, let me refer to a 2009 OECD report that helps us to add some insights into the situation of China's poverty.[48] The OECD recognizes that the living conditions in urban areas have improved considerably, as families can afford all sorts of current consumption goods (such as electrical appliances, colour TV, air-conditioning units, apartments etc.). It further estimates that a population of 50 million has an income equal to 30 per cent of the average US household. If this is a measure of the increasing Chinese middle class, we are very far from the optimistic estimates that have circulated recently.[49] However, it is true that a larger proportion of the urban population now enjoys a relatively fair standard of living, corresponding to the Chinese leadership's goal of building a moderately well-off society. However, the OECD also recognizes that in rural areas the standard of living is much lower, in spite of the fact that the poverty rate fell to 4 per cent in 2007, measured on consumption basis (quoting the above-mentioned World Bank report). Finally, the OECD confirms the findings reported above about disparities between regions and between rural and urban areas.

New Public Management and crime

Given the inequalities mentioned above, and the absence, until recently, of an overall governmental strategy for addressing the problems of disparities and poverty, one could expect, as we have seen for the West, an increase in crime. Already in 2005 Hu Angang showed that the number of crimes went up from 1986 to about 1991 – during the last years of the first decade of reforms when new forms of poverty emerged following the first wave of marketization – and then remained unchanged until 1998 but increased again dramatically from 1998 to about 2002, after the acceleration of reforms decided at the September 1997 Party Congress.[50]

Taking the data provided by China's *Statistical Yearbook* for criminal cases (Figure 6.3), the increase during the first decade of reforms is quite impressive: it increased 3.6 times, from 56 crimes per 100,000 people in 1978 to 204 in 1991. Then it decreased to reach 131 in 1997. However, after the 1997 Party Congress, it started again to increase from 1998 to reach 349 in 2001. Since then, after a small decrease between 2001 and 2002, it went up again to reach 445 in 2010. Therefore, criminal cases have increased 8.12 times from 1978 to 2010. Taking now the offences against public order (i.e. social unrest) we find a similar pattern. The rate for these types of crimes increased 2.7 times, from 104 crimes per 100,000 people in 1986 (first date for which these data are available) to 283 in 1993. Then it decreased to reach 259 in 1998. However, two years after the 1997 Party Congress, it again started to increase from 1999 to reach 951 in 2010. Therefore, from 1986 to 2010 crimes against public order have increased 9.14 times. Finally, adding criminal cases to offences against public order, we find that between 1986 and 2010 crimes per 100,000 people have increased from 155 (51 + 104) to 1,397 (445 + 951), that is, 8.78 times. The conclusion we can draw from these data is similar to the one we reached for Western countries: marketization in the absence of social policies aimed at supporting those who suffer from unemployment or from underpaid jobs and are therefore in a difficult financial situation (many of them in poverty) may lead to an increase in crime. This situation is not only socially unfair, but also regrettable from the point of view of the economy, as crime represents a cost that must be covered and may very well diminish the GDP increase.

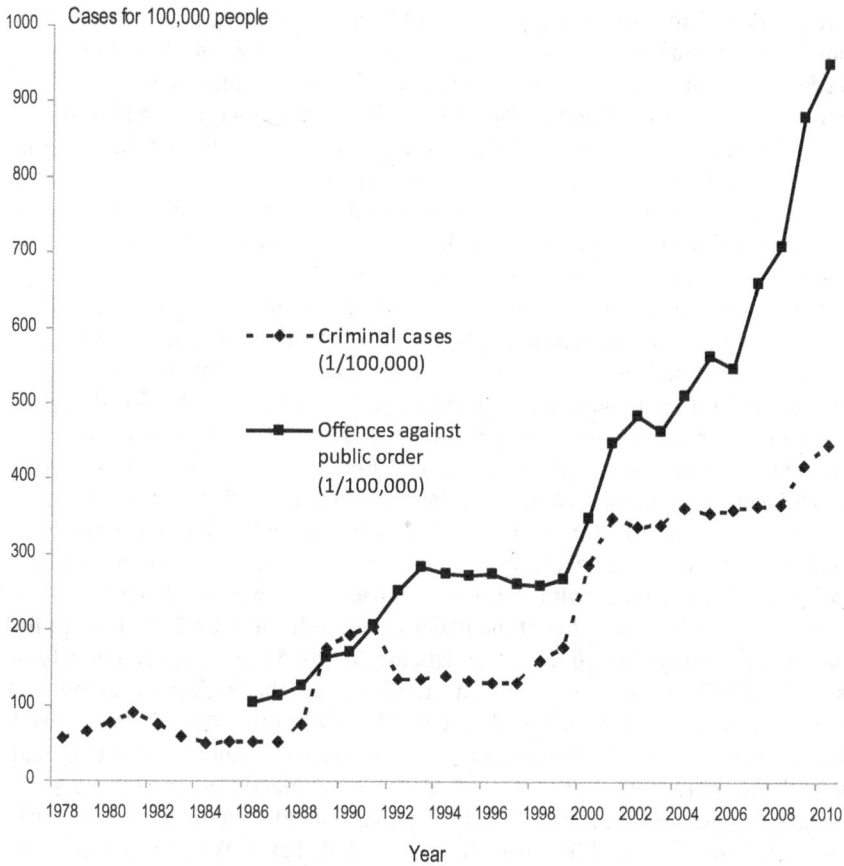

Figure 6.3 Crime rates in China, 1978–2010. Source: built by author with data provided by *China Statistical Yearbooks*, Beijing, People's Republic of China, tables 23-11 and 23-12, various years.

New Public Management and health

As we have already seen, health is the domain in which China has experienced the most difficult choices since the beginning of reforms and the demise of the planned economy. Experts are unanimous in criticizing the introduction of measures that, by making people pay for part of their health services, have brought the commodification of Chinese society to a point that large numbers of people have been excluded from health care. Moreover, the dismantling of the health system (which during the Mao era had allowed rural China to escape from traditional infectious and parasitic diseases) and the migration of medical personnel from the rural areas to the cities in search of better living and financial conditions have left large sectors of Chinese society without proper health services. Hence, the deterioration instead of the improvement of Chinese public health, as attested by many health indicators, such as life expectancy, is mentioned in one of the World Bank's influential annual reports.[51] In addition to this, the changing habits of the increasingly well-off urban population have fuelled the emergence and development of diseases typical of a well-off society, such as cardiovascular disease, cancer, obesity and diabetes.[52] Finally, insufficient regulation in favour of environmental protection has resulted in serious pollution of water, air and land that has not only devastated huge areas of the Chinese territory, but also contributed to the deterioration of China's public health.

Hu Angang divides China's health policies into four stages: the Mao golden stage during which, as mentioned before, traditional infectious and parasitic diseases were eradicated and a modest, but fair, medical system was made accessible to the entire population; the second stage, which Hu describes as 'slow progress' between the end of the Mao era (1978) and 2003, but that I would describe as 'significant regression' because, being based on the primacy of economic development over human capital development, it produced the problems mentioned before; third, the transition from 'growth-first' to 'health-first' from 2003 to 2009; and fourth the necessary 'build-up of healthy China.'[53] Let us see how China's health compares with Western countries as shown in Table 5.12, which presents WHO data for some of the major health indicators for 2008 (except for maternal mortality, for which WHO data are for 2005). We can see that China is well behind Western countries on practically all the indicators, except for adolescent fertility, for which, with a score of five per 1,000 girls, it does as well as countries such as Switzerland (four), Denmark, Italy and Sweden (six) and much better than Ireland (17), the UK (26), New Zealand (29) and the USA (an astonishing 41), and significantly better than all the other countries on the table (between 7 and 12). For life expectancy, China falls below Western countries by between four years less than the USA and eight years less than Switzerland and Italy. The data also show that for life expectancy China reached in 2008 the level Western countries had in 1990, that is, about 74–76 years. Nevertheless, if we take into consideration data between 1990 and 2008, we must recognize that China has made considerable progresses: infant mortality rate by age one decreased from 37 (per 1,000 births) in 1990 to 30 in 2000 and 18 in 2008 (nevertheless, well above Western countries, where it was between two for Sweden and seven for the USA); under-five mortality rate decreased from 46 (per 1,000 births) in 1990 to 36 in 2000 and 21 in 2008 (again, well above Western countries, where it was between three for Sweden and Finland and eight for the USA); finally, adult mortality rate (per 1,000 population) measured by the probability of dying between 15 and 60 decreased from 172 in 1990 to 135 in 2000 and 113 in 2008 (again, well above Western countries, where it was between 60 for Switzerland and 107 for the USA).

China's situation looks also worse than that of Western countries if we take WHO data for 2007 for health expenditure, as shown in Table 5.13. China's expenditure as percentage of GDP decreased from 4.6 in 2000 to 4.3 in 2007, whereas all Western countries increased their health expenditures in the same period.[54] All the other indicators in the table are less favourable to China. First, general government expenditure on health as percentage of total expenditure on health (44.7) is well below Western countries, except the USA, which spends only 45.5 per cent of its GDP, whereas the other Western countries spend between 71.8 (Spain) and 84.5 per cent (Denmark), with the exception of Switzerland (59.3 per cent). Second and consequently, China's private expenditure on health as percentage of total expenditure on health (55.3 per cent) exceeds by far all Western countries, which spent between 15.5 (Denmark) and 25.9 per cent (Belgium), with the exceptions of Switzerland with 40.7 and especially the USA with 45.5 per cent. Third, per capita total expenditure on health ($PPP 233) and per capita government expenditures on health ($PPP 104) are both well below Western countries. Of course, one has to take into consideration the considerable contextual differences between China and the West, but it remains that these data are a clear indicator of the improvement China must realize in the future in this domain. Here again, the WHO provides some data that show that between 2000 and 2007 China has already made some progress: in particular, per capita expenditures on health increased from $PPP 108 in 2000 to $PPP 233 in 2007. Only the general government expenditure on health as percentage of total government expenditure decreased from 11.1 to 9.9 per cent.

Some recent analyses and data provided by Hu Angang, allow us to understand what lies below the data presented above, and what are the real problems China's health policy has to address.

Table 6.10 is an excellent summary of the causes of China's health problems. The various dimensions of the reform process, namely the opening up to the global economy on one hand and the major domestic dimensions of reforms (marketization, urbanization and industrialization, and the ageing of the population) on the other, without a proper set of state policies aimed at providing accompanying measures to the process of modernization, lead inevitably to the social and economic problems mentioned in the first two columns of the table. There is no room here to develop the considerations suggested by this table.[55] It is nevertheless at least important to conclude that these problems are the consequence of the implementation of a set of policies: some of them were necessary for sustaining the modernization process and the improvement of the living conditions of the Chinese people, whereas some others, of a clear neoliberal inspiration, suggest that it is not enough to liberate market forces in order to obtain a balanced development beneficial to everybody. Without investment policies aimed at simultaneously developing hard infrastructures (e.g. railways, power plants) and soft infrastructures (e.g. health, education) the emergence of the problems underlined by Hu Angang's analysis was inevitable. Hu comments:

> The direct consequence of this model [of development] was that: (1) the number of unhealthy population grew larger; in this perspective, China was the largest country not only for total population, but also for unhealthy population; (2) the number of disease incidence in urban and rural areas was as high as 5 billion person/times of which nearly half did not consult a doctor; and (3) more than 80 per cent, or one billion, of the urban and rural population were not covered by medical insurance.[56]

Table 6.10 Health costs of economic transition and development in China

	Health costs	Impact on economy	Defects of government and health system
Marketization	Income gap, health problem of the poor	Human resources, social stability	Shortage of social security and basic public service
Industrialization	Environmental pollution, occupational disease, industrial accidents	Human resources	Lack of monitoring, restriction on pollution and occupational disease
Urbanization	Population mobility adding to disease infection	Human resources, economic operation	Lack of facilities, vaccination, monitoring of diseases, medical security for mobile population
Globalization	Mobilization of diverse factors leading to crisis spreading to public health	Economic operation, negative externality	System responsive to risks of globalization: bad International cooperation: not enough
Ageing	Large proportion of chronic diseases	Disease burden, resources consumptions	Communities' health establishments and volunteers not enough
Revolution of consumption	Tobacco consumption, automobile exhaust gases	Disease burden	Adjustment of consumption through economic means not adequate

Source: Hu Angang, Master's course, Tsinghua University, Beijing, 2010, lesson 12.

Table 6.11 gives a precise idea of the consequences on the Chinese population of the situation described above. The year 2003 is an important milestone as it is the year following the beginning of the Party's appointment of Hu Jintao as President of China and Wen Jiabao as Prime Minister, and the beginning of a new development strategy that 'puts people first', that is, a policy that starts investing heavily in the development of human capital.

Table 6.11 shows very well the new strategy of the Chinese leadership. The coverage of health insurance has been increased so that only 8.2 per cent of the population was not covered by the end of 2009, and it seems that, by the end of 2010, 100 per cent coverage was attained. Even if, as we shall see in the last part of this chapter, the insurance contribution to health care costs is rather modest, there is no doubt that this change represents a considerable improvement from the previous situation. Changes in the number of people affected by the types of diseases in the table are of course more modest than the coverage by health insurance: chronic diseases have even slightly increased, as well as the number of smokers and alcohol drinkers. This is because it is easier to increase the insurance coverage than to improve other factors crucial for the improvement of public health, such as the qualifications of the medical professions (especially in the

Table 6.11 People with health insecurity in China, 2003 and 2008

	2003		2008	
	million	%	million	%
People with chronic diseases	167	12.8	210	15.7
People not covered by social medical insurance	1,040	80.0	320	23.9
Lying-in women not delivering in hospital (rural)	2.86		2.74	
Smoking population	260	20.0	270	20.2
Regular alcohol drinkers	82	6.3	92.6	6.9
People without correct knowledge about ways of AIDS communication	330	25.4	260	19.5
People without regular physical exercises	890	68.5	840	62.9
People not covered by medical insurance	1,000	76.9	110*	8.2

Source: Hu Angang, Master's course, lesson 12.
* Data for 2009.

rural areas) or investment in the modernization of hospitals (again, especially in the rural areas) and in information campaigns aimed at changing the smoking and drinking habits of the population, to which we could add diseases such as obesity and diabetes deriving from new nutritional habits of the Chinese population, especially the young generation.

Finally, health is also a domain in which the disparities among different Chinese regions appear. Table 6.12 shows that in the urban areas, where the average income is higher than in rural areas, the percentage of people covered by health insurance was higher than in rural areas. Moreover, the percentage of medical expenses was considerably higher and the proportion of out of pocket payments for health care was considerably lower in urban than in rural areas.

Table 6.13 is a good illustration of Hu Angang's theory of 'one China, four worlds', which I have already mentioned above. Hu Angang has chosen four

Table 6.12 Comparison of three kinds of medical insurance in China, 2008

	% of the total population which is insured	Coverage of medical expenses as % of total medical expense	Average household annual income (RMB)	Percentage of total medical expenses paid out of pocket
Medical insurance for urban workers	94.8	63.2	12,776	31.8
Medical insurance for urban citizens	79.2	49.3	9,215	38.2
Medical insurance for rural population	80.2	26.6	4,473	56.0

Source: Elaborated by Hu Angang from China's Health Statistical Yearbook, 2009.

Table 6.13 Regional disparity in health: one China, four worlds, 2007–8

	HDI (2008)		Life expectancy (2007)	Doctors per 1,000 people (2007)	Hospital beds per 1,000 people (2007)
	HDI	HDI rank in China			
Beijing	0.891	2	80.09	4.79	6.99
Liaoning	0.835	7	75.2	2.14	4.31
Hubei	0.784	16	73.6	1.51	2.14
Tibet	0.630	31	67	1.56	3.10
Developed countries			78.6	3.14	8.57
In-transition countries			68.4	2.99	6.53
Average developing countries			67.3	1.12	2.08
Very underdeveloped countries			52.0	0.14	0.67

Source: Elaborated by Hu Angang from China's Health Statistical Yearbooks. Column with HDI added by author.

provinces representing the four worlds: one of the most developed (Beijing), one representing a slightly less developed coastal province (Liaoning), one of the inner provinces of central China (Hubei) and one of the least developed western provinces (Tibet). I have added an additional column with the HDI data we have already presented above in Table 6.8. We can see that the difference between Beijing and Liaoning (representing the first and the second worlds) is significant for each of the three indicators (i.e. life expectancy and numbers of doctors and beds per 1,000 people); and that, overall, Beijing (rank 2 in China for the HDI) bears comparison with developed countries, whereas, overall, Liaoning (rank 7 in China for the HDI) does almost as well as the in-transition countries. For Hebei (representing the third world with rank 16 in China for the HDI) the situation is slightly different from Liaoning, as it is comparable to in-transition countries for life expectancy, but does not do very well for number of doctors and number of beds per 1,000 people, for which it is closer to the average of developing countries. Finally, Tibet (occupying the last place in China for HDI, rank 31) is clearly close to the average developing countries on every count, although it does slightly better than the latter for the number of doctors and beds per 1,000 people.

A recent working paper published by the World Bank confirms the persistence of disparities: 'intra-provinces disparity in health outcomes remains high between and within rural and urban areas respectively'.[57] Of course, these findings must be qualified, as the reform of China's health system is quite recent. It was announced at the beginning of November 2007 that its implementation had just started, and it was designed to reach its goals by 2020. Nevertheless, the report recognizes that 'with respect to health indicators, some provinces have achieved equitable improvements.' For example, figure 12 on p. 24 of the paper shows that maternal mortality decreased significantly between 1990 and 2009 in both rural and urban areas; moreover, the difference between maternal mortality ratios in rural and urban areas was considerably reduced between 1990 and 2009: in 1990 it was 112.5 per 1,000 births for rural areas and 45.9 for urban areas, whereas in 2009 it was 34 and 26.6 respectively.

Conclusion

At the end of this journey into the consequences for China of the development strategy adopted by Deng Xiaoping that put economic development first, before human capital, our hypothesis according to which similar public policies produce similar results is confirmed. As for the Western countries, the greater space given to market mechanisms, and the emergence in China of economic actors behaving in similar ways to capitalist agents within Western economies, has produced a spectacular improvement of economic efficiency, but at the same time has also increased disparities. Even if (like the present writer) one does not require the establishment of a totally egalitarian society one would be at least worried if the improvement of economic efficiency went hand in hand with the emergence not only of considerably large disparities, but also of new forms of poverty. This situation was aggravated in China by the failure to replace the old solidarities of the Mao era with a modern set of social policies. These remarks constitute a verification of the second hypothesis, according to which one cannot simultaneously maximize economic efficiency and social equity. The difference is that in the West since the 1930s, and even more so after the Second World War, a Welfare State has been implemented in every country, even if with different scopes. When the wave of neoliberalism arrived at the beginning of the 1980s, the attack on the Welfare State had difficulties in dismantling what had been realized before, even if several serious regressions were realized following neoliberal prescriptions, as I have shown in Chapter 5.[58] On the contrary, in China the demise of the social functions of the SOEs of the Mao era created a vacuum that cannot be compared to the reduction of the Welfare State in Western countries, at least until the consequences of the 2008–11 crisis put additional pressure upon Western states urging them to overcome the crisis by further reducing Welfare State benefits, along with implementing several other austerity measures. In China, at a time when people were, from one day to the next, immersed in a severely competitive labour market, and left there without proper social insurances (unemployment, health and age), the road was left wide open to the emergence of important disparities and, considerably worse, to new forms of poverty that were to put millions of people under the poverty line as defined by international norms.

The third hypothesis, according to which differences in the implementation of NPM produce different outcomes, is also confirmed. Comparing Western countries and China we have seen that, in spite of the similarities mentioned above regarding the two first hypotheses, NPM prescriptions have been implemented in China in a different manner and with different outcomes. First, China's flexible (and, for Westerners, rudimentary) legal system has allowed experimenting with different solutions in practically all domains on a regional basis (e.g. introduction of market mechanisms, employment protection, health care) whereas in the West a well-established practice of public law requires the state to apply laws to all the citizens concerned as a set of 'impersonal general rules' in such a way as to safeguard the fundamental principles of legality and equal treatment. Second, the rather centralized structure of China's political system, in spite of considerable changes that opened it to outside interferences, has on one hand allowed China to implement the policy decisions (as soon as they are adopted after discussion) rapidly and consistently;[59] but, on the other hand, this has also made it difficult to discover (and accept) unwanted or unforeseen consequences of public policies, with the consequence of delaying the adoption of corrective measures. As we have already said, it is a pity the Chinese leadership has been rather slow in taking advantage of research already available at the end of the 1980s pointing out the negative consequences of the development strategy adopted in 1978. Nevertheless, it is also true that, once these problems were recognized by the Chinese leadership, China has been able to change the strategy of development, to abandon at least some of the neoliberal prescriptions in education and health, and to start to implement measures for rebalancing the Chinese society. This capacity, which corresponds to our fourth hypothesis, will be demonstrated in the last part of this chapter, and will become even more evident when we deal, in the general conclusion of this book, with the different responses given to the 2008–11 crisis by China and the West.

The rebalancing of Chinese society

In the 'Assessment and recommendation' introductory part of its 2009 report on China, the OECD considers that regarding poverty and, more generally, social security (1) imbalances remain, but are being addressed, (2) higher levels of social spending need to be sustained, (3) major social reforms have been undertaken but safety nets remain overly fragmented, (4) income inequality may no longer be on the rise though geographically disparities remain acute, (5) pension reforms have addressed only part of the challenges of an ageing population, the various pension regimes need to be gradually consolidated and the average retirement age needs to be increased, (6) progress in health care has been genuine but incomplete and a set of ambitious health care reforms are being rolled out but more may still be needed.[60] On its side, the World Bank has recently put forward a statement about the policy initiatives adopted by the Chinese leadership in response to these challenges that suggest that a broader poverty reduction agenda is evolving: (1) the launch, in 2000, of the Western Region development strategy, (2) restructuring of poverty alleviation investments, (3) development of the urban social security system, (4) a training programme to support transfer of rural surplus labour, (5) elimination of agricultural taxes, (6) supporting farm incomes, (7) a nationwide rural social assistance system, (8) a rural health insurance scheme, (9) urban residents' basic medical insurance, (10) a medical assistance scheme in rural and urban areas and (11) compulsory education finance reform.[61]

Defining the new development strategy

Let us now see the situation for some of the major policy initiatives taken by the Chinese leadership, and what their impact is on the reduction of inequalities and disparities, of which poverty is certainly one of the most disturbing manifestations. We start from the generally accepted idea that 'traditional' sources of inequality and poverty, those resulting from an inefficient planned economy, have been practically eliminated, and that new sources of poverty have emerged, especially an unequal primary distribution of income (i.e. resulting from the market) whose consequences have been further aggravated by the weakness (in some cases the absence) of public policies supporting the unemployed, the underemployed, the less educated and senior citizens, as well as those suffering from illnesses and accidents.

The first move away from a policy that based societal development primarily on the economy was suggested by a paper sent to China from the USA by two Chinese intellectuals. This document suggested that the development strategy should be directed by the central government, which therefore needed sufficient financial resources. To achieve this goal it was necessary to reorient China's fiscal system towards centralization. This report was circulated in China and is at the origin of the centralization of fiscal policy decided by Jiang Zemin in 1994, which gave to the central government more fiscal revenues and thus the financial power to implement the rebalancing policies adopted during the following years.[62]

This proposal, aimed at strengthening the fiscal capacity of central government, was based on previous research carried out during the 1980s by Hu Angang, first for his PhD thesis and then within the China Academy of Sciences (CAS). These researches, based upon the analysis of China's population and its relation to its territory, as well as on the general 'Chinese conditions' (which was to become a leitmotiv not only of Hu Angang's research but also of the Chinese leadership) forecast, already before the Tiananmen events of 1989, the problems China would face in the future as a consequence of the strategy of development that 'puts the economy first': economic and social disparities and environmental damages. These documents were known to the Chinese leadership, in particular thanks to one of the daughters of Deng Xiaoping who was also working within the CAS.[63]

Following the change in fiscal policy, at the 5th Plenum of the 14th CCP Central Committee in 1995 the government started to redefine the development strategy, comprising three dimensions: the development of the western provinces (2001); the rejuvenation of the old industrial bases in northern China (2004); and the development of the central provinces (2006). This new strategy (which looks like a correction of Deng's motto 'let some people get rich first') has given an incentive to a vast programme of investments in infrastructure in the northern, inner and western provinces. Even if one may regret, as I do, that at the beginning this programme gave priority to hard infrastructures and neglected soft infrastructure (and we have seen the negative consequences for public health in the preceding paragraphs) one must recognize that these investments have improved the physical assets of the less developed provinces and has prepared them, with the new policies that 'put people first', to start another long march, the one that will eventually raise these provinces close to the development level of the coastal ones in terms not only of economic but also of human development.

The investments in physical infrastructure needed to be complemented with some parallel investments in human capital.[64] This has been done first by abolishing some of the most irrational decisions taken in the past, and first of all by eliminating, between 2003 and 2006, the taxes and fees that peasants were obliged to pay and that constituted a heavy burden on their already meagre income. Second, fees were abolished for elementary and junior high school, in 2006 for rural areas in the western provinces and then in 2007 for the inner and eastern provinces,[65] and in 2008 for urban areas.[66] Then, at the Party Congress of November 2007 President Hu Jintao announced the adoption of China's new health system, which should provide universal coverage by the year 2020. Of course, the major domain in which the new policy trend manifests itself is that of social security. Social welfare is necessary not only if one's attitude is oriented by considerations of equity, but also because a well educated population protected by decent health, unemployment and old age insurances is better armed for contributing to the development of society and for assuring it the stability it needs. Finally in 2008 the new labour law improving the protection of employees and workers was adopted and implemented. The new contract law improves the protection of employees in case of redundancy and of abuse of short-term contracts (for example, after 10 years within the same company short-term contracts become illegal). Moreover, the Chinese government has established the principle of minimum wages, the provinces being able to fix them taking into consideration the conditions of the local labour market. Even if the minima are very low, this policy shows that the interests of the working people are being taken into consideration more seriously than in the past.[67] According to the National Population and Family Planning Commission, many provinces and municipalities have recently increased the minimum wage, and six of them have increased it by 20 per cent. The average minimum wage in all provinces in eastern and southern China now exceeds 1,000 RMB per month. Amongst them, Zhejiang (one of the richest provinces in China) has recently raised the minimum wage to 1,310 RMB per month, surpassing Guangzhou, where the minimum wage is 1,300 RMB, and Shanghai, where it is 1,280 RMB.[68] Moreover, the role of the All-China Federation of Trade Unions (ACFTU), which admitted representatives of the migrant workers for the first time at the national congress of October 2008, is becoming more active in the defence of employees, as has been recently recognized by the China Labour Bulletin, a very critical NGO based in Hong Kong.[69]

Finally, we should also very briefly take into consideration measures taken by China in the domain of environmental protection as this is necessary not only for sustaining the good health of the Chinese people, but also for supporting sustainable economic development. In its 2009 report commenting upon the realizations of China's Eleventh Five-Year Plan, the World Bank, in spite of considering that progress on the environmental objectives during the first two years of the Plan (i.e. between 2006 and 2008) has been mixed (especially insufficient progress in reducing energy intensity), recognizes that improvements were seen in reducing air and water pollution, treating industrial solid waste, increasing the efficiency of water use and expanding forest coverage.[70] Since then, China has embarked upon a whole set of measures aimed at reducing the impact of human activities over the environment.

Two types of measures are worth mentioning. First, a report from the Worldwatch Institute recognizes that China has become the major producer and implementer of clean energy equipment such as light bulbs, solar water heaters, solar photovoltaic cells and wind turbines, which reflect:

> a strong and growing commitment by the government to diversify its energy economy; reduce environmental problems, and stave off massive increases in energy imports. Around the world, governments and industries now find themselves struggling to keep pace with the new pacesetter in global clean energy development.[71]

Furthermore, the report explains that positive results have been achieved thanks to the implementation of a host of new policies and regulations that have resulted during the first three years of the Eleventh Five-Year Plan (2006–8) in a reduction of energy consumption per unit of GDP (the so-called energy intensity):

> by just over 10 percent, saving 290 million tons of coal equivalent (tce) and reducing the country's greenhouse gas emissions by 750 million tons of carbon dioxide-equivalent. This pace of energy conservation has rarely been achieved by the rest of the world.[72]

In spite of the persistence of problems for energy savings especially in the industry sector, the report is rather positive in recognizing that:

> China's rapid rise to global leadership in clean energy is rooted in an unusual level of cooperation between government and industry . . . with the aim of making the country an innovator as well as a low-cost manufacturer of cutting-edge technologies.[73]

Moreover, the Worldwatch Institute considers that, thanks to the policies mentioned above, 'one of the greatest promises of China's green transition is the potential for expanded employment in industries and economic sectors that can help slow down and possibly reduce the country's environmental impact.'[74]

On its side the World Bank has recently recognized that, 'over the last five years, China has increased its renewable energy generation to 8.8 percent of total primary energy consumption, making it one of the world's leading producers.'[75] Finally, for wind power, Pinsent Masons recognized recently that, 'at the end of 2010, China became the world's largest wind power developer, having overtaken the US in installed capacity.'[76]

The second type of measure in the domain of environmental protection is the development of 'eco-cities' in several parts of China, of which the most acclaimed example is the Sino-Singapore Tianjin Eco-city with the support of the Singapore government and the World Bank.[77] The new eco-city covers an area of 34.2 square kilometres and is designed to become a model of energy and resource efficiency while maintaining economic viability and social harmony. The project promotes green transport such as public transport, walking tracks and bicycle pathways, and green buildings with energy efficiency standards higher than the national standard. Although there have been a few failures (e.g. Dongtan and Huangbiayu), eco-cities are a necessity for the rapidly growing urbanization process. This is used by the government as a means to promote development and increase the per capita income of the Chinese people, especially those who are leaving the countryside for the urban areas. However, the government has understood that big cities may create more problems than they can solve. Hence, the project of building several cities anew, with the aim of building them 'green'. This is another example of the Chinese strategy of experimenting in some places, then evaluating the results, correcting them whenever necessary and diffusing the good practices in other parts of the country.

To conclude this part, let me mention another impressive example of the new development strategy, by taking the case of the municipality of Chongqing. I have already mentioned in Chapter 2 (pp. 38–40) the theory of the Tsinghua professor Cui Zhiyuan proposing a strategy that does not oppose but tries to integrate public and private property. In 2010 Cui was detached from Tsinghua University to Chongqing to act as assistant to the chairman of the State Assets Commission of Chongqing. For several years now Chongqing has been embarked upon a new development strategy that tries to realize just that objective. Should it succeed, no doubt the Chinese leadership will then have at its disposal a new development 'good practice' to be diffused to other parts of China with the purpose of rebalancing Chinese society. This experiment is interesting for different reasons. In 2000 the Chinese government established a 'Leadership Group for Western China Development' covering six provinces (Gansu, Guizhou, Qinghai, Shaanxi, Sichuan and Yunnan), five autonomous provinces (Guangxi, Inner Mongolia, Ningxia, Tibet and Xinjiang) and one municipality (Chongqing). In 2007, Chongqing was designated by the Chinese government as an experimental zone for integrating rural and urban development, along with Chengdu, the capital of Sichuan province, to which Chongqing belonged until 1997, when it acquired its autonomy as one of the four municipalities reporting directly to the central government.[78] According to Cui Zhiyuan 'stimulating Chinese domestic demand has become urgent . . . but the key to raise our domestic market is to raise the revenue of peasants. This is why Chongqing's experiment is of special importance',[79] as the municipality is a small replica of China with 'a population of 32.8 million, including 23.3 million farmers. Among them, 8.4 million farmers have become migrant workers, including 3.9 million working and living in urban areas of Chongqing.'[80] In this vast area of 82 square kilometres city billionaires live alongside poor farmers, with large inequalities in income, education, medical care and housing, thus reproducing some of the major structural features of the entire country I have described above.

Moreover, whereas there have been many privatizations in Chongqing, public assets have also multiplied by six to eight times. 'So, the Chongqing experience shows that public ownership of assets and private entrepreneurship are not necessarily contradictory and that they are not substitutes for each other.'[81]

Of course this strategy could not be implemented without a strong political leadership orienting the development and submitting private investments to the interests defined by the political leadership.[82] One of the first measures taken by the central government was to allow the provinces mentioned above (including Chongqing) 'to levy only 15 percent of [private] enterprise income tax while the national average was 33 percent until 2008 and now is 25 percent.' Whereas many western provinces went back to the 33 per cent tax, Chongqing kept it at the 15 per cent level, thus succeeding in attracting huge foreign investment (e.g. from Hewlett Packard and Foxconn) and 'Hewlett Packard has moved its financial accounting centre from Singapore [where the income tax is 17.5 per cent] to Chongqing [a very unusual move] because foreign investors have never set up their financial accounting centres in China before.'[83] Cui's comment on the outcomes of this strategy is quite revealing:

> Therefore, low taxation is good for private local entrepreneurship, but paradoxically it is only possible because the government benefits from the revenues of public-owned assets. This is why we can talk of a new model. It is not a return to pre-reform period, because back then China's many public assets did not generate market revenue. It gives some substance to this concept of a socialist market economy, and the coexistence of market forms of ownership.[84]

Another interesting aspect of Chongqing's experiment is represented by the use of collective land to improve the revenues of peasants; this is done thanks to the establishment of the first Land Exchange Certificate in 2008. Peasants who have converted their land into arable land can get a land certificate that can be sold in auctions organized by the Land Exchange Authority. The conversion must be approved by the municipality committee by a two-thirds majority vote. Similarly, the projects of developers who buy the land certificates must be approved by the Municipality. Cui explains:

> If a developer wins an auction and thus gets a 'land certificate', then it can use this quota to purchase land-use rights in urban areas and develop that land. This interesting institutional arrangement is in a sense similar to 'emission permits trading' in the current global climate change regime.[85]

Cui further comments:

> to understand the profound meaning of Chongqing's land exchange market, we need to know two of China's fundamental national policies: one is that China would like to speed up the synchronized development of urban and rural areas, especially to speed up the process of industrialization and urbanization. And the other is that China would like to maintain 1.8 billion mu of cultivated land to ensure the country's food supply.[86]

184 *The crisis of New Public Management in the West and in China*

At the auction held in April 2010 the auction price was 140,000 RMB for a one-mu land certificate, equivalent to 666.7 square metres. After the sale, peasants keep their land as arable land, and can choose to move to the urban area by obtaining a residence permit there, or they can stay in the rural area living in apartment blocks especially built for them by the municipality. To date 2.6 million peasants have obtained the urban residence permit, the most important change in the rural *hukou* system in China since the beginning of reforms.[87] Not only does this change allow peasants to benefit from the public services available in the urban areas, but, as Cui comments:

> This is a way for the peasants to share some of the land value increase of urbanization because, usually, in Beijing for instance, . . . only people who live near the cities, in the suburbs, can share some of the land value increase of urbanization when their land is confiscated . . . but here, even people living far from the city can get their share and get payment as long as they can convert rural land back to arable land.[88]

The peasants are free to use 85 per cent of the money they get from selling the Land Exchange Certificate, whereas 15 per cent goes to their village, and its use is subject to a two-thirds majority vote by the village committee.

Finally, in order to rebalance Chongqing society, the Chinese local and central leaderships have developed, in addition to the creation of the Land Exchange Certificate mentioned above, a whole set of public policies aimed at helping those who have suffered, and are still suffering, from the uneven development of China.[89] The most important measures are the following: first, a project to increase farmers' income to 10,000 RMB per household by 2013; second, a project for supporting the so-called 'left-behind children', that is, children of former peasant families whose parents are both working in the urban areas and are therefore leaving their child (or children) on their own in the countryside, with problems that are easy to imagine, including the development of asocial behaviour and risks of social unrest.[90] These programmes include the building of 400 new boarding schools and nursing centres in the countryside, the provision of 'surrogate' parents, support for almost half a million students attending boarding schools in the countryside, and exemption from tuition and housing costs for 57,000 left-behind children studying at vocational middle schools. Third, more generally, in the domain of education, the city has allocated 26.7 billion RMB in favour of mandatory education, and has financially supported 3.6 million students. Fourth, there is a programme to support lower middle-class people (many of whom are migrant workers and university graduates) who find it difficult to find decent lodgings in the 'new free market'. This task still needs to be sustained as 'about 30 percent of city residents with low and mid-level incomes were not able to purchase their own housing'; for this purpose the city has planned to build 30 million square metres of public housing for apartments of 35 to 80 square metres, with a lease that will be only up to 60 per cent of the same type of private housing.[91]

The Chongqing experiment has attracted not only domestic and foreign investment, but also the attention of leaders of other Chinese cities who have visited

The development of social security in China[92]

We have seen, at the end of the paragraphs on unemployment, that China has already invested in public policies supporting the unemployed, thanks to several measures such as unemployment allowances and retraining support. I will briefly summarize these measures hereafter and introduce information about the other social policies adopted and developed by China since the beginning of the twenty-first century in urban and rural areas. In the following paragraphs I will update the information given in my book on China's reforms. Table 6.14 summarizes some data on the main social insurances in urban areas of China.

The structure of social security in urban areas

Old age insurance

By the end of 2007, the number of people participating in the basic old age insurance scheme in urban China reached 201.37 million (Table 6.14), 182.35 million of whom were employees. The revenues of the scheme grew from 631

Table 6.14 People insured by the major social insurances in Chinese urban areas, 2001–10 (million)

| Year | Old age insurance | Medical insurance | | Work-related injury insurance | Maternity insurance | Unemployment insurance |
		For employed	For unemployed residents[a]			
2001	141.83	76.3	–	43.45	34.55	103.55
2002	147.36	94	–	44.06	34.88	101.82
2003	155.06	109.02	–	45.75	36.55	103.73
2004	163.53	124.04	–	68.45	43.84	105.84
2005	174.87	137.83	–	84.78	54.08	106.48
2006	187.66	157.32	–	102.68	64.59	111.87
2007	201.37	180.20	42.91	121.73	77.75	116.45
2008	218.91	199.96	118.26	137.87	92.54	124.00
2009	235.50	219.37	182.10	148.96	108.76	127.15
2010	257.07	237.35	195.28	161.61	123.36	133.76

Sources: Ministry of Labour and Social Security Statistical Communiqué for Social Security (2001–2007), Ministry of Human Resource and Social Security Statistical Communiqué for Social Security (2008–2010), Beijing, People's Republic of China.

a The medical insurance system for urban residents was introduced in 2007.

billion RMB in 2006 to 783.4 billion RMB in 2007, an increase of 24.2 per cent, 649.4 billion RMB of which was raised by premiums. State budgets at all levels contributed 115.7 billion RMB to the basic old-age insurance funds. In 2007, the total of retirees who had joined the revolutionary ranks before October 1949 and other retirees reached 49.54 million, and the total payment was 596.5 billion RMB, an increase of 21.8 per cent. The accumulated balance within the old age insurance reached 739.1 billion RMB by the end of 2007. According to the *China Statistical Yearbook 2010*, by the end of 2009, 235.5 million people were covered by old age insurance, corresponding to a coverage of 75.67 per cent, out of a total number of employed persons in urban areas of 311.2 million.[93]

One must be aware of the fact that the pension system is much more sophisticated in the urban areas than in the rural areas. In the case of health insurance alone (to be dealt with hereafter), there are numbers of different kinds of pension systems in urban areas. For example, the commercial pension may be correlated with the insurance fees and the number of years one has paid; governmental officials' pension will be slightly lower than the salary they earn at the time of their retirement. However, usually, many officials' salary level is to be raised by one level as a reward (say, from vice mayor's to mayor's) when they retire, so their pension might be slightly higher than their last salaries. It is impossible to list all the different systems, but for urban people an estimated average amount of pension could be expected to be more or less the same as the salaries they earn when they retire, and it will definitely be higher than the local low-income level.

In addition to participating in the compulsory basic old-age insurance, enterprises with sufficient financial capacity are encouraged to set up enterprise annuities for their employees.

By the end of 2007, 320,000 enterprises had set up annuity schemes, the number of employees covered by annuities reached 9.29 million and the size of annuity assets amounted to 151.9 billion RMB. In theory, the development space of enterprise annuities in China is very impressive. Professor Yang Yansui of Tsinghua University predicted that the total of China's annuities would reach 1,000 billion RMB by 2010[94] and according to the prediction of the World Bank it would be 15 trillion RMB by 2030.[95] In fact, by the end of 2010, 371,000 enterprises had set up annuities schemes, the number of employees covered by annuities reached 13.35 millions and the size of annuity assets amounted to 280.9 billion RMB.

Health insurance

As the reform of the economic system and the development of Chinese society were under way during the 1980s, the Chinese government began to undertake the reform of medical insurance. Several pilot experiments were carried out, the most significant, in my opinion, being the decision to require patients to pay for part of health services. This decision was concomitant with the requirement that hospitals (the main source of health care in China) cover their costs (after deduction of the subsidy paid by government) through the selling of services (both pharmaceuticals and treatments). This system, of clear neoliberal inspiration, had the catastrophic consequence of excluding from health care a huge percentage of the Chinese population.[96] After years of experimentation at the provincial level, a report of the NDRC concluded that the existing system had failed because of a considerable increase in cost, inefficiency and the exclusion of a large part of the population. The Party-State then set up a coordination group under the responsibility of the Ministry of Health and the NDRC. This group coordinated the works of several organizations: 12 agencies representing several ministries; the Universities of Peking, Fudan, Renmin and Tsinghua (in cooperation with Harvard) and the Normal University of Beijing; the WHO; and the private consulting company McKinsey. Several reports were presented by these organizations, and a final report was presented to the Chinese leadership for evaluation and final decision.

At the Party Congress of November 2007 President Hu Jintao announced the imminent publication of the new Chinese public health system. Of course, the implementation of this new health system will necessitate several years' work; completion is planned for the year 2020. Bearing that in mind, let us try to define the present situation of health insurance in China starting from the urban areas. Health policies in rural areas will be dealt with hereafter under 'the structure of social security in rural areas'.

By the end of 2007 (see Table 6.14), at the moment when the new health system was made public by President Hu Jintao, the number of people participating in the basic medical insurance system across China reached 223.11 million, an increase of 65.79 million from 2006, of whom 180.2 million were covered by the basic medical insurance for employees (representing an increase of 22.88 million) and 42.91 million were covered by the medical insurance for urban residents. The revenue of the basic medical insurance in 2007 was 225.7 billion RMB, an increase of 29.3 per cent from 2006, and the expenses were 156.3 billion RMB (an increase of 22.3 per cent). By the end of 2007, the accumulated balance within the basic medical insurance reached 247.7 billion RMB.[97] By the end of 2009, 401.5 million people were covered by the health insurance, representing a coverage of 64.56 per cent.[98]

As for what is actually paid to the patients, the coverages for hospitalization and for outpatient care are different (see Table 6.15). For the outpatient services, the insurance reimbursement cap is about 400 to 600 RMB per year. The exact number may vary slightly with local policies, one's insurance fees or hierarchical level for governmental health insurance. For the hospitalization costs, the reimbursement cap is much higher. For the urban health insurance, the cap is usually higher than for rural areas (which was, in 2010, about 60,000 RMB for one year in most provinces). Nevertheless, the exact amount varies significantly from area to area, and different insurance systems have their own caps. For example, for commercial health insurance, this cap may be correlated with the insurance fees; whereas, for governmental health insurance, the cap is correlated with local government's financial capacity (which varies considerably from one province to another) and one's hierarchical level. Generally speaking, an estimated cap of 100,000–200,000 RMB can be expected for urban health insurance.[99]

Table 6.15 Reimbursement caps to patients from health insurances in China, 2010 (RMB)

	Outpatient services	Hospitalization
Rural	400–600	60,000
Urban	400–600	100,000–200,000

Sources: based upon *China Statistical Yearbook* 2009 and 2010.

Unemployment insurance

The Chinese government has taken several measures for improving the unemployment insurance system and, thanks to the increase of the accumulated assets, the basic livelihood guarantee system for *xiagang* workers has been progressively integrated within the unemployment insurance programme since 2001. This task was completed by the end of 2005, and the concept of *xiagang* was cancelled.[100] Today, the government pays more attention to re-employment and regards it as the foundation of people's livelihood. The number of people covered by unemployment insurance in urban areas rose from 106.5 million in 2005 to 127.2 million in 2009 over a workforce of employed people of 311.2 million in urban areas, representing a coverage of 40.87 per cent (Table 6.14). In 2007 it provided unemployment insurance benefits of varying time limits to 2.86 million people throughout the year. The revenue of unemployment insurance in 2007 amounted to 47.2 billion RMB, an increase of 17.5 per cent from the previous year; the expenditure was 21.8 billion RMB, representing an increase of 9 per cent. By the end of 2007, the accumulated balance reached 97.9 billion RMB.[101] Finally, the exact unemployment insurance benefits also vary in different provinces; it usually ranges from 500 to 600 RMB per month.[102] The number of people covered by unemployment insurance in urban areas is increasing every year: in 2010 it reached 133.76 million people (Table 6.14).

Work-related injury insurance

By the end of 2009, the number of people participating in work-related injury insurance nationwide reached 148.96 million and increased by 11.09 million from 2008 (Table 6.14). It provided insurance benefits to 0.95 million insured people throughout the year. The revenue in 2009 was 24 billion RMB, an increase of 10.8 per cent from the previous year; the expenditure was 15.6 billion RMB, an increase of 22.7 per cent. By the end of 2009, the total accumulated balance was 40.4 billion RMB, and the reserves fund reached 6.5 billion RMB. According to the Statistical Communiqué of the Ministry of Human Resource and Social Security, in 2010 the number of people participating in work-related injury insurance nationwide reached 161.61 million, an increase of 12.65 millions from 2009 (Table 6.14). It provided insurance benefits to 1.141 million insured people throughout the year. The revenue in 2010 was 28.5 billion RMB, an increase of

18.7 per cent from the previous year; the expenditure was 19.2 billion RMB, an increase of 23.6 per cent. By the end of 2010, the total accumulated balance was 47.9 billion RMB, and the reserves fund reached 8.2 billion RMB.

Maternity insurance

Maternity insurance has also been extended to an increasing number of women, form 34.55 million in 2001 to 123.36 million in 2010, an increase of 3.56 times or 355 per cent (see Table 6.14, according to the 2010 Statistical Communiqué of the Ministry of Human Resources and Social Security). In 2010 this insurance provided benefits to 2.11 million insured women throughout the year. The revenue in 2010 was 16 billion RMB, an increase of 20.5 per cent from the previous year; the expenditure was 11 billion RMB, an increase of 24.5 per cent. By the end of 2010, the total accumulated balance was 26.1 billion RMB.

Social relief

In 1999, the Chinese government promulgated the 'Regulations on Guaranteeing Urban Residents Minimum Standard of Living'. It stipulates that urban residents with non-agricultural permanent residence permits whose family's per capita income is lower than the local urban residents' minimum standard of living can receive basic subsistence assistance from the local government; those with neither source of income nor working capability, nor legal guardian, supporter or fosterer, can receive in full the minimum living allowance according to the minimum living standard of local urban residents.

In 2009, there were 23.456 million urban residents nationwide drawing the minimum living allowance, which was an average of 172 RMB per person per month. A total of 48.21 billion RMB for the minimum living allowance was allocated from government budgets in 2009, of which 35.91 billion RMB was from the central budget.[103] Moreover, medical relief was carried out actively in urban areas. In 2009, 15.063 million people (or times) received medical relief. The total expense for medical relief in urban areas was 4.12 billion RMB, an increase of 38.7 per cent from the previous year. Chinese public authorities have progressively increased the minimum living standard line, as shown in Table 6.16.

The structure of social security in rural areas

Old age insurance

As the process of modernization developed from the beginning of the 1980s, the social structure in the rural areas also underwent important changes and a huge migratory movement developed from the rural to the urban areas. Consequently the reliability of family security and solidarity decreased. Taking stock of these changes, the Chinese government began to experiment in the 1990s with a socialized old age insurance system in accordance with the actual level of local

Table 6.16 The minimum living standard line in China, 2005 and 2010 (RMB per month)

City	Standard line	
	2005	2010
Beijing	300	361
Tianjin	265	283
Fuzhou	210–230	224
Nanchang	190	291
Jinan	230	323
Zhengzhou	200	263
Wuhan	220	287
Changsha	200	250
Shijiazhuang	220	249
Taiyuan	183	273
Changchun	169	273
Haerbin	200	254
Guangzhou	330	398
Nanning	210	365
Wulumuqi	161	n/a
Dalian	240	350
Qingdao	260	305
Ningbo	300	373
Shenzhen	344	415
Xiamen	265–315	285
Huhehaote	190	282
Shenyang	220	328
Shanghai	300	302
Nanjing	200–260	350
Urumqi	161	252
Haikou	221	320
Chengdu	195	275
Chongqing	210	165
Kunming	210	175
Guiyang	170	229
Lahsa	200	310
Xian	200	229
Lanzhou	190	240
Xining	165	203

	Standard line	
City	2005	2010
Yinchuan	180	228
Hangzhou	280–320	368
Hefei	230	262

Sources: Ministry of Civil Affairs, http://www.china.com.cn/city/txt/2006-11/25/content_7406758.htm (accessed 15 June 2007) and http://files2.mca.gov.cn/cws/201007/20100727185927248.htm (accessed 12 June 2011).

socio-economic development in the rural areas. However, as participation in the scheme was not compulsory, this resulted, by the end of 2007, in selective coverage in favour of the better-off rural households, and in a very low coverage ratio of 16.4 per cent, corresponding to 51.71 million people. In 2007 there were 37 million peasants receiving old-age pension benefits, at a total expense of 4 billion RMB. According to the Ministry of Human Resources and Social Security Statistical Communiqué for Social Security 2009 and *Statistical Yearbook 2010*, by the end of 2009, 86.91 million people were covered by old age insurance, corresponding to a coverage of 12.19 per cent.

This low coverage is also due to the fact that the national old age pension system has been adopted only recently. This system is implemented by the government but is quite similar to commercial insurance. One needs to pay a regular insurance fee for a certain number of years (which can vary slightly in different provinces) before being entitled to receive the pension. As for the amount of money to be paid for the pension, every province has its own sophisticated way of calculating, but there are several basic principles they share. For example, it will be correlated with the average salary for workers and officials in the province during the last year, with the purpose of assuring a basic income level for old people. Some other factors may also affect the pension, such as the years of affiliation and the insurance fees one has paid. Generally speaking, the exact amount of the pension received by the insured people varies significantly in different provinces and for different categories of people. An estimated average amount of pension could be expected to be a little lower than, but close to, the average income of local areas.

The new rural cooperative medical system

By the end of 2007, 2,448 counties had carried out this new system, covering 730 million rural residents, corresponding to a participation rate of 85.7 per cent. In 2007, 260 million participants (or times) received compensation from this system, equal to a total of 2.2 billion RMB.[104] It is estimated that by the year 2010 this system will cover all rural residents throughout China. In fact, data from *China Statistical Yearbook 2010* show that, at the end of 2009, 833.1 million people were insured, corresponding to a coverage rate of 117 per cent, higher than 100 per cent because some urban people, especially those who live in small towns, are also eligible for China's rural health care insurance system.

Similarly to what we said for urban health insurance concerning the amount that is actually paid to the patients from the insurance, in the rural areas too there are differences in the coverage of the patients' costs for hospitalization and for outpatient care (Table 6.15). For outpatient services, the insurance reimbursement cap is about 400–600 RMB for one year, the same as for urban areas. The exact number may vary slightly with local policies, one's insurance fees or the hierarchical level for governmental health insurances.

For the hospitalization costs, the reimbursement cap is much higher. For rural health insurance, this cap was raised in 2010 to about 60,000 RMB per year in most provinces. However, in rural areas, the differences are less important than in urban areas, because the health insurance system for rural people is a uniform system valid all over the country, the New Rural Cooperative Medical System, which is implemented compulsorily by the central government; consequently, local policies vary little in different rural areas.

Social relief

By the end of 2006, this system had been set up in 2,133 counties nationwide (out of a total of 2,863) and there were 15.091 million rural residents receiving the minimum living allowance. In 2007, social relief was expanded to all the counties of China, and 34.519 million people drew the benefits, corresponding to an increase of 19.43 million. Moreover, the state has set up medical relief for poor peasants. In 2007, 6.034 million peasants (or times) received medical relief, and 23.055 million peasants (or times) were subsidized by the state to participate in the new rural cooperative medical system. The total expense for medical relief in rural areas amounted to 2.35 billion RMB, an increase of 146 per cent from the previous year.

In 2009, there were 47.6 million rural residents nationwide drawing the minimum living allowance, which was an average of 68 RMB per person per month. A total of 36.3 billion RMB for the minimum living allowance was allocated from government budgets in 2009, of which 25.51 billion was from the central budget.[105] Moreover, medical relief was carried out actively in rural areas. In 2009, 47.891 million persons (or times) received medical relief. The total expense for medical relief in rural areas was 6.46 billion RMB.

Conclusion: evaluating the results of the re-balancing policy

The question to which we have to provide an answer in this conclusion is: to what extent has the Chinese leadership been able to reverse, or at least put an end to the development of inequalities within the Chinese society? Several data are available for answering this question. Coming back to Figure 6.1 and Table 6.6, we can see that for income inequalities between urban and rural areas, after several decades during which the gap had widened between 1984 and 2003 from a ratio of 1.84 to 3.23, between 2003 and 2009 it went up only from 3.23 to 3.33, and between

2007 and 2009 it stayed practically stable at 3.33. Moreover, we have also seen that, according to China's National Bureau of Statistics, the Gini index measuring income inequality between households has not increased since 2007, when it was 48. Of course, this new trend is quite recent, and we must wait to see if it will be confirmed in the future. Nevertheless, there are several indices that point to this outcome, namely the general improvements to social security and the education system that are being implemented and developed in all the Chinese provinces, as well as in the urban and rural areas. Several Chinese researchers have recently put forward the idea, based upon empirical evidence, that after a long period of 'divergence' attested by increasing gaps of practically all the resources that should be at the disposal of all social groups (health, education, physical infrastructure such as roads and railways, social insurances such as for unemployment, health and old age) a new era of 'convergence' has developed since the government opted for a policy 'that puts people first' in 2002.[106]

According to Hu Angang and Wang Shaoguang, the reasons for this change are to be found, first, in the new fiscal policy that since the mid-1990s gave more financial means to the central government; second, in the new regional integration and coordinated development strategy adopted in 1995 at the Fifth Plenum of the Fourteenth CCP Central Committee, which includes the Development of the West Regions Strategy (2001), Rejuvenation of Old Industrial Bases in Northeastern China (2004) and Rise of Central China Strategy (2006); and, third, in the massive migration of an estimated number of 120–200 million workers from the poor inland rural areas to the rich urban coastal areas, which contributes to reducing interregional disparities.[107] Already in an article published in 2008, Wang Shaoguang sustained the thesis that the evolution of disparities in China has followed a 'two-way movement': first divergence increased and then, from the mid-1990s, it started to diminish.[108] First, the total transfer from the central government to the local government has increased from just over 20 billion RMB in 1994 to 1,600 billion RMB in 2007. Second, the GDP of four large regions in China (i.e. east, northwest, mid and west) started to converge since 1993 (when divergence was the highest, between 12 and almost 20 per cent) to become quite small in 2005 (about 2 per cent difference). Third, as we have already seen above, the government has implemented a comprehensive social security system that, even if rather modest, has put at the disposal of the great majority of the Chinese people a variety of supports in both rural and urban areas.

Using the most recent data for his last Master's course on China's development, Hu Angang, confirming Wang's analysis, shows that from the 1980s to 2008 the gap between provinces has also declined. By taking four levels of average personal income, he shows that between 1980 and 1990 almost all the provinces (except Shanghai and Beijing) were in the 'low income group (less than $755)', whereas in 2008 none was any longer in that group, 12 were in the 'upper middle group (between $2995 and $9265)', 18 in the 'lower middle income group (between $755 and $2995)' and only one (Shanghai) in the 'high income group (above $9265)'.[109] Second, by taking the entire Chinese population, and distributing it amongst the same income groups, Hu obtains the data shown in Table 6.17.

Table 6.17 From convergence to divergence and to reconvergence: population distribution of different GDP per capita groups in China (%, 1980–2008)

	1980	1990	2000	2005	2008	Change (%) 1980–2005
High income: > $9,265	0.00	0.00	0.00	0.00	1.42	1.42
Upper middle income: $2,995–$9,265	0.00	0.00	2.38	3.46	36.87	36.87
Lower middle income: $755–$2,995	1.16	2.85	58.88	93.63	61.71	60.55
Low income: < $755	98.84	97.15	43.74	2.91	0.00	–98.84
China	100.00	100.00	100.00	100.00	100.00	

Source: Hu Angang, Master's course 2009–10, lesson 14.

This table shows that at the beginning of reforms almost every Chinese citizen was in the 'low income group' with less than $755. As reforms were implemented, a small minority jumped into the 'lower middle income group' (2.38 per cent in 2000, 3.46 per cent in 2005), whereas another small minority (2.91 per cent) stayed within the 'low income group'. However, as soon as the new rebalancing policies were implemented and started to produce their desired effects between 2005 and 2008, the 'upper middle income group' increased from 3.46 per cent to an astonishing 36.71 per cent, while the 'low income group' disappeared, the 'lower medium group' decreased from 93.63 per cent to 61.71 per cent, and the 'high income group' rose from zero to a modest 1.42 per cent. This is an encouraging sign towards the establishment of a modestly well-off society.

Third, Hu Angang takes the Engel coefficient as a measure of the improvement of the expenditure structure of the Chinese household's budget. In a few words, the Engel coefficient measures the changes in consumption over time as income increases, namely the decline of the percentage of income spent on basic goods such as food and clothing compared with other consumption items. The index is low when basic goods represent a low percentage in total spending, and it corresponds to the living standard of rich people, whereas it is high when the proportion of basic goods is high, and it corresponds to the living standard of poor people.[110] By taking an Engel coefficient of 30–40 per cent to define the 'rich group', 40–50 per cent for the 'well-off group', 50–60 per cent for the 'basic food and clothing group' and above 60 per cent for the 'absolute poverty group', Hu Angang obtains the figures presented in Table 6.18. One can see that at the beginning of reforms the great majority of the Chinese population (92.46 per cent) belonged to the absolute poverty group. As reforms were implemented, the great majority of the population (84.62 per cent) in 2007 was concentrated into the two upper groups (43.37 per cent in the 'rich group', and 41.25 per cent in the 'well-off group'), whereas only a small proportion (15.38 per cent) belonged to the 'basic food and clothing group' and none to the 'absolute poverty group'.

Then, by taking again the Engel coefficient, but now at the provincial level,

Table 6.18 From absolute poverty to well-off in China: population distribution of different Engel coefficient groups (%, 1978–2007)

	1978	1990	2000	2007
Rich (EC 30–40%)	0.00	0.00	6.41	43.37
Well-off (EC 40–50%)	0.00	10.21	55.81	41.25
Basic food and clothing (EC 50–60%)	7.54	53.79	15.38	15.38
Absolute poverty (EC > 60%)	92.46	36	0.00	0.00

Source: Hu Angang, Master's course 2009–10, lesson 14.

Hu demonstrates that between 1978 and 2007 there was a convergence movement through which the majority of the provinces tended to pass from the lowest groups to the highest, so that in 2007 the great majority of the provinces (26 out of 31) were concentrated within the two upper groups (13 in the 'rich group' and another 13 in the 'well-off group'), the remaining five provinces being within the 'basic food and clothing group'. Moreover, Hu shows that the same convergence movement towards the upper levels of a moderately well-off society can be observed for the average years of education and the HDI and its components (education, health and GDP per capita) for which disparities have declined. Nevertheless, Hu warns us that disparities persist for life expectancy (mainly between regions), literacy rate (mainly within regions), gross enrolment rate for education (mainly between regions), per capita income (mainly between regions) and the HDI (also mainly between regions).

This analysis based upon the Engel coefficient can be further developed and expanded by taking the data published recently by the National Population and Family Planning Commission of China.[111] The Commission takes the same data we used in Table 6.6 above, showing the per capita disposable nominal income of urban households and the per capita annual net nominal income of rural households from 1978 to 2009 (see Table 6.19). For both these sets of data the Commission then adds an index (with base 100 for 1978) and the Engel coefficients. The index shows that urban income has grown more than rural income (index 895.4 against 860.6). Nevertheless, the difference between the rural and urban coefficients, which was about 10 points in 1978, declined to 4.5 points in 2009, when the Engel coefficient was 41.0 for urban and 36.5 for rural families. This change means that the difference in consumption between rural and urban areas has declined, especially (given the nature of the Engel coefficient) the difference of the percentage of income devoted to basic goods. In other words the consumption habits of urban and rural households tend to converge. If we look at the evolution of the Engel coefficient between 1978 and 2009 in more detail, we see that it followed basically the same pattern as the rate between urban and rural incomes we found when we commented on Table 6.6. The difference between the urban and rural Engel coefficients started to decrease between 1978, when the difference was 10.2 points, and 1991, when it dropped to 3.8 points, the lowest difference for the whole period between 1978 and 2009. This trend very likely reflects the positive

Table 6.19 China's urban per capita nominal annual disposable income and rural per capita net nominal income and Engel coefficients in China, 1978–2009

Year	Urban per capita disposable nominal income		Rural per capita net nominal income		Engel coefficient (%)	
	Value (RMB)	Index (1978 = 100)	Value (RMB)	Index (1978 = 100)	Urban households	Rural households
1978	343.4	100.0	133.6	100.0	57.5	67.7
1980	477.6	127.0	191.3	139.0	56.9	61.8
1985	739.1	160.4	397.6	268.9	53.3	57.8
1990	1,510.2	198.1	686.3	311.2	54.2	58.8
1991	1,700.6	212.4	708.6	317.4	53.8	57.6
1992	2,026.6	232.9	784.0	336.2	53.0	57.6
1993	2,577.4	255.1	921.6	346.9	50.3	58.1
1994	3,496.2	276.8	1,221.0	364.3	50.0	58.9
1995	4,283.0	290.3	1,577.7	383.6	50.1	58.6
1996	4,838.9	301.6	1,926.1	418.1	48.8	56.3
1997	5,160.3	311.9	2,090.1	437.3	46.6	55.1
1998	5,425.1	329.9	2,162.0	456.1	44.7	53.4
1999	5,854.0	360.6	2,210.3	473.5	42.1	52.6
2000	6,280.0	383.7	2,253.4	483.4	39.4	49.1
2001	6,859.6	416.3	2,366.4	503.7	38.2	47.7
2002	7,702.8	472.1	2,475.6	527.9	37.7	46.2
2003	8,472.2	514.6	2,622.2	550.6	37.1	45.6
2004	9,421.6	554.2	2,936.4	588.0	37.7	47.2
2005	10,493.0	607.4	3,254.9	624.5	36.7	45.5
2006	11,759.5	670.7	3,587.0	670.7	35.8	43.0
2007	13,785.8	752.5	4,140.4	734.4	36.3	43.1
2008	15,780.8	815.7	4,760.6	793.2	37.9	43.7
2009	17,174.7	895.4	5,153.2	860.6	36.5	41.0

Source: National Population and Family Planning Commission of China, based upon China Statistical Yearbook 2010, http://www.npfpc.gov.cn/en/detail.aspx?articleid=101222122513548283 (accessed 22 March 2011).

impact of the reforms implemented in the rural areas. However, in 1992 the difference started to increase to reach 10.5 points in 1999 (the highest difference for the whole period), reflecting the impact of the reforms conducted in the industrial sector that favoured urban areas over the rural ones. Then we have, between 2000 and 2004, an intermediate period when the difference stabilized to around 9.5, reflecting the first impact of the rebalancing policies decided in 1995. Finally, after 2006, the difference started to drop significantly to reach 4.5 points in 2009, reflecting the positive impact of the policies implemented since the beginning of the leadership of Hu Jintao.

Let me conclude this chapter by referring to the conclusion that Hu Angang draws from his analysis. Taking stock of the progress realized but also of the disparities that persist today, very realistically Hu concludes that (1) the coordinated development strategy, and the related goal to the reduction of regional disparities, adopted by the Chinese leadership in 1995 at the Fifth Assembly of the Fourteenth Central Committee is an important task, but also a long-term one; (2) the convergence of regional disparities must first of all concern the convergence of public services delivery, then the dimensions of the HDI and finally economic development; (3) the convergence of regional development levels needs not only market mechanisms but also effective governance. By this, Hu remains faithful to the position already adopted in 1993 with Wang Shaoguang, considering that the state must play a central role in orienting the strategy of economic and social development in such a big and diverse country as China.[112]

It remains to be seen whether the Chinese leadership is willing and able to sustain the convergence trend in the future, especially after a new generation of leaders is appointed at the 2012 Party Congress. However, we can already proceed to a first test, represented by the challenge of the 2008–11 global crisis, and this will be the theme I will develop in the general conclusion of this book.

Conclusion

Chinese way, Western way, the 2008–11 crisis and beyond

The attentive reader has certainly remarked that Chapter 6 on the impact of New Public Management (NPM) on China's economy and society concludes with a long section on the rebalancing of Chinese society, whereas there is no such section in Chapter 5 on the impact of NPM in the West. There is a good reason for that: the West has not taken any significant measures to reduce income inequalities and poverty rates during the years of the triumph of neoliberalism and of its two armed wings, the 'Washington consensus' and the NPM (1979–2008). On the contrary, the persistent implementation of the neoliberal project in the West, which has in fact delegated to the market (or more precisely to the market 'freed' from state interferences) the task of developing and distributing wealth, has further deteriorated income inequality and poverty, as I have shown in Chapter 5.[1] Well-documented research shows that, since the beginning of capitalism, income inequalities have not ceased to increase, except during some limited periods such as the 30 years after the Second World War. However, from the beginning of the neoliberal era (1980s) inequalities started to increase again and then stabilized at a relatively high level.[2] This is one of the major sources of the 2008–11 crisis, as Joseph Stiglitz very well explains:

> in the years immediately preceding the crisis, . . . domestic demand had also been weakened by high oil prices. The problem of high oil prices and growing inequality – reducing domestic aggregate demand – afflicted many other countries [in addition to the USA]. Income inequality increased in more than three-quarters of OECD countries from the mid-1980s to the mid-2000s, and the past five years saw growing poverty and inequality in two thirds of OECD countries.[3]

Moreover, 'growing inequality in the US and elsewhere around the world . . . shifted money from those who would have spent it to those who didn't thus reducing global aggregate demand.'[4] As Stiglitz and associates have explained for years:

> in the world of globalization, global aggregate demand is what matters. If the sum total of what people around the world want to buy is less than what the world can produce, there is a problem – a weak global economy.[5]

Of course, one has to take into consideration that, during that period of time, China and the West were at different stages of their development: in principle there was more space for improvements in the equitable distribution of wealth in a developing country such as China than in the West. In fact, during the first phase of its development (1978–95) China increased its GDP and reduced poverty. Unfortunately, it also developed inequalities and damaged the environment (see above, Chapter 6). Nevertheless, as soon as these phenomena were brought to the attention of decision-makers by academic researchers and critical intellectuals, the Chinese leadership understood the danger that such phenomena could represent for the stability of the country and the quest for international power, and several measures were taken to rebalance economy and society (see above, Chapter 6). Moreover, the different ways these issues have been treated by Chinese and Western leaders is quite striking, and even more so after the outburst of the 2008–11 crisis. I will come back to this point.

In order to evaluate and appreciate the reactions of China and the West to these phenomena, let us first recall the four hypotheses upon which this book is based. First, by implementing the NPM management type defined in Chapter 3 (in particular privatization and deregulation), both China and the West have obtained, in addition to similar positive results for the economy (measured by GDP), similar negative social outcomes too: increasing unemployment or underemployment,[6] increasing income inequalities, increasing poverty rates (and/or appearance of new forms of poverty), increasing crime rates and the deterioration of public health. Thus, the implementation of a type (some would say a model) of public management produced similar results.

Second, similar results are not necessarily identical, as, in the process of implementing a model, one is confronted with the local conditions (i.e. particular features of economy, polity, legal system, political culture and the heritage of history). So we have seen that, in spite of the fact that practically all the Western countries have implemented NPM devices, those that have gone very far in implementing the NPM model, that is, the strong-NPM countries, have deteriorated income distribution and public health (with the exception of the UK), as well as poverty and crime rates much more than the weak-NPM countries, which have implemented only part of the NPM model.[7] Moreover, the overall impact of NPM has been, at least until the outburst of the 2008–11 crisis, more serious in China than in the West. This is because, before the implementation of NPM, Western countries had developed a whole set of social policies that NPM has limited, but not dismantled. Nevertheless, there is today enough evidence to show that the crisis and the way the West is dealing with it are unfortunately producing a convergent movement amongst Western countries, precisely a realignment of many of the continental European states alongside the English-speaking ones, especially the USA and the UK. If this movement is confirmed in the years to come, this means that inequalities and poverty rates of these countries will attain the US and UK levels in the near future. I will come back to the reasons that explain this important outcome below. As for China, the verification of the second hypothesis has allowed us to conclude that, after the abandonment of the Maoist safety nets, neoliberal policies aimed at improving economic efficiency have brutally deregulated the labour market, limited access to education and health (by making citizens pay for substantial parts of these services) and introduced pensions with very limited coverage, not to mention that until recently the urban areas have benefited from more efficient social policies than the countryside. Only since the mid-1990s and especially after 2002 has a vigorous strategy of establishing a modern safety net system been gradually implemented.

Third, both China and the West have improved the strength of their economy (measured by GDP), at least up to the outburst of the 2008–11 crisis, by giving more space to economic efficiency thanks to NPM devices. However, this has been obtained at the expense of social equity. This confirms that one cannot simultaneously maximize economic efficiency and social equity, and that, on the contrary, there is a trade-off between these two values. Fourth, when these phenomena appear in the process of implementation, as has been the case since the 2008–11 crisis, China has proved to be better armed to rapidly take adequate measures for re-establishing overall social stability and the smooth functioning of the economy. This leads me to the second reminder, which will also be useful for evaluating our findings related to this fourth hypothesis.

The second reminder focuses our attention on the fact that NPM is the legitimate son of neoliberalism and the twin brother of the 'Washington Consensus'. The 2008–11 crisis shows very clearly both this filiation and brotherhood. The measures taken by Western countries to overcome the crisis are mainly directed at saving the dominant layer of capitalism, the financial system, by taking a number of measures that not only are meant to save this system with the injection of huge amounts of public money (ironically in clear contradiction to the neoliberal ideology, according to which the state should not interfere with the 'natural' functioning of the market) but are also imposing drastic austerity policies that very clearly harm the citizens of the middle and lower classes, who are not responsible for the crisis, with the consequence of increasing inequalities, poverty rates and social exclusion. In fact, these measures impose privatization of public services, reduction of social security benefits, reduction of salaries (in both the private and public sectors), the increase of unemployment (especially for young people) and the increase of different forms of taxation that are more often directed at the lower and middle classes than to the rich, while those responsible for the crisis are practically untouched.[8] The similarity between these policies implemented today in developed countries and those imposed in the past upon developing countries is quite striking. Let me quote two examples.

First, on 5 August 2011, the President of the European Central Bank (ECB), Jean-Claude Trichet, co-signed a letter with his successor, Mario Draghi, addressed to the Italian Prime Minister, Silvio Berlusconi, informing him of the conditions imposed by the ECB on the acquisition of Italian government bonds. First, the ECB asks Berlusconi to proceed by decree, not by a bill of law. It then lists the reforms it expects from Italy. In terms of privatization, it mentions municipal services (public transport, roads and electricity supply, with the exception of water, which will remain public).[9]

Second, let me quote the remarks made by the President of the European Central Bank, Jean-Claude Trichet, introducing his last press conference, 6 October 2011:

> Fiscal consolidation and structural reforms must go hand in hand to strengthen confidence, growth prospects and job creation. The Governing Council therefore urges all euro area governments to decisively and swiftly implement *substantial and comprehensive structural reforms*. This will help these countries to strengthen competitiveness, increase the flexibility of their economies and enhance their longer-term growth potential. In this respect, *labour market reforms are key*, with a focus on the removal of rigidities and the implementation of measures which *enhance wage flexibility*. In particular, we should see the *elimination of automatic wage indexation clauses* and a strengthening of firm-level agreements. More generally, in these demanding times, moderation is of the essence in terms of both profit margins and wages. These measures should be accompanied by structural reforms that increase competition in product markets, particularly in services – including the liberalisation of closed professions – and, where appropriate, the *privatisation of services* currently provided by the public sector, thereby facilitating productivity growth and supporting competitiveness.[10]

If one adds to these two statements the measures already imposed by the ECB, the European Commission and the IMF (a new 'Unholy Alliance'?)[11] on several European countries, one cannot but conclude that the era of triumphant neoliberalism has not come to an end.[12] If we also take into consideration the well-documented tendencies towards concentration of, and interconnections between, capitalist companies, and the massive tax evasion or avoidance by multinational firms thanks to the persistence of the tax havens that they use for the purpose of hiding the exact amount of their profits,[13] we are forced to recall the prophetic statement of Fernand Baudel (already mentioned in Chapter 2):

> capitalism has always been monopolistic, and merchandise and capital have always circulated simultaneously, for capital and credit have always been the surest way of capturing and controlling a foreign market. Long before the twentieth century the exportation of capital was a fact of daily life, for Florence as early as the thirteenth century . . . Need I observe that all methods, dealings, and tricks [*ruses* in the French edition, p. 118] of the financial world were not born in 1900 or in 1914? Capitalism was familiar with them all, and, yesterday as today, its uniqueness and its strength lie in its ability to move from one trick to another, from one way of doing things to another, to change its plans ten times as the economic conjunctures dictate –, and as a result, to remain relatively faithful, consistent with itself.[14]

Nevertheless, when one knows that the neoliberal policies imposed on developing countries have not worked in the past, especially in Africa and South America (where they have on the contrary devastated the state's finances and whole sectors of society, such as health and education, without bringing to these countries the development they promised) how can Western leaders imagine that these same policies will work today for the Western developed world? Moreover, it seems that so far no serious measures have been taken to reduce unemployment and promote growth, nor to avoid the recurrence of similar crises in the future. This short-sighted attitude has discouraged those Western experts who hoped that the crisis would have brought to an end the irrational behaviour of political leaders who have surrendered to the dictates of the financial elite. Let me put this frustration in the words of Joseph E. Stiglitz:

> One might have thought that with the crisis of 2008 the debate over market fundamentalism . . . would be over. One might have thought that no one ever again . . . would argue that markets are self-correcting and that we can rely on the self-interested behaviour of market participants to ensure that everything works well. Those who have done well by market fundamentalism offer a different interpretation. Some say our economy suffered an 'accident' . . . those who held this position want us to return to the world before 2008 as quickly as possible.[15]

Finally, witnessing the consequences of neoliberal austerity policies, the protest movements of large sectors of the population of Western countries, and the violence that states may consider necessary for keeping the situation under control and implementing austerity policies, the former French Prime Minister Michel Rocard (a moderate social democrat) has declared to the influential French newspaper *Le Monde*:

> given the state of anger of the [Greek] people, one can forecast that no Greek government will be able to face this situation without the support of the army . . . This sad consideration is certainly also valid for Portugal and/or Ireland, and/or other, bigger countries. How far will we go?[16]

This quite evidently poses the question of democracy; not only have Western politics of liberal democratic countries been under the control of the financial elite for several decades, not only does the ECB ask a formally sovereign democratic state (Italy) to act by decree instead of using one of the typical instruments of democracy (the law) when demanding the implementation of severe austerity policies, not only do eminent political leaders manifest their disapproval when they learn that the Greek President envisages submitting these policies to universal referendum, but the risk of seeing police and military force resort to brutal force to silence those who dare protest has become a possibility, and in too many cases already a reality. The fundamental contradiction between the functioning of capitalism and democracy could not be more evident.[17]

The insistence of the present Western leadership upon the untouchable status of the neoliberal project, which has so blatantly failed, is particularly worrying for our future, because it is the sign of an incapacity to question past choices (and the ideology upon which they were based), and thereafter to redirect our policies away from the myths diffused by neoliberalism during the last 30 years. A myth, as I have defined it in the introduction of this book, is a set of ideas that one has defined once and for all, and considered to be valid everywhere, not subject to critique and reconsideration, and that moreover promises to realize objectives that in fact it is not capable of delivering. There is a terrible social, political and economic fraud embedded in neoliberalism that becomes apparent when one passes from that ideology to its implementation through the 'Washington Consensus' and NPM. This is in fact one of the functions of all ideologies: to convince the people of their validity, by promising results that everybody would be ready to adhere to enthusiastically, but that in fact ideologies cannot deliver. This is exactly what neoliberalism (and its armed wings of the 'Washington Consensus' and – for this book – NPM) have promised to realize: let the economy work according to its 'natural' laws, both nationally and internationally, let the market correct itself without state intervention (what Stiglitz has labelled 'market fundamentalism') and prosperity will become accessible to everybody. How far are we today from this promise! Prosperity for all did not materialize; on the contrary, neoliberalism has produced a huge redistribution of wealth away from labour to the advantage of capital, thereby increasing not only income inequalities, but also insecurity in the labour market and poverty rates.

Since at least the mid-1990s it was clear that NPM was a myth for at least part of society (people at the lower end of the wealth distribution); and after the 2008 crisis it has become apparent that NPM is also catastrophic for the entire economy and the middle class. Of course, defenders of NPM would say that NPM has nothing to do with all this; it is a box of technical tools aimed at improving public management. However, I have shown in this book that the reality is that the tools have been used instead to realize the ideological goals of neoliberalism, of which the NPM is one of the armed wings. The hammer has been used to harm people, not to drive nails. If we are tempted today to restore the economic system that produced the crisis, 'we will emerge with a society more divided and an economy more vulnerable to another crisis and less equipped to meet the challenges of the twenty-first century.'[18] This is the irrational character of neoliberalism. But beware; whereas it is irrational for society as a whole, it is very rational for those who have rationally and systematically implemented it and benefited from it, and would like today to restore it after its blatant failure. How can someone rationally propose, for the purpose of overcoming the crisis, to restore the system that led to the crisis, if not out of personal interest and greed?[19]

Today, the consequences of neoliberalism, and the popular protest movements that are developing all over the West against the way Western leaders try to come out from the crisis (which point dramatically to their badly concealed desire to restore the management of the economy as it was before) shows an increasing fracture between our economic and political leaders who run Western states and economies, on one hand, and the people, on the other. Not surprisingly, this situation has reminded me of the way I described elsewhere the situation in which China found itself at the end of the 1970s after the Cultural Revolution and that necessitated the reconciliation of the Chinese state, market and society.[20] Are we today in the West on the road of reconciliation? By concluding in October 2008 the manuscript of my book on China's reforms and commenting upon the 2008 crisis and the reactions to it by Western leaders that pointed, already then, to a restoration of the neoliberal project, I considered:

> that at the end of this process the cynical and disabused remark of Prince Salina in the famous Italian novel *The Leopard* will, once again, prove to be true: 'If we want everything to stay as it is, it is necessary to change everything . . .' waiting for the next, fatal and final crisis?[21] While it is certain that the seriousness of the present crisis needs some radical restructuring of the various components of society (in a new form of capitalism or in a completely different form of societal organization), it is today difficult to forecast how the West will succeed in reconciling state, economy and society.[22]

Three years after, I have no reason whatsoever to change this statement. Joseph Stiglitz also seems to predict the worst, as he has recently described the present Western strategy as a 'suicide pact'.[23]

Of course one may object that China has also taken some massive measures in order to overcome the crisis, and some even consider that China has 'overacted', thus running the risk of overheating its economy (i.e. fuelling inflation) and of investing without evaluating the risk of creating (again as in the 1990s) a considerable number of non-performing loans (NPL).[24] Quite true, but there is a considerable difference. Whereas, as mentioned above, the money spent by Western countries (i.e. the money of their taxpayers) was injected into the financial sector to avoid its collapse in the short run and, moreover, by simultaneously imposing drastic austerity policies upon their people, the Chinese government has taken the crisis as an opportunity for investing in projects that are meant to improve economy and society in the long run.[25] For years Western officials and mainstream economists (especially Americans) have blamed China for not having developed a 'modern and performing' financial sector independent from the Party-State, and insisted in particular on the huge amount of NPL. Many even forecast the collapse of China's financial sector. However, as Stiglitz remarks, 'the irony that it was US banks that collapsed, not those of China, has not escaped those on both sides of the Pacific.'[26] Taking a more general perspective (as I have already mentioned in Chapter 2) the New Left Chinese intellectual Wang Hui comments: 'China's economic development has broken many predictions – a seemingly endless string of theories that China would collapse began to appear after 1989 [a clear reference to the crackdown of the protests in Tiananmen Square in June of that year] but then it wasn't China that collapsed but those theories themselves.'[27] Talking about the difficulty in understanding China's development, one of the most knowledgeable Chinese economists comments:

> Even I, a scholar who has long been involved internally in China's reform and opening up, and who has studied China national conditions for more than

20 years, find it hard to get everything clear. Reading China is like reading an illegible script or 'a book from heaven' as the Chinese saying goes. It is very hard to understand, because China is so large, the situations are so complicated and the changes are so precarious that it is impossible to 'be foresighted'. It would be good enough to 'be hindsighted'. Modern China studies are harder and more complicated than was imagined.[28]

This suggests that one would expect, on the part of Western leaders and scholars, a more cautious and modest attitude when commenting upon China's public policies.

Here again, we have to take into consideration that China is today at a different stage of development from the West; local conditions favourable for overcoming the difficulties created by the crisis abound.[29] Nevertheless, it is one thing to be at a different stage of development that may offer some good prospects for overcoming the crisis, and it is another to take the right measures in order to seize that opportunity. Now that is just what China has done.[30] In October 2008 China introduced its fiscal stimulus to be implemented between 2008 and 2010. The decision was taken very rapidly and implementation has followed immediately. It is clear that a great part of the investments were already planned; their implementation has been simply accelerated as a timely response to the crisis. This may moderate the praise for China's rapid adoption of the stimulus, but it may be considered, on the contrary, as a sign that the Chinese leadership was already aware of the necessity of those investments, in line with decisions taken since 2002 in the framework of the new policy that departs from 'economic development first' to 'put people first'. The stimulus, as it was first announced in 2008, totalled 4 trillion RMB; it was revised in 2009 by the Chinese Parliament, while maintaining the total at 4 trillion RMB, to increase the amounts allotted to well-being expenditures such as health, education and housing for low-income residents, thus strengthening the 'people first policy' by revising the structure of the stimulus after 2009. The stimulus investments were attributed to infrastructure, that is, railways, roads, airports and electricity grid (1,500 million RMB); structural adjustment and technical reconstruction (370 million RMB); health and education (150 million RMB); rural residents' well-being (370 million RMB); energy savings and environmental protection (210 million RMB); housing for low-income residents (400 million RMB); and post-earthquake reconstruction in Sichuan province (1,000 million RMB). All these measure are in line with the construction of infrastructures necessary for the further development of the economy and for sustaining domestic demand, a *sine qua non* for diminishing dependency upon exports. The sources of financing are shared between the central government (1,180 million RMB) and local governments (3 trillion RMB, including 200 million RMB of local debt, policy-related loans and local enterprise bonds).[31]

It is generally admitted that the Chinese stimulus has worked, but at the cost of some negative outcomes.[32] After a temporary slowdown in the first half of 2009, the economy recovered to an astonishing GDP increase of 8.7 per cent year on year for 2009 (after an increase of 13 per cent in the fourth quarter of 2009) to reach 10.3 per cent in 2010, thus compensating for the temporary collapse of export; employment also grew and the massive unemployment among migrant workers never materialized. Nevertheless, there have also been costs. First, growth was based upon investments, which goes contrary to the declared aim of the government to rely more on consumption.[33] This is true, but one must take into consideration that the aim of the stimulus was to rapidly bring China out of the crisis, and there are signs that China is moving from investment to consumption. Moreover, other policies (i.e. social insurances) that help boost domestic demand by reducing the high propensity of the Chinese households to save are included in the stimulus – such as health and education – and, moreover, are already financed outside the stimulus package. Second, and more seriously, the stimulus has produced a huge amount of debts, especially at the local level, and has probably been invested in projects whose risk has not been properly calculated.[34] This may result not only in inefficiencies but also in financial and budgetary difficulties that China will have to address in a not too distant future. However, the Chinese leadership has demonstrated during the last 30 years its capability of mastering this type of problem; of course, on condition that the right measures be taken as soon as possible, such as a strengthening of the fiscal capacity of the central government (if it wants to take the responsibility of providing some services instead of the local authorities) as well as its capacity of controlling the spending habits of local governments.

In spite of the difficulties mentioned above, it seems that China has managed the crisis better than Western countries. One reason for this is that China's choice in favour of NPM devices has been oriented not by ideology but by pragmatism; the tools have been used to drive nails. At the beginning of the 1980s, the introduction of market mechanisms combined with privatization, deregulation and personal responsibility for facing unemployment, old age and education seemed to be the best means for rapidly developing the country and restoring China's power. However, when problems appear, as in the 2008–11 crisis, measures are taken without losing time discussing whether *laissez-faire* or Keynesianism is the best choice. On the contrary, in the West, the dominance of the upper layer of capitalism (finance) is clearly oriented towards the restoration of the system that led to the crisis. It also shows that the heritage of the socialist features that were so present during the Mao era are operating still today and orient the Party-State. True, socialism under Mao has produced negative and, on several occasions, even catastrophic outcomes such as the Great Leap Forward and the Cultural Revolution. Still, as I have argued elsewhere, since then China's decision-making system has been transformed into one whereby decisions are taken collectively, and moreover it has been opened to all kinds of sources of information (not only from stakeholders but also from research performed nationally and internationally), which makes the occurrence of similar mistakes unlikely.[35]

At the end of our journey into the world of NPM, it seems that the statement I put forward in Chapter 2, that China is on its way to succeeding in managing market mechanisms without introducing liberal democracy, seems to be correct for the time being. Nevertheless, I also pointed to the appearance of capitalist behaviours performed by the new Chinese capitalists. Even if China is not today a capitalist country, we cannot exclude the possibility that it may become capitalist in the future. The decision belongs to the Chinese leadership and to the Chinese people. Whatever the outcome, here are some suggestions not so much for avoiding the evolution towards capitalism (as there are several serious intellectuals both in the West and in China who think that capitalism must and can be rescued from the greed of the financial sector[36]) but to orient China's policies towards the satisfaction of its citizens, which should be the ultimate goal of any economic and political system, liberal or socialist. I hope that in this book I have suggested to the attentive reader some clues that should help him/her to decide which one is the best. Moreover, we can forecast that in a foreseeable future China will not change its political system, and hopes expressed by Western observers that the 2011 Arab Spring revolutions may spread to China are not taking into consideration the very different local situations.[37]

Taking into consideration the remarkable progress China has made since the beginning of reforms, but also the major challenges facing the Chinese leadership today (especially disparities, accumulation of huge amounts of wealth by rich families in the presence of very low income for the majority of workers and peasants, corruption, pollution, ageing of the population, to mention only a few), here are some suggestions the Chinese leadership may be willing to consider:

1. Further develop the policies that 'put people first' (especially social security, i.e. health, unemployment and old age insurance, housing, drinkable water and access to public services) that will help reduce disparities, especially income inequalities. As I have pointed out, in spite of the convergence trend that reduces disparities between provinces and groups of citizens, income inequalities between households are still today quite high, even if the increase seems to have been brought to a halt in 2007 at a Gini index equal to 48.[38] Moreover, the policies that 'put people first' constitute an important stimulus favouring the development of domestic demand that will reduce dependence upon investment and exports.
2. For this purpose it is also necessary to improve the well-being of the rural residents and migrant workers (the Chongqing experiment could be a source of information) and this will help the smooth management of the process of urbanization.
3. Further open up the decision-making process so that it can base its decisions upon information from experts (both national and international) and organized stakeholders, as well as ordinary people at the five levels of China's political and administrative organization.
4. Avoid all forms of market fundamentalism and keep on the road of Chinese pragmatism.
5. Keep politics in command over the economy and its actors.[39]
6. Therefore keep the new Chinese capitalists under control so that they do not develop behaviours similar to those of their Western colleagues that led to the dominance of the upper layer of capitalism (finance) and to the 2008–11 crisis.[40]

7 Keep the banks, and the central bank, under control.
8 Promote the development of the 'real market': a market economy based upon competition and transparency (see also point 19 below).[41]
9 For this purpose it is necessary to regulate the market so that it produces efficiently what society needs.
10 Be ready to substitute the market when it fails to produce what society needs; and maintain within the state sectors that may be considered as strategic for China's economy, and/or necessary for providing affordable services to the citizens.
11 Improve the local authorities' capacity to evaluate the opportunity of setting up public–private partnerships; improve their capacity to manage PPPs.
12 Further improve the management and efficiency of SOEs, including banks.
13 Support the development of Chinese brands.
14 Further eradicate corruption and tax evasion and avoidance.
15 Further increase the fiscal capacity of the central government and its capacity to control the spending of local authorities by setting up an efficient debt-reporting system on local governments.
16 Further develop the policy of reducing pollution and the use of scarce resources (green economy).
17 Keep developing and improving the education system (which should be free of charge at the compulsory level and affordable at the upper levels), as well as science and technology.
18 In the international arena be ready to take the lead in international organization when blockages appear, for example in climate change, international finance, tax evasion and avoidance, and more generally for the necessary restructuring of the international economic, financial and political system.
19 Continue the policy of opening up to the global economy, but practice selective protectionism, as recent economic history has shown and as the UK and the USA did before they became strong enough to promote global 'free trade'.
20 Establish and/or develop exchanges with the European Left (the American one being too weak and isolated and too much submerged by neoliberal ideology) as well as with European Green parties for exploring common solutions to national and international issues.
21 Last but not least, revise the old categories used today both in universities and in economic, political and media circles, such as 'capitalism', 'socialism', 'liberalism', 'free market', 'free trade' and 'protectionism'.

By succeeding in the above-mentioned issues and challenges, China could contribute in a significant way not only to the well-being of its own people but also to the rest of the world. Yet one question remains open: is there a 'China model'? This question has been debated by both Chinese and Western scholars and opinion leaders.[42] The tentative answer I can give, based on the findings presented in this book, as well as on my evaluation of China's reforms,[43] is, for the time being, negative. There is no China model; or more precisely, and maybe also paradoxically, the China model is that there is no model, but a continuous transformation of the ways of thinking and managing the modernization process of this great country. Given the success of China and the relative failure (and persistence) of the 'neoliberal model' in the West, I would be tempted to end this book by wishing good luck to my fellow Westerners, and by encouraging my Chinese friends to go ahead on the road of pragmatism and continuous transformation.[44]

Annex 1
New Public Management: another point of view[1]

In the 3 October [1997] issue of the *Journal de Genève* Prof. X tackles the criticisms addressed to the New Public Management (NPM), especially those of university professors, which, he says:

> are certainly understandable in the framework of ideological debates, but ignore the practice of NPM. Indeed, NPM is not a new neoliberal ideology ... but a new approach aimed at making the public service more efficient and more effective.

There, the tone is set! On one side the NPM practice, void of any kind of neoliberal ideology, and those who understand it, and on the other side university professors fond of ideological debates and ignorant of what is going on in the real world. Following the usual approach of defenders of NPM, the rest of the article stuns us with a series of slogans in tune with the signs of the times, without any kind of empirical evidence.

I will not comment on the self-proclaimed novelty of NPM (in fact a remake of recipes at least 50 years old), or on the absence of its neoliberal filiations. New Public Management is without doubt the very legitimate son of the renewal of liberalism, whether you like it or not. But then, why should one not recognize one's father? In order to please everybody? The Right as well as the Left?

But there is worse to come. Where the NPM really innovates is when it replaces the concept of the citizen with that of the customer. By doing so one confines the role of the individual-citizen to that of a buyer of products on a variety of markets. At the same time, one destroys the role of the individual-citizen as bearer of a set of rights and duties conferred upon him/her by the community (i.e. by his/her fellow citizens) through the democratic process.

One must say, to the credit of Prof. X, that he continues to use the word 'citizen'. But it is a simple exercise of style: it suffices to read the writings of the proponents of NPM to see that they explicitly introduce the market into the political sphere, and consequently it is the customer who becomes the major actor and not the citizen. Now, in a market, the customer acts as an individual, bearer of a solvent demand. In the democratic process of law formation the individual acts in so far as he/she is member of a community, independent of his/her financial capacity. The latter is taken into consideration only to correct the impact of the market (e.g. through progressive income taxation).

However, as somebody has already said, there is no limit to the worst. The defenders of NPM are very careful not to quote the 'performance' of the countries that have systematically implemented the recipes of NPM, either long ago (the USA) or since the 1980s (New Zealand and the UK). Serious research shows that these countries are the champions of inequality of income distribution. This would not in itself be regrettable if at the same time this did not lead to the appearance of increasing poverty rates.

Moreover, unemployment statistics, in appearance very flattering for NPM countries, become much less attractive when one takes into consideration the non-registered unemployed people, invalids, as well as the considerable increase of part-time, low-paid jobs (often with a considerable reduction of social security coverage). Moreover, statistics on criminality show that it is in these countries that the increase of petty crimes is the highest.

Finally, these same countries have initiated a considerable reduction of social security. In summary, NPM countries are those where the social breakdown is most significant. What will happen if this movement continues to develop? What do the NPM supporters say about this? Nothing or close to nothing. And for a good reason: NPM is not an ideology ... Really?

Should then university professors, who do not ignore the practice of NPM, ask the classical question of detective stories: whom does the crime benefit? This is in fact the question implicitly posed by the economist Paul Krugman regarding income distribution in the USA during the very highly NPM years of the Reagan era: 70 per cent of the increase in income (as there was an increase of income in spite of the economic crisis) went to the richest taxpayers (1 per cent of the total), whereas the 20 per cent at the bottom experienced an average decrease in income of 9 per cent.[2] It is also the question asked by the London *Times* for the United Kingdom and giving practically the same answer.[3]

Among the beneficiaries of NPM there is also a certain number of politicians favourable to a reduction and/or a revision of the role of the state, as well as civil servants trained at business schools that diffuse the NPM approach, which the American, New Zealand and British cases show very well. There are finally the consulting companies, private and public, that obtain mandates (very often on the basis of an exaggerated reputation) from the politicians and civil servants mentioned above. The circle is thus closed. It then suffices to explain to the people that NPM is the inevitable consequence of the globalization of the economy.

At this point, the reader not quite convinced by the NPM will ask the other classical question (but not the detective stories' one): what is to be done? I would tell him that there is nevertheless something to be glad of in our countries ravaged by the crisis, globalization and NPM. The citizen exists, as recent legislative elections in Italy, England, France and ... Geneva show, as well as the protest movements and strikes everywhere in Europe and even in the USA.[4] So what then? Would the citizen pose the same questions as the university professors well acquainted with the practice of NPM? Whom does NPM profit? And, finally, is the self-defining 'New Public Management' the latest manifestation (new in its form, but very traditional indeed) of some 'old private interests' in the public sphere?

Annex 2
The role of scientists in the definition of the strategies of reform[1]

I should like to say right from the beginning that the subject I was asked to address is 'the role of scientists in defining strategies for reform [of public management]', and not a critique of the strategies themselves. It should also be emphasized that, even defined so restrictively, this subject is a very difficult and controversial one, and I am even more embarrassed because I am myself a scientist, or at least an academic and a consultant; so I am judge and jury in dealing with this subject. Two premises, before entering the heart of the matter.

First, for a scientific analysis of the reform process, please refer to the paper of Prof. Christopher Pollit, who has worked and published extensively on public sector reforms.[2] For myself, I will rather deal with the relationship between scientists and the reform process, and finally what their role is in this adventure of public sector reform. I presume that Prof. Horber-Papazian [one of the organizers of this congress] asked me to address this issue and placed my presentation at the end of this half day, probably because she relies on my criticism, and even on my tendency to engage in polemical arguments. I am not in the habit of polemicizing, but occasionally I do, especially when my interlocutors are so armoured in their beliefs that it is necessary to shake them a little; and this is today the case for most proponents of New Public Management. So I shall effectively be quite critical in dealing with the interface between scientists and the process of public sector reform. I am all the more comfortable in doing so in that I am soon to retire, and I have furthermore just won two mandates that will keep me busy until retirement.[3] Therefore, I am no longer looking for other mandates and I feel quite free to say what I think today. This was the first premise.

A second premise is necessary to understand the following comments: I am, and I have always been a supporter of reforms of the administration, or even of the state, provided they can improve the situation of a community. On the occasions of several expert reports produced during the last 15 years at various levels of the federal structure, I had the opportunity to propose improvements for the organization and the management of public affairs, but I have always refused to promise miracles. Now, if you look at some of the literature (but still an important part of the literature) on the reforms that it would be necessary to introduce into our systems of public sector management, one is struck by the trend that has spread very rapidly in recent years, promising miracles: debureaucratization, decentralization, deregulation, to do more with less (which seems to be a new version of the squaring of the circle). We are witnessing a surge of expressions such as 'breaking through bureaucracy', 're-engineering', 'reinventing' and so on.

Moreover, as one's own consulting practice must be made consistent with practising what one preaches, it is inevitable that one is tempted to overdo it, proposing reforms more and more striking on the inexhaustible road of permanent performance improvement. For example, it is not surprising that one of the pundits of reforms (who was mentioned several times during this congress and again just a moment ago by my colleague Prof. Pollitt), David Osborne, who in 1993 modestly proposed to reinvent government, four years later invited us simply to banish bureaucracy.[4] Why not? But how? And with what real chances of success?

Those who have read and meditated a little on the work of Max Weber, and who have added to Weber's reflections (dating from the beginning of the twentieth century) the results of serious research published since, are well aware that bureaucracy is one of the social formations that it is most difficult to destroy, and that the forms of quasi-bureaucratic administrations that existed in the past, especially in antiquity, disappeared only at the same time as the actual disappearance of the very societies that they were supporting. So I think that it calls for at least some caution (and a certain modesty) when putting forward such shattering proposals. Alternatively, one must be much bolder and propose a complete restructuring of our society. It must be said that, following the wave of such proposals, a lot of politicians have produced (or reproduced) the same discourse, that is to say that they promise extraordinarily well-performing improvements in the management of public affairs.

It is in this context that I was asked to give my views on the role of scientists in defining strategies for reform. The debate is not new. Here again, as with other proposals of New Public Management, the novelty is relative. This does not rejuvenate me, because I remember that, when I was a student and a young assistant [in the 1960s], the debate was already raging within the discussions about the 'policy sciences' and 'policy analysis'. Two scenarios were then considered: first, scientists at the service of their own discipline, analysing phenomena independently, basing their work upon criteria of truth, rigour and objectivity, but also attentive to the weaknesses of their discipline; second, scientists at the service of politics, that is, they put their knowledge at the service of politicians and therefore ultimately to the aims, objectives and values of these latter.

Nevertheless, there is one fundamental difference from the debate that took place in the 1950s and 1960s and up to the late 1970s. Today, and more precisely after the first oil crisis, this debate takes place in the framework of a fiscal crisis, the growing indebtedness of the state, a crisis of the Welfare State, and the revival of liberal thought and globalization. And so the debate becomes much more crucial than 20 or 30 years ago. Indeed at that time the reform proposals were mainly aimed at improving the functioning of what existed. We thus witnessed a wave of proposals such as the PPBS (Planning, Programming and Budgeting System) in the United States, the 'rationalization of budgetary choices' in France, the zero-based budgeting, the management by objective and other reforms, but in fact the aim was to improve what already existed, without fundamentally questioning the role of the state, whereas today NPM is aiming exactly at that. Not only are the reforms aimed at improving the functioning of public administrations as they exist, but NPM proposes to review the role of the state, to revise its public policies, and therefore eventually to require the state to withdraw from part of the activities it carries out for the benefit of the community. The assumption is that by introducing market and quasi-market mechanisms (especially privatization, but also contracting out) one will improve the provision of public services. The problem is that by doing so one calls into question some fundamental values.[5]

I am talking about really heavy reforms relating to privatization in particular, outsourcing and contracting out of public services, and also the experiences of decentralization, the separation of strategic decisions (that is to say political decisions) and operational decisions (that is to say, administrative, operational or current decisions) such as the British so-called 'Next Step Agencies'. This is a whole set of reforms that it is absolutely essential to evaluate before concluding their state of superiority and efficiency. So I am really talking about something very weighty, which touches the heart of the system of values upon which the state activity is based.[6]

In this context, I see two types of betrayal on the part of scientists, therefore of myself and of my colleagues, and first of all the one I call 'the intellectual betrayal'. This is what I alluded to earlier, that is, promising something that one cannot deliver, to promise to banish bureaucracy, for example. This means very specifically to outlaw bureaucracy, something, I believe, we can hardly promise. Therefore, there is there, right at the beginning of the construction of a logic for apprehending reality, a formidable bias that is introduced by some scientists.

The second betrayal is what I call 'the professional betrayal'; because in the current context, or, to use a fashionable terminology, in today's market of consulting, characterized by fierce competition, one must absolutely get mandates for making his/her consulting business viable, in other words profitable. An independent consultant, who is engaged for an expertise, either directly by a public administration or by a consulting company, is often subjected to such pressures that he/she is led to betray the scientific principles of his/her profession.

In this respect I refer you to the editorial published in the July–August 1997 issue of the very serious *Public Administration Review* (American), by a US consultant, Mr David Lempert, who works in Washington, DC.[7] Mr Lempert is, like me, at the end of his career, so perhaps he can afford to say certain things. On the basis of his own experience and of other experts he knows personally, Mr Lempert bitterly complains about attempted corruption of consultants in the United States, and admits having been subjected to pressure from US government agencies or consulting firms for which he had been engaged on behalf of the American government. The aim of these pressures is to censor or change the results of an evaluation, conceal results from the public, change the conclusion of an expertise or get the experts to unanimously agree on the conclusions of expertise, thus excluding dissenting opinions and the like. That is then the situation that Mr Lempert denounces; and he appealed to the American Association for Public

Administration to support individual consultants who, without the support of an association, are completely helpless when faced with such pressures, are quickly blacklisted and can no longer practise their profession.

He also highlights through his analysis that the current practice of preferring an external expertise made by private consultants instead of one made by appointed public officials has produced the absolutely perverse result that he denounces. Indeed, public officials who provide expertise within the administration of the US are highly protected in case of pressure, so they can defend themselves, whereas the individual consultant outside the administrative system has virtually no chance of defending him-/herself. There there is something very disturbing that I wanted to bring to your attention.

Let me conclude my presentation with two remarks. First, it might be tempting to overstep the limits of the topic I have been asked to develop, and try to analyse the reform strategies that have been actually implemented in a number of countries, and try to determine what are the conditions that support or make difficult the implementation of a particular reform strategy. On this basis we could then advise the Prince, saying, for example, 'if in your country you have the same conditions as in New Zealand, then you can implement the New Zealand reform strategy, but if they do not exist, then you must adopt another alternative strategy', and so forth. This can be done, and some do it. However, by merely identifying the conditions governing the implementation of a strategy, we run the risk of forgetting that the outcomes of this strategy have an impact on society. And when the reform strategy has a fundamental impact on the role of the state, these consequences cannot be ignored. In other words, we really have to proceed to a prospective analysis; it is when we adopt a strategy of reform that we must be very clear about the probable consequences of the reforms that we want to implement.

To sum up very quickly, when one changes so radically the role of the state there is certainly an impact on the distribution of income; we cannot say, as do some colleagues who do not agree with my criticism, that it is not possible to establish a causal link between one type of public management (in this case, NPM) and the rest of society.[8] This is an absurdity, and politicians very well know that, if they seek election, it is precisely in order to have an impact on society and not just to make rhetorical speeches. It is certain that if we change the management style and the role of the state there will be an impact on the whole of society; and we must try to measure it. Then, we must pay attention to the distribution of income, changes in poverty rates, changes in crime rates, and changes in the health of the population. These are the four main indicators that should at least be considered in assessing the consequences of reform strategies that call into question the fundamental role of the state.[9] The reforms inspired by NPM have been implemented in different countries long enough for prospective analyses to be based on sound ex-post evaluation. But, alas, these analyses are still very rare. The way is thus open to purely ideological decisions.[10]

Second remark: we may rejoice with the politicians that the power of bureaucrats has at last been defeated thanks to NPM. But I am not so sure of this; I even believe, and there is already serious evidence that, for example, decentralization and the separation between strategic decisions and operational decisions are giving, on the contrary, more power to civil servants responsible for managing the 'Next Step Agencies'. However, I do not want to prevent anyone from rejoicing. Nevertheless, I think it is a brilliant mistake. Why? Well again, I think that by observing what is happening today in the process of public sector reform we discover the empirical confirmation of one of the most compelling theories of Max Weber; that is to say that, in a society like ours, the power of a bureaucracy can be defeated only by another bureaucracy.[11]

The power of a bureaucracy is based on what? Apart from its centrality in a social system, it is its knowledge, expertise and relevance to a given social system. So today we may have defeated the power and knowledge of traditional state officials, but by what other power and knowledge have we replaced them? By the knowledge and power of other bureaucracies, that of consulting firms, that of a new class of state officials, those who manage the 'Next Step Agencies', who have been carefully recruited from amongst those who share a certain point of view about the role of the state (and the New Zealand case is very instructive in this regard), and finally that of the international economic organizations. All these new bureaucracies share a common knowledge, socially relevant, which tends to prevail over everything and everyone. And the basis of this knowledge is constituted by what my colleague Prof. Pollitt has called 'managerialism', that is to say, a particular conception of the role of the state and of its functioning, according to which public management must be based on the model of private sector management: on market mechanisms or, alternatively, quasi-market mechanisms. To implement this project one obviously needs a particular expertise; but, if that expertise is going to be imposed everywhere upon everybody, we will certainly have succeeded in defeating the power of traditional civil servants with the result of submitting ourselves to the authority of other bureaucrats, those I just mentioned. With what results for the values of democracy, equity, security, efficiency and freedom?

Notes

Introduction

1 I will explain this statement in Chapter 2. For the moment it suffices to say that, for Braudel, the production–consumption activities have produced, at the end of a long history, a three-layer hierarchical structure with, from the bottom, material life, markets and capitalism. For a summary of Braudel's approach see Fernand Braudel, *Afterthoughts on Material Civilization and Capitalism* (The Johns Hopkins Symposia in Comparative History), Baltimore, The Johns Hopkins University Press, 1979. Braudel's approach and other works of Braudel will be quoted in Chapter 2.
2 Christopher Hood, 'The New Public Management in the 1980s: variations on a theme', *Accounting, Organization and Society*, 1995, vol. 20, no. 2/3, pp. 93–109, and 'Contemporary public management: a new global paradigm?', *Public Policy and Administration*, 1995, vol. 10, no. 2, pp. 104–117; as well as three texts by Lawrence E. Lynn: 'The New Public Management as an International Phenomenon: Questions of an American Skeptic', paper prepared for the conference on the New Public Management in International Perspective, St. Gallen, July 1996; 'Dividing the job: intergovernmental dimension', *Public Manager*, Fall 1992, pp. 7–10; and *Public Management as Art, Science, and Profession*, Chatham, NJ, Chatham House, 1996. See also the last book by Laurence E. Lynn Jr., *Public Management: Old and New*, New York, Routledge, 2006.
3 For a definition of the Weberian ideal-type methodology see Max Weber, 'Die "Objectivität" sozialwissenschaftlicher und sozialpolitischer Erkenntnis', *Gesammelte Aufsätze zur Wissenschaftslehre*, Tübingen, J.C.B. Mohr, 1988, pp. 146–214; English translation: 'Objectivity in social science and social policy', in *Methodology of Social Sciences*, New Brunswick, NJ, Transactions, 2011, pp. 49–112.
4 Ma Jun and Zhang Zhibin, 'Remaking the Chinese administrative state since 1978: the double-movements perspective', *Korean Journal of Policy Studies*, 2009, vol. 23, no. 2, pp. 225–226. To sustain their claim they quote in particular an article by J.A. Worthley and K.K. Tsao, 'Reinventing government in China', *Administration & Society*, 1999, vol. 31, no. 5, pp. 571–87. Ma Jun is a professor and director of the Centre for Public Administration Research at Sun Yat-sen University. Zhang Zhibin is an assistant professor of public administration at the School of Humanities & Social Sciences, Nanyang Technological University, Singapore.
5 In their conclusion Ma and Zhang consider that NPM 'at best provides an incomplete picture of the inherent logic of rebuilding the Chinese administrative state during the reform era': ibid., p. 246. Granted. However, as they admit, the logic of Chinese reforms (especially the process of marketization, a typical NPM policy device) was the dominant policy option followed by the Chinese leadership from 1978 up to about the mid-1990s.

6 At the moment of finalizing the manuscript of this book, November 2011, the crisis that broke out in 2008 was still going on, and may not have come to an end by the time when the book is published in 2012. Nevertheless, in this book I will refer to this crisis as the 2008–11 crisis whenever appropriate, hoping that by then the crisis may have come to an end.
7 Paolo Urio, 'La gestion publique au service du marché', in Marc Hufty (ed.), *La pensée comptable: Etat, néolibéralisme, nouvelle gestion publique*, Paris, Presses Universitaires de France, Collection Enjeux, Cahier de l'IUED, Genève, 1999, pp. 91–124; Paolo Urio, *Reconciling State, Market, and Society in China: The Long March towards Prosperity*, London, Routledge, 2010; Urio (ed.) *Public Private Partnerships: Success and Failure Factors for In Transition Countries*, Lanham, MD, University Press of America, 2010.
8 *Littré: Dictionnaire de la langue française*, vol. 3, Monte Carlo, Editions du Cap, 1962, p. 4072.
9 Practically all the good Western dictionaries mention the same meanings of 'myth'. For the following paragraphs I have used more particularly the *Sabatini Coletti Dictionary of the Italian language*, the *Zingarelli Dictionary of the Italian Language*, the *Larousse Maxipoche*, and Craig Calhoun (ed.), *Dictionary of the Social Sciences*, *Oxford Reference Online*, Oxford University Press, 2002, http://www.oxfordreference.com/pub/views/home.html (accessed 13 June 2010).
10 Against the myth of liberal democracy one can consult the works of Luciano Canfora, *La democrazia: Storia di un'ideologia*, Bari, Laterza, 2004 (English translation: *Democracy in Europe: A History of an Ideology*, Oxford, Wiley-Blackwell, 2006; French translation: *La démocratie: Histoire d'une idéologie*, Paris, Seuil, 2006); *Exporter la liberté: Echec d'un mythe*, Paris, Ed. Desjonquères, 2008; and *L'imposture démocratique: Du procès de Socrate à l'élection de G.W. Bush*, Paris, Flammarion, 2003. Against the myth of the classless society one can consult the works of Raymond Aron, *Les étapes de la pensée sociologique*, Paris, Gallimard, 1967; *Le Marxisme de Marx*, Paris, Editions de Fallois, 2002.
11 Note that some authors prefer to use the term 'fetishism' instead of 'myth', e.g. Alain Bihr, *La novlangue néolibérale: La rhétorique du fétichisme capitaliste*, Lausanne, Page Deux, 2007. Although I recognize the interest of this approach, in this book I will limit myself to 'myth' to qualify the ideological and rhetorical usages of the major components of neoliberal discourse.
12 Umberto Galimberti, *I miti del nostro tempo*, Milan, Feltrinelli, 2009. Galimberti's books have been translated into several languages (German, French, Spanish and even Japanese) but it is a pity that, to my knowledge, none has been translated into English.
13 Galimberti also deals with the myths of technology, and of the new information technologies, which are clearly linked to the ones in which I am interested, but I will not dwell upon them directly in this book. Galimberti also has a chapter on the myth of power, which, surprisingly, he places among the individual myths.
14 Ibid., pp. 11–12; my free translation and interpretation, therefore without quotation marks.

1 From public administration to New Public Management

1 Paolo Urio, *L'évaluation comme instrument d'apprentissage et de changement organisationnel: L'exemple des programmes cantonaux de promotion de la santé*, report presented to the Swiss National Foundation for Scientific Research, National Programme 27, 1996; Paolo Urio and Véronique Meckx, *Le budget de la Confédération: Le système politique suisse face à l'équilibre des finances fédérales*, Lausanne, Editions Réalités Sociales, 1996.

2 It is of course difficult to pinpoint an exact date for the commencement of such a complex change. In fact, the origins of NPM can be traced back to the beginning of the 1970s. See, for example, David Harvey, *A Brief History of Neoliberalism*, Oxford, Oxford University Press, 2004, pp. 39–63.
3 By the way, this was exactly the motto of the American version of NPM, the National Performance Review (NPR), under Vice-President Al Gore: 'We have customers, the American people.' The other motto was 'Red Tape to Results. Creating a Government that works better and costs less.' On the role of the concept of the customer and the role of the private sector as a model for reorganizing (and reinventing) the public sector within the NPR see Al Gore, *Businesslike Government: Lessons Learned from America's Best Companies*, Washington, DC, US Government Printing Office, 1994, and *The Gore Report on Reinventing Government*, New York, Times Books, 1993.
4 After the Second World War, a group of liberal intellectuals met at a Swiss resort above Montreux, the Mount Pèlerin, between 1 and 10 April, and founded the Mount Pèlerin Society. Thirty-six intellectuals, mainly economists, attended, amongst them Friedrich von Hayek, Milton Friedman, Maurice Allais, Bertrand de Jouvenel, Fritz Machlup, Salvador de Madariaga, Ludwig von Mises, Michael Polanyi, Karl Popper, George Stigler, William Rappard, who was the first director of the Graduate Institute of International Studies in Geneva, and Wilhelm Röpke, was my professor at this same Institute at the beginning of the 1960s. It is amongst its members that we can find some of the most influential founders of neoliberalism, such as Hayek and Friedman. Some other liberal economists have not supported the most radical form of neoliberalism, for example Wilhelm Röpke, who, with Walter Eucken, is considered to be the founder of the *soziale Marktwirtschaft* (social market economy); still others have been very critical of capitalism, for instance Karl Polanyi. Several members of the society have received the Nobel Prize in economics: Friedrich von Hayek, Maurice Allais, Milton Friedman, George Stigler, James M. Buchanan, Gary Becker and Ronald Coase.
5 I refer here for the first time in this book to the concept of 'customer' that the NPMists propose to use instead of the concept of 'citizen', this change being due, as I will explain later, to the use of neoclassical economic theory and its central concept of economic efficiency for improving the management of the state.
6 See, for example, Harvey, *A Brief History of Neoliberalism*, pp. 10–11. It is not necessary to discuss here the various schools under the general label of 'Keynesianism', such as neo-Keynesianism or post-Keynesianism. For a discussion of the various Keynesian schools and their position regarding the monetarist school see Joseph Stiglitz, *Freefall: America, Free Markets, and the Sinking of the World Economy*, New York, Norton, 2010, Chapter 9, especially pp. 257–274.
7 On these aspects and for a general and enlightening analysis of the origins of the present crisis see Stiglitz, ibid.
8 Milton Friedman, *Capitalism and Freedom*, Chicago, The University of Chicago Press, preface to the second edition, 1982 (first edn 1962), proudly advertised on the front page 'With a new Preface by the Author, Winner of the Nobel Prize in Economics', pp. vi–vii. There is nevertheless a difference: neoliberals were supported, psychologically and financially, by the political and economic Right during that period, which financed university chairs and research, congresses and publications. If only we could have benefited from a small fraction of that support!
9 Paolo Urio, 'La gestion publique au service du marché', in Hufty (ed.), *La pensée comptable*, pp. 91–124.
10 World Bank, *China 2020: Development Challenges in the New Century*, 18 September 1997, Report no. 17027-CHA, World Bank, p. ix.
11 Let us remark that in this chapter I use the terms 'market' and 'market economy' without addressing the fundamental question of the relationship between these terms

and 'capitalism'. For the moment, these terms can be used without comment; the reader will certainly understand in what sense I use them here. Nevertheless, the discussion of these terms will be absolutely necessary for clarifying in what sense, in my opinion, we can compare the reforms of public management introduced in China and the West from the 1980s. I will show then, starting from the fundamental work of Fernand Braudel, that there is a big difference between the Chinese and the Western 'markets', the latter being dominated by the upper layer of the production and consumption processes, that is, capitalism in which the economic and especially the financial elites are in command, whereas in China the economy is dominated by the political elite (the Communist Party), which develops, orients, controls or restrains the freedom of the Chinese private entrepreneurs. Finally, let me note, in order to avoid misunderstanding, that I usually use the term 'market mechanisms' and not 'market economy' when referring to the case of China. More on these and other related aspects in the second chapter.

12 The additional research needed was conducted in part at the University of Geneva, thanks to several PhD dissertations under my supervision, as well as research on one of the dimensions of NPM, the public–private partnerships (covering China, Poland, Russia and Ukraine) financed by the Geneva International Academic Network, that will be duly quoted in this book. Books and article referred in this introduction will be presented in more detail in the following chapters, where they will be duly quoted.

13 In French: *L'administration dans tous ses états: réalisations et conséquences.*

14 I will mention these mandates in more detail hereafter.

15 David Lempert, 'Holding accountable the powers that be: protecting our integrity and the public we serve', *Public Administration* Review, July/August 1997, pp. ii–v.

16 My speech was subsequently published in a collective book: 'Le rôle du scientifique dans la définition des stratégies de réformes', in Yves Emery (ed.), *L'administration dans tous ses états: réalisations et conséquences*, Lausanne, Presses Polytechniques et Universitaires Romandes, pp. 187–195. An English translation of my speech is provided in Annex 2 below.

17 In fact I had accepted an invitation to sit within the group of experts for the National Research Programme (promoted by the Swiss Government) on the domain of transportation in Switzerland. Very likely I was asked to join this group because in the late 1970s I had contributed to interuniversity research on the Swiss Motorway Policy, as well as (between 1987 and 1993) to an expert report for the Swiss Federal Agency for National Roads on the oppositions to the construction of motorways. However, for several reasons (the main one being the heavy load of the management of the Chinese training programme) I took part in only a couple of meetings.

18 In the second chapter, I will come back to these two aspects of neoliberalism (NPM and the 'Washington consensus'). For the moment it suffices to mention the definition of the 'Washington consensus' given by John Williamson, *Latin American Adjustment: How Much Has Happened*, Washington, DC, Institute for International Economics, 1990, and 'Democracy and the Washington Consensus', *World Development*, 1993, vol. 21, no. 8, p. 1331. Williamson's 10 prescriptions reflecting his interpretation of the Washington consensus in the early 1990s are (1) exhibit fiscal discipline, (2) redirect public expenditure, (3) reform taxes, (4) implement financial liberalization, (5) adopt a single, competitive exchange rate, (6) liberalize trade, (7) eliminate barriers to foreign direct investment, (8) privatize state-owned enterprises, (9) deregulate market entry and competition and (10) ensure secure property rights. For a critique see Joseph E. Stiglitz, *Post Washington Consensus*, published on the Website of the Initiative for Policy Dialogue, Columbia University, Working Paper Series, 2005, available online at http://www.gsb.columbia.edu/ipd/ (accessed 6 June 2009), and Yujiro Hayami, 'From the Washington Consensus to the Post-Washington Consensus: retrospect and prospect', *Asian Development Review*, 2003, vol. 20, no. 2, pp. 40–65.

19 On these aspects see the works of Ha-Joon Chang, *Bad Samaritans: The Myth of Free Trade and the Secret History of Capitalism*, New York, Bloomsbury, 2008; *Globalization, Economic Development and the Role of the State*, New York, Zed Books, 2003; *Kicking Away the Ladder: Development Strategy in Historical Perspective*, London, Anthem Press, 2003; Ha-Joon Chang and Ilene Grabel, *Reclaiming Development: An Alternative Economic Policy Manual*, New York, Zed Books, 2004; Ha-Joon Chang (ed.), *Institutional Change and Economic Development*, Tokyo, United National University Press, 2007; and Ha-Joon Chang (ed.), *Rethinking Development Economics*, London, Anthem Press, 2003; and those of Joseph E. Stiglitz: *Globalization and Its Discontents*, New York, W.W. Norton, 2002; *The Roaring Nineties: Why We Are Paying the Price for the Greediest Decade in History*, London, Penguin Books, 2003; *Making Globalization Work: The Next Steps to Global Justice*, London, Penguin, 2006; and *Freefall*; see also Joseph E. Stiglitz and Andrew Charlton, *Fair Trade for All: How Trade Can Promote Development*, Oxford, Oxford University Press, 2005.
20 It suffices to note here strategic management and competency frameworks, as they were being developed especially in England. Moreover, these are not the most typical tools of NPM, as they belong to any reform strategy aimed at improving the transparency, effectiveness and efficiency of the public sector.
21 The Civil Service College changed its structure and its name in 2006 to become the National School of Government.
22 Paolo Urio, *Reconciling State, Market and Society in China: The Long March towards Prosperity*, London, Routledge, 2010.
23 The famous article by Robert Merton ('The unanticipated consequences of purposive social action', *American Sociological Review*, vol. 1, 1936, pp. 894–904) has launched a whole series of empirical researches on the dysfunctioning inside public and private bureaucracies, of which I will mention here only those of Alwin A. Gouldner, *Patterns of Industrial Bureaucracy*, Glencoe, IL, Free Press, 1953, and Philip Selznick, *TVA and the Grass Roots*, Berkeley, University of California Press, 1949.
24 It is exactly for this reason that Herbert Simon proposed in the mid-1940s to separate the decision-making process into two phases: the first, during which values are chosen, is the domain of politics; the second, when the most appropriate means are chosen, is the domain of administration. Then, in his attempt to construct a scientific theory of the decision-making process, Simon (who won the Nobel Prize in economics in 1984) leaves aside the first phase because he considers that choices of values cannot be subject to scientific inquiry and decision. Herbert Simon, *Administrative Behaviour: Decision-Making Processes in Administrative Organizations*, fourth edition updated with extensive new commentaries by the author, New York, Free Press, 1997 (first edition 1945).
25 On the concept of political culture see Gabriel A. Almond and Sidney Verba, *The Civic Culture*, Boston, Little, Brown & Co., 1963; Gabriel A. Almond and G.B. Powell, *Comparative Politics: A Developmental Approach*, Boston, Little, Brown & Co, 1966; Lucian W. Pye, *Aspects of Political Development*, Boston, Little, Brown & Co., 1968.
26 On this last point see, for example, Daniel A. Bell (ed.), *Confucian Political Ethics*, Princeton, NJ, Princeton University Press, 2008, and Daniel A. Bell, *China's New Confucianism: Politics and Everyday Life in a Changing Society*, Princeton, NJ, Princeton University Press, 2008.
27 I have already sustained this idea in my book *Reconciling* (especially ch. 1). Some scholars may contest the assertion that the fundamental goal of the Chinese government (in fact, for me, of all Chinese governments since the mid-nineteenth century) has been the restoration of China as a world power. I will come back to this point in Chapter 4 and provide some evidence supporting this assertion.

28 François Jullien develops this idea in several books; the reader will find them with a short and clear explanation in François Jullien, *Conférence sur l'efficacité*, Paris, Presses Universitaires de France, 2005, section entitled 'Dans les arts de la guerre chinoise: notion de potentiel de situation', pp. 29–31. See among his numerous works also *Eloge de la fadeur*, Paris, Ed. Philippe Picquier, 1991; *Les transformations silencieuses*, Paris, Grasset, 2009; *Procès ou création: Une introduction à la pensée chinoise*, Paris, Seuil, 1989; *La propension des choses: Pour une histoire de l'efficacité en Chine*, Paris, Seuil, 1992; *Traité de l'efficacité*, Paris, Grasset, 1996. An interesting application of this type of reasoning is provided by the world-famous Chinese classic on war: Sun Tzu, *The Art of War*, Boulder, CO, Westview Press, 1994. For an application of the works of Jullien to current situations (both in the public and in the private sectors) see the very interesting work of a French-Chinese economist, consultant to several French enterprises active in China: André Chieng, *La pratique de la Chine*, Paris, Grasset, 2006.

29 Although the origins of liberalism can be traced back to Greek philosophy and Roman law, the generally accepted opinion is that the origins of the economic dimension of liberalism, that is, capitalism (understood as a set of practical, actual behaviours organizing the economy), can be placed some time during the sixteenth century (or even during the twelfth century). On the other hand, the origins of the political dimension of liberalism, namely liberal democracy (understood as a set of practical, actual behaviours organizing the polity), can be placed during the eighteenth century (the Age of Enlightenment, and the French and American Revolutions). For example, the founding writings of modern capitalism (the economic dimension of liberalism) were published towards the end of the eighteenth and the beginning of the nineteenth centuries: Adam Smith, *An Inquiry into the Nature and Causes of the Wealth of Nations*, 1776; David Ricardo, *On the Principles of Political Economy and Taxation*, 1817. The major works on socialisms were published after those dates.

30 Gideon Rachman, 'Conservatism overshoots its limits', *Financial Times* (London), 6 October 2008.

2 Comparing New Public Management in China and in the West

1 I have proposed an interpretation of China's reforms in Paolo Urio, *Reconciling State, Market and Society in China*, London, Routledge, 2010.

2 According to the French historian Fernand Braudel, markets have existed since ancient times. Moreover, it is important to distinguish, in analysing the historical process, three hierarchical levels of the organization of production and consumption: material life, market and capitalism. I will come back to this important point in the following paragraphs, where I will refer the reader to Braudel's main works.

3 Marie-Claire Bergère, *Capitalisme et capitalistes en Chine*, Paris, Perrin, 2007, pp. 23–24.

4 For an account of the Chinese contribution to science and technology (well before the European contributions since the Renaissance) see Robert Temple, *The Genius of China: 3,000 Years of Science, Discovery and Invention*, London, Prion, 1998 (introduced by Joseph Needham), and John M. Hobson, *The Eastern Origins of Western Civilisation*, Cambridge, Cambridge University Press, 2004 (ch. 3 and 9 on Chinese influence on the West).

5 See the seven volumes of the monumental history of Chinese science and technology by Joseph Needham, and especially vol. 7: *Science and Civilisation in China*, vol. VII: 2 (edited by K.G. Robinson), Cambridge, Cambridge University Press, 2004; for a short presentation on the relations between China and the West see Joseph Needham, *The Grand Titration: Science and Society in East and West*, London, Allen & Unwin, 1969 (French translation: *La science chinoise et l'Occident*, Paris, Seuil, 1973).

6 Bergère, *Capitalisme et capitalistes en Chine*; the whole book admirably illustrates this perspective.
7 This is the substantive content that Fareed Zakaria, the influential editor of *Newsweek* magazine, who also has a special programme on CNN (Cable News Network), gives to liberal democracy. See Fareed Zakaria, 'The rise of illiberal democracy', *Foreign Affairs*, vol. 76, no. 6, November–December 1997, pp. 22–43.
8 See the reaction of some American opinion leaders after the decisions taken in 2008 by the Obama administration to overcome the crisis. These decisions have introduced some doubts even amongst the ranks of the most fervent defenders of American-style capitalism, who have started to ask a question that would have been unthinkable a few months before: 'Are we all socialists now?' This is the title of an article published online by the influential American think tank Reason Foundation (which posts online the motto 'Free minds, Free markets'). Available online at http://www.reason.com (accessed 7 March 2009). On President Obama's side, *Newsweek* does not even use the question mark, commenting on a debate between American politicians on Fox News Channel, when a right-wing politician violently questioned Obama's policy. The revealing title of the article is 'We are all socialists now', with a subtitle written, I guess, with some regret: 'In many ways our economy already resembles a European one. As boomers age and spending grows we will become even more French.' *Newsweek* quite reasonably comments:

> If we fail to acknowledge the reality of the growing role of government in the economy, insisting instead on fighting 21st-century wars with 20th-century terms and tactics, then we are doomed to a fractious and unedifying debate. The sooner we understand where we truly stand, the sooner we can think more clearly about how to use government in today's world'
> 16 February 2009, available online at http://www.newsweek.com (accessed 7 March 2009).

It seems that the time is over when the majority of American opinion leaders used to look down with condescension on the intrusive, inefficient and big French government. Let us note that the most radical critics of capitalism do not hesitate to say that 'the spectre of socialism is haunting the American elite', World Socialist Web Site, available online at http://www.wsws.org (accessed 9 March 2009).
9 For the origins of capitalism, its major economic characteristics and its link to the state, see, for example, Pierre Rosanvallon, *Le capitalisme utopique: Histoire de l'idée de marché*, Paris, Seuil, 1979, and *Le libéralisme économique: Histoire de l'idée de marché*, Paris, Plon, 1979; Ellen Meiskins Wood, *The Origins of Capitalism*, revised and expanded edition, London, Verso, 2002. For different types of capitalism: Tom Bottomore, *Theories of Modern Capitalism*, London, Allen & Unwin, 1985; Peter A. Hall and David Soskice (eds), *Varieties of Capitalism: The Institutional Foundations of Comparative Advantage*, Oxford, Oxford University Press, 2001; Gosta Esping-Andersen, *The Three Worlds of Welfare Capitalism*, Princeton, NJ, Princeton University Press, 1990; Robert E. Goodin, Bruce Heady, Ruud Muffels and Henk-Jan Dirven, *The Real Worlds of Welfare Capitalism*, Cambridge, Cambridge University Press, 1999. For a contemporary Western critique: Ellen Meiskins Wood, *Empire of Capital*, London, Verso, 2003, and *Democracy against Capitalism*, Cambridge, Cambridge University Press, 1995; Daniel Bell, *The Cultural Contradictions of Capitalism*, twentieth anniversary edition with a new afterword by the author, New York, Basic Books (Perseus Books), 1996, and *Beyond Liberal Democracy: Political Thinking for an East Asian Context*, Princeton, NJ, Princeton University Press, 2006; Roberto Mangabeira Unger, *What Should the Left Propose?*, London, Verso, 2005, and *Free Trade Reimagined*, Princeton, NJ, Princeton University Press, 2007; Joseph E. Stiglitz, *Globalization and Its Discontents*, New York, W.W. Norton, 2002. For the rise of market economy and an international comparison about 'the

wealth of nations' see, among the vast literature: Immanuel Wallerstein, *The Modern World System*, New York, Academic Press, 2 volumes, 1974–1980; Braudel works will be quoted in the next note; David S. Landes, 'The fable of the dead horse, or the Industrial Revolution revisited', in Joel Mokyr (ed.), *The British Industrial Revolution: An Economic Perspective*, 2nd edn, Boulder, CO, Westview Press, 1998, and *The Wealth and Poverty of Nations: Why Some Are So Rich and Some So Poor*, New York, Norton, 1999 (with two chapters on China and Japan); Ha-Joon Chang, *Bad Samaritan: The Myth of Free Trade and the Secret History of Capitalism*, New York, Bloomsbury, 2008. For a return to an interpretation of capitalism faithful to the 'founding fathers' (especially Adam Smith) and the validity of the foundations of capitalism see Amartya Sen, 'Capitalism beyond the crisis', *New York Review of Books'*, vol. 56, no. 5, 26 March 2009, available online at http://www.nybooks.com (accessed 27 April 2009).

10 Fernand Braudel, *Ecrits sur l'histoire*, Paris, Flammarion, 1969 (English translation: *On History*, Chicago, University of Chicago Press, 1992); *Civilisation matérielle, économie et capitalisme (XVe–XVIIIe siècle)*, Paris, A. Colin (Edition Livre de poche), 1979, vol. 1: *Les structures du quotidien*; vol. 2: *Les jeux de l'échange*; vol. 3: *Le temps du monde* (English translation: *Civilization and Capitalism: 15th–18th Century*, vol. 1: *The Structure of Everyday Life*; vol. 2: *The Wheels of Commerce*; vol. 3: *The Perspective of the World*, Berkeley, University of California Press, 1992). For a summary of the main findings and ideas of *Civilization and Capitalism*, see the texts of three conferences given at the Johns Hopkins University in 1976, published in English before the publication of the three volumes of *Civilization and Capitalism*: *Afterthoughts on Material Civilization and Capitalism* (The Johns Hopkins Symposia in Comparative History), Baltimore, Johns Hopkins University Press, 1979 (French edition: *La dynamique du capitalisme*, Paris, Flammarion, 1985). Braudel's perspective has been further developed (although with some differences) by Immanuel Wallerstein, who directed the 'Fernand Braudel Centre for the Study of Economies, Historical Systems, and Civilizations' at Binghamton University (New York) until 2005; his major works are *The Modern World System, vol. I: Capitalist Agriculture and the Origins of the European World-System in the Sixteenth Century*; *vol. II: Mercantilism and the Consolidation of the European World-Economy, 1600–1750*, New York, Academic Press, 1974 and 1980. For a summary of Wallerstein's approach, see Immanuel Wallerstein, *World Systems Analysis: An Introduction*, Durham, NC, Duke University Press, 2004.

11 The importance and originality of Braudel's analysis of capitalism has been very well captured by Immanuel Wallerstein (in fact his intellectual successor) in a short article, the title of which translates the revolutionary character of Braudel's analysis: 'Braudel on capitalism, or everything upside down', *Journal of Modern History*, June 1991, no. 6, pp. 354–361. For a critique of Braudel's Eurocentric biases see Jack Goody, 'The theft of "capitalism": Braudel and global comparison', Chapter 7 of *The Theft of History*, Cambridge, Cambridge University Press, 2006, pp. 180–211. Goody admits that Braudel is 'much subtler about the question of European advantage [than Weber and Marx]'. Nevertheless, he considers that 'his sources are inevitably largely European and partake of some of those prejudices about that advantage' (ibid., p. 184). Granted. However, this does not diminish the value of Braudel's analysis of the essence of capitalism that I use in this chapter and in this book.

12 Braudel, *Afterthoughts*, p. 113.

13 Ibid., p. 5.

14 Let us note that for Braudel 'material life' is sometimes defined as a 'no economy', sometimes as a 'very elementary economy', for example in the introductory remarks to the second volume of *Civilisation matérielle, économie et Capitalisme*, p. 7. For me, what is important is that Braudel shows that, since the twelfth century, markets have emerged out of the 'material life' well before capitalism (ibid., p. 15), and this is

a sufficient reason for not considering capitalism as the sole possible form of market economy. Moreover, Braudel's *Civilization and Capitalism* shows that markets were already present in Africa, India, China and Islamic countries. For the emergence of a market in China see *Civilisation matérielle, économie et Capitalisme*, vol. 2, and especially pp. 116, 120–125, 139–140, 146 and 255–256. On the emergence of capitalism see ibid., pp. 268–287 for the use of 'capital, capitalist, and capitalism', and for the emergence of capitalism in China see ibid., and more especially pp. 354–356 and 708–23. Also the interested reader may consult the remarkable works of the French sinologist Marie-Claire Bergère, *L'âge d'or de la bourgeoisie chinoise*, Paris, Flammarion, 1986, and *Capitalismes et capitalistes en Chine*.

15 The exact sentences in French are the following:

> Je suis sûr que cette division est tangible, que les agents et les hommes, que les actes, que les mentalités ne sont pas les mêmes à ces étages différents. Que les règles de l'économie de marché qui se retrouvent à certains niveaux, telles que les décrits l'économie classique, jouent beaucoup plus rarement sous leur aspect de libre concurrence dans la zone supérieure, qui est celle des calculs et de la spéculation. Là commence une zone d'ombre, de contre-jour, d'activités d'initiés que je crois à la racine de ce que l'on peut comprendre sous le mot de capitalisme, celui-ci étant une accumulation de puissance (qui fonde l'échange sur un rapport de force autant et plus que la réciprocité des besoins), un parasitisme social, inévitable ou non, comme tant d'autres. . . . Pour cette zone qui n'est pas la vraie économie de marché, mais si souvent sa franche contradiction, il me fallait un mot particulier. Et celui qui se présentait irrésistiblement, c'était celui de capitalisme.
> *Civilisation matérielle, économie et Capitalisme*, vol. 2, pp. 8–9; see also pp. 542–546

16 Braudel, *Afterthoughts*, pp. 113–114.
17 The exact sentence in French:

> Le caractère partiel de l'économie de marché peut tenir, en effet, soit à l'importance du secteur d'autosuffisance, soit à l'autorité de l'état qui soustrait une partie de la production à la circulation marchande, soit tout autant, ou plus encore, au simple poids de l'argent qui peut, de mille façons, intervenir artificiellement dans la formation des prix.
> *Civilisation et Capitalisme*, p. 262

18 Western countries are reluctant to recognize China as a market economy because, if they do, it will be more difficult to prove that China manipulates the market through state intervention.
19 In December 2006 the State Assets Supervision and Administration Commission (SASAC) published a list of seven sectors critical to the national economy and in which public ownership is considered essential: armaments, electrical power and distribution, oil and chemicals, telecommunications, coal, aviation, and shipping. Moreover, to reorient state capital away from non-critical areas to priority sectors, SASAC said China would reduce the number of central SOEs by at least one-third to between 80 and 100 before 2010 through mergers. Finally, it announced that 'China aims to build between 30 and 50 large, internationally competitive companies by 2010', http://www.xinhuanet.com/english/ (accessed 21 January 2007).
20 See Bruce J. Dickson, *Red Capitalists in China: The Party, Private Entrepreneurs, and Prospects for Political Change*, Cambridge, Cambridge University Press, 2003, and *Wealth into Power: The Communist Party's Embrace of China's Private Sector*, New York, Cambridge University Press, 2008.
21 I was pleased to see, on reading Joseph Stiglitz's book on the crisis, that he also uses 'market mechanisms' when referring to the reform introduced in East Asian countries, including China: Joseph E. Stiglitz, *Freefall*, p. 245.

22 This is the result of the research based upon interviews of a sample of Chinese entrepreneurs by Jie Chen and Bruce J. Dickson, 'Allies of the State: democratic support and regime support among China's private entrepreneurs', *China Quarterly*, December 2008, vol. 196, pp. 780–804.
23 See Chapter 6, where I refer to the Chongqing experiment as an example of development policy that uses state ownership for improving the situation of peasants compared with urban residents.
24 Urio, *Reconciling*. Let us note that safety nets are still in the development phase, but coverage is already today almost universal, even if rather limited. I will come back to this important point in Chapter 6.
25 Commenting on China's reaction to the 2008–11 crisis, Barry Naughton, writing for the *China Leadership Monitor* (of the influential Hoover Institution at Stanford University) considers that:

> there are strong political forces that benefit from government patronage and extension of government power, and those interest groups do not show the slightest sign of being in retreat. . . . This continued failure to tackle some hard issues, trim back the power and resources controlled by the state . . . has made most economists increasingly frustrated. . . . it is very difficult to get change out of a political system that seems to be succeeding so brilliantly on its own terms.
>
> Barry Naughton, 'The turning point: first steps toward a post-crisis economy', *China Leadership Monitor*, no. 31, Winter 2009–10, p. 7.

In the following number of the *China Leadership Monitor* (no. 32), commenting upon Premier Wen Jabao's report to the Chinese parliament, Naughton confirms his statement: 'This is probably the most unambiguous movement to reemphasize centralization and administrative instruments to govern the economy since the term "socialist market economy" was incorporated into the official Chinese rhetoric in September 1992'.(Barry Naughton, 'Reading the NPC: post-crisis economic dilemmas of the Chinese leadership', *China Leadership Monitor*, no. 32, Spring 2010, p. 5). Naughton papers are accessible at http://www.hoover.org/publications/china-leadership-monitor (accessed 30 July 2010). For an evaluation and critique of the Chinese banking system see James Riedel, Jing Jin and Jian Gao, *How China Grows*, Princeton, NJ, Princeton University Press, 2007. In an article published by the *Financial Times* Henry Sender considers that Chinese commercial banks 'remain an instrument of the state despite of being publicly traded' ('China's listed banks still at behest of state', *Financial Times*, 7 December 2010).
26 On China's 'informal economy', which, depending on definition, may include at least part of Braudel's 'material life', see Angang Hu and Zhao Li, 'The emergence of informal sector and the development of informal economy in China's transition: a historical perspective (1952–2004)', paper presented at the World Bank Annual Meeting, ABCDE (Annual Bank Conference on Development Economics), Tokyo, 29–30 May 2006, kindly provided by the authors; a slightly different version has circulated internally (in Chinese): 'Informal economy and development growth in the urban areas of China', *Reports of National Conditions*, Special Edition no. 6, 26 June 2006, Center for China Studies, Tsinghua University.
27 I have analysed these problems in Urio, *Reconciling*, especially ch. 2 and 3.
28 References to typologies of capitalism are provided later in this chapter.
29 See for example the working papers of Barry Naughton in the *China Leadership Monitor*, available on the internet at http://www.hoover.org/publications/china-leadership-monitor.
30 This is the case of the Fourth International; see its website, http://www.wsws.org, which has developed the most radical criticism of the present Chinese political system, which it describes as Stalinist.
31 By saying that Marxist and liberal frameworks of analysis are 'outdated' I do not mean, of course, that they cannot be useful for understanding present-day society.

Many of their elements retain their heuristic value today, as do many important elements of ancient Greek and Chinese philosophy. However, just like any theoretical framework, they were conceived within a historical era and must therefore be 'updated' to today's situation, which may, and in fact does, present several new aspects that the 'old' frameworks could not reasonably foresee.

32 Anthony Giddens, *The Third Way: The Renewal of Social Democracy*, Cambridge, Polity Press, 1998, and *The Third Way and Its Critics*, Cambridge, Polity Press, 2000.

33 A good example, among many, is given by one of the most eminent representatives of the Swiss Socialist Party, Jean-Noël Rey, former secretary general of the Socialist group at the Swiss parliament, former director general of the Swiss Post and former member of the Swiss parliament: 'We cannot decide in 2011 to overcome capitalism. This good old rhetoric of the 1980s has had its day. Today, people need something concrete' (*La Tribune de Genève*, 23 March 2011, p. 5). The exact sentence in French is: 'On ne peut pas en 2011 décider du dépassement du capitalisme. Cette bonne vielle rhétorique des années 80 a fait son temps. Aujourd'hui les gens ont besoin du concret.'

34 Moreover, the increasing complexity of public policies as well as their interactions (which further increase complexity) has reduced the impact that citizens can exert on the policy process and limits their role to the choice of members of parliaments and governments.

35 Ezra Suleiman, *Dismantling Democratic States*, Princeton, NJ, Princeton University Press, 2003.

36 Urio, *Reconciling*, pp. 198–199. It is interesting to note, in this context, that two of the major international organizations that are at the core of the international neoliberal system were presided over until April 2011 by two eminent representatives of the French socialist party: Pascal Lamy, director-general of the World Trade Organization, and Dominique Strauss-Kahn, managing director of the International Monetary Fund (IMF). It is interesting to note that Strauss-Kahn declared in an interview with the French TV Station TF2 (20 February 2011) that the IMF has changed and that he is very much worried by the consequences of the crisis on ordinary people. Good news indeed, but at that time there were few signs that the IMF was really working in favour of policies that would help ordinary people to overcome the crisis. So, in spite of the positive evaluations of Strauss-Kahn's work by Joseph Stiglitz ('The IMF's switch in time', *Project Syndicate*, May 2011, available online at http://www.project-sydicate.org, accessed 29 August 2011), we had just to wait and see. But we did not wait for long. In May 2011 Strauss-Kahn resigned and was replaced by the French minister of the economy, Christine Lagarde, who, upon taking office, declared that she would continue on the line defined by her predecessor. Knowing that Lagarde is a strong defender of capitalism and has supported the neoliberal policies of the French government, one can conclude that the Strauss-Kahn presidency at the head of the IMF did not represent a clear departure from the IMF traditional line in favour of capitalism and neoliberal policies. I will come back to this important point in the conclusion to this book. For a radical critique of liberal democracy see the works of Luciano Canfora, *L'imposture démocratique: Du procès de Socrate à l'élection de G.W. Bush*, Paris, Flammarion, 2003; *Democracy in Europe: A History of an Ideology*, New York, Wiley, 2006 (English translation of *La democrazia: Storia di un'ideologia*, Bari, Laterza, 2004); *Exporter la liberté: Echec d'un mythe*, Paris, Ed. Desjonquères, 2008.

37 Among the many interpretations of the 2008–11 crisis one can consult the analysis of two of the most popular 'main-stream critical economists': Nouriel Roubini and Stephen Mihn, *Crisis Economics: A Crash Course in the Future of Finance*, New York, Penguin, 2010; Stiglitz, *Freefall*; 'The triumphant return of John Maynard Keynes', *The Economists' Voice*, Project Syndicate, The Berkeley Electronic Press, December 2008, available online at http://www.project-sydicate.org (accessed 6 January 2009); 'Turn left for sustainable growth', *Economists' Voice*, http://www.

bepress.com/ev, September 2008; *Around the World with Joseph Stiglitz: Perils and Promises of Globalization*, documentary film realized by the author, 2009. For a Marxist critique see Bellamy John Foster and Fred Magdoff, *The Great Financial Crisis: Causes and Consequences*, New York, Monthly Review Press, 2009.

38 Guy Sorman, 'Goodbye to Europe's cradle-to-grave gravy', *Shanghai Daily*, 19 October 2010. It seems that this article has been published all over the world, for example in the *Project Syndicate* under the title 'The welfare state, RIP', *Project Syndicate*, 8 October 2010 (http://www.project-syndicate.org, accessed 8 November 2010), and in Sorman's blog in the Swiss weekly *L'Hebdo*, 'La mort annoncée de l'Etat Providence', 14 October 2010.

39 For a better understanding of this type of reasoning see Guy Sorman's radical defence of liberal economy: *Economics Does Not Lie: A Defense of the Free Market in a Time of Crisis*, New York, Encounter Books, 2009 (first published in French, *L'économie ne ment pas*, Paris, Fayard, 2008). A year before, the same author published a violent criticism of China: *The Empire of Lies: The Truth about China in the Twenty-First Century*, New York, Encounter Books, 2008 (first published in French with a much less 'marketing' title: *L'année du coq: chinois et rebelles*, Paris, Fayard, 2006). These ideas are very close to one of the types of capitalist Welfare States proposed by Gosta Esping-Andersen, which I will deal with later in this chapter: the liberal Welfare State type.

40 Li Minqi, *The Rise of China and the Demise of the Capitalist World Economy*, New York, Monthly Review Press, 2008.

41 He Li, 'Debating China's economic reform: New Leftists vs. liberals', *Journal of Chinese Political Science*, 2010, no. 15, pp. 1–23. The best account on Chinese intellectuals by a Western scholar is, to my knowledge, Joseph Fewsmith, *China since Tiananmen: The Politics of Transition*, Cambridge, Cambridge University Press, 2001, second edition, revised and expanded, 2008. On Chinese intellectuals see also: Louis Baeck, 'Discours intellectuels sur la mondialisation en Chine', *Monde chinois*, 2007, no. 9, pp. 55–71; Xu Youyu, 'The debates between liberalism and the New Left in China since the 1990s', *Contemporary Chinese Thought*, 2003, no. 34 (3), pp. 3–17; He Li, 'China's New Left and its impact on political liberalization', *EAI Background Brief no. 401*, 26 August 2008; Simon Shen, 'The response of Chinese intellectuals to the US War on Terror', *Journal of Chinese Political Science*, 2007, vol. 12, no. 3, pp. 238–280. On ideology and Party legitimization see Bruce Gilley and Heike Holbig, 'The debate on Party legitimacy in China: a mixed quantitative/ qualitative analysis', *Journal of Contemporary China*, 2009, March, pp. 339–358; Heike Holbig, 'Remaking the CPC's ideology: determinants, progress, and limits under Hu Jintao', *Journal of Current Chinese Affairs*, 2009, no. 3, pp. 35–61; Bruce Gilley and Heike Holbig, 'Reclaiming legitimacy in China', *Politics and Policy*, 2010, vol. 38, no. 3, pp. 395–422 (first published as 'In Search of Legitimacy in Post-revolutionary China: Bringing Ideology and Governance Back In', German Institute of Global and Area Studies, Working Paper no. 127, March 2010).

42 Arif Dirlik, 'Introduction', *Boundary 2*, 2008, no. 2, p. 11, special number dedicated to China. Dirlik goes on to say (ibid.):

> This recognition that the revolution was not an act of madness but had on its side a historical logic goes against the grain these days – not just of the leaders of the Communist Party, but of China scholars inside and outside the PRC.

43 Urio, *Reconciling*, pp. 77–78. This conclusion is confirmed by a Chinese scholar, He Li, 'Debating China's economic reform', especially p. 2. See also Dominik Mierzejewski, ' "Not to oppose but to rethink": the New Left discourse on the Chinese reforms', *Journal of Contemporary Eastern Asia*, 2009, vol. 8, no. 1, pp. 15–29.

44 See the interesting case of the Tsinghua professor Hu Angang in Urio, *Reconciling*, p. 227, n. 4.

45 He Li, 'Debating', p. 5.
46 The best analysis of the opposition between neoliberals and New Left intellectuals is that of Zheng Yongnian, *Globalization and State Transformation in China*, Cambridge, Cambridge University Press, 2004, Chapter 8: 'Contending visions of the Chinese state: New Liberalism vs. the New Left', pp. 162–186. For several interesting complements see He Li, 'China's New Left and its impact on political liberalization'. In these two sources the reader who is fluent in Chinese will find numerous references to works published in Chinese. For the best account from a Western scholar see Fewsmith, *China since Tiananmen*.
47 'The world's top 100 public intellectuals', *Foreign Policy*, May–June 2008, no. 166, pp. 58–61.
48 During the 1980s Li Minqi was a student at Peking University's Economic Management Department (today the Guanghua Economic Management School, a neoliberal think tank, influenced by the 'Chicago School') and was among the demonstrators on Tiananmen Square in 1989. Later, influenced by the writings of Mao, he evaluated the Tiananmen events and became 'a leftist, a socialist, a Marxist, and eventually, a Marxist–Leninist–Maoist' (Li Minqi, *The Rise of China*, p. xiv). A year later he 'gave a political speech on campus of Peking University, which cost [him] two years of imprisonment' (ibid.). Then he developed his analysis, being influenced by the writings of Marx, Engels, Lenin, Mao and Baran, Sweezy's *Monopoly Capital* and Immanuel Wallerstein's *The Capitalist World Economy*. He came to the USA in 1994 and studied economics at the University of Massachusetts. He now teaches economics at the University of Utah, USA. He explains his intellectual path in the preface to *The Rise of China*, pp. ix–xix.
49 Li Minqi, *The Rise of China*, p. ix.
50 Ibid., p. xvi. The book, *Capitalist Development and Class Struggle in China*, is available at Li's website: http://www.econ.utah.edu/~mli/index.htm.
51 Let us note for the sake of clarity that Li considers that China has become a capitalist country, as neo-Marxists generally do. For a detailed recent explanation see Li's article 'The rise of the working class and the future of the Chinese revolution', *Monthly Review*, June 2011, available on http://monthlyreview.org (accessed 15 July 2011).
52 Li Minqi, *The Rise of China*, pp. 175–176.
53 See for example the analysis of the 2008 crisis provided by contributors to the *Monthly Review* (http://www.monthlyreview.org/), for example Bellamy John Foster and Fred Magdoff, *The Great Financial Crisis*, and Fred Magdoff and Michael D. Yates, *The ABC of the Economic Crisis*, New York, Monthly Review Press, 2009.
54 Immanuel Wallerstein, 'Structural crises', *New Left Review*, March–April 2010, pp. 133–142; the quotation is from p. 138.
55 Interview given by I. Wallerstein to *Le Monde*, published 12 October 2008 (my translation from the French).
56 Cui Zhiyuan, 'How to comprehend today's China', *Contemporary Chinese Thought*, Summer 2006, vol. 37, no. 4, pp. x–xx (translated from the Chinese original published in *Dushu – Reading*, March 2004, no. 3, pp. 3–9). See also his 'Privatization and consolidation of democratic regimes: an analysis and an alternative', *Journal of International Affairs*, Winter 1997, vol. 50, no. 2, pp. 675–692, in which he evaluates the privatization strategies followed by Russia and eastern Europe and proposes an alternative strategy for China. After obtaining his PhD at Chicago University, Cui spent several years in the USA as a visiting scholar at Harvard Law School; he now teaches public policy at the School of Public Policy and Management at Tsinghua University, Beijing. Between 2010 and 2011 he spent a year as adviser to the local government of the Chongqing municipality, one of the most rapidly developing municipalities in China.
57 For more detail on Cui's 'petty bourgeois socialism' see his article 'Liberal socialism and the future of China: a petty bourgeois manifesto', in Tian Yu Cao (ed.), *The*

Chinese Model of Modern Development, London, Routledge, 2005, pp. 157–174. In a recent article Li Minqi, in a much more radical approach, comes to consider that the present development of capitalism makes the proletariat (again) the force that will overthrow the bourgeoisie: 'with massive proletarianization in Asia, world-historical conditions are finally approaching what, in line with Marx, will lead to the victory of the proletariat and the downfall of the bourgeoisie' ('The rise of the working class and the future of the Chinese revolution', *Monthly Review*, June 2011, available on http://monthlyreview.org, accessed 15 July 2011).

58 John Stuart Mill, *Principles of Political Economy* (with Chapters on Socialism), New York, Oxford University Press (Oxford World's Classics), 1994.
59 Cui, 'How to comprehend today's China', p. 4.
60 Quoted by Zheng Yongnian, *Globalization and State Transformation in China*, p. 179.
61 Ibid.
62 Ibid., p. 180. Let us note that other New Left intellectuals are re-evaluating the positive aspects of the Maoist era, which for a long time have been left aside as they have been discredited by the mistakes perpetrated by Mao, especially the Great Leap Forward and the Great Cultural Revolution. For example, the Tsinghua professor Hu Angang is working on a revision of the history of the Peoples' Republic of China since its beginning to the present day. It will comprise three volumes, the first of which is already available in Chinese.
63 Cui, 'Privatization and consolidation of democratic regimes', pp. 684 and 689–691. Given the discussion on capitalism presented above I will rather speak of 'the best features of market economy and socialism' instead of 'the best features of traditional capitalism and traditional socialism'.
64 Ibid., pp. 685–686 and 689–691. For a more detailed explanation of Meade's theory see the whole Cui article, where one can find other references, and J.E. Meade, *Liberty, Equality and Efficiency*, New York, New York University Press, 1993.
65 This has been recognized by the Chinese leadership. See for example Vice-Premier Li Keqiang, reported by Reuters:

> 700 million farmers couldn't benefit from the country's rapid growth and prosperity . . . This is about the accelerating change of the economy's development model – its development should be fast, but stable in the long run and allow all Chinese to participate in the fruits of reform . . . Restructuring income distribution, improving public service and establishing a social security system will help develop the untapped purchasing potential of more than one million Chinese.
> Quoted by *Caijing*, 5 January 2011, http://emglish.caijing.com.cn/ajax/ensprint. html (accessed 8 June 2011)

66 Interview given by Cui Zhiyuan to Emilie Frenkiel, 'From scholar to official: Cui Zhiyuan and Chongqing city's local experimental policy', *La vie des idées (Books & Ideas)*, 25 January 2011, p. 3, http://www.booksandideas.net (accessed 15 May 2011).
67 Discussion with Wang Hui, Beijing, 12 October 2010. See Wang Hui, interview by Pankaj Mishra, 'China's New Leftist', published by the *New York Times*, 15 October 2006, as well as his major works translated into English: *China's New Order*, Cambridge, MA, Harvard University Press, 2003; and *The End of the Revolution: China and the Limits of Modernity*, London, Verso, 2009.
68 Wang Hui, *The End of the Revolution*, p. xvii. On Wang Hui's interpretation of the Tiananmen events of June 1989, see his article 'How Tiananmen protesters led to the new market economy. China: unequal shares', available on http://christusrex.org/www1/news/hui-4-02.html (accessed 10 July 2011).
69 Wang Hui, *The End of the Revolution*, p. xxi. Here Wang Hui refers to the motto attributed to Deng Xiaoping, 'crossing the river by feeling the stones', meaning that it is necessary to advance step by step on the road (or through the river) of reforms.

70 Ibid., p. xxiii.
71 Ibid.
72 Ibid., p. xxv.
73 Ibid. On the role of interest groups in China see Scott Kennedy, *The Business of Lobbying in China*, Cambridge, MA, Harvard University Press, 2005.
74 Wang Hui, *The End of the Revolution*, p. xxvii.
75 Ibid., p. xxix.
76 Ibid., p. xxx.
77 Ibid.
78 Ibid., pp. xxxi–xxxii. By using the term 'depoliticization' Wang Hui refers to the title of an article he published in 2006: 'Depoliticized politics, from East to West', *New Left Review*, 2006, no. 41, September/October, pp. 29–45, reproduced as Chapter 1 in *The End of Revolution*, pp. 3–18.
79 Ibid., p. xxxii.
80 Zhang Yongle, 'No forbidden zone in reading? *Dushu* and the Chinese intelligentsia', *New Left Review*, 2008, January/February, pp. 5–26. On p. 5, Zhang, who considers *Dushu* 'probably China's leading intellectual journal for the past decade, as well as the most controversial', informs us that:

> in July 2007 . . . Wang Hui and Huang Ping were being dismissed from the monthly magazine by its parent company, SDX Publishing. . . . The official grounds for this seemed scarcely plausible: initially there was talk of falling circulation, although in fact the number of *Dushu* subscribers had risen under Wang and Huang from around 60.000 to well over 100.000. SDX then announced that it was implementing a company policy requiring that all chief editors be full-time . . . The company could provide no explanation, however, as to why it had suddenly 'remembered' this policy . . . The editors detractors argued that the two turned the journal, 'universally recognized' by the Chinese intelligentsia in the 1980s and early 1990s, into a platform for a small 'new-left clique'.

81 The China Beat website (http://www.thechinabeat.org/?s=Wang+Hui&paged=2, accessed 8 February 2011) has posted information according to which Wang Hui:

> has been accused of plagiarism in an article . . . published in an academic literary journal (*Wenyi Yanjiu*) in which the Nanjing University literature professor Wang Binbin charges that Wang Hui's dissertation on Lu Xun, (fangkan juewang), published in 1985 when he was a doctoral student at Nanjing University and later the basis of a book published in the early 1990s, contains several passages lifted from other works and used without citation.

The link 'About' of the China Beat site informs readers that:

> Launched in early 2008, The China Beat provides context and criticism on contemporary China from China scholars and journalists. Based around a group of active contributors at the University of California, Irvine, including co-founders Kenneth Pomeranz and Jeffrey Wasserstrom, the blog draws on a global group of China watchers in the US, China, the UK, Australia, Japan, Canada, Taiwan, and many other locations.

82 Let us note that, whereas I place Hu Angang in the company of other New Left intellectuals, some other scholars classify him as a statist or neo-statist, being one of the first (with Wang Shaoguang) to propose a centralization of the Chinese fiscal system in order to give more power to the central government (e.g. Joseph Fewsmith, *China since Tiananmen*, p. 132) or a statist within the general category of the Left (Zheng Yongnian, *Globalization and State Transformation in China*, p. 181) whereas some others consider him as a representative of the New Left, or even 'the beacon theoretician of the Marxist wing of the Party' (for example Agnès Andrésy, *Le Président*

chinois Hu Jintao: Sa politique et ses réseaux. Who's Hu?, Paris, L'Harmattan, 2008, p. 71, my translation from the French). For a short story of the development of Hu's research and the impact he has had on China's public policies see Urio, *Reconciling*, pp. 104–110.
83 Hu Angang, 'Corruption: an enormous black hole: public exposure of the economic costs of corruption', Chapter 11 of Hu Angang, *Economic and Social Transformation in China*, London, Routledge, 2007, pp. 217–223; 'Second transition of the Communist Party of China: from economic development to institution building', ibid., Chapter 12, pp. 224–246.
84 Several discussions with Hu Angang, Beijing, 2005–2011, especially September–October 2010 and October 2011. Hu Angang is Professor at the School of Public Policy and Management of Tsinghua University, where he directs the Centre for China Studies, which he founded in 2000. The Centre has become one of the most influential think tanks in China and provides policy advice to the Chinese leadership, for example for the preparation of the Eleventh and Twelfth Five-Year Plans. See Hu Angang, 'Predictions for the next five years: interview with Prof. Hu Angang', *Beijing Review*, September 2010, vol. 53, no. 37, pp. 28–31, and 'A plan is born', ibid., pp. 32–33, as well as the major works of Hu Angang published in English: *Economic and Social Transformation in China*; *Roadmap of China's Rise*, London, Routledge, 2011; and *China in 2020: A New Type of Superpower*, Washington, DC, Brookings Institution, 2011. Hu has also put forward proposals in the domain of climate change that have not been totally accepted by the Chinese government: Hu Angang, 'A new approach at Copenhagen', available on China Dialogue's website: http://www.chinadialogue.net (accessed 7 September 2009). Nevertheless, Hu declared that he always started in the minority, but finally he ended up in the majority, meaning by that that his innovative ideas have taken some time before they were recognized as good ideas by the Chinese leadership.
85 Hu Angang, *China in 2020*.
86 Hu Angang, 'How do I conduct China study?', first handout for the course for the Master in International Development: 'China Economic Development: Theory and Practice', Beijing, School of Public Policy and Management, Tsinghua University, 2007.
87 Wang Shaoguang is presently professor at the Chinese University, Hong Kong, and at the School of Public Policies and Management at Tsinghua University. After studying law at Peking University in the late 1970s, he obtained his PhD in political science at Cornell University in 1990; between 1990 and 2000 he taught at Yale University, where he met Hu Angang, who was at Yale as a visiting scholar in 1992–3. Wang moved to Hong Kong in 2000.
88 Wang Shaoguang and Hu Angang, *The Political Economy of Uneven Development: The Case of China*, New York, M.E. Sharpe, 1999. The first policy research-oriented works of Hu Angang, available to the Chinese leadership before the end of 1988, and published in English at the beginning of the 1990s, are the following: Hu Angang, Wang Yi *et al.*, *Survival and Development: A Study of China's Long Term Development*, Beijing, Science Press, 1992; and Hu Angang and Zou Ping, *China's Population Development*, Beijing, China's Science and Technology Press, 1991. For a brief analysis of these two books see Urio, *Reconciling*, pp. 104–108.
89 Opinion expressed during the Glasshouse Forum, Paris, 23–24 February 2009: 'Is there a China model? A summary and video documentation of a China–West intellectual summit', Maison Louis Carré, Paris, 2009. See also his evaluation of China's development strategy: Wang Shaoguang, 'The great transformation: two-way movement in China since the 1980s', *Social Sciences in China* (in Chinese, *Zhong Guo She Hui Ke Xue*), 2008, no. 1, pp. 129–148, also published with some differences as 'Great social transformation afoot in China', *China Economist*, July 2008, pp. 55–69, and, in a more complete form, as 'The great transformation: the double movement in China', *Boundary 2*, 2008, no. 2, pp. 16–47.

90 For more details on the role of New Left intellectuals, and more particularly of Hu Angang, see Urio, *Reconciling*, pp. 104–10.
91 Emilie Frenkiel 'Political change and democracy in China: an interview with Wang Shaoguang', *La vie des idées (Books and Ideas)*, 15 July 2009, pp. 3–4, http://www.booksandideas.net (accessed 15 May 2011).
92 Ibid., p. 4.
93 Karl Polanyi, *The Great Transformation: The Political and Economic Origins of Our Time*, Boston, Beacon Press, 2001, with an introduction by Joseph E. Stiglitz and a new introduction by Fred Block (1st edn 1944).
94 Wang Shaoguang, 'Great social transformation afoot in China', p. 55.
95 Wang Shaoguang, 'China in transition', *L'Annuaire du Collège de France*, 2010, no. 109, 24 June, http://annuaire-cdf.revues.org/427 (accessed 29 April 2011). Let us note that the explicit reference Wang makes to redistributive policies as a means to correct the market's negative outcomes (a clear social-democratic strategy adopted by Western governments) is in contradiction with Cui Zhiyuan's ideas, according to which, as we have seen above, the Chinese 'socialist market economy' is not a compromise between capitalism and socialism, as is clearly the case for the strategy followed by Western social democracies.
96 Hu Angang, PowerPoint Presentation for the Master's course 2009–10, taught at Tsinghua University.
97 Wang Shaoguang, 'The great transformation'.
98 He Li, 'Debating', p. 2.
99 On the importance of neoliberals in China, in addition to the references in notes 41 and 46, see Wang Hui, 'The year 1989 and the historical roots of Neoliberalism in China', Chapter 2 of *The End of the Revolution*, pp. 19–66. On Chinese think tanks see Joseph Fewsmith, 'Where do correct ideas come from? The Party school, key think tanks, and the intellectuals', in David M. Finkelstein and Marianne Kivlehan (eds), *China's Leadership in the 21st Century: The Rise of the Fourth Generation*, New York, M.E. Sharpe, 2003, pp. 152–164, and Cheng Li, 'China's new think tanks: where officials, entrepreneurs, and scholars interact', *China Leadership Monitor*, no. 29, available on http://www.hoover.org/publications/china-leadership-monitor (accessed 20 October 2009); in Li's n. 12 there are several additional references.
100 He Li, 'Debating', p. 6, attributes this statement to the liberal scholar Liu Junning. Also in this sense see Zheng Yongnian, *Globalization and State Transformation in China*, p. 167.
101 Zheng Yongnian, ibid., pp. 167 and 169.
102 An example of the intervention of neoliberals in the decision-making process is given by the *Caijing Magazine* in an article summarizing the debates about the new Chinese health system, in particular the discussion held on 7 March 2009 between officials of the Ministry of Health and members of the Chinese People's Political Consultative Conference (CPPCC), in which sit representatives of the so-called 'democratic parties' as well as other representatives of civil society. Some members of the Conference 'expressed reservations about . . . the efficiency of reform if the government – not the market – becomes the dominant force in distributing health care resources'. Professor Gu Xin, professor of public administration at Peking University and State Council appointed specialist for evaluating medical insurance for township residents, has expressed the idea that 'the market is usually more effective than executive administration, especially in China where administrative professionalism is low'. Finally, the *Caijing* article reports that 'some CPPCC delegates suggested that all medical institutions should be market-oriented.' These opinions would be quite alarming, should they be heard and implemented by the Chinese leadership in this domain, as, to quote just one aspect of the present Chinese situation in health care, patients in recent years have covered 50 per cent of all medical costs from their own pockets, according to China Health Economic Institute, quoted by this *Caijing* article, and we know that the marketization of the health sector has cut access to

health care for large sectors of the Chinese population, which cannot afford to pay out of pocket (*Caijing Magazine Online*, 19 March 2009, available online at http://www.english.cajing.com.cn, accessed 4 May 2009).
103 Zheng Yongnian, *Globalization and State Transformation in China*, p. 174.
104 On the issues related to the 2012 Party Congress see the papers published online (http://www.hoover.org/publications/china-leadership-monitor) by the *China Leadership Monitor*, and more particularly Alice Miller, 'The 18th Central Committee Politburo: a quixotic, foolhardy, rashly speculative, but nonetheless ruthlessly reasoned projection', *China Leadership Monitor*, June 2010, no. 33; Cheng Li, 'China's midterm jockeying: gearing up for 2012 (Part 1: provincial chiefs)', *China Leadership Monitor*, February 2010, no. 31, 'China's midterm jockeying: gearing up for 2012 (Part 2: cabinet ministers)', *China Leadership Monitor*, May 2010, no. 32; 'China's midterm jockeying: gearing up for 2012 (Part 3: military leaders)', *China Leadership Monitor*, June 2010, no. 33; 'China's midterm jockeying: gearing up for 2012 (Part 4: top leaders of major state-owned enterprises)', *China Leadership Monitor*, Spring 2011, no. 34.
105 To summarize the last paragraphs on NPM in the West, it is evident that I adopted a Weberian methodology: first I defined an ideal type of NPM and then, on the basis of this ideal type, I tried to understand how different Western countries have organized their public management and with what consequences.
106 This is done, as I will maintain hereafter, through the twin brother of NPM, the 'Washington consensus'.
107 Some authors do this in a way that is not acceptable methodologically, because they compare two very different elements: on one hand the 'theoretical' features of NPM, most of the time imported from the private sector (e.g. competition, decentralization) and therefore with little empirical evidence that they will actually work within the public sector, as well as the 'theoretical' benefits that NPM will bring to the public sector; and on the other hand the 'actual' dysfunctions of traditional management (inefficiency, red tape etc.), leaving aside the positive 'actual' outcomes of traditional management.
108 'Washington consensus' is the name that the economist John Williamson gave in 1989 to a list of 10 policy recommendations for countries willing to reform their economies imposed upon developing countries by the US Treasury, the World Bank and, especially, the IMF. Williamson's 10 prescriptions reflecting his interpretation of the Washington consensus in the early 1990s are listed in Chapter 1 note 18. See John Williamson (ed.), *Latin American Adjustment: How Much Has Happened*, Washington, DC, Institute for international Economics, 1990, and John Williamson, 'Democracy and the Washington consensus', *World Development*, 1993, vol. 21, no. 8, p. 1331.
109 Compare my list presented in Chapter 3 with Williamson's list.
110 This interpretation is generally admitted in the literature. Nevertheless, some scholars have criticized this interpretation; see, for example, Scott Kennedy, 'The myth of the Beijing consensus', first draft, prepared for the conference 'Washington consensus versus Beijing consensus', National Taiwan University Centre for China Studies and University of Denver Center for China–US Cooperation, Denver, Colorado, May 30–31, 2008, pp. 2–9. On pp. 4–5 Kennedy writes:

> Williamson, though, is most upset that the WC [Washington consensus] is often conflated with the economic ideology of Neoliberalism. Williamson likes to point out that he and a famous critic of the WC, Joseph Stiglitz (2002 [*Globalization and Its Discontents*]) actually agree on the substance of what makes good economic policies, but that Stiglitz has mistaken the WC for the policies of the IMF and neoliberal ideology.
>
> I prefer to stay with the dominant interpretation, shared by scholars such as Joseph Stiglitz.

111 This is what I have already maintained, by providing some empirical evidence, in Urio, *Reconciling*.
112 See, for example, Joshua Cooper Ramo, 'The Beijing consensus', London, The Foreign Policy Centre, May 2004, http://www.fpc.org.uk (accessed 6 June 2009); Joseph Stiglitz, 'Post Washington consensus', Columbia University, Initiative for Policy Dialog, Working Paper Series, 2005, http://www.gsb.columbia.edu/ipd/ (accessed 6 June 2009); Yujiro Hayami, 'From the Washington consensus to the post-Washington consensus: retrospect and prospect', *Asian Development Review*, 2003, vol. 20, no. 2, pp. 40–65; Huang Ping, 'Beijing consensus or Chinese experience or what?', unpublished paper, Chinese Academy of Social Sciences, Beijing, 2005; Scott Kennedy, 'The myth of the Beijing consensus'; Stefan Halper, *The Beijing Consensus: How China's Authoritarian Model Will Dominate the Twenty-First Century*, New York, Basic Books, 2010.
113 Gideon Rachman, 'Conservatism overshoots its limits', *Financial Times* (London), 6 October 2008.
114 Urio, *Reconciling*.
115 This is also true for other in-transition countries such as Poland, Ukraine and Russia. I have directed a research project dealing with one aspect of NPM in these countries: Paolo Urio (ed.), *Public Private Partnerships: Success and Failure Factors for In-Transition Countries*, Lanham, MD, University Press of America, 2010.
116 The most impressive example is that of the China Centre for Economic Research at Peking University: in 2005 among its 24 professors 21 held degrees from American universities, one from the UK, one from Belgium and one from Japan; Cheng Li, 'China's new think tanks', where one can find a comprehensive presentation of China's think tanks.
117 Urio, *Public Private Partnerships*, p. 330.
118 This is a distinction I have introduced ibid., pp. 6, 49–50 and 55–56. I have labelled 'hard infrastructure' those that provide services in which the physical component is very important (such as transportation and energy), and 'soft infrastructure' those aimed more specifically and directly at improving human capital (such as education and health). For the link between hard and soft infrastructure see ibid., pp. 41–43.
119 For in-transition countries the most recent references are Ha-Joon Chang, *Bad Samaritans*, and José Antonio Ocampo and Joseph E. Stiglitz (eds), *Capital Market Liberalization and Development*, Oxford, Oxford University Press, 2008. Although this book deals mainly with capital market liberalization, several contributions deal more generally with neoliberal orthodoxy. See also Joseph E. Stiglitz, *Globalization and Its Discontents*; *The Roaring Nineties*; *Making Globalization Work*; Stiglitz and Charlton, *Fair Trade for All*; Chang, *Institutional Change and Economic Development*. For developed countries see Suleiman, *Dismantling Democratic States*. I would add that some scholars, who have been researching NPM during the last 20 years or so, are now taking stock of the flaws of this movement and are returning to Max Weber for the purpose of (re)constructing a New Weberian Bureaucracy: Geert Bouckaert, 'La réforme de la gestion publique change-t-elle les systèmes administratifs?', *Revue française d'administration publique*, 2003, no. 105–106, pp. 39–54; Laurence E. Lynn, Jr, 'What is a neo-Weberian state? Reflections on a concept and its implementations', draft, 24 January 2008.
120 José Antonio Ocampo, Shari Spiegel and Joseph E. Stiglitz, 'Capital market liberalization and development', in José Antonio Ocampo and Joseph E. Stiglitz (eds), *Capital Market Liberalization and Development*, pp. 3–4. Moreover, they inform us that 'Theoretical and empirical research over the past quarter century have helped explain why the market economy often does not function as well as free market advocates had hoped.' The OECD presents a similar faith in market mechanisms. I have criticized its last publication on a special variant of contracting out, namely public–private partnerships (OECD, *Public–Private Partnerships: In Pursuit of Risk*

Sharing and Value for Money, Paris, OECD, 2008) in Urio (ed.), *Public Private Partnerships*, pp. 338–344.

121 The main references I have used are Peter A. Hall and David Soskice (eds), *Varieties of Capitalism: The Institutional Foundations of Comparative Advantage*, Oxford, Oxford University Press, 2001; Bruno Amable, *Les cinq capitalismes: Diversité des systèmes économiques et sociaux dans la mondialisation*, Paris, Seuil, 2005; Gosta Esping-Andersen, *The Three Worlds of Welfare Capitalism*, Princeton, NJ, Princeton University Press, 1990; and Esping-Andersen, *Welfare States in Transition*, London, Sage, 1996. Other interesting works are Peter Flora, *Growth to Limits: The Western European Welfare States since World War II*, Berlin, De Gruyter, 1986; Marco Giugni (ed.), *The Politics of Unemployment in Europe*, Burlington, VT, Ashgate, 2009; Manlio Cinalli and Marco Giugni, 'Welfare states, political opportunities, and claim-making in the field of unemployment politics', in Marco Giugni (ed.), *The Contentious Politics of Unemployment in Europe: Welfare States and Political Opportunities*, Houndmills, Palgrave, 2010, pp. 9–42.

122 Esping-Andersen, *The Three Worlds*, pp. 3–5.

123 Ibid., pp. 26–28.

124 Let us note that the Esping-Andersen typology is still used today by serious researchers. See, for example, Eric Crettaz and Giuliano Bonoli, 'World of working poverty: cross-national variation in the mechanisms that lead poverty among workers', Luxembourg Income Study, Working Paper no. 539, July 2010. For a critique see Andreas Tiemann, 'Stability of Gosta Esping-Andersen's *The Three Worlds of Welfare Capitalism*', Luxembourg Income Study Working Paper Series, no. 449, September 2006. For a critique, comparison and integration with other approaches see Torben Iversen and John D. Stephens, 'Partisan politics, the welfare state, and three worlds of human capital formation', *Comparative Political Studies*, 2008, vol. 41, no. 4/5, pp. 600–637. In this article (p. 601) the authors say:

> Recently, the theory [i.e. that of Esping-Andersen, which is described as 'Power Resource Theory' according to which 'the size and structure of the Welfare State is a function of the historical strength of the political left, mediated by alliances with the middle class', ibid., p. 600] has come under attack for neglecting the role of employers in the rise and design of the modern welfare state . . . It has also been challenged from a variety of capitalism perspectives (Hall & Soskice [*Varieties of Capitalism*, quoted above, note 121]) by scholars who propose that different systems of social protection are efficient complements to distinct modes of capitalist production, or welfare production regimes . . . In this article, we show that the Power Resource Theory and Welfare Production Regime approaches are consistent with one another and can productively be combined to make sense of many puzzling differences in the structure and functioning of Esping-Andersen's different worlds of welfare capitalism. Such a synthesis also helps explain more recent changes.

125 Hall and Soskice, *Varieties of Capitalism*, pp. 6–7.

126 Ibid., pp. 19–21.

127 Ibid., p. 173.

128 Amable, *Les cinq capitalismes*, pp. 23–25, 136–151 and 221–232.

129 Ibid., p. 222, fig. 5.1.

130 One could even consider that the USA was a strong-NPM country well before the Ronald Reagan administration (1980–88), as the USA has always been against 'big government', has developed a weak Welfare State and has always given preference to the 'free market' over state intervention.

131 Richard Wilkinson and Kate Pickett, *The Spirit Level: Why More Equal Societies Almost Always Do Better*, London, Allen Lane, Penguin Books, 2009. The results of this research will be briefly presented at the end of Chapter 5.

132 F.A. von Hayek, *The Fatal Conceit: The Errors of Socialism*, University of Chicago Press, 1988, p. 99.
133 At least until the spring of 2011 when the European Union and the IMF, under pressure from financial markets, started to put a lot of pressure on several European countries, especially Greece, Portugal, Spain and Italy, to implement the policies needed to reduce their debt.
134 For example the PhD thesis by Matteo Guidotti: *The Good Governance Agenda and Public Administration Reforms: An Institutional Political Analysis. The Case of the Commune Level One-Stop Programme in Vietnam*, unpublished PhD thesis, University of Geneva, 2010.
135 The use of contracting out in France and the UK before NPM has been mentioned by Simon Domberger, *The Contracting Organization: A Strategic Guide to Outsourcing*, New York, Oxford University Press, 1998. For a recent defence of PPPs see European Union, Communication from the Commission to the European Parliament, The Council, the European Economic and Social Committee and the Committee of the Regions, *Mobilising Private and Public Investment for Recovery and Long Term Structural Change: Developing Public Private Partnerships*, Brussels, 19 November 2009, COM (2009) 615 final. Other similar initiatives are being taken within the United Nations Economic Commission for Europe (UNECE). On the huge literature on PPPs I refer to the references quoted in Urio (ed.) *Public Private Partnerships*.
136 See for example the case of the USA as mentioned by J.E. Stiglitz:

> The seasonally adjusted rate of 'Total unemployed, plus all marginally attached workers plus total employed part-time for economic reasons, as a percentage of all civilian labor force plus all marginally attached workers' was 17.5 percent in October 2009 [well above the official unemployment rate]. Bureau of Labor Statistics, 'Current Population Survey: Labour force Statistics, Table U-6 . . .'
> Joseph E. Stiglitz, *Freefall*, note 18 of Chapter 1, p. 305; see also comments on pp. 17–18.

137 The LIS working papers are available on the LIS site: http://www.lisproject.org/.
138 Paul Krugman, 'The rich, the right and the facts: deconstructing the income distribution debate', *American Prospect*, Fall 1992, pp. 19–31, http://epn.org/prospect.html (accessed 3 July 1996).
139 Of course it is necessary to take into consideration the size of the household, the poverty line being increased less than proportionally to the number of people in the household for the purpose of taking into consideration economies of scale.
140 Let us note that this decision can considerably change the size of the poor population for both methods (absolute and relative), as in many countries low incomes are concentrated within a very narrow range of values. Therefore, by moving the poverty line upwards or downwards one can considerably change the size of the population living under the poverty line.
141 Andrea Brandolini, Silvia Magri and Timothy M. Smeeding, 'Asset-based measurement of poverty', *Journal of Policy Analysis and Management*, 2010, vol. 29, no. 2, pp. 267–284. In particular the authors warn us that 'our empirical comparative results, however tentative because of data problems, suggest that asset-related measures of poverty have distinctive informative value with respect to income-based statistics and other statistics such as material hardship' (p. 281).
142 The Oxford Poverty & Human Development Initiative website: http://www.ophi.org.uk.
143 David Woodward, *How Poor Is "Poor"? Towards a Rights-Based Poverty Line*, London, NEF (The New Economic Foundation), 2010.
144 Ibid., pp. 2–3.
145 UNDP website, http://hdr.undp.org/en/ (accessed 10 March 2011). Moreover, UNDP gives the following additional explanations:

Why change the indicators for measuring education and income? The indicators were changed for several reasons. For example, adult literacy used in the old HDI (which is simply a binary variable – literate or illiterate, with no gradations) is an insufficient measure for getting a complete picture of knowledge achievements. By including average years of schooling and expected years of schooling, one can better capture the level of education and recent changes. Gross Domestic Product (GDP) is the monetary value of goods and services produced in a country irrespective of how much is retained in the country. Gross National Income (GNI) expresses the income accrued to residents of a country, including international flows such as remittances and aid, and excluding income generated in the country but repatriated abroad. Thus, GNI is a more accurate measure of a country's economic welfare. As shown in the Report, large differences could exist between the income of a country's residents, measured by GNI or GDP.

For more details and the complete list of the new indices (for the inequality-adjusted HDI, gender inequality and poverty) see the 2010 Report available on the UNDP website.

146 United Nations Development Programme (UNDP), *Human Development Report 2010*, New York, Palgrave Macmillan for UNDP, 2010, pp. 217–218.
147 See, for example, Perry Anderson, *The Origins of Postmodernity*, London, Verso, 1998; David Harvey, *The Condition of Postmodernity*, Oxford, Blackwell, 1990; Ronald Inglehart, *Modernization and Postmodernization: Cultural, Economic, and Political Change in 43 Societies*, Princeton, NJ, Princeton University Press, 1997; Arif Dirlik and Zhang Xudong (eds), *Postmodernism and China*, Durham, NC, Duke University Press, 2000.

3 The foundation of the Western experiment

1 Paolo Urio, 'La gestion publique au service du marché', in Marc Hufty (ed.), *La pensée comptable: Etat, néolibéralisme, nouvelle gestion publique*, Paris, Presses Universitaires de France, pp. 91–124.
2 This is the case for the book that has become the foundation of NPM in the USA: David Osborne and Ted Gaebler, *Reinventing Government: How the Entrepreneurial Spirit is Transforming the Public Sector*, New York, Plume Book, 1993. See the opinion of Riccardo Petrella, 'Les nouvelles Tables de la Loi' (or 'The new Tables of the Law'), *Le Monde Diplomatique*, October 1995.
3 World Bank, *China 2020: Development Challenges in the New Century*, 18 September 1997, Report no. 17027-CHA, World Bank, p. ix. At the beginning of ch. 3 of this same report, the World Bank further explains what is the role of good government: 'Good markets start with good government. This is true because effective governments serve markets rather than make markets serve government' (ibid., p. 23). For an application to the international level of this way of thinking see the project of Multilateral Agreement on Investment (MAI), negotiated within the OECD, available on the internet in English (http://www.citizen.org) and in French (http://www.monde-diplomatique.fr/md/dossier/ami/). For comment, see Lori M. Wallach, 'Le nouveau manifeste du capitalisme mondial', *Le Monde Diplomatique*, February 1998, p. 22. See also for the Anti-Counterfeiting Trade Agreement, Florent Latrive, 'Traité secret sur l'immateriel', *Le Monde Diplomatique*, March 2010, pp. 1 and 6; on the Trans-Pacific Partnership (TPP) Agreement see Jane Kelsey, 'International civil society demands end to secrecy in TPPA talks', media release, 16 February 2011, http://tppwatch.org, accessed 29 March 2011; and on the General Agreement on Trade and Services (GATS), Jane Kelsey, *Serving Whose Interests? The Political Economy of Trade in Services Agreements*, Abingdon (UK), Routledge Cavendish, 2008.

4 Gideon Rachman, 'Conservatism overshoots its limits', *Financial Times* (London), 6 October 2008. See also Joseph E. Stiglitz, 'Turn left for sustainable growth', *Economists' Voice*, http://www.bepress.com/ev, September 2008 (accessed 28 October 2008), and P.K. Rao, 'Letter: comment on Stiglitz's Turn Left for Sustainable Growth', *Economists' Voice*, http://www.bepress.com/ev, November 2008 (accessed 30 November 2008).
5 Thus, for instance in 1947, when the future Nobel prizewinner Herbert Simon attacks the classical theory of the organization (regarding which it is sufficient to mention here the distinguished names of W.T. Taylor and H. Fayol), he does not hesitate to qualify as 'proverbs' the principles of organization that were presented by his predecessors as scientific principles.
6 Concerning the impossibility of discovering a new paradigm of public management, I would restrict myself to citing two texts of Christopher Hood: 'The New Public Management in the 1980s: variations on a theme', *Accounting, Organization and Society*, 1995, vol. 20, no. 2/3, pp. 93–109, and 'Contemporary public management: a new global paradigm', *Public Policy and Administration*, 1995, vol. 10, no. 2, pp. 104–117; as well as three texts by Lawrence E. Lynn: *The New Public Management as an International Phenomenon: Questions of an American Skeptic*, paper prepared for the conference on the New Public Management in International Perspective, St. Gallen, July 1996; 'Dividing the job: intergovernmental dimension', *Public Manager*, Fall 1992, vol. 21, no. 3, pp. 7–10; and *Public Management as Art, Science, and Profession*, Chatham, NJ, Chatham House, 1996. See also the last book by Laurence E. Lynn Jr., *Public Management: Old and New*, New York, Routledge, 2006. Some authors discuss the possible demise of NPM: Ewan Ferlie and Gianluca Andresani (eds), 'Overview of: Roundtable: Understanding current developments in public-sector management – New Public Management, governance or other theoretical perspectives?', *Public Management Review*, 2006, vol. 8, no. 2, pp. 390–94; and Tom Christensen and Per Laegreid, *Transcending New Public Management: The Transformation of Public Sector Reform*, Aldershot (UK), Ashgate, 2007.

On the validity of the Weberian model, I would limit myself to mentioning two articles: Ronald C. Moe, 'The "reinventing government" exercise: misinterpreting the problem, misjudging the consequences', *Public Administration Review*, March–April 1994, vol. 54, no. 2, pp. 111–122, and Ronald C. Moe and Robert S. Gilmour, 'Rediscovering principles of public administration: the neglected foundation of public law', *Public Administration Review*, March–April 1995, vol. 55, no. 2, pp. 135–144. On the validity of the Keynesian approach, the reader will profit from reading Paul Krugman, *Peddling Prosperity*, New York, W.W. Norton & Co., 1994, particularly 'The attack on Keynes', pp. 23–54, 'The budget deficit', pp. 151–169, and 'In the long run Keynes is still alive', pp. 197–220.
7 The 'unholy trinity' expression has been used by Ha-Joon Chang, *Bad Samaritans: The Myth of Free Trade and the Secret History of Capitalism*, New York, Bloomsbury Press, 2008, p. 32.
8 Milton Friedman bitterly complains about this in the preface to the second edition of his *Capitalism and Freedom*, Chicago, Chicago University Press, 1982. Nevertheless there is a difference: the critics of NPM did not benefit, by a long way, from the same support the neoliberals gained after the Second World War from the private sector in financing university chairs, research, conferences and publications.
9 This has also been the case for non-profit organizations such as university faculties and research centres. For charity's sake I will not mention examples.
10 It is impossible to mention in any detail at this point the abundant literature on these concepts. I limit myself here to referring the hard-pressed reader to Keith Dowding, *The Civil Service*, London, Routledge, 1995, pp. 31–51.
11 It is sufficient here to mention the famous article by the future President of the United States Woodrow Wilson, 'The study of administration', *Political Science Quarterly*,

June 1887, pp. 197–222, reprinted in *Political Science Quarterly*, December 1941, pp. 481–506.

12 The English language has forged a new expression to make the reader aware of these phenomena: the 'working poor'. These people are employed, but their income is not sufficient to place them above the poverty line, thus necessitating state assistance or help from private organizations. This expression effectively brings into focus the anomaly of the existence of this phenomenon in our very rich civilization, in which work is the privileged means for achieving the individual's life expectations: these persons work, but do not succeed in getting beyond the vicious circle of poverty. Note that this expression is beginning to be used in English even in French publications (e.g. *L'Hebdo*, 8 January 1998, p. 40). On the vicious circle of poverty see, for example, Samuel Bowles, Steven N. Durlauf and Karla Hoff (eds), *Poverty Traps*, New York, Russel Sage Foundation, 2006.

13 On these aspects, one may refer to the book by three Geneva economists: Gabrielle Antille, Beat Bürgenmeier and Yves Flückiger, *L'économie suisse au futur: une réforme en trois piliers*, Lausanne, Réalités Sociales, 1997.

14 Paolo Urio and Véronique Merckx, *Le budget de la Confédération: Le système politique Suisse face à l'équilibre des finances fédérales*, Lausanne, Réalités Sociales, 1996, p. 14. The use of the adjective 'providential' was meant to refer to the French expression equivalent to the English 'welfare state', *l'état-providence*, meaning by this that the Left saw in the NPM the last chance of rescuing the welfare (i.e. 'providential') state.

15 The most renowned book by David Osborne and Ted Gaebler, *Reinventing Government*, was summarized in a series of articles published in *Domaine Public*, a bi-monthly published in Lausanne by a group of people from, or close to, the Swiss Socialist Party. The articles were then collected together in a brochure of which several thousand copies were sold. This text was frequently referred to in the media of the French-speaking part of Switzerland. The same goes for the 10 principles of NPM defined by these two authors, which have become a sort of new 'Tables of the Ten Commandments'. See for a similar interpretation the article by Riccardo Petrella, 'Les nouvelles Tables de la Loi'.

16 Jean-Daniel Delley, 'Nouvelle gestion publique: le débat n'est pas clos', *Domaine Public* (Lausanne), 9 January 1997, p. 4. (My translation from the French.)

17 Note, in passing, that the non-mechanical application of a model is a banality, which no theoretician or practitioner of the organization would even mention, it being so obvious.

18 Let us remind the reader that there are at least three characteristics that confer to the market its undisputable supremacy over any other way of organizing the economy whenever economic efficiency is the goal: (1) multiple actors on the supply and the demand sides, to guarantee competition, diminish production costs and avoid inefficient dominant positions, (2) transparency (i.e. complete and inexpensive information), to guarantee the rationality of the economic actors' decisions in the market, and (3) no obstacles to exit from and entry into the market, to avoid keeping inefficient producers in activity. Moreover, it was assumed that markets were self-correcting over time, and this should avoid state intervention.

19 Joost Mönks, 'New Public Management: pas de modèle unique!', *Journal de Genève*, 16 December 1997, p. 2 (my translation from the French).

20 Despite the somewhat polemic character of this first part of my article, I have not allowed myself to mention the author who has declared on several occasions that with NPM it means not applying theories, but doing a job of tinkering (in French *bricolage*, referring to a 'do-it-yourself job'). I wondered what private enterprise would hire a consultant who offered his advice on doing a do-it-yourself-job.

21 To my knowledge, the best critique of NPM has been made by Iva Bolgiani, *L'application des nouvelles méthodes de gestion publique dans les secteurs sanitaire*

et hospitalier: risques et opportunités, Muri (Switzerland), Publications of the Swiss Society for Health Policy, no. 66, 2002; for an analysis of NPM see ch. 4, pp. 12–15 and 37–71, and ch. 14, pp. 259–264; for the evaluation of NPM in the Swiss health system see ch. 5–7, pp. 77–148, where the author evaluates the first three types, Efficiency, Decentralization and Excellence, listed by Ferlie and colleagues (see next note). Urio and Bolgiani have summarized their description and understanding of the four types of NPM in Paolo Urio and Iva Bolgiani, 'La nuova gestione pubblica', in Marco Meneguzzo, Domenico Ferrari, Christian Vitta and Karin Zanolini (eds), *Management pubblico in Ticino*, Milan, McGraw-Hill, 2007, pp. 87–97. For an analysis of Weber's theory and methodology applied to public administration see Paolo Urio, *Le role politique de l'administration publique*, Lausanne, LEP, 1984, pp. 45–59.

22 Ewan Ferlie, Lynn Ashburner, Louise Fitzgerald and Andrew Pettigrew, *The New Public Management in Action*, Oxford: Oxford University Press, 1996, pp. 10–15. Max Weber's work quoted is 'Bureaucracy', in H.H. Gerth and C.W. Mills (eds), *From Max Weber: Essay in Sociology*, New York, Oxford University Press, 1946, pp. 328–340.

23 Max Weber, 'Die "Objectivität" sozialwissenschaftlicher und sozialpolitischer Erkenntnis', in *Gesammelte Aufsätze zur Wissenschaftslehre*, Tübingen, J.C.B. Mohr, 1988, pp. 146–214; English translation, 'Objectivity in social science and social policy', in *Methodology of Social Sciences*, New Brunswick, NJ, Transactions, 2011, pp. 49–112.

24 Rachman, 'Conservatism overshoots its limits'. By referring to the promotion of democracy, quite rightly Rachman points to one important aspect of the international dimension of neoliberalism that I have not explicitly dealt with in this book, but is clearly linked to the international armed wing of neoliberalism mentioned above, that is, the 'Washington consensus', through which the West has granted loans to developing countries on condition that they transform their political system according to the standards of the liberal state.

25 Bolgiani, *L'application des nouvelles méthodes*, p. 261.

26 François Bouvard, Thomas Dohrmann and Nick Lovegrove, 'The case for government reform now', *McKinsey Quarterly*, 2009, no. 3, pp. 1–13.

27 Friedman, *Capitalism and Freedom*, pp. 35–36. The list comprises, among other policies, parity piece support programmes for agriculture; rent control or more general price and wage control; legal minimum wage rates, or legal maximum prices; detailed regulation of industries; control of radio and television; present social security programmes, especially compulsory old age and retirement programmes; so-called 'public housing' and a host of other subsidy programmes directed at fostering residential construction such as Federal Housing Administration and Veteran Affairs guarantee of mortgage; national parks; the legal prohibition on carrying of mail for profit; and publicly owned and operated toll roads.

28 It is quite surprising that in the definition and comments on their typology they never mention privatization.

29 This was for example the slogan of the US version of NPM, the National Performance Review (NPR) under the responsibility of Vice-President Al Gore: 'Creating a Government that works better and costs less' was the title on the cover page of the reports of the NPR.

30 This is clearly the strategic goal pursued by the British government since at least the 1990s, as the seminars organized for British civil servants at the Civil Service College at Sunningdale (near London) very well demonstrate, linking strategic management, excellence models, competency frameworks, performance management and human resource management (with the introduction of performance-related pay).

31 See, nevertheless, the citation above of the article by Joost Mönks, 'New Public Management: pas de modèle unique!'

32 This seems to be the case, as attested by the appearance (or reappearance) and the development of 'alternative' social movements practically everywhere in the West, in the form of Marxian, anti-capitalist or ecological movements.
33 See, for example, Ernst Buschor, 'Introduction: from advanced public accounting via performance measurement to New Public Management', in Ernst Buschor and Kuno Schedler (eds), *Perspectives on Performance Management and Public Sector Accounting*, Bern, Haupt, 1994, pp. vii–xviii.
34 See, for example, Francis Fukuyama, *The End of History and the Last Man*, New York, Free Press, 1992; Daniel Bell, *The End of Ideology: On the Exhaustion of Political Ideas in the Fifties*, Cambridge, MA, Harvard University Press, 1960.
35 Jean-François Leuba, 'Avant qu'il ne soit trop tard', *Journal de Genève*, 22 November 1996 (my translation from the French). See also the Swiss minister Pascal Couchepin, 'Le marché c'est comme l'orthographe, ça ne suffit pas', *Journal de Genève*, 8 March 1996. Even the founder and president of the World Economic Forum in Davos admitted in early 1997 that an equilibrium between economic competitiveness and social responsibility is from now on necessary; 'Klaus Schwab souscrit à l'idée de l'exception culturelle', *Le Courrier* (Geneva), 4/5 January 1997.
36 The thesis of the primacy of the economic field in order to guarantee the freedom of individuals has been very clearly asserted by Milton Friedman, *Capitalism and Freedom*, ch. 1, 'The relation between economic freedom and political freedom', pp. 7–21, and ch. 2 'The role of government in a free society', pp. 22–36.
37 Pierre de Senarclens, 'Vers une dérive des civilisations ?' *Journal de Genève*, 10 March 1997 (my translation from the French).
38 Note that the illusion of an 'empowerment' of the citizen found amongst NPM followers stems essentially from the fact that the few success stories of NPM that they cite are situated precisely at the local level.
39 Urio, 'La gestion publique au service du marché', p. 98.
40 It is interesting to note the opinion of *Forbes Magazine International*:

> China has so far escaped the worst of the Asian economic crisis, in part because its currency isn't fully convertible and is therefore not vulnerable to attacks by currency speculators. Also, unlike Thailand and South Korea, China has current account surpluses, huge foreign-exchange reserves and relatively little short-term foreign debt.
> Andrew Tanzer, 'Will China bite the bullet?', *Forbes Magazine International*, 29 December 1997

41 Urio, 'La gestion publique au service du marché', p. 98. In effect, the reference made to globalization must be related to the fascination that most of the NPM followers have with the liberalization of international trade, the market, as well as the concepts that are closely linked to it: competition and competitiveness. On the crisis of economic thinking, one could read Paul Ormerod, *The Death of Economics*, London, Faber and Faber, 1994, and the more recent and severe book by James K. Galbraith, *The Predator State: How Conservatives Abandoned the Free Market and Why Liberals Should Too*, New York, Free Press, 2008. For a historical analysis of the weaknesses of the liberal thesis according to which free trade has a positive impact on economic development anywhere and at any time, see Paul Bairoch, *Economics and World History: Myths and Paradoxes*, New York, Harvester Wheatsheaf, 1993 (French version: *Mythes et paradoxes de l'histoire économique*, Paris, La Découverte, 1999).
42 It is enough to mention, by way of example, Michael Hammer, one of the authors most referred to in this context: Michel Hammer and James Champy, *Re-engineering the Corporation: A Manifesto for Business Revolution*, New York, HarperCollins, 1993.

43 This neologism reflects the intentions of the author: Jan-Erik Lane, *Public Sector Reform, Rationale, Trends and Problems*, London, Sage, 1997, pp. 1–16.
44 It is the famous article by Robert Merton ('The unanticipated consequences of purposive social action', *American Sociological Review*, 1936, vol. 1, pp. 894–904) that has launched a whole series of empirical researches on the dysfunctioning inside public and private bureaucracies, of which I will mention here only those of Alwin A. Gouldner, *Patterns of Industrial Bureaucracy*, Glencoe, IL, Free Press, 1953, and Philip Selznick, *TVA and the Grass Roots*, Berkeley, University of California Press, 1949.
45 Michel Crozier, *Le phénomène bureaucratique*, Paris, Seuil, 1964 (English translation: *The Bureaucratic Phenomenon*, New Brunswick, NJ, Transactions, 2009, with an introduction by Erhard Friedberg).
46 Max Weber, *Wirtschaft und Gesellschaft*, Tübingen, Mohr, 1922 and 1956 (this last critical edition edited by J. Winckelmann). Let us remark that some authors consider that some of the characteristics of traditional quasi-bureaucracies persisted even after the collapse of the society of which they were the support. This is in fact my case when analysing the transition from imperial bureaucracy and the republican administration (both the Nationalist republic and the Communist one): Paolo Urio, *Reconciling State, Market and Society in China: The Long March towards Prosperity*, London, Routledge, 2010.
47 For Weber, bureaucracy exists only in a system of legitimate legal-rational power. In the two other types of legitimate power (traditional and charismatic) there exist other types of administrations.
48 Let us recall that the Weberian ideal-type is a pure utopian rationalization, not a representation of reality. It is a heuristic instrument, whose value is measured only against its effectiveness in the process of research, not by its correspondence to reality. Critiques of Weber too often forget this, and, as can be expected, the NPM followers are prevalent amongst their number. See Max Weber, 'Objectivity in social science and social policy', in *Methodology of Social Sciences*. It is within this essay that Weber has explained his ideal-type methodology, taking the example of 'abstract economic theory'. The following passage (pp. 89–90) is worth quoting:

> We have in abstract economic theory an illustration of those synthetic constructs which have been designated as '*ideas*' of historical phenomena. It offers us an ideal picture of events on the commodity-market under conditions of a society organized on the principles of an exchange economy, free competition and rigorously rational conduct. This conceptual pattern . . . brings together certain relationships and events of historical life into a complex, which is conceived as an internally consistent system. Substantively, this construct in itself is like a *utopia* which has been arrived at by the analytical accentuation of certain elements of reality. Its relationship to the empirical data consists solely in the fact that where market-conditioned relationships of the type referred to by the abstract constrict are discovered or suspected to exist in reality to some extent, we can make the *characteristic* features of this relationship pragmatically *clear* and *understandable* by reference to an *ideal-type*. This procedure can be indispensable for heuristic as well as expository purposes. The ideal typical concept will help to develop our skill in imputation in *research*: it is no 'hypothesis' but it offers guidance to the construction of hypotheses. It is not a *description* of reality but it aims to give unambiguous means of expression to such a description. . . . An ideal type is formed by the one-sided *accentuation* of one or more points of view and by the synthesis of a great many diffuse, discrete, more or less present and occasionally absent *concrete individual* phenomena, which are arranged according to those one-sidedly emphasized viewpoints into a unified *analytical* construct (*Gedankenbild*). In its conceptual purity, this mental construct (*Gedankenbild*) cannot be found empirically anywhere in reality. It is a *utopia*.

49 It is too early to evaluate whether the initiatives taken recently to overcome the crisis and to reorganize the international economic system are sufficiently innovative to lead us to revise our evaluation. For the moment, it seems that nothing radical has changed.
50 One can contest the use of the word 'consensus'. Talking of consensus in the international system would require at least a simple majority of international actors, and not only the World Band, the IMF and the USA.
51 I put the US first, even if the majority of analysts take the first election of Margaret Thatcher (1979) as the starting point in the implementation of NPM at the national level, as the first election of Ronald Reagan occurred the following year. Nevertheless, it is clear that the USA has implemented public policies hostile to 'big government' practically since the beginning of the Union with the result that the size of the US state in the economy is one of the lowest among OECD countries and US social public policies are more modest than in European countries.
52 John Williamson, 'Democracy and the Washington consensus', *World Development*, 1993, vol. 21, no. 8, pp. 1329–1336; John Williamson (ed.), *Latin American Adjustment: How Much Has Happened*, Washington, DC, Institute for International Economics, 1990; Joshua Copper Ramo, *The Beijing Consensus*, London, Foreign Policy Centre, 2004; Yujiro Hayami, 'From the Washington consensus to the post-Washington consensus: retrospect and prospect', *Asian Development Review*, 2003, vol. 20, no. 2, pp. 40–65.
53 See, for example, Ohmae Kenichi, *The End of the Nation State: How Capital, Corporations, Consumers and Communication are Reshaping Global Markets*, New York, Free Press, 1995. See the recent example of the Treaty on the MAI, the Anti-Counterfeiting Trade Agreement, the TPP and GATS, mentioned above in note 3.
54 These agents are the financial elite that dominates powerful states (mainly Western, and especially the USA and the EU), multinational Western corporations, ideologists of economic globalization (university professors, consulting firms, most of the time specialized in business administration), and journalists and owners of mass media organized at the national level in the most powerful and influential countries (again the USA and the EU) and especially at the global level.
55 On the unexpected effects of deregulation, see Steven K. Vogel, *Freer Markets, More Rules*, Ithaca, NY, Cornell University Press, 1966. On the problematic of (de)regulation see Matthew Bishop, John Kay and Colin Mayer (eds), *The Regulatory Challenge*, Oxford, Oxford University Press, 1995; John Francis, *The Politics of Regulation: A Comparative Perspective*, Oxford, Blackwell, 1993; Giandomenico Majone (ed.), *Deregulation or Re-regulation? Regulatory Reform in Europe and in the United States*, London, Pinter, 1990; and John J. Dilulio Jr. (ed.), *Deregulating the Public Service: Can Government Be Improved?*, Washington, DC, Brookings Institution, 1994.
56 Read again the heavily loaded title of the book by Gaebler and Osborne already mentioned in note 2: *Reinventing Government: How the Entrepreneurial Spirit Is Transforming the Public Sector.*
57 The most striking cases can be confirmed in which the official is responsible for passing contracts with private enterprises on behalf of the state. For the USA, see Nicholas Henry, *Public Administration and Public Affairs*, Englewood Cliffs, NJ, Prentice Hall, 1995, p. 239.
58 This means, as we have seen above, that the implementation of laws in individual cases must not be based upon personal considerations, that is, must be impersonal in order to comply with the principle of equal treatment. See Michel Crozier, *Le phénomène bureaucratique*.
59 See, for example, Joseph E. Stiglitz, *Around the World with Joseph Stiglitz: Perils and Promises of Globalization*, documentary film by the author, 2009.

60 Excessiveness is shown by the size of budgets, whereas irrationality is attributed to the so-called watering-can politics, which results in making not only the poorest benefit from social security but also those who do not really need it. See in this sense Guy Sorman, 'Good-by to Europe's cradle-to-grave gravy', *Shanghai Daily*, 19 October 2010, also published in *Project Syndicate* under the title 'The welfare state, RIP', *Project Syndicate*, 8 October 2010 (http://www.project-syndicate.org, accessed 8 November 2010) and in Sorman's blog in the Swiss weekly *L'Hebdo*, 'La mort annoncée de l'Etat Providence', 14 October 2010.

61 Roberto Mangabeira Unger, *What Should the Left Propose?*, London, Verso, 2005, p. 1; Joseph E. Stiglitz, 'Turn left to sustainable growth' and 'The triumphant return of John Maynard Keynes', *Economists' Voice*, Project Syndicate, Berkeley Electronic Press, December 2008, http://www.project-sydicate.org (accessed 6 January 2009).

62 In some cases one could even envisage privatizing unprofitable economic activities, but with the safeguard of obtaining state intervention (i.e. subsidies) in case of difficulties. The rationale of promoters of NPM for this transfer is that in any case the private sector is more efficient than the public one; consequently, even if the state must provide some subsidies (i.e. taking some money from taxpayers) the cost of producing the service will be lower than provision by a state-owned enterprise.

63 Besides the authors already mentioned above, let us add, for the UK, Ferlie *et al.*, *The New Public Management in Action*, particularly pp. 1–16, as well as Isaac-Henry Kester, Chris Painter and Chris Bernes, *Management in the Public Sector*, London, Thomson, 1997; and, for the USA, Donald F. Kettl, *Sharing Power: Public Governance and Private Markets*, Washington, DC, Brookings Institution, 1993. For the Weberian methodology for defining typologies see note 48 above and pp. 1–2 and pp. 71–75.

64 This is in fact the position of Milton Friedman, *Capitalism and Freedom*, especially ch. 1 and 2.

65 A good example is given by the policy of contracting out established by the British Conservative government in the 1980s and followed by the New Labour government after 1997. See, for example, *Deregulation and Contracting Out Act*, 1994, London, HMSO; *Competition and Service: The Impact of the Local Government Act 1988*, London, HMSO, 1993; *Competing for Quality: Buying Better Public Services*, Cm. 1730, HMSO, London, 1991; and Kieron Walsh, *Competitive Tendering for Local Authority Services, Initial Experiences*, London, HMSO, 1991 (research conducted at the University of Birmingham for the Department of Environment). A good example of competition in health services is given by the reforms introduced in the UK National Health Service: Kieron Walsh, Nicholas Deakin, Paula Smith, Peter Spugeon and Neil Thomas, *Contracting for Change: Contracts in Health, Social Care, and Other Local Government Services*, Oxford, Oxford University Press, 1997. For a critique see Allyson M. Pollock, *NHS plc: The Privatisation of Our Health Care*, London, Verso, 2004, and Colin Leys and Stewart Player, *The Plot against the NHS*, Pontypool (UK), Merlin Press, 2011; for the USA see Douglas Conrad, Robert Bonney, Michael Sachs and Robert Smith, *Managed Care Contracting*, Chicago, IL, Health Administration Press, 1996.

66 Woodrow Wilson, 'The study of administration', and Herbert Simon, *Administrative Behaviour: A Study of Decision-Making Processes in Administrative Organization*, New York, Free Press, 1945, third reviewed and enlarged edition, 1976, ch. 3, pp. 45–60.

67 The classical example is the one of the numerous British state-owned enterprises that have been privatized and for which the state has instituted regulatory bodies. These exist in a considerable number of fields: airports, telecommunications, gas, electricity, water and railways in particular.

68 Competitive tendering became compulsory in the UK on a local level in many sectors under the government of Margaret Thatcher; local authorities were freed from the obligation of compulsorily tendering public services by the New Labour government in 2002. See the study by Walsh and colleagues, *Contracting for Change*.
69 See, for example, some remarkable exceptions within the UK version of contracting out, the Private Finance Initiative (PFI), within which the duration of the contracts can be much longer; for instance, for prisons and hospitals the length of the contract is generally between 15 and 30 years or more. For hospitals see, for example, Pollock, *NHS plc*.
70 I have developed this argument in Paolo Urio, 'L'avenir des contrats de prestations', in François Bellanger and Thierry Tanquerel (eds), *Les contrats de prestation*, Geneva, Helbing & Lichtenhahn, 2002, pp. 109–130.
71 Another advantage of decentralization according to NPM is greater motivation, which encourages the spirit of enterprise in employees from decentralized units, because they enjoy greater autonomy. On the UK Next Step Agencies see Neil Elder and Edward Page, *Accountability and Control in Next Steps Agencies*, London, Palgrave Macmillan, 2006, and the *Next Steps Agencies in Government Reviews*, published each year by the UK Cabinet Office.
72 Vice-President Al Gore, 'Creating a Government that works better, and costs less', Reports of the National Performance Review, Washington, DC, 7 September 1993.
73 Also here there is nothing really new. Since 1941, James Burham announces the seizing of power by the managers in a prophetic book, *The Managerial Revolution*, New York, John Day, 1941, translated into French as *L'ère des organisateurs*, Paris, Calmann-Lévy, 1947, with a preface by Léon Blum, new edition 1969, with a new foreword by the author. More than half a century after the first edition, Burham's prophecy has come true, even beyond all expectations: not only the managers have taken power, but also, and above all, the account managers.
74 This inevitably leads to a revision of the laws of working relations, thereby considerably reducing trade unions' rights, as was the case in the countries that have systematically implemented the project of NPM, such as the United Kingdom and New Zealand.
75 To mention the most important ones: natural monopolies, oligopolies, dominant positions, cartel practices, externalities, lack of transparency (incomplete information and information asymmetry) and access difficulties.
76 In *Peddling Prosperity*, p. 181, Paul Krugman comments on the imminent privatization of British Rail:

> At the time of writing, the Major government has declared its intention to privatize British Rail, with an enthusiasm and lack of concern for consequences that suggest that little has been learned. Conservatives in Britain apparently have not yet realized that markets are not magical. They can work well when conditions are right, but leaving a natural monopoly free to do its worst is blind ideology.

For a more radical critique of 'market fundamentalism' see Stiglitz, *Globalization and Its Discontents*, New York, W.W. Norton, 2002; *Making Globalization Work: The Next Steps to Global Justice*, London, Penguin, 2006; 'Post Washington consensus', Columbia University, Initiative for Policy Dialogue, Working Paper Series, 2005, http://www.gsb.columbia.edu/ipd/ (accessed 6 June 2009); 'The triumphant return of John Maynard Keynes'; James K. Galbraith, *The Predator State*; Ha-Joon Chang, *Bad Samaritans*.
77 These values can be briefly defined as equity, sustainability and security. I have developed this approach elsewhere: Paolo Urio (ed.), *Public Private Partnerships: Success and Failure Factors for In-Transition countries*, Lanham, MD, University Press of America, 2010, especially ch. 2 and 8.
78 For a history of reforms in the USA, see the works of Lawrence Lynn mentioned

in note 6 of this chapter. See also Paul C. Light, *The Tides of Reform: Making Government Work 1945–1995*, New Haven, CT, Yale University Press, 1997; for an evaluation of the US National Performance Review see Donald F. Kettl and John J. Dilulio (eds), *Inside the Reinvention Machine: Appraising Governmental Reform*, Washington, DC, Brookings Institution, 1995.

79 See, for example, Michael Parkin and David King, *Economics*, Wokingham (UK), Addison-Wesley, 1995, pp. 550–556; David H. Rosembloom, *Public Administration*, New York, McGraw-Hill, 1998, pp. 417–418, 425 and 439; and Donald F. Kettl, *Sharing Power*, ch. 2, pp. 21–40.

80 Amongst the numerous publications on the origins and explanation of the present financial and economic crisis one can refer to Joseph E. Stiglitz, *Freefall: America, Free Markets, and the Sinking of the World Economy*, New York, Norton, 2010, and *The Stiglitz Report: Reforming the International Monetary and Financial Systems in the Wake of the Global Crisis*, New York, New Press, 2010; Nouriel Roubini and Stephen Mihn, *Crisis Economics: A Crash Course in the Future of Finance*, New York, Penguin, 2010; Isaac Joshua, *La grande crise du XXI siècle: une analyse marxiste*, Paris, La Découverte, 2009; John Bellamy Forster and Fred Magdoff, *The Great Financial Crisis: Causes and Consequences*, New York, Monthly Review Press, 2009.

81 For the theory of transaction costs, the imperative references are Oliver E. Williamson, *The Economic Institutions of Capitalism*, New York, Free Press, 1985, and *Markets and Hierarchies*, New York, Free Press, 1975, which owe much to the research of Ronald H. Coase. In the case of the British National Health Service, which has not been privatized, but into which a whole series of 'marketizations' has been introduced, let us mention Chris Barnes and David Cox, 'Patients, power and policy: NHS management reforms and consumer empowerment' in Kester *et al* (eds), *Management in the Public Sector*, p. 186:

> A major matter of contention has been the increase in transaction costs that this mode of managing causes. Contract managers, accountants, purchasing teams, marketing teams, information officers, audit teams all struggle to achieve the cost savings/quality improvements required but they are not caring for patients directly and they all require salaries, cars, computers, clerical support, and so on.

82 See, for example, for the British National Health Service, Pollock, *NHS plc*.
83 Ronald C. Moe, 'The "reinventing government" exercise', and Ronald C. Moe and Robert S. Gilmour, 'Rediscovering principles of public administration'.
84 In this context I use the terms 'contract' and 'contractualization' in the generic sense, covering contracts (i.e. formal agreements between two parties each one possessing a legal personality) and agreements between ministers and state agencies, in which only one party, the state, possesses a legal personality, for example the 'Next Step Agencies' of the United Kingdom.
85 To my knowledge this expression was first put forward by David Osborne and Ted Gaebler, *Reinventing Government: How the Entrepreneurial Spirit Is Transforming the Public Sector*, New York, Plume, 1993, ch. 1 entitled 'Catalytic government: steering rather than rowing', pp. 25–48. See also John Barlow and Manfred Röber, 'Steering not rowing: co-ordination and control in the management of public services in Britain and Germany', *International Journal of Public Sector Management*, 1996, vol. 9, no. 5/6, pp. 73–89.
86 The other objective is to discover the training needs and define the content of the training programmes for civil servants, especially for the senior ones. After several years of this experience, the Civil Service College changed its name to National School of Government at the end of 2006 to become a new department separated from the Cabinet Office. Nevertheless, in 1 April 2011 it rejoined the Cabinet Office, and ceased to be a non-ministerial department.

250 *Notes*

In 2010–11 the National School came under review as part of two key policy initiatives: the Public Body Review Programme; and the Next Generation HR programme. The Public Body Programme concluded that the School should be brought back within a department to increase control and accountability. This led to the School re-joining the Cabinet Office on 1 April 2011.
National School of Government, *Annual Report and Accounts 2010–11*, London The Stationery Office, 2011

87 Nicholas Henry, *Public Administration and Public Affairs*, p. 239.

During Reagan's two terms as president (1981–89) 7,462 federal officials were prosecuted – that is, were indicted, convicted (3,226) or awaiting trial – for public corruption. Compare this figure to the total number of prosecutions of federal officials for public corruption during the preceding eight years (1972–80): 1,694.

For an analysis of political corruption in South-East Asia, France and the UK see John Girling, *Corruption, Capitalism and Democracy*, London, Routledge, 1997. Even in Switzerland, a latecomer to NPM, a certain number of cases of corruption of officials (particularly linked to the drawing up of contracts with private enterprises) have been reported recently by the press. See the Geneva newspaper *Le Courrier*, 28 October 2011, according to which 'the legal rules are sufficient for fighting against corruption, but sentences by courts are rare; the implementation of laws is being questioned' (my translation from the French).

88 Urio, 'La gestion publique au service du marché'.

4 The foundation of Chinese New Public Management

1 This chapter is based upon Paolo Urio, *Reconciling State, Market and Society in China: The Long March towards Prosperity*, London, Routledge, 2010.
2 For this reason, the analysis I have presented in the preceding chapter on the implementation of the principle of economic efficiency also applies to the Chinese case, as China also seeks to improve economic efficiency through the implementation of some of the NPM devices. On this dimension, the two cases must be evaluated on the basis of the same criteria: the impact of NPM on economic efficiency and equity.
3 I have analysed the development of Chinese political culture from the Empire to the present in Urio, *Reconciling*, ch. 1.
4 Sun Tzu, *Art of War*, Boulder, CO, Westview Press, 1994.
5 For an interpretation of the strategy followed by Deng Xiaoping to implement this new way of organizing the Chinese economy and society, see Urio, *Reconciling*, especially ch. 1 and 2 and the references given there.
6 Jacques Gernet, *Chine et christianisme: La première confrontation*, Paris, Gallimard, 2nd edn, 1991, pp. 252–253 (my free translation from the French) quoted by Michèle Pirazzoli-T'Serstevens, *Giuseppe Castiglione, 1688–1766, Peintre et architecte à la cour de Chine*, Paris, Thalia, 2007, pp. 9–10.
7 Pirazzoli-T'Serstevens, *Giuseppe Castiglione*; see also, for instance, the title of the following book, which underlines the fact that Castiglione is considered as a Chinese painter: Michel Cartier (ed.), *Giuseppe Castiglione dit Lang Shining, 1688–1766, Jésuite italien et peintre chinois*, Paris, Favre, 2004.
8 Pirazzoli-T'Serstevens, *Giuseppe Castiglione*, p. 195.
9 The Chinese still remember that event as one of the most barbaric acts perpetrated by Western people. In one of the recent booklets for tourists published in English and Chinese by the Foreign Language Press one can read:

In October [1860] Yuanmingyuan was plundered and set fire to by the British and French troops. Within a few days, the cultural artefacts and treasures in the garden which had been accumulated in the course of several generations were almost totally plundered or destroyed. The tragic destruction of the famous garden was a catastrophe in the modern history of civilization of China and the world. . . . Today the ruins of Yuanmingyuan have become a symbol of China's modern history. The glory and splendour of yesterday can no longer be found . . . There are only the broken walls and columns of the Western Buildings and other ruins for people to ponder on the past . . . Today's Yuanmingyuan, with its unique tragic beauty and sense of history, reminds people of the past and urges them to study the rise and fall, order and disorder of a nation. The soul-stirring power embodied in Yuanmingyuan and its special historic place are far more than what are to be found in the ruins on an imperial scenic garden.

Zhu Jie and Lan Peijing, *Yuanmingyuan Garden*, Beijing, Foreign Language Press, 2000, without pagination

10 Patricia Buckley Ebrey (ed.), *The Cambridge Illustrated History of China*, Cambridge, Cambridge University Press, 1999, p. 245.
11 Bai Shouyi (ed.), *Précis d'histoire de Chine*, Beijing, Editions en langues étrangères, 1988, pp. 465 and 468–469, emphasis added, my free translation from the French; the quotation marks are in the original text. At that time Professor Bai Shouyi was director of the Faculty of History and in charge of the Institute of History of the Normal University, Beijing.
12 Kenneth Lieberthal, *Governing China: From Revolution through Reform*, New York, Norton, 1995, p. 23, emphasis added.
13 John King Fairbank and Merle Goldman:

While at the end of the twentieth century China appeared to be on its way to *fulfilling the dream of China's reformers since the late nineteenth century to make China 'rich and powerful'* and *recapture its traditional greatness*, there was a question whether its leaders would be able to lead China to its destination without basic changes in its political structure.

John King Fairbank and Merle Goldman, *China: A New History*, Cambridge, MA, Harvard University Press, 2006, second enlarged edition, p. 344; quotation marks original, emphasis added

14 Lieberthal, *Governing China*, p. 22, emphasis added.
15 Immanuel C.Y. Hsü, *The Rise of Modern China*, New York, Oxford University Press, 1995, pp. 660–661 and 803, emphasis added by us.
16 Hu Sheng (chief editor), *A Concise History of the Communist Party of China*, Beijing, Foreign Language Press, 1994, pp. 837 and 849, emphasis added.
17 He Ping, *China's Search for Modernity: Cultural Discourse in the Late 20th Century*, Oxford, Palgrave Macmillan, 2002, p. 1, emphasis added.
18 See He Li 'Debating China's economic reform: New Leftists v. Liberals', *Journal of Chinese Political Science*, 2010, no. 15, p. 11. See also Jonathan Fenby, *History of Modern China. The Fall and Rise of a Great Power: 1850–2008*, London, Penguin Books, 2008.
19 Hu Angang, *China in 2020: A New Type of Superpower*, Washington, DC, Brookings Institutions, 2011.
20 Ibid., p. 140, emphasis added.
21 Ibid., p. 13.
22 This part is based upon the works of the French philosopher François Jullien, more particularly *Eloge de la fadeur*, Paris, Philippe Picquier, 1991; *Les transformations silencieuses*, Paris, Grasset, 2009; *Procès ou création: Une introduction à la pensée chinoise*, Paris, Seuil, 1989; *La propension des choses: Pour une histoire de l'efficacité en Chine*, Paris, Seuil, 1992; *Traité de l'efficacité*, Paris, Grasset, 1996.
23 Sun Tzu, *Art of War*.

24 I have developed this in more detail in *Reconciling*, especially in ch. 2 and 3.
25 Zhu Suli, 'The Party and the courts', in Randall Peerenboom (ed.), *Judicial Independence in China: Lessons for Global Rule of Law Promotion*, Cambridge, Cambridge University Press, 2010, pp. 52–68. After having reminded the Western reader that the

> CPC has ... inherited from its former political enemy [the Nationalist Party] the legacy of having to construct and rule a nation-state through the leadership of a single political party – a party that, as proposed early in the nineteenth century by Sun Yat-sen, had to be above the nation-state
>
> ibid., p. 54

Zhu Suli goes on to say:

> Yet this kind of interference [of the party on the judiciary] might actually be beneficial for a majority of Chinese who do not care about foreign interference [of Western people suggesting that China should imitate the Western legal system] but seek justice and social solidarity. From a Western constitutional perspective, such an interference seems to be improper. But from a political perspective, it is hard to see why legal control over a case is always and necessarily more just or reasonable than political control.
>
> ibid., p. 57

26 André Chieng, *La pratique de la Chine*, Paris, Grasset, 2006, pp. 224–225.
27 Let us remark that after China's accession to the WTO the performance of the Chinese SOEs and banks has improved tremendously.
28 Milton Friedman, *Capitalism and Freedom*, Chicago, University of Chicago Press, second edition 1982 (first edition 1962), ch. 1 and 2.
29 See, for example, Nicolas Zufferey, *Introduction à la pensée chinoise*, Paris, Hachette, 2008, pp. 65–66.
30 However, see the different opinion of Zhang Zhibin (of the Nanyang Technological University, Singapore), who considers (quoting B. Naughton, but without providing reference) that reforms started first in industry, in 'Competition or privatization: China's experience in SOE reforms', *Journal of the Washington Institute of China Studies*, Spring 2006, vol. 1, no. 1, p. 39, and n. 4.
31 In December 2006 the State Assets Supervision and Administration Commission (SASAC) published a list of seven sectors critical to the national economy and in which public ownership is considered essential: armaments, electrical power and distribution, oil and chemicals, telecommunications, coal, aviation, and shipping. Moreover, to reorient state capital away from non-critical areas to priority sectors, SASAC said China will reduce the number of central SOEs by at least one-third to between 80 and 100 before 2010 through mergers. Finally, it announced that 'China aims to build between 30 and 50 large, internationally competitive companies by 2010' (Xinhua, 18 December 2006, http://www.xinhuanet.com/english/, accessed 21 January 2007).
32 Many Western observers of modern China use the expression 'Party-State' to translate the symbiosis existing between the Communist Party of China and the state's organs at the five administrative levels of the Chinese state. At each of these five levels the Party hierarchy is superior to the state's hierarchy.
33 On this point see the interesting analyses of Cui Zhiyuan, 'Privatization and consolidation of democratic regimes: an analysis and an alternative', *Journal of International Affairs*, Winter 1997, pp. 675–692, and Roberto Mangabeira Unger and Cui Zhiyuan, 'China in the Russian mirror', *New Left Review*, November 1994, pp. 78–87.
34 I have developed this reference to socialisms in more detail in Chapter 2.

35 The theory of the Three Represents affirms that the Party represents the advanced social productive forces, the advanced culture and the interests of the overwhelming majority of the Chinese people. This is quite a radical change from the previous ideology, which considered that the Party represented the interests of the proletariat.
36 This is confirmed by Jie Chen and Bruce J. Dickson, 'Allies of the state: democratic support and regime support among China's private entrepreneurs', *China Quarterly*, December 2008, pp. 780–804.
37 I have analysed these aspects in more detail in Urio, *Reconciling*, especially ch. 1. On the persistence of socialism in China see the opinion of the Hong Kong professor Wang Shaoguang in 'Is there a China model? A summary and video documentation of a China–West intellectual summit', Maison Louis Carré, Paris, Glasshouse Forum, Paris, 23–24 February 2009. See also his evaluation of China's development strategy: Wang Shaoguang, 'The great transformation: two-way movement in China since the 1980s' (in Chinese: 'Zhong Guo She Hui Ke Xue'), *Social Sciences in China*, 2008, no. 1, pp. 129–148.
38 Urio, *Reconciling*.
39 On Chinese think tanks see Joseph Fewsmith, 'Where do correct ideas come from? The party school, key think tanks, and the intellectuals', in David M. Finkelstein and Marianne Kivlehan (eds), *China's Leadership in the 21st Century: The Rise of the Fourth Generation*, New York, M.E. Sharpe, 2003, pp. 152–164, and Cheng Li, 'China's new think tanks: where officials, entrepreneurs, and scholars interact', *China Leadership Monitor*, no. 29, http://www.hoover.org/publications/china-leadership-monitor (accessed 20 October 2009); n. 12 of the latter gives several additional references. The article provides a comprehensive description of the system of China's think tanks, including their hierarchical status, as 10 of them constitute a sort of 'top ten', given the close link they have with the 'super think tank', the China Centre for International Economic Exchange set up in March 2009 by the State Council and presided over by former Vice-Premier Zeng Peiyan.
40 Cheng Li, 'China's new think tanks', pp. 3–5.
41 Ibid., p. 16.
42 Let me quote three reports prepared under the auspices of the World Bank with teams of Western and Chinese experts: World Bank, *China: Deepening Public Service Unit Reform to Improve Service Delivery*, Beijing, Citic Publishing House, 2005; World Bank, *From Poor Areas to Poor People: China's Evolving Poverty Reduction Agenda. An Assessment of Poverty and Inequality in China*, March 2009, http://www.worldbank.org (accessed 5 September 2009); World Bank, *Mid-term Evaluation of China's 11th 5 Year Plan*, 2008, http://www.worldbank.org (accessed 15 June 2009). This last example is quite exceptional as it was prepared at the request of the Development Planning Department of China's National Development and Reform Commission (NDRC) under the authority of the Prime Minister. I do not know of any other country that has submitted to the scrutiny of an international organization the major planning instrument of its societal development.
43 On the role of the Party Schools see David Shambaugh, 'Training China's political elite: the Party School system', *China Quarterly*, December 2008, pp. 827–844. According to Shambaugh the Party Schools are 'a critically important mechanism for maintaining control over the 6,932,000 Party cadres and many of the 33,578,000 cadres in the state system' (p. 828).
44 Several professors of the Central Party School attended the training seminars organized within the Sino-Swiss Management Training Programme in the Public Sector of China, of which I was the director on the Swiss side between 1997 and 2003. Back in Beijing, some of these professors have introduced into their teaching elements of NPM they have learned in Europe.

45 The Shanghai-Pudong Party School (the China Executive Leadership Academy Pudong, CELAP) has a website (in English) that gives information about the activities of the school, including the list of courses and seminars, as well as the names of foreign experts who have contributed to the training of Chinese officials: http://218.78.215.163:8080 (in English) and http://www.celap.org.cn/Template/home/welcome.html (in Chinese).
46 The NDRC has a website: http://en.ndrc.gov.cn (in English) and http://www.ndrc.gov.cn (in Chinese).
47 On the development of NGOs in China see, for example, Yiyi Lu, *Non-governmental Organizations in China*, London, Routledge, 2008, and the review published in English by the Research Centre on NGOs (directed by Professor Wang Ming) within the School of Public Policy and Management at Tsinghua University. For NGOs in the domain of environmental protection see Ran Yan, *L'éducation à l'environnement en Chine*, unpublished dissertation for the Master in Asian Studies, University of Geneva, under the supervision of Professor Paolo Urio, 2005. For NGOs in the social domain see Yuan Ying, *La transformation des rôles de l'Etat dans la politique de la réinsertion des chômeurs en Chine*, unpublished dissertation for the Master in Asian Studies, University of Geneva, under the supervision of Professor Paolo Urio, 2005.
48 See Urio, *Reconciling*, pp. 104–111.

5 The Western experiment

1 Let us remark that this opinion is not shared by everybody; in particular, neo-Marxists have pointed to the decreasing profit at the end of the so-called Dream Era of the Keynesian compromise between capital and labour. This has led capitalists to seek better opportunities for profit outside the traditional area of capitalism, for example in China and other fast-developing countries, where labour is much cheaper than in the West, and labour and environmental legislation are less strict. See, for example, John Bellamy Foster and Fred Magdoff, *The Great Financial Crisis: Causes and Consequences*, New York, Monthly Review Press, 2009; David Harvey, *The Enigma of Capital: And the Crises of Capitalism*, London, Profile Books, 2010; Isaac Joshua, *La grande crise du XXI siècle. Une analyse marxiste*, Paris, La Découverte, 2009.
2 UNDP, *Human Development Report 2009*, New York, Palgrave Macmillan, 2009, pp. 195–198; UNDP, *Human Development Report 2010*, New York, Palgrave Macmillan, 2010, pp. 143–146 and 202–209.
3 Just one recent example: several French municipalities that had contracted out the provision of domestic water have recently municipalized the enterprises concerned because the selling price was too high and the investments in maintenance have not been sufficient; *Le Courrier* (Geneva), 11 August 2010.
4 For example, savings of 15–30 per cent have been reported: United Kingdom, DETR (Department of the Environment, Transport and Regions), *Research Summary: CCT and Local Authority Blue-Collar Services*, http://www.local-regions.detr.gov.uk/bestvalue/cct/mayhead.htm (accessed 7 April 2001). See also the study by Kieron Walsh, *Competitive Tendering for Local Authority Services, Initial Experiences*, London, HMSO, 1991.
5 See the example taken from the experience of the UK, mentioned hereafter under 'New Public Management and unemployment'.
6 Isaac-Henry Kester, Chris Painter and Chris Barnes, *Management in the Public Sector*, London, Thomson, 1996, p. 117; OCDE, *Gestion publique*, Etudes hors série no. 10, Paris, OECD, 1995, p. 20.
7 Quoted by the *Journal de Genève*, 28 April 1997, p. 7
8 Ibid.
9 For New Zealand, see Jane Kelsey, *Economic Fundamentalism*, London, Pluto Press, 1995 (published in New Zealand in 1995 as *The New Zealand Experiment: A World*

Model for Structural Adjustment? by Auckland University Press) and her more recent book *Reclaiming the Future: New Zealand and the Global Economy*, Wellington, NZ, Bridget Williams Books, 1999. For the USA, Economic Policy Institute, *The State of Working America*, Washington, DC, published every year and available on the institute's website: http://epinet.org.

10 Lawrence Mishel, Jared Bernstein and John Schmitt, *The State of Working America 1998–99*, Ithaca, NY, Cornell University Press, 1999; David K. Shiper, *The Working Poor: Invisible America*, New York, Knopf, 2004.

11 Swiss Federal Statistical Office, *Les working poor en Suisse*, Neuchâtel, Swiss Federal Statistical Office, 2004, p. 6.

12 Paul Krugman, 'The rich, the right and the facts, deconstructing the income distribution debate', *American Prospect*, Fall 1992, no. 11, pp. 19–31, http://epn.org/prospect.html (accessed 3 July 1996).

13 Arlock Sherman and Chad Stone, *Income Gap between Very Rich and Everyone Else More Than Tripled Last Three Decades, New Data Show*, Washington, DC, Centre on Budget and Policy Priorities, 15 June 2010.

14 Alyssa Goodman and Steven Webb, *The Distribution of UK Household Expenditure, 1979–1992*, London, Institute of Fiscal Studies, 1995, http://www1.ifs.org.uk/ (accessed 15 July 1996). The study separates taxpayers into 10 groups from the poorest to the richest. The income variations (average) are: first group −18%, second group −1%, third group +4%, fourth group +13%, fifth group +22%, sixth group +28%, seventh group +32%, eighth group +39%, ninth group +46%, tenth group +61%. See also Alissa Goodman, Paul Johnson and Steve Webb, *Inequality in the U.K.*, Oxford, Oxford University Press, 1997.

15 Jonathan Bradshaw and Jun-Rong Chen, 'Poverty in the UK: a comparison with nineteen other countries', Luxembourg Income Study Working Paper Series, no. 147, October 1996, p. 1.

16 For international comparison purposes, see the research of the Luxembourg Income Study at http://lissy.ceps.lu/index.htm, where one can consult some very interesting research papers.

17 Timothy Smeeding, *Globalisation, Inequality and the Rich Countries of the G-20: Evidence From The Luxembourg Income Study (LIS)*, July 2002, http://www.LIS.org (accessed 7 March 2003).

18 Robert Joyce, Alastair Muriel, David Phillips and Luke Sibieta, *Poverty and Inequality in the UK*, London, Institute of Fiscal Studies, 2010, p. 30.

19 The Gini index is well known, but nevertheless it is necessary to make a few remarks on its use. First of all we remind the reader that the Gini coefficient can range from 0 to 1; it is sometimes multiplied by 100 to range between 0 and 100. Too often only the Gini coefficient is quoted without describing the proportions of the quantiles used for measurement, but its accuracy depends on the choice of quantiles. Moreover, being based on income, it does not reflect the distribution of wealth, which can be quite different. Also, small changes from one year to the next must be treated with care because they may be not statistically significant, as was the case for the small increase in the US index between 1991 and 1992.

20 The index can be based upon gross income, or net or disposable income, i.e. after taxes and social benefits; in the UK it is calculated both before and after housing expenses. The case of the US is worth mentioning: the increase of Gini index proceeds the NPM Reagan years and it started already at the end of the 1960s, and this is sometimes used to deny a causal relation between the US NPM and the increase of inequalities in this country. Nevertheless, we remind the reader what we said when presenting the NPM pioneers in Chapter 2, page 54, note 130: these are the UK, US and New Zealand, but we said that in fact the US have for a very long time practiced a form of NPM, if we recognize that since the beginning of the Union public policies have been oriented by an aversion towards 'big government' and a preference for the private sector. The consequence has been a smaller size of the state compared to

OECD countries, and more modest social policies compared to the European countries, well before the 'official' American NPM began under the form of the National Performance Review (NPR) during the Clinton-Gore administration.
21 Let us note that although the Gini index is the most commonly used measure of inequality, other measures, some of them more sophisticated, have been developed. For more information about the Gini index and other methods for measuring inequality one can consult for example 'Measuring inequality' on the World Bank website: http://web.worldbank.org/.
22 John Weeks, 'Inequality trends in some developed OECD countries', DESA Working Paper No. 6, ST/ESA/2005/DWP/6October 2005, p. 5.
23 It is interesting to note that according to the New Zealand Institute, http://www.nzinstitute.org (accessed 15 March 2011):

> New Zealand had much more unequal distribution in the 1980s, which deteriorated rapidly over a decade [i.e. during the implementation of strong NPM] and has been approximately flat recently . . . the Ministry of Social Development reports 'the Gini declined from 2001 and in 2007, mainly reflecting the impact of transfers incorporated in the Working for Families package' as those welfare transfers worked to reduce inequality. The most recent data point an uptick from 31.7 in 2007 to 32.3 in 2009, representing an increase in inequality.

24 United Nations Development Programme (UNDP), *Human Development Report 2010*, New York, Palgrave Macmillan, 2010.
25 I will again comment on this figure in Chapter 6 dealing with the case of China.
26 Andrea Brandolini and Timothy M. Seeding, 'Inequality patterns in western-type democracies: cross-country differences and time changes', LIS Working Paper No. 458, April 2007.
27 Andrea Brandolini and Timothy Seeding, 'Inequality patterns in western-type democracies: cross-country differences and time changes', Centre for Household, Income, Labour and Demographic Economies, Working Papers, ChilD no. 08/2007, p. 30, available at www.child-centre.it, accessed 22 November 2011.
28 *The State of Working America, 2008*, Economic Policy Institute, http://www.epi.org/ (accessed 13 June 2009).
29 Timothy Seeding, 'Poor people in rich nations: the United States in comparative perspective', *Journal of Economics Perspectives*, winter 2006, vol. 20, no. 1, pp. 69–90.
30 Bradshaw and Chen, 'Poverty in the UK'. The countries were the following: Australia, Belgium, Canada, the Czech Republic, Denmark, Finland, Germany, Hungary, Israel, Italy, the Netherlands, Norway, Poland, Russia, Slovakia, Spain, Sweden, Taiwan, the UK and the USA. In Table 5.5 I have excluded the eastern European countries, as well as Israel and Taiwan.
31 Jane Kelsey, *Economic Fundamentalism*, p. 33.
32 A word of warning: unfortunately the two research projects are based upon different methodologies for measuring poverty around 1990 and 2000. Bradshaw and Chen define the poverty line as 50 per cent of the mean income, whereas Smeeding uses 50 per cent of the median income. Consequently we cannot compare the two distributions by using the percentages. However, we can use the rankings, as I suggested when introducing the section on NPM and poverty.
33 Smeeding, 'Poor people in rich nations', p. 74
34 Economic Policy Institute, *The State of Working America 2006–7*, Washington, DC, http://epinet.org.
35 Ibid.
36 Note, however, that we can compare only the ranking of these countries and not the child poverty percentage as these two analyses are based upon different data. Nevertheless, as I have already noted on several occasions, this does not forbid us to use the ranking when comparing the positions of the countries under consideration.

37 This classification has been used by the Tsinghua professor Hu Angang, for example, to put forward a practical proposal to define the engagements to be made by countries differentiating their commitments according to their level of pollution and their belonging to one of the above-mentioned categories; the first group being linked by formal and compulsory engagements to reduce pollution, the other groups being only encouraged to do so. Moreover, countries could pass from one group to the other according to their changes in HDI and level of pollution. I have briefly discussed this proposal in Paolo Urio, *Reconciling State, Market and Society in China: The Long March towards Prosperity*, London, Routledge, 2010, pp. 116–117.
38 United Nations Development Programme (UNDP), *Human Development Report 2009*, New York, Palgrave Macmillan, 2009, pp. 171–174.
39 I have not taken into consideration the latecomers in the European Union, namely all the former communist countries of eastern Europe, for the purpose of having a homogeneous set of Western countries having attained a comparable level of development. Of course Spain, Portugal and Greece are not at the same level as the other European countries but are members of the European Union and are ranked well before the eastern European countries, with the exception of the Czech Republic.
40 I have added China for the purpose of the comparison I will make in Chapter 6.
41 Peter H. Hall and David Soskice, (eds), *Varieties of Capitalism: The Institutional Foundations of Comparative Advantage*, Oxford, Oxford University Press, 2001; Bruno Amable, *Les cinq capitalismes: diversité des systèmes économiques et sociaux dans la mondialisation*, Paris, Seuil, 2005.
42 Smeeding, 'Poor people in rich nations'.
43 M. Jäntti and S. Danziger, 'Income poverty in advanced countries', LIS Working Paper No. 193, March 1993. The country with the lowest likelihood of escaping from poverty was the USA, whereas the countries with the greatest probability were the Netherlands, Finland, Sweden, France, Luxembourg, Ireland and Germany; Canada was placed in between.
44 Jo Blanden, *Essays on Intergenerational Mobility and Its Variation over Time, Place and Family Structure*, unpublished PhD thesis, University of London, 2005; Jo Blanden, Paul Gregg and Stephen Machin, 'Educational inequality and intergenerational mobility' in S. Machin and A. Vignoles (eds), *What's the Good Education? The Economics of Education in the United Kingdom*, Princeton, NJ, Princeton University Press, 2005; Jo Blanden, Paul Gregg and Stephen Machin, *Intergenerational Mobility in Europe and North America*, a report supported by the Sutton Trust, London, Sutton Trust, April 2005.
45 Blanden et al., *Intergenerational mobility*, p. 2. This research concludes that Germany also looks more mobile than the UK and USA, but a small sample size prevented drawing a firm conclusion.
46 Ibid., p. 7.
47 Ibid., p. 14. On this last point, this research concludes that 'equalizing educational attainments by redistribution alone would be unrealistic. To improve this situation we also need to use more direct means such as early years' education, improved schools for poor communities and financial support to pursue post-compulsory education.'
48 See, for example, Richard B. Freeman, 'Why so many young American men commit crimes and what might we do about it?', *Journal of Economic Perspectives*, vol. 10, no. 1, pp. 25–42. See also Ian Irvine and Kuan Xu, 'Crime, punishment and measurement of poverty in the United States, 1979–1997', LIS Working Paper Series, Working Paper No. 333, November 2002.
49 See Allyson M. Pollock, *NHS plc: The Privatization of Our Health Care*, London, Verso, 2004; Colin Leys and Stewart Player, *The Plot against the NHS*, Pontypool (UK), Merlin Press, 2011.
50 I was lucky enough to be able to find these data on the website of Interpol when I was preparing my 1999 article. Unfortunately Interpol no longer provides these data on its website.

51 Let us note that at that time Switzerland was far from having adopted the core of NPM as I have described it in this book. Therefore Switzerland was at that time a non-NPM country with which the three beacon NPM countries could be compared.
52 Let us note that Switzerland started to adopt some of the NPM prescriptions a few years later.
53 On the case of New Zealand see Jane Kelsey, *Economic Fundamentalism* and *Reclaiming the Future*.
54 See, for example, David C. Anderson, 'The mystery of the falling crime rate', *American Prospect*, May–June 1997, no. 32, pp. 49–55.
55 From Irvine and Xu, 'Crime, punishment and measurement of poverty in the United States', and Roy Walmsley, *World Prison Population List*, 8th edition, London, King's College, 2008. For the comparison we are limited by the choice made by Irvine and Xu. For 2007–8 it is interesting to note that the rates for the other European countries were between 63 for Denmark and 100 for the Netherlands, with the exceptions of Iceland (44), Monaco (105), Greece (109) and Luxembourg (155). Let us note that Ireland presented a fairly low 76 rate.
56 Let us note that other continental European countries that were not included in the 2000 research present in 2007–8 a low prisoner rate, for example Denmark (63), Finland (64) and Switzerland (76).
57 On the NHS see Charles Webster, *The National Health Service: A Political History*, Oxford, Oxford University Press, 1998; Robert Maxwell (ed.), *Reshaping the National Health Service*, New Brunswick, NJ, Transaction Books, 1988; Howard Mellett, Neil Marriott and Stephen Harries, *Financial Management in the NHS*, London, Thomson, 1993; Calum Paton, *Competition and Planning in the NHS*, 2nd edition, Cheltenham (UK), Stanley Thornes, 1998. For a critique of the NHS reforms introduced by Conservatives and then confirmed and developed by New Labour, see Allyson M. Pollock, *NHS plc*; Alison Talbot-Smith and Allyson M. Pollock, *The New NHS: A Guide*, London, Routledge, 2006; and Leys and Player, *The Plot against the NHS*. Let us also remark that the NHS is presently under attack from the new government. See Tony Delamothe and Fiona Godlee, 'Dr Lansley's monster', *British Medical Journal*, 21 January 2011, http://www.bmj.com/content/342/bmj.d408.full (accessed 15 August 2011):

> What do you call a government that embarks on the biggest upheaval of the NHS in its 63 year history, at breakneck speed, while simultaneously trying to make unprecedented financial savings? The politically correct answer has got to be: mad.

58 New Zealand's health and disability system has a mix of public and private ownership and funding that has developed in complexity over time. Like most OECD countries, New Zealand's health and disability system is predominantly funded from general taxation. In New Zealand hospitals are public and treat citizens or permanent residents free of charge. Most of the day-to-day business of the system, and around three-quarters of the funding, is administered by District Health Boards (DHBs). Under this devolved system DHBs plan, manage, provide and purchase services for the population of their district. This includes funding for primary care, public health services, care for the aged services and services provided by other non-governmental health providers including Maori and Pacific providers. Under the Labour coalition governments (1999–2008), there were plans to make primary health care available free of charge. At present government subsidies exist in health care. For more information see New Zealand, Ministry of Health, *The New Zealand Health and Disability System: Organizations and Responsibilities*, November 2008, http://www.health.govt.nz/publication/new-zealand-health-and-disability-system-organisations-and-responsibilities-briefing-minister-health, accessed 18 June 2009.

59 Guttmacher Institute, *U.S. Teenage Pregnancy, Births and Abortions: National and State Trends by Race and Ethnicity*, January 2010, http://www.guttmacher.org/ (accessed 4 October 2010). This report comments:

> Recent research concluded that almost all of the decline in the pregnancy rate between 1995 and 2002 among 18–19-year-olds was attributable to increased contraceptive use. Among women aged 15–17, about one-quarter of the decline during the same period was attributable to reduced sexual activity and three-quarters to increased contraceptive use. But, for the first time since the early 1990s, overall rates of pregnancy and birth – and, to a lesser extent, rates of abortion – among teenagers and young women increased from 2005 to 2006. It is too soon to tell whether this reversal is simply a short-term fluctuation, a more lasting stabilization or the beginning of a longer-term increase. Preliminary data on births for 2007 show further increase in the birth-rate among all women, including teenagers and those aged 20–24.

60 It is of course too early to evaluate the impact of the US health reform on the American people, of which until recently more than 40 million were without health insurance. It is clear that the impact of the new system will take several years to produce overall results. In this respect it is interesting to note that recently some big US employers have already started to ask the US government for exemptions. This is the case for McDonald's, according to the *Wall Street Journal*, 30 September 2010.

61 For a critical review of the literature see Magnus Sverke, Johnny Hellgren and Katharina Näswall, *Job Insecurity: A Literature Review*, The National Institute for Working Life and The Swedish Trade Unions in Co-operation, Report No. 1, 2006. See also M. Bartley, A. Sacker and P. Clarke, 'Employment status, employment conditions, and limiting illness: prospective evidence from the British household panel survey 1991–2001', *Journal of Epidemiology and Community Health*, vol. 63, no. 3, pp. 501–506; Jussi Vahtera, Mika Kivimäki, Jaana Pentti, Anne Linna, Marianna Virtanen, Pekka Virtanen and Jane E. Ferrie, 'Organizational downsizing, sickness absence, and mortality: 10-town prospective cohort study', *British Medical Journal*, November 2007, pp. 1–5; Jane E. Ferrie, 'Is job insecurity harmful to health?', *Journal of the Royal Society of Medicine*, February 2001, vol. 94, pp. 71–76; Mika Kivimäki, Jussi Vahtera, Jaana Pentti and Jane E. Ferrie, 'Factors underlying the effect of organizational downsizing on health employees: longitudinal cohort study', *British Medical Journal*, April 2000, vol. 320, pp. 971–975.

62 Joan Benach, Carles Muntaner, Haejoo Chung, Orielle Solar, Vilma Santana, Sharon Friel, Tanja A.J. Houweling and Michael Marmot, 'Reducing the health inequalities associated with employment conditions', *British Medical Journal*, June 2010, vol. 340, p. 1392.

63 Ibid., p. 1394.

64 Gian-Franco Domenighetti, Barbara D'Avanzo and Brigitte Bisig, *Health Effects of Job Insecurity*, Lausanne, HEC, 1999.

65 Michel Husson, 'Les inégalités à l'échelle mondiale', *Chronique internationale de l'IRES*, May 2011, no. 130, pp. 55–63. The studies mentioned are A. Atkinson, T. Piketty and E. Saez, 'Top incomes in the long run of history', NBER, Working Paper No. 15408, October 2009; Branko Milanovic, 'Global income inequality', IMF Institute, March 2010; and PNUD, *La vraie richesse des nations: Les chemins du développement humain*, http://tinyurl.com/pnud2010.

66 Richard Wilkinson and Kate Pickett, *The Spirit Level: Why More Equal Societies Almost Always Do Better*, London, Allen Lane, 2009.

67 For the reader more particularly interested in the USA, let us note that these authors have also collected data allowing comparing the member states of the USA.

68 Ibid., pp. 173–177.

6 The Chinese experiment

1. For a more detailed analysis of the origins, rationale and overall outcomes of China's reforms I refer to my book on China's reforms and to the references quoted there, Paolo Urio, *Reconciling State, Market, and Civil Society in China: The Long March towards Prosperity*, London, Routledge, 2010.
2. World Bank, *China 2020*, seven volumes, Washington, DC, World Bank, 1997, vol. 1, p. 4. On the development of China's economy since 1978 there are not only very pessimistic analyses such as the one by Gordon G. Chang, *The Coming Collapse of China*, New York, Random House, 2001, but also several more balanced and objective ones. There is a vast literature by Chinese scholars working in mainland China available in English. See, in particular, Hu Angang, *Economic and Social Transformation in China*, London, Routledge, 2007, and *Roadmap of China's Rise*, London, Routledge, 2011; and Wang Yahua and Hu Angang, 'Multiple forces driving China's economic development: a new analytic framework', *China & World Economy*, 2007, vol. 15, no. 3, pp. 103–120. See also Chi Fulin, *Reform Determines Future of China*, Beijing, Foreign Language Press, 2000, *China's Economic Reform at the Turn of the Century*, Beijing, Foreign Language Press, 2000, and *Starting Point: Thirty Years of Reform in China*, Beijing, Foreign Language Press, 2008; Wu Jinglian, 'China's economy: 60 years of progress', *Caijing*, 30 September 2009, http://english.caijing.com.cn/ (accessed 6 October 2009). From Western scholars, for a general overview of China's economic transformation the best (in my opinion) recent account by a Western scholar is Barry J. Naughton, *The Chinese Economy: Transition and Growth*, Cambridge, The Press, 2007; and for an account that retraces the reforms from the perspective of the development of the new 'Chinese capitalists' see Marie-Claire Bergère, *Capitalismes et capitalistes en Chine: des origines à nos jours*, Paris, Perrin, 2007. From other Western scholars, see, for example, the works of Peter Nolan, *China and the Global Business Revolution*, Houndmills (UK), Palgrave, 2001, *China and the Global Economy*, Houndmills (UK), Palgrave, 2001, *Transforming China: Globalization, Transition and Development*, London, Anthem Press, 2004, and *China at the Crossroads*, Cambridge, Polity Press, 2004; see also Nicholas R. Lardy's works: *China's Unfinished Economic Revolution*, Washington, DC, Brookings Institution Press, 1998, and *Integrating China into the Global Economy*, Washington, DC, Brookings Institution Press, 2002. Books dealing with the economy in a larger perspective: Lin Yi-Min, *Between Politics and Markets, Firms, Competition, and Institutional Change in Post-Mao China*, Cambridge, Cambridge University Press, 2001; Fred C. Bergsten, Gill Bates, Nicholas Lardy and Derek J. Mitchell, *China: the Balance Sheet. What the World Needs to Know about the Emerging Superpower*, New York, Public Affairs, 2006, and Fred C. Bergsten, Charles Freeman, Nicholas Lardy, and Derek J. Mitchell, *China's Rise: Challenges and Opportunities*, Washington, DC, Peterson Institute for International Economics, Center for Strategic and International Studies, 2009. On the development of the private sector see Ross Garnaut and Ligang Song (eds), *China's Third Economic Transformation: The Rise of the Private Economy*, London, Routledge, 2004; Gregory C. Chow, *China's Economic Transformation*, Oxford, Blackwell, 2002, and *Interpreting China's Economy*, Singapore, World Scientific, 2010.
3. According to IMF Data Bank 2009 for 2008, NBSC for 2009 and, for the forecast for 2010, the World Bank's Quarterly Update, November 2010.
4. World Bank, *From Poor Areas to Poor People: China's Evolving Poverty Reduction Agenda. An Assessment of Poverty and Inequality in China*, March 2009, p. iii, http://www.worldbank.org (accessed 25 March 2009). Moreover, the World Bank considers that 'measured by the new international poverty standard of $1.25 per person per day (using 2005 Purchasing Power Parity for China), the levels of poverty are higher, but the decline since 1981 is no less impressive (from 85 in 1981 to 27 per cent in 2004)'.

5 World Bank, Quarterly Update, November 2010; press release no. 2011/163/EAP; and Louis Kuijs, 'A remarkable stable outlook for China', 2 February 2011, http://blogs.worldbank.org/eastasiapacific (accessed 2 March 2011).
6 For a complete evaluation of China's position in the world see Hu Angang, *China in 2020: A New Type of Superpower*, Washington, DC, Brookings Institution, 2011.
7 The EU comprises 27 states: Austria, Belgium, Bulgaria, Cyprus, the Czech Republic, Denmark, Estonia, Finland, France, Germany, Greece, Hungary, Ireland, Italy, Latvia, Lithuania, Luxembourg, Malta, the Netherlands, Poland, Portugal, Romania, Slovakia, Slovenia, Spain, Sweden and the United Kingdom. The Eurozone comprises 17 states: Austria, Belgium, Cyprus, Estonia, Finland, France, Germany, Greece, Ireland, Italy, Luxembourg, Malta, the Netherlands, Portugal, Slovakia, Slovenia and Spain.
8 CIA (Central Intelligence Agency), *Factbook 2010*, US Government, https://www.cia.gov/library/publications/the-world-factbook/ (accessed 7 March 2011).
9 On this important point see Albert Keidel, *The Causes and Impact of Chinese Regional Inequalities in Income and Well-Being*, place, Carnegie Endowment for International Peace, December 2007, in which he demonstrates that, in spite of increasing disparities, both urban and rural areas have an increase in their per capita income. Moreover, using a historical approach (considering data every five years between 1985 and 2005) Keidel shows that rural per capita income has grown in all regions, but more in the coastal regions (between 7.4 and 8.5 per cent) than in the interior (between 6 and 6.7 per cent). Taking then into consideration consumption expenses, the divergence is confirmed and the ranking of regions is the same, even if the size of the divergence is smaller than for income.
10 This is based upon the calculation done by the CIA, which places China's per capita GDP at $PPP7,400 (slightly lower than the World Bank data for 2010, $PPP7,536; see Table 6.2). The UNDP Human Development report estimates China's per capita GDP at $PPP7,258 in 2008. Whichever is the preferred calculation, the ranking of China's per capita GDP will not be substantially different.
11 See Chapter 2, pp. 61–62, and Chapter 5, p. 130, for the old and new definitions of HDI used in the following paragraphs.
12 It must be said, however, that, whereas the HDI allows a comparison of countries using an overall indicator of their performance, it nevertheless masks differences within these same countries. I will come back to this important aspect of China's development.
13 UNDP, *Human Development Report, 2010*, New York, Palgrave Macmillan, 2010, pp. 149–50.
14 Ibid., p. 105.
15 Hu Angang, *Great Transformations in China: Challenges and Opportunities*, Beijing, Tsinghua University, October 2004, p. 149, n. 1. In his book *China's New Development Strategy*, Hu demonstrates that farmers have been left far behind the urban regions (especially in the coastal provinces): Hu Angang, *China's New Development Strategy*, 3rd edition (in Chinese), Zhejiang, People's Publishing House of Zhejiang, 2004. I am grateful to Yuan Ying for having translated several chapters of this book.
16 Only about 5 per cent of China's workforce is engaged in what Hu Angang calls the knowledge society, which comprises people working in sectors such as technology, education, health, finance, business (sic) and the civil service. In order to narrow the gap, Hu suggests that the government should speed up the process of urbanization, invest more in the economically backward western provinces and accelerate the development of manufacturing, service and knowledge sectors; Hu Angang, 'China's economic growth, human resources development and poverty reduction (1978–2003'), a contribution to the International Population and Development Forum, Eliminating Poverty, Wuhan City, Hubei Province, China, 7–9 September 2004, and *Economic and Social Transformation in China*, ch. 5, 'China's economic growth and

poverty reduction (1978–2002)', pp. 97–132, ch. 6, 'China's macro-economy and health', pp. 133–151, and ch. 7, 'Health insecurity: the biggest challenge to human security in China', pp. 152–166.

17 I remind the reader that this is based upon the calculation made by the CIA, which places China's per capita GDP at US$7,400.

18 Luo Xubei and Zhu Nong, 'Rising income inequality in China: a race to the top', World Bank, East Asia and Pacific Region, Poverty Reduction and Economic Management Department, Policy Research Paper, No. 4700, August 2008, p. 20:

> education is one of the key paths out of poverty. Among those with nine years or more of education, the poverty rate is only two percent, compared to a 10 percent national average in China. Inequality of access to education is an important source of inequality across people contemporaneously and across generations.

19 Unless otherwise mentioned, the following paragraphs are based upon Hu Angang, *China in 2020: A New Type of Superpower*, and on the PowerPoint presentation of lesson 11 for the Master course 2009–10 taught at Tsinghua University.

20 According to the latest UNDP data (i.e. for end 2008) presented in its 'China profile', http://hdr.undp.org (accessed on 13 January 2011), the adult literacy rate (for both sexes as a percentage of people aged 15 and above) is 94.2 per cent; the combined gross enrolment ratio in education (for both sexes) is 68.7 per cent; expenditure on education is 2.3 per cent of GDP; the mean length of schooling of adults is 7.5 years; and the expected length of schooling of children is 11.4 years.

21 *South China Morning Post*, 30 March 2011, http://www.scmp.com (accessed 30 March 2011). The article goes on to say:

> China shot up from sixth place (4.4 per cent of the total) to second place with 10.2 per cent over the two periods. Although the US still leads the world, its share of global authorship has fallen to 21 per cent from 26 per cent. 'China's rise up the rankings has been especially striking,' the report said. 'China has heavily increased its investment in R&D [research and development], with spending growing by 20 per cent per year since 1999 to reach over US$100 billion a year today,' it added. However, the report also pointed out that the quantity of published scientific research did not necessarily translate into quality. One real index of the value of any scientific research is the number of times it is cited by peer scientists in their work. Although China has risen in the citation rankings as well, its performance on this measure lags behind its publication rate. 'It will take some time for the absolute output of emerging nations to challenge the rate at which this research is referenced by the international scientific community,' the report said.

22 Hu, lesson 12, Master's course 2009–10.

23 Amongst the many books on China's inequalities and disparities one can consult Wang Shaoguang and Hu Angang, *The Political Economy of Uneven Development: The Case of China*, New York, M.E. Sharpe, 1999; Hu Angang, *Economic and Social Transformation in China* and *Roadmap of China's Rise*; Wang Hui, *The End of the Revolution: China and the Limits of Modernity*, London, Verso, 2009; Martin King White (ed.), *One Country, Two Societies: Rural–Urban Inequality in Contemporary China*, Cambridge, MA, Harvard University Press, 2010.

24 Luo and Zhu, 'Rising income inequality in China', p. 20: 'Before 1978, China was a poor society and the issue of uneven distribution had not surfaced. The reforms have unleashed market forces, and improved economic efficiency. As a result, the economy grew, and disparity in income rose.'

25 See in this sense the interesting article by a journalist of the *Financial Times*, James Kynge, 'West miscasts Tiananmen protesters', *Financial Times*, 3 June 2009. After reminding us that he covered the 1989 events as part of a team of Reuter's reporters, Kynge writes:

I cannot help feeling troubled. . . . I'm concerned because I don't think we – the western media – got the narrative of those days quite right. . . . The powerful iconography of those days . . . supports a clear dichotomy between good and evil, freedom and repression, democracy and dictatorship. In a world of moral fluidity, Tiananmen is an anchor, a gratifyingly fixed reference for our judgments of others. But is it? I don't deny the atrocity of the event . . . I do question, however, the western media's basic assertion that the demonstrations had been 'pro-democracy'. Even now, a raft of editorials commemorating the event's 20th anniversary repeats the mantra that the students were 'demanding democracy'. The reality was less coherent, as shown in *Beijing Coma*, a recent novel by Ma Jian, a Chinese writer who experienced the demonstrations first hand. By interweaving individual motives and broad themes, Ma shows that the movement never adhered to tidy definitions. It was, above all, the unburdening of the hopes of a generation easing itself free of the strictures left from Chairman Mao's rule. Almost everything fell within its scope: campaigns against corruption, nepotism, inflation, police brutality, bureaucracy, official privilege, media censorship, human rights abuses, cramped student dormitories and the smothering of democratic urges. But to say the demonstrations were to 'demand democracy' is an oversimplification. . . . [the protesters] were motivated more by outrage at the betrayal of socialist ideals than by aspirations for a new system. The mood in the square was at least as much conservative as it was activist.

26 Contrary to this dominant opinion see the interesting paper by Albert Keidel, *China's Economic Rise: Fact and Fiction*, Carnegie Endowment for International Peace, July 2008, who sustains, with some reason in my opinion, that China's 'success in recent decades has not been export-led but driven by domestic demand, its rapid growth can continue well into the twenty-first century, unfettered by world market limitations'; and the critique by James A. Dorn (a specialist of China at the Cato Institute in Washington, DC, and editor of the *Cato Journal*), 'Caveats on reform', *South China Morning Post*, 28 July 2008. The UNDP has recently shared the same opinion as Keidel: 'Contrary to popular opinion, foreign direct investment and export growth have not been major drivers. Instead, much of China's growth occurred through township and village enterprises, businesses owned and operated by local governments' (*Human Development Report 2010*, p. 105).
27 Conference at Tsinghua University, 29 March 2005.
28 However, we must consider that part of this unemployment is being absorbed by the urban areas, thanks to the vast process of migration from the rural areas. The number of migrant workers is today estimated at between 120 and 200 million people.
29 Conference at Tsinghua University, January 2005.
30 For more information on the development of China's social policies see Urio, *Reconciling*, pp. 126–152.
31 For more details on the situation of social insurance in the rural areas see Urio, ibid.
32 World Bank, *China: Promoting Growth with Equity*, 2003, Washington, DC, World Bank, p. 10.
33 Luo and Zhu, 'Rising income inequality in China', p. 3.
34 World Bank, *From Poor Areas to Poor People*, p. 34.
35 This statement refers to the generally accepted criterion by experts of inequality, as measured by the Gini index, according to which public authorities should start worrying when the index reaches 40 because this level of inequality could be the cause of social and political unrest. Some experts put the worrying line at a higher level, and some fix it at 45.
36 *China Daily*, 12 May 2010: 'The Gini coefficient . . . has reached 47 in China, overtaking the recognized warning level of 45, government-affiliated experts have said.'
37 Ibid.

38 See nevertheless the work of three Chinese researchers: Jr-Tsung Huang, Chun-Chien Kuo and An-Pang Kao, 'The inequality of regional economic development in China between 1991 and 2001', *Journal of Chinese and Business Studies*, September 2003, vol. 1, no. 3, pp. 273–285. For one of the first appraisals of China's uneven economic development see Wang Shaoguang and Hu Angang, *The Political Economy of Uneven Development*.
39 I have summarized some of these works in Urio, *Reconciling*, pp. 84–91.
40 For more detail see Wang Xiaolu, 'Who's in first? A regional development index for the PRC', Asian Development Bank Institute, Discussion Paper no. 66, May 2007.
41 For more detail see Yang Yongheng and Hu Angang, 'Investigating regional disparities of China's human development with cluster analysis: a historical perspective', *Social Indicators Research*, 2008, no. 86, pp. 417–432.
42 Ibid., p. 431.
43 For comments on the 2006 data see Urio, *Reconciling*, pp. 88–89.
44 For example, Luo and Zhu, 'Rising income inequality in China', p. 4: 'Higher income provinces have smaller urban–rural income gaps, while difference in rural–urban incomes in the poorer regions is particularly pronounced.'
45 OECD, *OECD Rural Policy Reviews: China*, Paris, OECD, 2009, p. 20. These data confirm those of the Oxford Poverty and Human Development Initiative mentioned in the next paragraph. See also OECD, *OECD Economic Surveys: China*, Paris, OECD, 2010; World Bank, *From Poor Areas to Poor People*.
46 World Bank, *From Poor Areas to Poor People*, pp. iii and 1–17; David Dollar, 'Remarkable progress, remaining vulnerability among China's poor', World Bank, http://web.worldbank.org (accessed 18 May 2009).
47 The MPI reflects both the incidence of poverty – the proportion of the population that is multidimensionally poor – and the average intensity of their deprivation – the average proportion of indicators in which they are deprived. The MPI is calculated by multiplying the incidence of poverty by the average intensity across the poor. A person is identified as poor if he or she is deprived in at least 30 per cent of the weighted indicators; Sabina Alkire and Maria Emma Santos, 'China country briefing', *Oxford Poverty & Human Development Initiative (OPHI) Multidimensional Poverty Index Country Briefing Series*, 2010, http://www.ophi.org.uk/policy/multidimensional-poverty-index/mpi-country-briefings/ (accessed 3 April 2011).
48 *OECD Rural Policy Reviews: China*, pp. 21–23. For more detail see ch. 5, which looks at the evolution of inequality over the past decade and at the impact of some of the government programmes introduced in recent years.
49 See, for example, Diana Farrell, Ulrich A. Gersch and Elisabeth Stephenson, 'The value of China's emerging middle class', *McKinsey Quarterly*, 2008 Special Edition, pp. 62–69.
50 Hu Angang, comments on Paolo Urio Conference on 'New Public Management in the West', PowerPoint presentation, based upon *China's Statistical Yearbook*, Tsinghua University, 29 March 2005.
51 World Bank, *The World Bank Report 2008: The Challenges of a Changing World*, Washington, DC, World Bank, p. 83.
52 There is a huge literature on this topic. See, for example, the following articles published in leading journals: David Blumenthal and William Hsiao, 'Privatization and its discontents: the evolving Chinese health care system', *New England Journal of Medicine*, September 2005, vol. 353, no. 11, pp. 1165–70; Winnie Yip and William Hiao, 'China's health care reform: a tentative assessment', *China Economic Review*, 2009, no. 20, pp. 613–619; Winnie Chi-Man, William Hiao, Qingyue Meng, Wen Chen and Xiaoming Sun, 'Realignment of incentives for health-care providers in China', *The Lancet*, 27 March 2010, pp. 1120–30. See also *The Lancet* series on health system reform in China, various dates since 2008. Even international economic organizations generally favourable to policies of neoliberal inspiration have

pointed to the negative consequences of China's health policies until recently; see, for example, World Bank, *The World Bank Report 2008*, p. 83:

> China's deregulation of the heath sector in the 1980s, and the subsequent steep increase in reliance on out-of-pocket spending, is a case in point and a warning to the rest of the world. A spectacular deterioration of health-care provision and social protection, particularly in rural areas, led to a marked slowdown in the increase of life expectancy.

See also Ren Bo and Liu Jingjing, 'Local government costs and doctors' pay are among the unfinished issues for health care reformers, whose task appears far from done', *Caijing Magazine Online*, 19 March 2009, http://www.english.cajing.com.cn (accessed 4 May 2009). For an overall presentation of China's health and poverty problems, Hu Angang, *Economic and Social Transformation in China*, and 'A healthy China: progress and problems', ch. 4 in Hu, *China in 2020*, pp. 65–81.

53 Information from Hu Angang's Master's course, Lesson 12, Tsinghua University, Beijing, 2010, and 'Prof. Angang Hu's PowerPoint on China's Health Development', Tsinghua University, 2010, kindly provided by the author.
54 I remind the reader that the level of health expenditure is not necessarily a favourable sign, as it must be correlated with the major health indicators, as I argued above when dealing with Western countries.
55 I have developed considerations about the problems the Chinese leadership has to face since the mid-1990s in Urio, *Reconciling*, pp. 68–76 and 171–182. I have developed considerations about the importance of simultaneously investing in hard and soft infrastructure in Paolo Urio (ed.), *Public Private Partnerships: Success and Failure Factors for In-Transition Countries*, Lanham, MD, University Press of America, 2010, especially ch. 2 and conclusion.
56 Hu, Master's course.
57 Hana Brixi, Yan Mu, Beatrice Targa and David Hipgrave, 'Equity and Public Governance in health system reform: challenges and opportunities for China', World Bank, Policy Research Working Paper 5530, January 2011, pp. 7 and 24.
58 See the different opinion of Ezra Suleiman, *Dismantling Democratic States*, Princeton, NJ, Princeton University Press, 2003, who shows that NPM has not only limited the Welfare State but in fact also gone very far along the road of dismantling democratic states.
59 On the opening up of the Chinese decision-making system see Chapter 3.
60 *OECD Rural Policy Reviews: China*, pp. 11–17.
61 Untitled document, World Bank website, http://web.worldbank.org/WBSITE/EXTERNAL/COUNTRIES/EASTASIAPACIFICEXT/CHINAEXTN/0,,contentMDK:22131856~pagePK:141137~piPK:141127~theSitePK:318950,00.html (accessed 5 April 2011).
62 Hu Angang spent one year as a postdoctoral scholar in the department of economics at Yale University between 1992 and 1993, where he worked with another Chinese scholar, Wang Shaoguang. In 1993 Hu and Wang wrote a report (Wang Shaoguang and Hu Angang, 'Strengthen the role of the central government during the transition towards a market economy', known as the 'report on China's state capacities') first sent to China as a manuscript and later published in Shenyang, Liaoning People's Press, 1993.
63 The first policy research-oriented works of Hu Angang available to the Chinese leadership before the end of 1988 and published in English at the beginning of the 1990s are the following: Hu Angang, Wang Yi, *et al.*, *Survival and Development: A Study of China's Long Term Development*, Beijing, Science Press, 1992; Hu Angang and Zou Ping, *China's Population Development*, Beijing, China's Science and Technology Press, 1991. For a brief analysis of these two books see Urio, *Reconciling*, pp. 104–108.

64 See Wang Shaoguang, 'Great social transformation afoot in China', *China Economist*, July 2008, pp. 55–69.
65 State Council of China, 'Circular of the State Council concerning promoting the reform in rural compulsory education's funding insurance system' [Guowuyuan Guanyu Shenhua Nongcun Yiwujiaoyu Jingfei Baozhang Jizhi Gaige De Tongzhi], 24 December 2005, http://www.gov.cn/zwgk/2006-02/07/content_181267.htm (accessed 15 June 2007).
66 State Council of China, 'Circular of the State Council concerning remitting the urban compulsory education's tuition and miscellaneous fees' [Guowuyuan Guanyu Zuohao Mianchu Chengshi Yiwujiaoyu Jieduan Xuesheng Xuezafei Gongzuo De Tongzhi], 12 August 2008, http://www.gov.cn/zwgk/2008-08/15/content_1072915.htm (accessed 15 June 2007).
67 The highest minimum wage was first established on 1 July 2009 by the Shenzen government at 1,000 RMB, an increase of 20 per cent.
68 National Population and Family Planning Commission, 'Minimum wage goes up highest in east China's Zhejiang', 12 April 2011, http:/npfpc.gov.cn/en/ (accessed 4 April 2011). Moreover, the commission quotes the owner of Zhejiang Fuyang Jin'aobo Shoe Co., Hu Xudong, who declared that 'My factory raised the average monthly salary by 20 per cent earlier this year, from 1500 Yuan to 1800 Yuan, in response to the severe labour shortage before the latest Spring Festival.' The commission adds: 'Hu's factory used to raise the monthly salary it paid by 10 per cent each year.'
69 The China Labour Bulletin website (http://www.china-labour.org.hk/en/, accessed 4 May 2009) recognizes that, in spite of the fact that 'workers feel left out in the cold and are increasingly bypassing the union altogether in their attempts to defend their rights [as evidenced by the fact that] workers now stage strikes and protests in a deliberate attempt to force local governments to intervene in their disputes with management', 'all the conditions for positive change within the union are present, and that there were signs in 2008 of union officials taking a more robust and pragmatic approach to protecting workers' rights'. The China Labour Bulletin publishes on its website news, information and reports on the situation of the workers in mainland China.
70 World Bank, *Mid-Term Evaluation of China's 11th 5 Year Plan*, Washington, DC, 2009, http://www.worldbank.org (accessed 15 June 2009). I have summarized China's environmental problems and policies in Urio, *Reconciling*, pp. 95–101 and 112–117. See also UNDP, *China Human Development Report 2009/10: China and Sustainable Future: Towards a Low Carbon Economy and Society*, Beijing, China Publishing Group Corporation, April 2010, commissioned by UNDP China and coordinated by Renmin University of China.
71 World Watch Institute, *Renewable Energy and Energy Efficiency in China: Current Status and Prospects for 2020*, Worldwatch Report 182, Washington, DC, World Watch Institute, 2010, p. 5.
72 Ibid. The report mentions the National Renewable Energy Law, the National Medium and Long-Term Development Plan for Renewable Energy and the Medium and Long-Term Energy Conservation Plan as well as the infrastructure-intensive government stimulus programme launched in late 2008 and the measures included in the Eleventh Five-Year Plan.
73 Ibid., p. 6.
74 Jiahua Pan, Haibing Ma and Ying Zhang, *Green Economy and Green Jobs in China: Current Status and Potentials for 2020*, Worldwatch Report 185, Washington, DC, Worldwatch Institute, 2011, p. 5.
75 World Bank, 'Empowering China's green growth', 31 May 2011, http://www.worldbank.org/en/news/2011/05/31/empowering-chinas-green-growth.print (accessed 8 June 2011).

76 Pinsent Masons, 'Update', March 2011, received through the author's e-mail subscription. Pinsent Masons LLP, based in London, is a full-service commercial law firm, which ranks in the top 15 in the UK. It has 270 partners and over 1,000 lawyers worldwide, with a total staff of 1,708 and offices in Beijing, Brussels, Dubai, Edinburgh, Glasgow, Hong Kong, Shanghai and Singapore; http://www.pinsentmasons.com/Default.aspx?page=0 (accessed 15 July 2011).
77 This paragraph is based upon information obtained from the World Bank site and from a visit to Tianjin in September 2010: World Bank, 'Chinese eco-city project gets boost from Global Environment Facility', press release, 22 July 2010, http://www-worldbank.org/en/news/2010/07/22/Chinese-eco-city-project-gets-boost-global-environment-facility (accessed 12 August 2010).
78 Let me remind the reader that these four municipalities enjoy a status equivalent to that of a province and report directly to the central government. The other three municipalities are Beijing, Shanghai and Tianjin.
79 Interview with Cui Zhiyuan given to Emilie Frenkiel, 'From scholar to official: Cui Yuan and Chongqing city's local experimental policy', *La vie des idées* (*Books & Ideas*), 25 January 2011, p. 3, http://www.booksandideas.net (accessed 15 May 2011). For an original theoretical analysis of the Chongqing experiment see Cui Zhiyuan, 'Partial intimations of the coming whole: the Chongqing Experiment in light of the theories of Henry George, James Meade, and Antonio Gramsci', *Modern China*, 2011, vol. 37, no. 6, pp. 646–660. I completed this article during a discussion with Cui Zheyuan, 29 September 2011, in Beijing. For additional factual information see Philip C.C. Huang, 'Chongqing: equitable development driven by a "third hand"?', *Modern China*, 2011, vol. 37, no. 6, pp. 569–622. For a Western point of view, see Jon Sigurdson and Krystyna Palonka, 'Innovative city in west China Chongqing', Working Paper 239, Stockholm School of Economics (EIJS), February 2009.
80 Xinghua News Agency, 'China's Chongqing starts household registration reform', 29 July 2010, http://news.xinhuanet.com/english2010/china/2010-07-29/c_13420830.htm (accessed 15 August 2010).
81 Cui in Frenkiel, 'From scholar to official', p. 4.
82 The new Party secretary of Chongqing, appointed in late 2007, Bo Xilai, is a member of the politburo and is considered a new rising star within the Chinese political leadership; his father, Bo Yobo, belongs to the first generation of Chinese leaders.
83 Cui in Frenkiel, 'From scholar to official', p. 5.
84 Ibid.
85 Cui, 'Partial intimations of the coming whole', p. 650.
86 Ibid., p. 649.
87 The *hukou* system was introduced in the 1960s in order to solve the economic crisis and famines. It divides citizens into several groups: agricultural residents, non-agricultural residents, permanent residents and temporary residents. In the logic of the planned economy, the system restricted peasants from entering cities, which guaranteed the labour force in rural areas but deprived them of many rights, including social security benefits, enjoyed by urban residents. Since peasants started to migrate to the urban areas, attracted by better job opportunities after the beginning of reforms, the consequence of this system has been that the migrants, who are still tied to their rural *hukou*, cannot enjoy the same benefits as the residents with the city *hukou*.
88 Cui in Frenkiel, 'From scholar to official', pp. 6–7.
89 The information presented in the following paragraphs is taken from Li Xiguang, 'China model and dream of Chongqing', draft paper for a conference given in Chongqing, 18 September 2010, kindly provided by the author. Li Xiguang is professor and president of the Tsinghua Centre for International Communication. See also Huang, 'Chongqing'.
90 According to a research paper mentioned by Li ('China model and dream of Chongqing', p. 10) there are today in Chongqing 2.35 million adolescents (out of

a total of 4.4. million) who belong to families with one or both parents working in urban areas.
91 Ibid., p. 14.
92 See, for example, Zhao Litao and Lim Tin Seng (eds), *China's New Social Policy: Initiatives for a Harmonious Society*, Hackensack, NJ, World Scientific, 2010 (for a summary see Urio, *Reconciling*, pp. 119–155); Hu Angang, *Economic and Social Transformation in China*; Kuo Ming-Cheng, Hans F. Zacher and Chan Hou-Sheng (eds), *Reform and Perspectives on Social Insurance: Lessons from the East and West. A Comparative Study of Social Insurance in China, EU, Germany, Great Britain, Japan, Sweden, Taiwan, and the USA*, The Hague, Kluwer Law International, 2002; François-Xavier Merrien, Raphaël Parchet, and Antoine Kernen, *L'état social: Une perspective internationale*, Paris A. Colin, 2005 (with a chapter on China).
93 In 2009 the total number of employed persons, aged 16 years and over, in urban and rural areas was 779.95 million.
94 Yang Yansui, 'The third choice of pension fund management', *Labour and Social Security Notes*, 2004.
95 Huang Zhouhui, 'Enterprises annuity: how many shares can it occupy?', http://www.ycwb.com/gb/content/2004-04/23/content_680652.htm (accessed 9 May 2008).
96 There is a huge literature on this topic already mentioned in note 52 above.
97 It must be noted that some Chinese professors specializing in this field pointed out that the accumulated rate was too high, which violated the basic principle of medical insurance.
98 According to *China's Statistical Yearbook 2010*, there are 621.86 million people holding the urban *hukou* (i.e. the urban residence permit), so I simply calculated the coverage of health insurance in urban areas at 64.56 per cent. However, as is well known, about 43.35 million out of 401.4 million covered by the basic medical insurance are the peasant workers with rural *hukou*, so the exact percentage of people covered by the health system with urban *hukou* is 57.59 per cent.
99 I should warn the reader that the figures given for health insurance are only estimates; the exact number varies significantly from area to area, from sector to sector and from system to system. China is too large to adopt a uniform policy for health insurance. In fact, the central government allows local officials to have their own insurance policies that best fit local situations and their financial capacities.
100 Let me remind the reader that *xiagang* people were still on the payroll of enterprises and bureaucracies and benefited from very small allowances, even if they were no longer working for their employer.
101 Ministry of Labour and Social Security Statistical Communiqués for Social Security (2001–7) and *China Statistical Yearbook 2010*, *China Statistical Year Book* (2006–9), Beijing, People's Republic of China.
102 It has not been possible to determine the exact benefit level of insurance for unemployed people but, according to the system, the benefit level will range between the *dibao* line (minimum living standard line) and the lowest salary line.
103 Ministry of Civil Affairs, '2009 statistical communiqué of civil affairs development', http://cws.mca.gov.cn/article/tjbg/201006/20100600081422.shtml (accessed 15 May 2011).
104 National Bureau of Statistics, '2007 statistical communiqué on national economy and social development', http://www.stats.gov.cn (accessed 20 May 2008).
105 Source: Ministry of Civil Affairs, '2009 statistical communiqué of civil affairs development', http://cws.mca.gov.cn/article/tjbg/201006/20100600081422.shtml (accessed 10 May 2010).
106 Hu, Master's course 2009–10, lesson 14; Wang Shaoguang, 'The great transformation: two-way movement in China since the 1980s' (in Chinese: Zhong Guo She Hui Ke Xue), 2008, *Social Sciences in China*, no. 1, pp. 129–148, also published as 'Great social transformation afoot in China', *China Economist*, July 2008, pp. 55–69,

and in a more complete form as 'The great transformation: the double movement in China', *Boundary 2*, 2008, vol. 35, no. 2, pp. 16–47; and 'China in transition', *L'Annuaire du Collège de France*, 24 June 2010, no. 109, http://annuaire-cdf.revues.org/427 (accessed 29 April 2011).
107 This conclusion was also partially confirmed by research conducted by Albert Keidel as early as the mid-2000s that proved that migrant workers, by sending back money to their families in the rural areas, contributed to the improvement of their standard of living for both income and consumption: Albert Keidel, *The Causes and Impact of Chinese Regional Inequalities in Income and Well-Being*.
108 Wang, 'The great transformation: two-way movement in China since the 1980s'. I also consulted Wang's PowerPoint presentation on 'The great transformation: double movement in China', conference given at the School of Public Policy and Management, Tsinghua University, 2008, which presents some additional data.
109 Hu, Master's course 2009–10, lesson 14.
110 For more detailed explanations see, for example, University of Zurich, 'Economic and social history online', http://www.eso.uzh.ch/modul3/HowToPre_en.html?lesson.section=unit&section.label=HowToPre_4
111 National Population and Family Planning Commission of China, 'Per capita annual income and Engel's coefficient of urban and rural households, 1978–2009', 22 December 2010, http://www.npfpc.gov.cn/en/detail.aspx?articleid=101222122513548283 (accessed 22 March 2011).
112 Wang and Hu, 'Strengthen the role of the central government'.

Conclusion

1 Remember the statement of the World Bank, already mentioned in Chapter 1, addressed to China in 1997 according to which 'the [Chinese] government must begin serving markets'; World Bank, *China 2020: Development Challenges in the New Century*, 18 September 1997, Report no. 17027-CHA, World Bank, p. ix.
2 In this sense see Michel Husson, 'Les inégalités à l'échelle mondiale', *Chronique internationale de l'IRES*, May 2011, no. 130, pp. 55 and 60–61. The studies upon which this article is based are quoted in note 65 of Chapter 5 above. The case of the evolution of the UK Gini index illustrates this trend very well. We have presented it in Chapter 5, Figure 5.2.
3 Joseph E. Stiglitz, *Freefall: America, Free Markets, and the Sinking of the World Economy*, New York, Norton, 2010, p. 19 and n. 21, p. 305, based upon data from OECD, *Growing Unequal? Income Distribution and Poverty in OECD Countries*, Paris, October 2008. The whole Stiglitz book provides a convincing explanation of the crisis.
4 Stiglitz, *Freefall*, pp. 19–20.
5 Ibid., p. 20. Stiglitz goes on to explain that the other source of weak global aggregate demand is that:

> developing countries have put aside hundreds of billions of dollars in reserve to protect themselves from the high level of global volatility that has marked the era of deregulation, and from the discomfort they feel at turning to the IMF for help. ... The oil-rich countries too were accumulating reserves – they knew that the high price of crude was not sustainable [and finally, as] export-led growth had been lauded as the best way for developing countries to grow ... many turned to a policy of keeping their exchange rate competitive. And this meant buying dollars, selling heir own currencies, and accumulate reserves.
>
> ibid.

6 Under 'underemployment' I put both involuntary part-time employment and underpaid jobs (i.e. under the poverty line), as well as people who have become unable

to work as a consequence of stress and other type of disabilities contracted in the workplace; in other words all the negative consequences (in addition to unemployment) of the deregulation of the labour market.

7 Let me remind the reader that within strong-NPM countries the UK is an exception as far as public health is concerned, thanks to the National Health Service (NHS), in spite of reforms based upon the NPM model introduced by both the Conservative and New Labour governments. Let us also remark that the NHS is presently under attack from the new government. See UK Department of Health, *Working Together for a Stronger NHS*, London, HMSO, 2011, and the comment in the *British Journal of Medicine* by Tony Delamothe and Fiona Godlee, 'Dr Lansley's monster', *BMJ*, 21 January 2011, 342, d408, http://www.bmj.com/content/342/bmj.d408.full (accessed 15 August 2011):

> What do you call a government that embarks on the biggest upheaval of the NHS in its 63 year history, at breakneck speed, while simultaneously trying to make unprecedented financial savings? The politically correct answer has got to be: mad.

See also Nicholas Timmins (Public Policy Editor), 'No "US-style system" for NHS, says regulator', *Financial Times*, 13 May 2011.

8 At the moment of writing this conclusion (November 2011) the attention is focused on Greece, where this type of measures is probably the most severe; but similar actions are being taken all over the West, especially in Portugal, Spain and Italy, but also in the USA, the UK, France and Germany. For the identification of those who are responsible for the crisis the best account is that of Stiglitz, *Freefall*, which mentions in the first place leaders of the financial sector (head of central banks – especially the US Federal Reserve – banks and investment companies, and traders), mainstream economists and leading mass media who have approved the neoliberal project, politicians who have listened to both the above-mentioned leaders of financial institutions and economists, and last but not least rating agencies that have attributed the highest rates to financial institutions for a long time, and until the eve of their collapse. Chief executives of multinational companies and banks, and traders, continue to draw enormous salaries and bonuses. According to Nomi Prins, Standard & Poor's 'rubber-stamped $14 trillion of toxic assets in the five years leading up to the crisis of 2008. This green light enabled Wall Street to thrive while it manufactured these assets and sold them globally'; 'Debt from bailouts did not pan out', 10 August 2011, http://www.nomiprins.com/articles/ (accessed 27 October 2011). Before becoming a journalist, Nomi Prins worked on Wall Street as a managing director at Goldman Sachs, and ran the international analytics group at Bear Stearns in London.

9 The letter was to remain secret, but the influential Italian newspaper *Il Corriere della Sera* published it the day after, as reported by the French newspaper *Le Figaro*, 8 August 2011, http://www.lefigaro.fr/conjoncture/2011/08/08/04016–20110808ART-FIG00475-la-bce-met-de-facto-l-italie-sous-tutelle.php (accessed 15 November 2011). Let us remark that the exclusion of water from privatization, which might have signalled a change in policy, is not in fact an extraordinary concession made by the ECB. In my opinion, the ECB would have made itself ridiculous if it had asked for water privatization after an overwhelming majority of Italian citizens had refused water privatization in a national referendum only a few months before.

10 As reported by the British newspaper the *Daily Telegraph*, 6 November 2011, 'European Central Bank president Jean-Claude Trichet held his final press conference in Berlin on Thursday. Here is his opening statement in full', http://www.telegraph.co.uk/finance/financialcrisis/8811287/Jean-Claude-Trichet-ECB-statement-in-full.html (accessed 6 November 2011). Emphasis added by the present author.

11 The 'Unholy Alliance' is a label that Ha-Joon Chang has attached to the World Bank, the IMF and the WTO for their structural adjustment policies imposed upon

developing countries, as already mentioned above in Chapter 3; see *Bad Samaritans: The Myth of Free Trade and the Secret History of Capitalism*, New York, Bloomsbury, 2008, p. 32.
12 This situation unfortunately contradicts the statement made by Joseph E. Stiglitz in December 2009 announcing the 'The triumphant return of John Maynard Keynes', *The Economists' Voice*, Project Syndicate, Berkeley Electronic Press, December 2008, http://www.project-sydicate.org (accessed 6 January 2009). We are instead witnessing 'the triumphant persistence of neoliberalism'.
13 On the concentration and interconnections of multinational companies see the results of a research by a team of the Swiss Federal Polytechnics in Zurich that has identified a network of 43,060 transnational companies that are interconnected thanks to the exchange of shares, of which 147 are mega-societies that control about 40 per cent of the wealth of the entire network, see Stefania Vitali, James B. Glattfelder and Stefano Battiston, 'The network of global corporate control', http://arxiv.org/PS_cache/arxiv/pdf/1107/1107.5728v2.pdf (accessed 30 October 2011); also Dan Braha, Blake Stacey and Yaneer Bar-Yam, 'Corporate competition: A self–organized network', *Social Networks*, 2011, 33, pp. 219–30, http://necsi.edu/affiliates/braha/Journal_Version_SON_Braha.pdf (accessed 30 October 2011).

On the persistence of tax evasion and avoidance, in spite of the attacks launched on tax heavens by the OECD and the G20, see the Tax Justice Network (http://taxjustice.blogspot.com/) and its last report: Robert S. McIntyre, Matthew Gardner, Rebecca J. Wilkins, Richard Phillips, *Corporate Taxpayers & Corporate Tax Dodgers 2008–10*, Washington, DC, Citizens for Tax Justice, November 2011. For example, according to a report of Citizens for Tax Justice, a public interest research and advocacy organization, '280 most profitable US corporations shelter half their profits from taxes. "These 280 corporations received a total of nearly $224 billion in tax subsidies," said Robert McIntyre, Director at Citizens for Tax Justice and the report's lead author. "This is wasted money that could have gone to protect Medicare, create jobs and cut the deficit." 30 Companies average less than zero tax bill in the last three Years, 78 had at least one no-tax year', 2 November 2011, http://ctj.org/ctjreports/2011/11/corporate_taxpayers_corporate_tax_dodgers_2008-2010.php (accessed 4 November 2011).
14 Fernand Braudel, *Afterthoughts on Material Civilization and Capitalism* (The Johns Hopkins Symposia in Comparative History), Baltimore, MD, Johns Hopkins University Press, 1979, pp. 113–114.
15 Stiglitz, *Freefall*, p. xiii. According to Stiglitz, increasing taxes to increase government spending and lower deficits and debt is the best way to kick-start the economy; moreover, the austerity that is going on in Europe, America and so forth is effectively a suicide pact for our economies (in a speech in Toronto, end of October 2011, as reported by the Toronto *Globe and Mail*, 25 October 2011, http://www.theglobeandmail.com/report-on-business/economy/government-stimulus-measures-too-feeble-stiglitz/article2213385/, accessed 5 November 2011).
16 *Le Monde*, 3 October 2011, http://www.lemonde.fr/idees/article/2011/10/03/un-systeme-bancaire-a-repenser_1581472_3232.html (accessed 30 October 2011), my translation from the French. The exact passage in French is:

> dans l'état de colère où va se trouver ce peuple, on peut douter qu'aucun gouvernement grec ne puisse tenir sans appui de l'armée . . . Cette réflexion triste vaut sans doute pour le Portugal et/ou l'Irlande, et/ou d'autres, plus gros . . . Jusqu'où ira-t-on?

17 See my evaluation of Western liberal democracy given in Chapter 2.
18 Stiglitz, *Freefall*, p. xiii.
19 It is interesting to quote in this context the interview given by the famous Swiss entrepreneur Nicolas G. Hayek to the German review *Cicero* a few weeks before his death:

> Unfortunately, during the second half of the last century, a large part of Swiss finance has taken example, increasingly and without any critical attitude, from the Anglo-Saxon stock exchanges and financial markets. Yet the new Anglo-Saxon financial mentality has only one goal – money, money and again money, as soon and as much as possible, at any cost. This behaviour is extremely harmful for industry . . . it is harmful for the entire human race. All these hypocrite acrobats, these preachers of finance, this plethora of speculators, . . . all these people help neither the industry nor the whole of American industry. Fortunately, they are only a small number, but there are still too many crooks and cheats.
>
> *L'Hebdo*, 1 July 2011 (my translation from the French)

20 Urio, *Reconciling State, Market and Society in China: The Long March towards Prosperity*, London, Routledge, 2010, especially p. xx.
21 Urio, *Reconciling*, pp. 202–203; Giuseppe di Lampedusa, *The Leopard*, New York, Pantheon-Random House, 2007. The exact sentence in Italian is: 'Se vogliamo che tutto rimanga come è, bisogna che tutto cambi!'
22 Urio, *Reconciling*, pp. 202–203.
23 See reference in note 15 above. On the crisis of capitalism see the most recent articles of Joseph E. Stiglitz published online by the Project Syndicate: 'Gambling with the planet', April 2011; 'The IMF's switch in time', May 2011; 'The ideological crisis of Western capitalism', July 2011; 'A contagion of bad ideas', August 2011, http://www.project-sydicate.org (all accessed 29 August 2011).
24 For a brief discussion of the development and management of NPL see Urio, *Reconciling*, pp. 92–93 and 111, where you will find some additional references.
25 Whereas the bailout of Wall Street by the Troubled Asset Relief Program voted by US Congress on 3 October 2008 amounted to $750 billion, the total US bailout is estimated at $9.2 trillion, of which $4,792 billion went to Wall Street, $2,824 billion to GSEs (government-sponsored enterprises; GSEs hold or pool approximately $5 trillion worth of mortgages, according to Wikipedia; http://en.wikipedia.org/wiki/Government-sponsored_enterprise, accessed 6 October 2011) and $1,663 billion to US citizens (according to Nomi Prins and Krisztina Ugrin, 'Bailout report', 1 October 2011, http://www.nomiprins.com, accessed 6 October 2011, where one can find the details of who gave it and who got it). The European bailout package approved in May 2010 is estimated at nearly $1 trillion according to the *New York Times* (http://www.nytimes.com/2010/05/11/opinion/11tue2.html, accessed 28 September 2011). Speaking on 27 September 2011 before the members of the European Parliament, the President of the European Commission, José Manuel Barroso, declared that:

> in the last three years, Member States – I should say taxpayers – have granted aid and provided guarantees of € 4.6 trillion to the financial sector. It is time for the financial sector to make a contribution back to society. That is why I am very proud to say that today the Commission adopted a proposal for the Financial Transaction Tax.
> European renewal – State of the Union Address 2011, available at http://europa.eu/rapid/pressReleasesAction.do?reference=SPEECH/11/607&format=HTML&aged=0&language=EN&guiLanguage=en (accessed 20 October 2011)

Nevertheless, according to the Geneva newspaper *Le Courier*, 29 September 2011, the UK has threatened to oppose its veto as this tax would harm the London financial market.
26 Stiglitz, *Freefall*, p. 301, n. 12.
27 Wang Hui, *The End of the Revolution: China and the Limits of Modernity*, London, Verso, 2009, p. xvii.
28 Hu Angang, 'How to know about contemporary China', Foreword to Urio, *Reconciling*, p. xii.

29 Two remarks. First, by taking the present distribution of the 800 million people constituting the potential Chinese work force within the three sectors (see above, Table 6.1), considering that just under 40 per cent or 320 million are (officially) still in agriculture, even by subtracting some 120 million migrant workers (who are still under the rural *hukou* regime) and further subtracting another 50 million who will be necessary for agriculture once China has completed its transition to an industrial and service economy (i.e. about 6 per cent of the working population as in today's developed countries), there still remain today about 150 million people in agriculture who can be transferred into the other two sectors over a period of time. This will help keep the cost of labour low, even if the trend is towards increasing salaries. As for the increase of salaries that may diminish China's competitive advantage in the global market, another remark is interesting. According to calculations made by Oxford University about China's level of poverty presented above, by taking the World Bank $2 per day level, we see that there were in 2003 in China 481 million people (i.e. 36 per cent of the total population) under this level. Even if the number of poor people has decreased since 2003, this gives a considerable margin for improving the income of these people (most of them in the inner and western provinces), thus boosting internal demand. This will help China not only to improve the living conditions of these people but also to reduce its dependency upon the export-led strategy of development.

30 For information about China's stimulus package I am indebted to several articles by Barry Naughton published online by the China Leadership Monitor of the influential Hoover Institution at Stanford University, available at http://www.hoover.org/publications/china-leadership-monitor (especially nos. 28, 29, 31 and 32); as well as to Wei Xing, Assistant Professor at the School of Public Policy and Management, who provided an unpublished paper. However I will mainly rely upon Christine Wong, 'The fiscal stimulus programme and public governance issues in China', *OECD Journal of Budgeting*, 2011, vol. 11, no. 3, pp. 1–21.

31 In fact, the stimulus can be estimated at 5.4 trillion RMB, if to the fiscal stimulus of 4 trillion RMB we add 16 key science and technology projects (600 million RMB) and social security (mainly health, 800 million RMB); if we also add 10 industrial revitalization projects, not included in the 5.4 trillion RMB, we would get a total between 6 and 8 trillion RMB (according to Wei Xing, unpublished paper). Moreover, in 2010 the central government decided on an additional allocation of 572 million RMB. Some experts evaluate the total investment at 9.5 trillion RMB, according to Wong, 'The fiscal stimulus programme', p. 9.

32 In this sense see Wong, ibid., pp. 16–17.

33 Geoff Dyer, 'Economy: move from investment to consumption', *Financial Times*, 27 October 2010.

34 Jamil Anderlini, 'Banking: bad loans seem set to worsen', *Financial Times*, 27 October 2010.

35 Urio, *Reconciling*, pp. 183–190.

36 I have quoted on several occasions Joseph E. Stiglitz, but there are many others such as Nouriel Roubini and Paul Krugman. Amongst the many Marxist analyses, in my opinion the best one is Bellamy John Foster and Fred Magdoff, *The Great Financial Crisis: Causes and Consequences*, New York, Monthly Review Press, 2009. For a philosophical analysis see Slavoj Zizek, *First as Tragedy, Then as Farce*, London, Verso, 2009. For a revival of Marxism see Meghnad Desai, *Marx's Revenge: The Resurgence of Capitalism and the Death of Statist Socialism*, London, Verso, 2002. For an appreciation of the interest of Marxism for the twenty-first century see Eric Hobsbawm, *How to Change the World: Tales of Marx and Marxism*, London, Little, Brown, 2011.

37 For an excellent account of these differences see Bruce J. Dickson, 'No "Jasmine" for China', *Current History*, September 2011, pp. 211–216; and for an evaluation of

the 2011 Arab revolutions, Emmanuel Todd, *Allah n'y est pour rien! Sur les révolutions arabes et quelques autres*, Loubiana, Arretsurimage, 2011.
38 According to the official statistics of the National Bureau of Statistics of China (NBSC).
39 One of the sources of the crisis in the West is that for a long time, but more so since the beginning of the neoliberal era (1980), the economy has been in command.
40 Do not forget that the crisis, a consequence of neoliberalism, the 'Washington Consensus' and NPM, has emerged because of the irresponsible behaviour of economic forces ('interests, ideas, and ideologies' in the words of Stiglitz, *Freefall*, p. xvii) that managed to convince politicians of the benefit for society at large of privatization and deregulation.
41 The question of the opening of the economy by eliminating all obstacles to the entrance and exit of goods and service is highly debatable, as it is linked to the question of the validity of global market liberalization, which corresponds to another aspect of market fundamentalism. See Paul Bairoch, *Economics and World History: Myths and Paradoxes*, New York, Harvester Wheatsheaf, 1993, and the recent appeals to a kind of 'soft' or selective protectionism for the purposes of protecting national jobs, health and environment; for example the French demographer and historian Emmanuel Todd, *Après la démocratie*, Paris, Gallimard, 2008, especially the Conclusion, 'Le protectionnisme, dernière chance de la démocratie européenne'; and one of the candidates to the primaries of the French Socialist Party, Arnaud Montebourg, *Votez pour la démondialisation!*, Paris, Flammarion, 2011.
42 On question of the 'China model' see the opinion of a group of renowned Chinese and Western scholars in two collective books: Cao Tian Yu (ed.), *The Chinese Model of Modern Development*, London, Routledge, 2005; S. Philip Hsu, Yu-Shan Wu and Suisheng Zhao (eds), *In Search of China's Development Model: Beyond the Beijing Consensus*, London, Routledge, 2011; and also Glasshouse Forum, Paris, 23–24 February 2009, 'Is there a China model? A summary and video documentation of a China–West intellectual summit', Maison Louis Carré, Paris, 2009.
43 Urio, *Reconciling*.
44 A clear reference to the interpretation of Chinese thought and strategy by the French philosopher François Jullien, as explained in Chapter 1 (see note 28 for references) and Chapter 4. Let me also remind the reader that in Table III.1 I have cautiously written for the topic 'Institutional choice': 'In search of the China "model" for democracy and economy'.

Annex 1

1 This is a free translation of Paolo Urio, 'New Public Management: un autre son de cloche', *Le Journal de Genève*, 27 October 1997, p. 2. I have added some references to the original article for the purpose of clarifying some points.
2 Paul Krugman, 'The rich, the Right and the facts: deconstructing the income distribution debate', *American Prospect*, Fall 1992, pp. 19–31, http://epn.org/prospect.html (accessed 15 April 1996).
3 *The Times* (London), 7 April 1997.
4 Let us note that a few years later the Right came back to power in these countries, in spite of the development of many anti-capitalist and anti-globalization movements. This shows the strength of neoliberal discourse on the citizens of these countries. We see in the chapters of this book how well the NPM countries have done after 1997 and especially during the 2008–11 crisis.

Annex 2

1. Free translation of Paolo Urio, 'Le rôle du scientifique dans la définition des stratégie de réforme', text of a conference given at the international congress on 'The administration in all its moods: realizations and consequences', University of Lausanne, 11–12 February 1999, published by Yves Emery (ed.), L'administration dans tous ses états: realisations et consequences, Lausanne, Presses Polytechniques et Universitaires Romandes, 2000, pp. 187–193.
2. Christopher Pollit, 'Reinvention and the rest: reform strategies in the OECD world', ibid., pp. 217–245.
3. These are two mandates of the Swiss government, one for the training of senior officials of the People's Republic of China, the other for the training of professors of the National Institute of Public Administration in Hanoi.
4. David Osborne and Ted Gaebler, *Reinventing Government: How the Entrepreneurial Spirit is Transforming the Public Sector*, New York, Plume, 1993; David Osborne and Peter Plastrik, *Banishing Bureaucracy*, New York, Plume, 1998.
5. This is certainly true for much of the reform proposals; I leave aside the purely technical proposals such as analytical accounting, which can improve and give more transparency to the management of state finances.
6. These are the values of democracy, equity, security, efficiency and freedom, whose conciliation and/or arbitration are at the heart of political debate.
7. David Lempert, 'Holding accountable the powers that be: protecting our integrity and the public we serve', *Public Administration Review*, July–August 1997, pp. ii–v. On p. iv, Mr Lempert publishes a contract template, which should be signed by the two parties of an expertise mandate. It is my opinion that such a template should be published by all academic journals specializing in public administration and management.
8. I informed the audience that I was about to publish a chapter on this point: Paolo Urio, 'La gestion publique au service du marché', in Marc Huffy (ed.), *La pensée comptable: Etat, Néolibéralisme, Nouvelle Gestion Publique*, Paris, PUF, 1999, pp. 91–123.
9. In this book I have added a fifth indicator: employment and unemployment.
10. Just one example, the opinion of Paul Krugman at the moment when the British government announced the privatization of British Rail:

    At the time of writing, the Major government has declared its intention to privatize British Rail, with an enthusiasm and lack of concern for consequences that suggest that little has been learned. Conservatives in Britain apparently have not yet realized that markets are not magical. They can work well when conditions are right, but leaving a natural monopoly free to do its worst is blind ideology.
    Paul Krugman, *Peddling Prosperity: Economic Sense and Nonsense in the Age of Diminishing Expectations*, New York, W.W. Norton, 1994, p. 181.

11. Max Weber was referring to private bureaucracies as the only probable limit to public bureaucracies.

Bibliography

Alkire, S. and Santos, M.E. (2010) 'China country briefing', Oxford Poverty & Human Development Initiative (OPHI) Multidimensional Poverty Index Country Briefing Series, available at http://www.ophi.org.uk/policy/multidimensional-poverty-index/mpi-country-briefings/, accessed 3 April 2011.
Almond, G.A. and Verba, S. (1963) *The Civic Culture*, Boston: Little, Brown & Co.
Almond, G.A. and Powell, G.B. (1966) *Comparative Politics: A Developmental Approach*, Boston: Little, Brown & Co.
Amable, B. (2005) *Les cinq capitalismes: Diversité des systèmes économiques et sociaux dans la mondialisation*, Paris: Seuil.
Anderson, P. (1998) *The Origins of Postmodernity*, London: Verso.
Andrésy, A. (2008) *Le Président chinois Hu Jintao: Sa politique et ses réseaux. Who's Hu?*, Paris: L'Harmattan.
Antille, G., Bürgenmeier, B. and Flückiger, Y. (1997) *L'économie suisse au futur: Une réforme en trois piliers*, Lausanne, Réalités Sociales.
Aron, R. (1967) *Les étapes de la pensée sociologique*, Paris: Gallimard.
Aron, R. (2002) *Le Marxisme de Marx*, Paris: Editions de Fallois.
Baeck, L. (2007) 'Discours intellectuels sur la mondialisation en Chine', *Monde chinois*, no. 9, pp. 55–71.
Bai, S. (ed.) (1988) *Précis d'histoire de Chine*, Beijing: Editions en langues étrangères.
Bairoch, P. (1993) *Economics and World History: Myths and Paradoxes*, New York: Harvester Wheatsheaf (French version: *Mythes et paradoxes de l'histoire économique*, Paris: La Découverte, 1999).
Barlow, J. and Röber, M. (1996) 'Steering not rowing: co-ordination and control in the management of public services in Britain and Germany', *International Journal of Public Sector Management*, vol. 9, no. 5/6, pp. 73–89.
Barnes, C. and Cox, D. (1997) 'Patients, power and policy: NHS management reforms and consumer empowerment', in Kester, I.-H., Painter, C. and Barnes, C. (eds) *Management in the Public Sector*, London: Thomson.
Bartley, M., Sacker, A. and Clarke, P. (2009) 'Employment status, employment conditions, and limiting illness: prospective evidence from the British household panel survey 1991–2001', *Journal of Epidemiology and Community Health*, March, pp. 501–506.
Bell, D. (1960) *The End of Ideology: On the Exhaustion of Political Ideas in the Fifties*, Cambridge, MA: Harvard University Press.
Bell, D. (2008) *China's New Confucianism: Politics and Everyday Life in a Changing Society*, Princeton, NJ: Princeton University Press.
Bell, D.A. (ed.) (2008) *Confucian Political Ethics*, Princeton, NJ: Princeton University Press.

Benach, J., Muntaner, C., Chung, H., Solar, O., Santana, V., Friel, S., Houweling, T.A.J. and Mormot, M. (2010) 'Reducing the health inequalities associated with employment conditions', *British Medical Journal*, vol. 340, pp. 1392–1395.

Bergère, M.-C. (1986) *L'âge d'or de la bourgeoisie chinoise*, Paris: Flammarion.

Bergère, M.-C. (2007) *Capitalismes et capitalistes en Chine: Des origines à nos jours*, Paris: Perrin.

Bergsten, C.F., Bates, G., Lardy, N. and Mitchell, D. (2006) *China: The Balance Sheet. What the World Needs to Know about the Emerging Superpower*, New York: Public Affairs.

Bergsten, C.F., Freeman, C., Lardy, N. and Mitchell, D. (2009) *China's Rise: Challenges and Opportunities*, Washington, DC: Peterson Institute for International Economics, Center for Strategic and International Studies.

Bihr, A. (2007) *La novlangue néolibérale: La rhétorique du fétichisme capitaliste*, Lausanne: Page Deux.

Bishop, M., Kay, J. and Mayer, C. (eds) (1995) *The Regulatory Challenge*, Oxford: Oxford University Press.

Blanden, J. (2005) *Essays on Intergenerational Mobility and Its Variation over Time, Place and Family Structure*, PhD thesis, University of London.

Blanden, J., Gregg, P. and Machin, S. (2005) 'Educational inequality and intergenerational mobility', in Machin, S. and Vignoles, A. (eds), *What's the Good Education? The Economics of Education in the United Kingdom*, Princeton, NJ: Princeton University Press.

Blanden, J., Gregg, P. and Machin, S. (2005) *Intergenerational Mobility in Europe and North America*, a report supported by the Sutton Trust, London: Sutton Trust, April.

Blumenthal, D. and Hsiao, W. (2005) 'Privatization and its discontents: the evolving Chinese health care system', *New England Journal of Medicine*, vol. 353, no. 11, September, pp. 1165–1170.

Bolgiani, Iva, (2002) *L'application des nouvelles méthodes de gestion publique dans les secteurs sanitaire et hospitalier: risques et opportunités*, Muri (Switzerland): Publications of the Swiss Society for Health Policy, no. 66.

Bouvard, F., Dohrmann, T. and Lovegrove, N. (2009) 'The case for government reform now', *McKinsey Quarterly*, no. 3, pp. 1–13.

Bowles, S., Durlauf, S.N. and Hoff, K. (eds) (2006) *Poverty Traps*, New York: Russel Sage Foundation.

Bradshaw, J., and Chen, J.-R. (1996) 'Poverty in the UK: a comparison with nineteen other countries', Luxembourg Income Study Working Paper Series, no. 147, October.

Braha, D., Stacey, B. and Bar-Yam, Y. (2011) 'Corporate competition: a self-organized network', *Social Networks*, no. 33, pp. 219–30, available at http://necsi.edu/affiliates/braha/Journal_Version_SON_Braha.pdf, accessed 30 October 2011.

Brandolini, A. and Smeeding, T.M. (2007) 'Inequality patterns in Western-type democracies: cross-country differences and time changes', LIS Working Paper no. 458, April.

Brandolini, A., Magri, S. and Smeeding, T.M. (2010) 'Asset-based measurement of poverty', *Journal of Policy Analysis and Management*, vol. 29, no. 2, pp. 267–284.

Braudel, F. (1969) *Ecrits sur l'histoire*, Paris: Flammarion (English translation: *On History*, Chicago: Chicago University Press, 1992).

Braudel, F. (1979) *Afterthoughts on Material Civilization and Capitalism* (The Johns Hopkins Symposia in Comparative History), Baltimore, MD: Johns Hopkins University Press (French edition: *La dynamique du capitalisme*, Paris, Flammarion, 1985).

Braudel, F. (1979) *Civilisation matérielle, économie et capitalisme (XVe–XVIIIe siècle)*, Paris: A. Colin (Edition Livre de poche), *vol. 1: Les structures du quotidien; vol. 2:*

Les jeux de l'échange; vol. 3: Le temps du monde (English translation: *Civilization and Capitalism: 15th–18th Century, vol. 1: The Structure of Everyday Life; vol. 2: The Wheels of Commerce; vol. 3: The Perspective of the World*, Berkeley: University of California Press, 1992).

Brewer, M., Goodman, A., Muriel, A. and Sibieta, L. (2007) *Poverty and Inequality in the UK*, London: Institute of Fiscal Studies.

Brixi, H., Mu, Y., Targa, B. and Hipgrave, D. (2011) 'Equity and public governance in health system reform: challenges and opportunities for China', World Bank, Policy Research Working Paper 5530, January.

Buckley Ebrey, P. (ed.) (1999) *The Cambridge Illustrated History of China*, Cambridge: Cambridge University Press.

Buschor, E. (1994) 'Introduction: from advanced public accounting via performance measurement to new public management', in Buschor, E. and Schedler, K. (eds), *Perspectives on Performance Management and Public Sector Accounting*, Bern: Haupt.

Canfora, L. (2006) *La democrazia. Storia di un'ideologia*, Bari, Laterza, 2004 (English translation: *Democracy in Europe: A History of an Ideology*, Oxford: Wiley-Blackwell (French translation: *La démocratie. Histoire d'une idéologie*, Paris: Seuil, 2006).

Canfora, L. (2008) *Exporter la liberté: Echec d'un mythe*, Paris: Ed. Desjonquères.

Canfora, L. (2003) *L'imposture démocratique: Du procès de Socrate à l'élection de G.W. Bush*, Paris, Flammarion.

Cao, T.Y. (ed.) (2005) *The Chinese Model of Modern Development*, London: Routledge.

Cartier, M. (ed.) (2004) *Giuseppe Castiglione dit Lang Shining, 1688–1766, Jésuite italien et peintre chinois*, Paris: Favre.

Chang, G.G. (2001) *The Coming Collapse of China*, New York: Random House.

Chang, H.-J. (2003) *Globalization, Economic Development and the Role of the State*, New York: Zed Books.

Chang, H.-J. (2003) *Kicking Away the Ladder: Development Strategy in Historical Perspective*, London: Anthem Press.

Chang, H.-J. (2008) *Bad Samaritans: The Myth of Free Trade and the Secret History of Capitalism*, New York: Bloomsbury.

Chang, H.-J. and Grabel, I. (2004) *Reclaiming Development: An Alternative Economic Policy Manual*, New York: Zed Books.

Chang, H.-J. (ed.) (2007) *Institutional Change and Economic Development*, Tokyo: United National University Press.

Chang, H.-J. (ed.) (2003) *Rethinking Development Economics*, London: Anthem Press.

Chen, J. and Dickson, B.J. (2008) 'Allies of the state: democratic support and regime support among China's private entrepreneurs', *China Quarterly*, vol. 196, December, pp. 780–804.

Cheng, L. (2009) 'China's new think tanks: where officials, entrepreneurs, and scholars interact', *China Leadership Monitor*, no. 29, available at http://www.hoover.org/publications/china-leadership-monitor, accessed 20 October 2009.

Cheng, L. (2011–12) 'China's midterm jockeying: gearing up for 2012', four articles published by the *China Leadership Monitor*, nos. 31 (February 2010), 32 (May 2010), 33 (June 2010) and 34 (Spring 2011), available at http://www.hoover.org/publications/china-leadership-monitor, accessed 15 September 2011.

Chi, F. (2000) *Reform Determines Future of China*, Beijing: Foreign Language Press.

Chi, F. (2000) *China's Economic Reform at the Turn of the Century*, Beijing: Foreign Language Press.

Chi, F. (2008) *Starting Point: Thirty Years of Reform in China*, Beijing: Foreign Language Press.

Chi-Man, W., Hiao, W., Meng, Q., Chen, W. and Sun, X. (2010) 'Realignment of incentives for health-care providers in China', *The Lancet*, vol. 375, no. 9720, 27 March, pp. 1120–1130.
Chieng, A. (2006) *La pratique de la Chine*, Paris: Grasset.
Chow, G.C. (2002) *China's Economic Transformation*, Oxford: Blackwell.
Chow, G.C. (2010) *Interpreting China's Economy*, Singapore: World Scientific.
Crettaz, E. and Bonoli, G. (2010) 'World of working poverty: cross-national variation in the mechanisms that lead poverty among workers', Luxembourg Income Study, Working Paper no. 539, July.
Christensen, T. and Laegreid, P. (2007) *Transcending new public management: the transformation of public sector reform*, Aldershot (UK): Ashgate.
Cinalli, M. and Giugni, M. (2010) 'Welfare states, political opportunities, and the claim-making in the field of unemployment politics', in Giugni, M. (ed.), *The Contentious Politics of Unemployment in Europe: Welfare States and Political Opportunities*, Houndmills: Palgrave.
Crozier, M. (2009) *Le phénomène bureaucratique*, Paris: Seuil, 1964 (English translation: *The Bureaucratic Phenomenon*, with an introduction by Erhard Friedberg, New Brunswick, NJ: Transaction Publishers).
Cui, Z. (1997) 'Privatization and consolidation of democratic regimes: an analysis and an alternative', *Journal of International Affairs*, vol. 50, no. 2, Winter, pp. 675–692.
Cui, Z. (2005) 'Liberal socialism and the future of China: a petty bourgeois manifesto', in Cao, T.Y. (ed.), *The Chinese Model of Modern Development*, London Routledge.
Cui, Z. (2006) 'How to comprehend today's China', *Contemporary Chinese Thought*, vol. 37, no. 4, pp. x–xx (translated from the Chinese original published in *Dushu* [Reading], no. 3., March 2004, pp. 3–9).
Cui, Z. (2011) 'Partial intimations of the coming whole: the Chongqing experiment in light of the theories of Henry George, James Meade, and Antonio Gramsci', *Modern China*, vol. 37, no. 6, pp. 646–660.
Desai, M. (2002) *Marx's Revenge: The Resurgence of Capitalism and the Death of Statist Socialism*, London: Verso.
Dickson, B.J. (2003) *Red Capitalists in China: The Party, Private Entrepreneurs, and Prospects for Political Change*, Cambridge: Cambridge University Press.
Dickson, B.J. (2008) *Wealth into Power: The Communist Party's Embrace of China's Private Sector*, New York: Cambridge University Press.
Dickson, B.J. (2011) 'No "Jasmine" for China', *Current History*, September, pp. 211–216.
Dilulio, J.J. Jr. (ed.) (1994) *Deregulating the Public Service: Can Government Be Improved?*, Washington, DC: Brookings Institution.
Dirlik, A. (2008) 'Introduction', *Boundary 2*, no. 2 (special number dedicated to China), pp. 1–13.
Dirlik, A. and Zhang, X. (eds) (2000) *Postmodernism and China*, Durham, NC: Duke University Press.
Dollar, D. (n.d.) 'Remarkable progress, remaining vulnerability among China's poor', World Bank site, http://web.worldbank.org, accessed 18 May 2009.
Domberger, S. (1998) *The Contracting Organization: A Strategic Guide to Outsourcing*, New York: Oxford University Press.
Domenighetti, G.-F., D'Avanzo, B. and Bisig, B. (1999) *Health Effects of Job Insecurity*, Lausanne: HEC.
Dowding, K. (1995) *The Civil Service*, London: Routledge.
Economic Policy Institute (various years) *The State of Working America*, Washington, DC: Economic Policy Institute, available at http://epinet.org, accessed 20 January 2012.

Elder, N. and Page, E. (2006) *Accountability and Control in Next Steps Agencies*, London: Palgrave Macmillan.
Esping-Andersen, G. (1990) *The Three Worlds of Welfare Capitalism*, Princeton, NJ: Princeton University Press.
Esping-Andersen, G. (1996) *Welfare States in Transition*, London: Sage.
Fairbank, J.K. and Goldman, M. (2006) *China: A New History* (second enlarged edition), Cambridge, MA: Harvard University Press.
Farrell, D., Gersch, U.A. and Stephenson, E. (2008) 'The value of China's emerging middle class', *McKinsey Quarterly*, Special Edition, pp. 62–69.
Fenby, J. (2008) *History of Modern China. The Fall and Rise of a Great Power: 1850–2008*, London: Penguin Books.
Ferlie, E., Ashburner, L., Fitzgerald, L. and Pettigrew, A. (1996) *The New Public Management in Action*, Oxford: Oxford University Press.
Ferrie, J.E. (2001) 'Is job insecurity harmful to health?', *Journal of the Royal Society of Medicine*, vol. 94, February, pp. 71–76.
Fewsmith, J. (2001) *China since Tiananmen: The Politics of Transition*, Cambridge: Cambridge University Press (second edition, revised and expanded, 2008).
Fewsmith, J. (2003) 'Where do correct ideas come from? The Party school, key think tanks, and the intellectuals', in Finkelstein, D.M. and Kivlehan, M. (eds), *China's Leadership in the 21st Century: The Rise of the Fourth Generation*, New York: M.E. Sharpe.
Finkelstein, D.M. and Kivlehan, M. (eds) (2003) *China's Leadership in the 21st Century: The Rise of the Fourth Generation*, New York: M.E. Sharpe.
Flora, P. (1986) *Growth to Limits: The Western European Welfare States since World War II*, Berlin: De Gruyter.
Forster, J.B. and Magdoff, F. (2009) *The Great Financial Crisis: Causes and Consequences*, New York: Monthly Review Press.
Francis, J. (1993) *The Politics of Regulation: A Comparative Perspective*, Oxford: Blackwell.
Freeman, R.B. (1996) 'Why so many young American men commit crimes and what might we do about it?', *Journal of Economic Perspectives*, vol. 10, no. 1, pp. 25–42.
Frenkiel, E. (2011) 'From scholar to official: Cui Zhiyuan and Chongqing city's local experimental policy', interview with Cui Zhiyuan, *La vie des idées (Books & Ideas)*, 25 January, p. 3, available at http://www.booksandideas.net, accessed 15 May 2011.
Friedman, M. (1982) *Capitalism and Freedom* (second edition), Chicago: University of Chicago Press (first edition, 1962).
Fukuyama, F. (1992) *The End of History and the Last Man*, New York: Free Press.
Galbraith, J.K. (2008) *The Predator State*, New York: Free Press.
Galimberti, U. (2009) *I miti del nostro tempo*, Milan: Feltrinelli.
Garnaut, R. and Song, L. (eds) (2004) *China's Third Economic Transformation: The Rise of the Private Economy*, London: Routledge.
Gernet, J. (1991) *Chine et christianisme: La première confrontation* (edition revue et corrigée), Paris: Gallimard.
Giddens, A. (1998) *The Third Way: The Renewal of Social Democracy*, Cambridge: Polity Press.
Giddens, A. (2000) *The Third Way and Its Critics*, Cambridge: Polity Press.
Gilley, B. and Holbig, H. (2009) 'The debate on Party legitimacy in China: a mixed quantitative/qualitative analysis', *Journal of Contemporary China*, vol. 18, no. 59, March, pp. 339–358.

Goodman, A. and Webb, S. (1995) *The Distribution of UK Household Expenditure, 1979–1992*, London: Institute of Fiscal Studies, available at http://www1.ifs.org.uk/, accessed 5 July 1996.

Goodman, A., Johnson, P. and Webb, S. (1997) *Inequality in the UK*, Oxford: Oxford University Press.

Goody, J. (2006) 'The theft of "capitalism": Braudel and global comparison', in Goody, J., *The Theft of History*, Cambridge: Cambridge University Press.

Gore, A. (1993) *The Gore Report on Reinventing Government*, New York: Times Books.

Gore, A. (1994) *Businesslike Government: Lessons Learned from America's Best Companies*, Washington, DC: US Government Printing Office.

Gouldner, A.A. (1953) *Patterns of Industrial Bureaucracy*, Glencoe, IL: Free Press.

Guidotti, M. (2010) *The Good Governance Agenda and Public Administration Reforms: An Institutional Political Analysis. The Case of the Commune Level One-Stop Programme in Vietnam*, PhD thesis, University of Geneva.

Guttmacher Institute (2010) *U.S. Teenage Pregnancy, Births and Abortions: National and State Trends by Race and Ethnicity*, January, available at http://www.guttmacher.org/, accessed 4 October 2010.

Halper, S. (2010) *The Beijing Consensus: How China's Authoritarian Model Will Dominate the Twenty-First Century*, New York: Basic Books.

Hall, P.H. and Soskice, D. (eds) (2001) *Varieties of Capitalism: The Institutional Foundations of Comparative Advantage*, Oxford: Oxford University Press.

Harvey, D. (1990) *The Condition of Postmodernity*, Oxford: Blackwell.

Harvey, D. (2004) *A Brief History of Neoliberalism*, Oxford: Oxford University Press.

Harvey, D. (2010) *The Enigma of Capital and the Crises of Capitalism*, London: Profile Books.

Hayami, Y. (2003) 'From the Washington Consensus to the post-Washington Consensus: retrospect and prospect', *Asian Development Review*, vol. 20, no. 2, pp. 40–65.

He, L. (2008) 'China's New Left and its impact on political liberalization', EAI Background Brief no. 401, 28 August.

He, L. (2010) 'Debating China's economic reform: New Leftists v. liberals', *Journal of Chinese Political Science*, no. 15, pp. 1–23.

He, P. (2002) *China's Search for Modernity: Cultural Discourse in the Late 20th Century*, Oxford: Palgrave Macmillan.

Henry, N. (1995) *Public Administration and Public Affairs*, Englewood Cliffs, NJ, Prentice-Hall.

Hobsbawm, E. (2011) *How to Change the World: Tales of Marx and Marxism*, London: Little, Brown.

Holbig, H. (2009) 'Remaking the CCP's ideology: determinants, progress, and limits under Hu Jintao', *Journal of Current Chinese Affairs*, no. 3, pp. 35–61.

Holbig, H. and Gilley, B. (2010) 'Reclaiming legitimacy in China', *Politics and Policy*, vol. 38, no. 3, pp. 395–422 (first published as 'In search of legitimacy in post-revolutionary China: bringing ideology and governance back in', German Institute of Global and Area Studies, Working Paper no. 127, March 2010).

Hood, C. (1995) 'The New Public Management in the 1980s: variations on a theme', *Accounting, Organization and Society*, vol. 20, no. 2/3, pp. 93–109.

Hood, C. (1995) 'Contemporary public management: a new global paradigm?', *Public Policy and Administration*, vol. 10, no. 2, pp. 104–117.

Hsü, I.C.Y. (1995) *The Rise of Modern China*, New York: Oxford University Press.

Hsu, S.P., Wu, Y.S. and Zhao, S. (eds) (2011) *In Search of China's Development Model: Beyond the Beijing Consensus*, London: Routledge.

Hu, A. (2004) *Great Transformations in China: Challenges and Opportunities*, Beijing: Tsinghua University.

Hu, A. (2004) *China's New Development Strategy* (third edition, in Chinese), Zhejiang: People's Publishing House of Zhejiang.

Hu, A. (2007) *Economic and Social Transformation in China*, London: Routledge.

Hu, A. (2007) 'China's economic growth and poverty reduction (1978–2002)', in Hu, A., *Economic and Social Transformation in China*, London: Routledge.

Hu, A. (2007) 'China's macro-economy and health', in Hu, A., *Economic and Social Transformation in China*, London: Routledge.

Hu, A. (2007) 'Health insecurity: The biggest challenge to human security in China', in Hu, A., *Economic and Social Transformation in China*, London: Routledge.

Hu, A. (2007) 'Corruption: an enormous black hole: public exposure of the economic costs of corruption', in Hu, A., *Economic and Social Transformation in China*, London: Routledge.

Hu, A. (2010) 'Predictions for the next five years', *Beijing Review*, vol. 53, no. 37, pp. 28–31.

Hu, A. (2011) *China in 2020: A New Type of Superpower*, Washington, DC: Brookings Institution.

Hu, A. (2011) *Roadmap of China's Rise*, London: Routledge.

Hu, A. (2011) *China by 2030: A Changing World towards Common Prosperity* (in Chinese), Beijing: Renmin University Press.

Hu, A. and Yi, W. et al. (1992) *Survival and Development: A Study of China's Long Term Development*, Beijing: Science Press.

Hu, A. and Ping, Z. (1991) *China's Population Development*, Beijing: China's Science and Technology Press.

Hu, A. and Zhao, L. (2006) 'The emergence of informal sector and the development of informal economy in China's transition: a historical perspective (1952–2004)', paper presented at the World Bank Annual Meeting, ABCDE (Annual Bank Conference on Development Economics), Tokyo, 29–30 May, kindly provided by authors.

Hu, A. and Zhao, L. (2006) 'Informal economy and development growth in the urban areas of China', *Reports of National Conditions*, Special Edition no. 6, 26 June (in Chinese), Centre for China Studies, Tsinghua University.

Hu, S. (chief editor) (1994) *A Concise History of the Communist Party of China*, Beijing: Foreign Language Press.

Huang, J.-T., Kuo, C.-C. and Kao, A.-P. (2003) 'The inequality of regional economic development in China between 1991 and 2001', *Journal of Chinese and Business Studies*, vol. 1, no. 3, pp. 273–285.

Huang, P.C.C. (2011) 'Chongqing: equitable development driven by a "third hand"?', *Modern China*, vol. 37, no. 6, pp. 569–622.

Husson, M. (2011) 'Les inégalités à l'échelle mondiale', *Chronique internationale de l'IRES*, no. 130, May, pp. 55–63.

Irvine, I. and Xu, K. (2002) 'Crime, punishment and the measurement of poverty in the United States, 1979–1997', LIS Working Paper no. 333, November.

Inglehart, R. (1997) *Modernization and Postmodernization: Cultural, Economic, and Political Change in 43 Societies*, Princeton, NJ: Princeton University Press.

Iversen, T. and Stephens, J.D. (2008) 'Partisan politics, the welfare state, and three worlds of human capital formation', *Comparative Political Studies*, vol. 41, no. 4/5, pp. 600–637.

Joshua, I. (2009) *La grande crise du XXI siècle: Une analyse marxiste*, Paris: La Découverte.
Joyce, R., Muriel, A., Phillips, D. and Sibieta, L. (2010) *Poverty and Inequality in the UK*, London: Institute of Fiscal Studies.
Jullien, F. (1989) *Procès ou création: Une introduction à la pensée chinoise*, Paris: Seuil.
Jullien, F. (1991) *Eloge de la fadeur*, Paris: Ed. Philippe Picquier.
Jullien, F. (1992) *La propension des choses: Pour une histoire de l'efficacité en Chine*, Paris: Seuil.
Jullien, F. (1996) *Traité de l'efficacité*, Paris: Grasset.
Jullien, F. (2005) *Conférence sur l'efficacité*, Paris: Presses Universitaires de France.
Jullien, F. (2009) *Les transformations silencieuses*, Paris: Grasset.
Keidel, A. (2007) 'The causes and impact of Chinese regional inequalities in income and well-being', Carnegie Endowment for International Peace, December.
Keidel, A. (2008) 'China's economic rise: fact and fiction', Carnegie Endowment for International Peace, July.
Kelsey, J. (1995) *Economic Fundamentalism*, London: Pluto Press (published in New Zealand as *The New Zealand Experiment: A World Model for Structural Adjustment?*, Auckland: Auckland University Press, 1995).
Kelsey, J. (1999) *Reclaiming the Future: New Zealand and the Global Economy*, Wellington, NZ: Bridget Williams Books.
Kelsey, J. (2008) *Serving Whose Interests? The Political Economy of Trade in Services Agreements*, New York: Routledge Cavendish.
Kenichi, O. (1995) *The End of the Nation State: How Capital, Corporations, Consumers and Communication Are Reshaping Global Markets*, New York: Free Press.
Kennedy, S. (2005) *The Business of Lobbying in China*, Cambridge, MA: Harvard University Press.
Kester, I.-H., Painter, C. and Barnes, C. (1996) *Management in the Public Sector*, London: Thomson.
Kettl, D.F. (1993) *Sharing Power: Public Governance and Private Markets*, Washington, DC: Brookings Institutions.
Kettl, D.F. and Dilulio, J.J. (eds) (1995) *Inside the Reinvention Machine: Appraising Governmental Reform*, Washington, DC: Brookings Institution.
Kivimäki, M., Vahtera, J., Pentti, J. and Ferrie, J.E. (2000) 'Factors underlying the effect of organizational downsizing on health employees: longitudinal cohort study', *British Medical Journal*, vol. 320, April, pp. 971–975.
Krugman, P. (1992) 'The rich, the Right and the facts, deconstructing the income distribution debate', *American Prospect*, Fall, pp. 19–31, available at http://epn.org/prospect.html, accessed 3 July 1996.
Krugman, P. (1994) *Peddling Prosperity*, New York: W.W. Norton & Co. (particularly 'The attack on Keynes', pp. 23–54, 'The budget deficit', pp. 151–169, and 'In the long run Keynes is still alive', pp. 197–220).
Lane, J.-E. (1997) *Public Sector Reform, Rationale, Trends and Problems*, London: Sage.
Lardy, N.R. (1998) *China's Unfinished Economic Revolution*, Washington, DC: Brookings Institution Press.
Lardy, N.R. (2002) *Integrating China into the Global Economy*, Washington, DC: Brookings Institution Press.
Lempert, D. (1997) 'Holding accountable the powers that be: protecting our integrity and the public we serve', *Public Administration Review*, vol. 57, no. 4, July/August, pp. ii–v.
Leys, C. and Player, S. (2011) *The Plot against the NHS*, Pontypool, UK: Merlin Press.
Li, M. (2008) *The Rise of China and the Demise of the Capitalist World Economy*, New York: Monthly Review Press.

Li, M. (2011) 'The rise of the working class and the future of the Chinese Revolution', *Monthly Review*, vol. 63, no. 2, June, available at http://monthlyreview.org, accessed 15 July 2011.

Li, X. (2010) 'China model and dream of Chongqing', draft paper for a conference given in Chongqing, 18 September, kindly provided by the author.

Lieberthal, K. (1995) *Governing China: From Revolution through Reform*, New York: Norton.

Light, P.C. (1997) *The Tides of Reform: Making Government Work 1945–1995*, New Haven, CT: Yale University Press.

Lin, Y.-M. (2001) *Between Politics and Markets, Firms, Competition, and Institutional Change in Post-Mao China*, Cambridge: Cambridge University Press.

Lister, J. (2008) *The NHS after 60: For Patients or Profit?*, London: Middlesex University.

Luo, X. and Nong, Z. (2008) 'Rising income inequality in China: a race to the top', World Bank, East Asia and Pacific Region, Poverty Reduction and Economic Management Department, Policy Research Paper, no. 4700, August.

Lynn, L.E. (1992) 'Dividing the job: intergovernmental dimension', *Public Manager*, vol. 21, no. 3, Fall, pp. 7–10.

Lynn, L.E. (1996) 'The new public management as an international phenomenon: questions of an American skeptic', paper prepared for the conference on the New Public Management in International Perspective, St. Gallen, July.

Lynn, L.E. (1996) *Public Management as Art, Science, and Profession*, Chatham, NJ: Chatham House.

Lynn, L.E. (2006) *Public Management: Old and New*, New York: Routledge.

Ma, J. and Zhibin, Z. (2009) 'Remaking the Chinese administrative state since 1978: the double-movements perspective', *Korean Journal of Policy Studies*, vol. 23, no. 2, pp. 225–252.

McIntyre, R.S., Gardner, M., Wilkins, R.J. and Phillips, R. (2011) 'Corporate taxpayers & corporate tax dodgers 2008–10', a joint project of Citizens for Tax Justice and the Institute on Taxation and Economic Policy, Washington, DC, November.

Magdoff, F. and Yates, M.D. (2009) *The ABC of the Economic Crisis*, New York: Monthly Review Press.

Majone, G. (ed.) (1990) *Deregulation or Re-regulation? Regulatory Reform in Europe and in the United States*, London: Pinter.

Meade, J.E. (1993) *Liberty, Equality and Efficiency*, New York: New York University Press.

Meiskins Wood, E. (1995) *Democracy against Capitalism*, Cambridge: Cambridge University Press.

Meiskins Wood, E. (2002) *The Origins of Capitalism* (revised and expanded edition), London: Verso.

Meiskins Wood, E. (2003) *Empire of Capital*, London: Verso.

Merton, R. (1936) 'The unanticipated consequences of purposive social action', *American Sociological Review*, vol. 1, pp. 894–904.

Mierzejewski, D. (2009) 'Not to oppose but to rethink: the New Left discourse on the Chinese reforms', *Journal of Contemporary Eastern Asia*, vol. 8, no. 1, pp. 15–29.

Mishel, L., Bernstein, J. and Schmitt, J. (1999) *The State of Working America 1998–99*, Ithaca, NY: Economic Policy Institute.

Mishel, L., Bernstein, J. and Allegretto, S. (2007) *The State of Working America 2006–7*, Ithaca, NY: Economic Policy Institute.

Moe, R.C. (1994) 'The reinventing government exercise: misinterpreting the problem, misjudging the consequences', *Public Administration Review*, vol. 54, no. 2, March–April, pp. 111–122.

Moe, R.C. and Gilmour, R.S. (1995) 'Rediscovering principles of public administration: the neglected foundation of public law', *Public Administration Review*, vol. 55, no. 2, March–April, pp. 135–144.

Naughton, B.J. (2007) *The Chinese Economy: Transition and Growth*, Cambridge, MA: MIT Press.

Naughton, B.J. (2009–10) 'The turning point: first steps toward a post-crisis economy', *China Leadership Monitor*, no. 31, Winter, available at http://www.hoover.org/publications/china-leadership-monitor, accessed 15 May 2010.

Naughton, B.J. (2010) 'Reading the NPC: post-crisis economic dilemmas of the Chinese leadership', *China Leadership Monitor*, no. 32, Spring, available at http://www.hoover.org/publications/china-leadership-monitor, accessed 19 August 2010.

Needham, J. (1954–2004) *Science and Civilisation in China*, 7 volumes, New York: Cambridge University Press.

Needham, J. (1969) *The Grand Titration: Science and Society in East and West*, London: Allen & Unwin (French translation: *La science chinoise et l'Occident*, Paris: Seuil, 1973).

New Zealand, Ministry of Health (2008) 'The New Zealand health and disability system: organizations and responsibilities', November.

Nolan, P. (2001) *China and the Global Business Revolution*, Houndmills, UK: Palgrave.

Nolan, P. (2001) *China and the Global Economy*, Houndmills, UK: Palgrave.

Nolan, P. (2004) *Transforming China: Globalization, Transition and Development*, London: Anthem Press.

Nolan, P. (2004) *China at the Crossroads*, Cambridge, UK: Polity Press.

Ocampo, J.A., Spiegel, S. and Stiglitz, J.E. (2008) 'Capital market liberalization and development', in Ocampo, J.A. and Stiglitz, J. (eds), *Capital Market Liberalization and Development*, Oxford: Oxford University Press.

OECD (1995) 'Gestion publique', Etudes hors série no. 10, Paris.

OECD (2008) 'Public–private partnerships: in pursuit of risk sharing and value for money', Paris.

OECD (2008) 'Growing unequal? Income distribution and poverty in OECD countries', Paris, October.

OECD (2009) 'OECD rural policy reviews: China', Paris.

OECD (2010) 'Employment outlook 2009', Paris.

Ormerod, P. (1994) *The Death of Economics*, London: Faber and Faber.

Osborne, D. and Gaebler, T. (1993) *Reinventing Government: How the Entrepreneurial Spirit Is Transforming the Public Sector*, New York: Plume.

Pan, J., Ma, H. and Zhang, Y. (2011) *Green Economy and Green Jobs in China: Current Status and Potentials for 2020*, Washington, DC: Worldwatch Institute, Worldwatch Report 185.

Peerenboom, R. (ed.) (2010) *Judicial Independence in China: Lessons for Global Rule of Law Promotion*, Cambridge: Cambridge University Press.

Petrella, R. (1995) 'Les nouvelles Tables de la Loi', *Le Monde Diplomatique*, October.

Pirazzoli-T'Serstevens, M. (2007) *Giuseppe Castiglione, 1688–1766, peintre et architecte à la cour de Chine*, Paris: Thalia.

Polanyi, K. (2001) *The Great Transformation: The Political and Economic Origins of Our Time*, with an introduction by Joseph E. Stiglitz and a new introduction by Fred Block, Boston: Beacon Press (first edition, 1944).

Pollock, A.M. (2004) *NHS plc: The Privatization of Our Health Care*, London: Verso.

Prins, N. (2011) 'Debt from bailouts didn't pan out', 10 August, available at http://www.nomiprins.com/articles/, accessed 27 October 2011.

Pye, L.W. (1968) *Aspects of Political Development*, Boston: Little, Brown & Co.
Rachman, G. (2008) 'Conservatism overshoots its limit', *Financial Times*, 6 October.
Ramo, J.C. (2004) *The Beijing Consensus*, London: Foreign Policy Centre.
Ran, Y. (2005) *L'éducation à l'environnement en Chine*, Master's dissertation, University of Geneva.
Rao, P.K. (2008) 'Letter: comment on Stiglitz's Turn Left for Sustainable Growth', *Economists' Voice*, November, available at http://www.bepress.com/ev, accessed 30 November 2008.
Ren, B. and Liu, J. (2009) 'Local government costs and doctors' pay are among the unfinished issues for health care reformers, whose task appears far from done', *Caijing Magazine Online*, 19 March, available at http://www.english.cajing.com.cn, accessed 4 May 2009.
Riedel, J., Jin, J. and Gao, J. (2007) *How China Grows*, Princeton, NJ: Princeton University Press.
Roubini, N. and Mihn, S. (2010) *Crisis Economics: A Crash Course in the Future of Finance*, New York: Penguin.
Selznick, P. (1949) *TVA and the Grass Roots*, Berkeley: University of California Press.
Sen, A. (2009) 'Capitalism beyond the crisis', *New York Review of Books*, vol. 56, no. 5, 26 March, available at http://www.nybooks.com, accessed 27 April 2009.
Shambaugh, D. (2008) 'Training China's political elite: the Party School system', *China Quarterly*, vol. 196, December, pp. 827–844.
Shen, S. (2007) 'The response of Chinese intellectuals to the US War on Terror', *Journal of Chinese Political Science*, vol. 12, no. 3, pp. 238–280.
Shipler, D.K. (2004) *The Working Poor: Invisible America*, New York: Knopf.
Sigurdson, J. and Palonka, K. (2009) 'Innovative city in west China Chongqing', Stockholm School of Economics (EIJS), Working Paper 239, February.
Simon, H. (1945) *Administrative Behaviour: A Study of Decision-Making Processes in Administrative Organization*, New York: Free Press (third reviewed and enlarged edition, 1976).
Smeeding, T. (2002) 'Globalisation, inequality and the rich countries of the G-20: evidence from the Luxembourg Income Study (LIS)', July, available at http://www.LIS.org, accessed 7 March 2003.
Smeeding, T. (2006) 'Poor people in rich nations: the United States in comparative perspective', *Journal of Economic Perspectives*, vol. 20, no. 1, pp. 69–90.
Smeeding, T. (2001) 'US poverty in a cross-national context', LIS Working Paper no. 244, United Nations Human Development Report.
Sorman, G. (2008) *The Empire of Lies: The Truth about China in the Twenty-First Century*, New York: Encounter Books (first published in French: *L'année du coq: chinois et rebelles*, Paris: Fayard, 2006).
Sorman, G. (2009) *Economics Does Not Lie: A Defense of the Free Market in a Time of Crisis*, New York: Encounter Books (first published in French: *L'économie ne ment pas*, Paris: Fayard, 2008).
Sorman, G. (2010) 'Good-by to Europe's cradle-to-grave gravy', *Shanghai Daily*, 19 October (also published in *Project Syndicate* under the title 'The welfare state, RIP', *Project Syndicate*, 8 October 2010, available at http://www.project-syndicate.org, accessed 8 November 2010; and in Sorman's blog in the Swiss weekly *L'Hebdo*, 'La mort annoncée de l'Etat Providence', 14 October 2010).
Stiglitz, J.E. (2002) *Globalization and Its Discontents*, New York: W.W. Norton.

Stiglitz, J.E. (2005) 'Post Washington consensus', Columbia University, Initiative for Policy Dialogue, Working Paper Series, available at http://www.gsb.columbia.edu/ipd/, accessed 6 June 2009.

Stiglitz, J.E. (2006) *Making Globalization Work: The Next Steps to Global Justice*, London: Penguin.

Stiglitz, J.E. (2008) 'Turn left for sustainable growth', *Economists' Voice*, September, http://www.bepress.com/ev, accessed 28 October 2008.

Stiglitz, J.E. (2008) 'The triumphant return of John Maynard Keynes', *Economists' Voice*, Project Syndicate, Berkeley Electronic Press, December, available at http://www.project-sydicate.org, accessed 6 January 2009.

Stiglitz, J.E. (2009) *Around the World with Joseph Stiglitz: Perils and Promises of Globalization*, documentary film by the author.

Stiglitz, J.E. (2010) *Freefall: America, Free Markets, and the Sinking of the World Economy*, New York: Norton.

Stiglitz, J.E. (2010) *The Stiglitz Report: Reforming the International Monetary and Financial Systems in the Wake of the Global Crisis*, New York: New Press.

Stiglitz, J.E. (2011) 'Gambling with the planet', *Project Syndicate*, April, available at htpp://www.project-sydicate.org, accessed 29 August 2011.

Stiglitz, J.E. (2011) 'The IMF's switch in time', *Project Syndicate*, May, available at http://www.project-sydicate.org, accessed 29 August 2011.

Stiglitz, J.E. (2011) 'The ideological crisis of Western capitalism', *Project Syndicate*, July, available at http://www.project-sydicate.org, accessed 29 August 2011.

Stiglitz, J.E. (2011) 'A contagion of bad ideas', *Project Syndicate*, August, available at http://www.project-sydicate.org, accessed 29 August 2011.

Suleiman, E. (2003) *Dismantling Democratic States*, Princeton, NJ: Princeton University Press.

Sun, T. (1994) *The Art of War*, Boulder, CO: Westview Press.

Sverke, M., Hellgren, J. and Näswall, K. (2006) 'Job insecurity: a literature review', National Institute for Working Life and Swedish Trade Unions in Co-operation, Report no. 1.

Talbot-Smith, A. and Pollock, A.M. (2006) *The New NHS: A Guide*, London: Routledge.

Tiemann, A. (2006) 'Stability of Gosta Esping-Andersen's The Three Worlds of Welfare Capitalism', Luxembourg Income Study Working Paper Series, no. 449, September.

Todd, E. (2008) *Après la démocratie*, Paris: Gallimard.

United Nations Development Programme (UNDP) (1997–2008) *China Human Development Reports*, n.p.: UNDP.

UNDP (2010) *China Human Development Report 2009/10: China and Sustainable Future: Towards a Low Carbon Economy and Society*, Beijing: China Publishing Group Corporation, April, commissioned by UNDP China and coordinated by Renmin University of China.

UNDP (2004–5) *Human Development Reports*, New York: UNDP.

UNDP (2006–10) *Human Development Reports*, New York: Palgrave Macmillan.

Unger, R.M. (2005) *What Should the Left Propose?*, London: Verso.

Unger, R.M. and Cui, Z. (1994) 'China in the Russian mirror', *New Left Review*, no. I/208, November, pp. 78–87.

Urio, P. (1984) *Le role politique de l'administration publique*, Lausanne: LEP.

Urio, P. (1999) 'La gestion publique au service du marché', in Hufty, M. (ed.), *La pensée comptable: Etat, néolibéralisme, nouvelle gestion publique*, Paris: Presses Universitaires de France, Collection Enjeux, Cahier de l'IUED, Genève, pp. 91–123.

Urio, P. (2000) 'Le rôle du scientifique dans la définition des stratégies de réformes', in Emery, Y. (ed.), *L'administration dans tous ses états: Réalisations et conséquences*, Lausanne: Presses Polytechniques et Universitaires Romandes, pp. 187–193.

Urio, P. (2002) 'L'avenir des contrats de prestations', in Bellanger, F., and Tanquerel, T. (eds), *Les contrats de prestation*, Geneva: Helbing & Lichtenhahn, pp. 109–130.

Urio, P. (2010) *Reconciling State, Market and Society in China: The Long March towards Prosperity*, with a foreword by Hu Angang, London: Routledge.

Urio, P. (ed.) (2010) *Public Private Partnerships: Success and Failure Factors for In-Transition Countries*, Lanham, MD: University Press of America.

Urio, P. (ed.) (1996) 'L'évaluation comme instrument d'apprentissage et de changement organisationnel: l'exemple des programmes cantonaux de promotion de la santé', report presented to the Swiss National Foundation for Scientific Research, National Programme 27.

Urio, P. and Meckx, V. (1996) *Le budget de la Confédération: Le système politique suisse face à l'équilibre des finances fédérales*, Lausanne: Editions Réalités Sociales.

Urio, P. and Bolgiani, I. (2007) 'La nuova gestione pubblica', in Meneguzzo, M., Ferrari, D., Vitta, C. and Zanolini, K. (eds), *Management pubblico in Ticino*, Milan: McGraw-Hill.

Vahtera, J., Kivimäki, M., Pentti, J., Linna, A., Virtanen, M., Virtanen P. and Ferrie, J.E. (2004) 'Organizational downsizing, sickness absence, and mortality: 10- town prospective cohort study', *British Medical Journal*, 23 February 2004, available at http://www.bmj.com, accessed 27 November 2007.

Vitali, S., Glattfelder, J.B. and Battiston, S. (n.d.) 'The network of global corporate control', University of Zurich, available at http://arxiv.org/PS_cache/arxiv/pdf/1107/1107.5728v2.pdf, accessed 30 October 2011.

Vogel, K., (1966) *Freer Markets, More Rules*, Ithaca, NY: Cornell University Press.

Wallerstein, I. (1974–80) *The Modern World System, vol. I: Capitalist Agriculture and the Origins of the European World-System in the Sixteenth Century*; *vol. II: Mercantilism and the Consolidation of the European World-Economy, 1600–1750*, New York: Academic Press.

Wallerstein, I. (1991) 'Braudel on capitalism, or everything upside down', *Journal of Modern History*, vol. 63, June, pp. 354–361.

Wallerstein, I. (2004) *World Systems Analysis: An Introduction*, Durham, NC: Duke University Press.

Wallerstein, I. (2010) 'Structural crises', *New Left Review*, no. 62, March–April, pp. 133–142.

Walmsley, R. (2008) *World Prison Population List* (eighth edition), London: King's College.

Walsh, K. (1991) *Competitive Tendering for Local Authority Services, Initial Experiences*, London: HMSO.

Walsh, K., Deakin, N., Smith, P., Spugeon, P. and Thomas, N. (1997) *Contracting for Change: Contracts in Health, Social Care, and Other Local Government Services*, Oxford: Oxford University Press.

Wang, H. (2003) *China's New Order*, Cambridge, MA: Harvard University Press.

Wang, H. (2006) 'Depoliticized politics, from East to West', *New Left Review*, no. 41, September/October, pp. 29–45.

Wang, H. (2006) 'China's New Leftist', interview with Pankaj Mishra, *New York Times*, 15 October.

Wang, H. (2009) *The End of the Revolution: China and the Limits of Modernity*, London: Verso.

Wang, H. (n.d.) 'How Tiananmen protesters led to the new market economy. China: unequal shares', available at http://christusrex.org/www1/news/hui-4-02.html, accessed 10 July 2011.
Wang, S. (2008) 'The great transformation: two-way movement in China since the 1980s' (in Chinese: 'Zhong guo she hui ke xue'), *Social Sciences in China*, no. 1, pp. 129–148 (also published as 'Great social transformation afoot in China', *China Economist*, July 2008, pp. 55–69; and, in more complete form, as 'The great transformation: the double movement in China', *Boundary 2*, vol. 35, no. 2, 2008, pp. 16–47).
Wang, S. (2010) 'China in transition', *L'Annuaire du Collège de France*, no. 109, 24 June, available at http://annuaire-cdf.revues.org/427, accessed 29 April 2011.
Wang, S. and Hu, A. (1992) 'Strengthen the role of the central government during the transition towards a market economy', (known as the report on China's state capacities) first sent to China from the US as a manuscript in and later published in Shenyang, Liaoning People Press, 1993 (in Chinese).
Wang, S. and Hu, A. (1999) *The Political Economy of Uneven Development: The Case of China*, New York: M.E. Sharpe.
Wang, X. (2007) 'Who's in first? A regional development index for the PRC', Asian Development Bank Institute, Discussion Paper no. 66, May.
Wang, Y. and Hu, A. (2007) 'Multiple forces driving China's economic development: a new analytic framework', *China & World Economy*, vol. 15, no. 3, pp. 103–120.
Weber, M. (1985) *Wirthschaft und Gesellschaft*, Tübingen: J.C.B. Mohr (first published 1956, first edition by Marianne Weber, 1922).
Weber, M. (1988) 'Die "Objectivität" sozialwissenschaftlicher und sozialpolitischer Erkenntnis', in Weber, M., *Gesammelte Aufsätze zur Wissenschaftslehre*, Tübingen: J.C.B. Mohr (English translation: 'Objectivity in social science and social policy', in Weber, M., *Methodology of Social Sciences*, New Brunswick, NJ: Transactions, 2011).
Weeks, J. (2005) 'Inequality trends in some developed OECD countries', DESA Working Paper no. 6, ST/ESA/2005/DWP/6October.
Wilkinson, R. and Pickett, K. (2009) *The Spirit Level: Why More Equal Societies Almost Always Do Better*, London: Allen Lane.
Williamson, J. (1990) *Latin American Adjustment: How Much Has Happened*, Washington, DC: Institute for International Economics.
Williamson, J. (1993) 'Democracy and the Washington Consensus', *World Development*, vol. 21, no. 8, pp. 1329–1336.
Williamson, O.E. (1975) *Markets and Hierarchies*, New York: Free Press.
Williamson, O.E. (1985) *The Economic Institutions of Capitalism*, New York: Free Press.
Wilson, W. (1887) 'The study of administration', *Political Science Quarterly*, June, pp. 197–222 (reprinted in *Political Science Quarterly*, December 1941, pp. 481–506).
Wong, C. (2011) 'The fiscal stimulus programme and public governance issues in China', *OECD Journal of Budgeting*, vol. 11, no. 3, pp. 1–21.
Woodward, D. (2010) *How Poor Is 'Poor'? Towards a Rights-Based Poverty Line*, London: New Economic Foundation.
World Bank (1997) *China 2020: Development Challenges in the New Century*, World Bank, 18 September, Report no. 17027-CHA, World Bank.
World Bank (2003) *China: Promoting Growth with Equity*, Washington, DC: World Bank.
World Bank (2005) *China: Deepening Public Service Unit Reform to Improve Service Delivery*, Beijing: Citic Publishing House.
World Bank (2008) *The World Bank Report 2008: The Challenges of a Changing World*, Washington, DC: World Bank.

World Bank (2008) 'Mid-term evaluation of China's 11th 5 Year Plan', available at http://www.worldbank.org, accessed 15 June 2009.
World Bank (2009) 'From poor areas to poor people: China's evolving poverty reduction agenda. An assessment of poverty and inequality in China', March, available at http://www.worldbank.org, accessed 5 September 2009.
World Bank (various dates) 'Quarterly update, China', available at http://www.worldbank.org/cn.
World Health Organization (2010) *World Health Statistics 2010*, Geneva: WHO.
World Watch Institute (2010) 'Renewable energy and energy efficiency in China: current status and prospects for 2020', Washington, DC, World Watch Institute, Worldwatch Report 182.
Wu, J. (2009) 'China's economy: 60 years of progress', *Caijing*, 30 September, available at http://english.caijing.com.cn/, accessed 6 October 2009.
Xu, Y. (2003) 'The debates between liberalism and the New Left in China since the 1990s', *Contemporary Chinese Thought*, vol. 34, no. 3, pp. 3–17.
Yang, Y. and Hu, A. (2008) 'Investigating regional disparities of China's human development with cluster analysis: a historical perspective', *Social Indicators Research*, no. 86, pp. 417–432.
Yip, W. and Hiao, W. (2009) 'China's health's care reform: a tentative assessment', *China Economic Review*, vol. 20, no. 4, pp. 613–619.
Yuan, Y. (2005) *La transformation des rôles de l'Etat dans la politique de la réinsertion des chômeurs en Chine*, Master's dissertation, University of Geneva.
Zakaria, F. (1997) 'The rise of illiberal democracy', *Foreign Affairs*, vol. 76, no. 6, pp. 22–43.
Zhang, Y. (2008) 'No forbidden zone in reading? Dushu and the Chinese intelligentsia', *New Left Review*, no. 49, January/February, pp. 5–26.
Zhang, Z. (2006) 'Competition or privatization: China's experience in SOE reforms', *Journal of the Washington Institute of China Studies*, vol. 1, no. 1, pp. 37–59.
Zhao, L. and Seng, L.T. (eds) (2010) *China's New Social Policy: Initiatives for a Harmonious Society*, Hackensack, NJ: World Scientific.
Zheng, Y. (2004) *Globalization and State Transformation in China*, Cambridge: Cambridge University Press.
Zhu, S. (2010) 'The party and the courts', in Peerenboom, R. (ed.), *Judicial Independence in China: Lessons for Global Rule of Law Promotion*, Cambridge: Cambridge University Press, pp. 52–68.
Zizek, S. (2009) *First as Tragedy, Then as Farce*, London: Verso.
Zufferey, N. (2008) *Introduction à la pensée chinoise*, Paris: Hachette.

Index

absolute truth 68, 69
academic institutions, management of 13
'Administration in All Its Moods: Realizations and Consequences' 18
administrative inflation 84–5
Afterthoughts on Material Civilization and Capitalism (Braudel, F.) 219n1
Alkire, Sabina 264n47
All-China Federation of Trade Unions (ACFTU) 180
Allais, Maurice 221n4
Almond, Gabriel A. 223n25
Amable, Bruno 51, 53–4, 238n121, 238n128
American Prospect (Krugman, P.) 15
An-Pang Kao 264n38
Anderlini, Jamil 273n34
Anderson, David C. 258n54
Anderson, Perry 240n147
Andresani, Gianluca 241n6
Antille, Gabrielle 242n13
Aron, Raymond 220n10
Asian crisis (1997) 79
Atkinson, A., Piketty, T. and Saez, E. 259n65
audits, generalization of 87
Australia 44, 53, 54, 57; anti-poverty effect of government spending in 125, 127; Gini indexes of disposable and market income in 120; HDI ranking of 130–3; income inequality in 115, 116, 118; inequality patterns in 121
Austria 52, 53, 54; anti-poverty effect of government spending in 126; child poverty in 128; HDI ranking of 130–3; health expenditures in 139–40; health indicators in 138; income inequality in 118; inequality patterns in 121

Baeck, Louis 230n41
Bai Shouyi 94, 251n11
Bairoch, Paul 150, 244n41, 274n41
Baran, Paul A. 231n48
Barlow, John 249n85
Barnes, Chris 249n81, 254n6
Barroso, José Manuel 272n25
Bartley, M., Sacker, A. and Clarke, P. 259n61
Battiston, Stefano 271n13
Becker, Gary 221n4
Belgium 52, 53, 54, 57; anti-poverty effect of government spending in 125, 126, 127; child poverty in 128; HDI ranking of 130–3; health expenditures in 139–40; health indicators in 138; income inequality in 115, 116, 118; inequality patterns in 121; unemployment in 113
Bell, Daniel A. 223n26, 225n9, 244n34
Bellanger, François 248n70
Benach, Joan *et al.* 259n62
Bergère, Marie-Claire 27, 224n3, 225n6, 226–7n14, 260n2
Bergsten, Fred C. *et al.* 260n2
Berlusconi, Silvio 201
Bernes, Chris 247n63
Bernstein, Jared 255n10
Bihr, Alain 220n11
Bishop, Matthew 246n55
Bisig, Brigitte 259n64
black listing, threat of 18
Blair, Tony (and government of) 90, 111, 115
Blanden, Jo 131, 257n44, 257n45, 257n47
Blum, Léon 248n73
Blumenthyal, David 264–5n52
Bo Xilai 267n82
Bo Yobo 267n82

Bolgiani, Iva 73–4, 242–3n21, 243n25
Bonoli, Giuliano 238n124
Bottomore, Tom 225n9
Bouckaert, Geert 237n119
bourgeois socialism 38
Bouvard, François 243n26
Bowles, Samuel 242n12
Bradshaw, J. and Chen, J.-R. 125, 127
Bradshaw, Jonathan 255n15, 256n30, 256n32
Braha, Dan 271n13
Brandolini, A. and Smeeding, T.M. 120, 121
Brandolini, Andrea 56, 239n141, 256n27
Braudel, Fernand 8, 9, 33, 37, 39, 47, 107, 165, 202, 219n1, 221–2n11, 224n2, 226–7n14, 226n10, 226n11, 227n15–17, 228n26, 271n14; on capitalism 28–30; on economic activity 29–30; historical perspective on China and West 28–9; market and capitalism in case of China, approach to 30–2
British Civil Service College 20, 243n30, 249–50n86
British Medical Journal 141, 258n57, 259n61
British Rail 248n76, 275n10
British Telecom 20
Brown, Gordon (and government of) 115
Buchanan, James M. 221n4
bureaucracies: disappearance of, only with the disappearance of the society it supports 80; private bureaucracies 81; process of bureaucratization 81–2; radical challenging of 80–1
Bürgenmeier, Beat 242n13
Burham, James 248n73
Buschor, Ernst 244n33

Caijing Magazine 235–6n102
Calhoun, Craig 220n9
Canada 44, 52, 53, 54, 57; anti-poverty effect of government spending in 125, 126, 127; child poverty in 128; Gini indexes of disposable and market income in 120; HDI ranking of 130–3; income inequality in 115, 116; inequality patterns in 121
Canfora, Luciano 220n10, 229n36
Cao Tian Yu 274n42
capital, freedom and dominance of 34
capital markets 50
capitalism 8, 24, 26, 27, 28–31, 32–3, 34, 36, 37–8, 39; call for Chinese control over 208–9; capitalist states, typologies of 53–4; competition, capitalism and 30; development after Great Depression 34; international dimension of 47, 49; Li Minqi's view on 36–7; long-term trends and emergence of 29; 'Mediterranean' capitalism 53, 54; monopolistic nature of 30, 202; neo-Marxist view 36–7; strength of 37; types of 54–5; Welfare States and public management in West 51–2, 53, 54–5; in West 97
Capitalism and Freedom (Friedman, M.) 16, 74
Cardinal Principles of Party leadership 99–100
Castiglione, Giuseppe 92–3
Central Party School in Beijing 103, 253n44
centralization 44, 179, 228n25, 233–4n82; need for 83
Centre for Economic Research at Peking University 102
Champy, James 244n42
Chan Hou-Sheng 268n92
Chang, Gordon C. 260n2
Chang, Ha-Joon 223n19, 225–6n9, 241n7, 270–1n11
Chang Xiuze 164
Charlton, Andrew 223n19
Cheing, André 252n26
Chen, Jie 228n22, 253n36
Chen, Jun-Rong 255n15, 256n30, 256n32
Chen Zhu 103
Cheng Li 102, 235n99, 236n104, 237n116, 253n39, 253n40
Chi Fulin 260n2
Chi-Man, Willie *et al.* 264–5n52
Chieng, André 98, 224n27
China: adaptation to international finance 79; analysis of NPM in 11–12; capitalism, call for control over 208–9; challenges for today's leadership, suggestions for addressing 208–10; Chinese brands, development of 209; Chinese state, Party hierarchy and levels of 252n32; Civil Affairs, Ministry of 190–1, 268n103, 268n105; corruption, eradication of 209; as country embracing NPM 2–3; decision-making, openness in 208; economic developments, 'illegible script' of 205–6; economic developments, suggestions for progress on 208–9; education improvement policies 209; European Left, development of exchanges with 209; fiscal capacity, control over 209; foundation of NPM in 8, 91–105; fundamental goal,

Index 293

realization of 23; global economy, opening-up of 209; HDI ranking of 130–3; Health Economic Institute 235–6n102; *hukou* system in rural areas 184, 267n87, 268n98, 273n29; human capital, development of 23; implementation of NPM in 49–50; income improvements in, potential for 273n29; international leadership 209; international training programme in 18–21; knowledge society in 261–2n16; Labour Bulletin 180, 266n69; market fundamentalism, avoidance of 208; market mechanisms, implementation in 23; market mechanisms, management of 207–8; minimum wage, establishment of 266n67; National Bureau of Statistics (NBSC) 150, 151, 167, 260n3, 268n104, 274n38; National Development and Reform Commission (NDRC) 253n42, 254n46; National Population and Family Planning Commission 266n68, 269n111; Organization, Department of 21; Party schools, system of 103, 253n43, 254n45; Permanent Committee of the Politburo 21; perspective on 'Chinese market' and democratic model 35–47; pollution reduction policies 209; pragmatism in 22–3, 207; privatization of state-owned enterprises (SOEs) 20; public management reforms, results of 4, 7, 8–9, 12; public–private partnerships (PPPs) 209; 'putting people first', call for 208; reaction to crisis of 2008–11, opportunity for 205; 'real market' in, promotion of 209; reality and planning in 23; reform process in, markets and 25; reforms in, major dimensions of (1978–2011) 108; revision of old economic categories, need for 209; rural and migrant residents, welfare of 208; socialist development strategy, stages of 95–6; society's needs, call for market subservience to 209; State Assets Supervision and Administration Commission (SASAC) 227n19, 252n31; State Council circulars 255n 66, 266n65; state-owned enterprises (SOEs), efficiency of 209; stimulus package, post 2008–11 crisis 206–7, 273n30, 273n31; tax evasion, eradication of 209; Three Represents, theory of 45, 101, 253n35; 'Washington consensus', rejection of 19; wealth distribution, space for equity in 200; West and, differences in development stages 63, 200, 206; work force potential 273n29; *see also* Chinese experiment with NPM; Chinese New Public Management (NPM), foundation of; comparison of NPM in China and West

China: Promoting Growth with Equity (World Bank) 160
China Beat (website) 233n81
China by 2030: A Changing World towards Common Prosperity (Hu Angang) 148, 149
China Compendium of Statistics 1949–2008 (National Bureau Statistics) 150, 151
China Daily 164, 263n36
China Leadership Monitor 228n25, 253n39
China Statistical Abstract 2010 (National Bureau Statistics) 150, 151, 167
China Statistical Yearbooks (1978–2010) 170–1, 186, 188, 191–2, 196, 268n98. 268n101
Chinese experiment with NPM 145–97; agriculture, employment and GDP changes in 146; All-China Federation of Trade Unions (ACFTU) 180; annuity schemes 186; China Reform Foundation 165; Chongqing experimental zone 182–5; clean energy, production of 181; 'Coordinated Human Development', aim of 166; crime rates, NPM and 170–1; development, definition of new strategy for 179–85; development strategy, fiscal policy and new dimensions of 179–80; disparities, persistence and challenges of 197; disposable income (urban) and nominal income (rural) compared 196; economic indicators (2004–10) 146–7; economic perspective 145–59; economy and related domains, spectacular development of 146–8; educational development, improvements in 158–9; energy intensity, reductions in 181; Engel coefficient groups, population distributions of 195; European Union (EU), position of China in purchasing power parity *vis-à-vis* 147–9; exports in proportion to world totals 149; fiscal capacity, strengthening of 179; Gini index of income inequality 164, 193; health, NPM and 171–7; health costs of economic development 173–4; health indicators (WHO data) 172–3; health insecurity 174–5; health insurance in urban areas 186–8; human

294 Index

capital, improvements in 158–9; Human Resources and Social Security, Ministry of 164; income distribution and inequality, NPM and 164–8; income inequality in, comparison with West 165–6; India, position of China in purchasing power parity *vis-à-vis* 148; industrial output in proportion to world totals 150; industry, employment and GDP changes in 146; inequalities, development of 159–78; infrastructural investment 180; Japan, position of China in purchasing power parity *vis-à-vis* 148; laid-off people (*xiagang*) 162, 163; marketization, positive outcomes of 145–59; maternity insurance in urban areas 189; medical insurance 175; minimum living standard line 190–1; National Bureau of Statistics (NBSC) 193; National Development and Reform Commission (NDRC) 164; National Economic Research Institute 165; National Population and Family Planning Commission 195; OECD, imbalances report 178; OECD, poverty assessment 168–9, 169–70; old age insurance in rural areas 189–91; old age insurance in urban areas 185–6; Oxford Poverty & Human Development Initiative's (OPHI) multidimensional poverty index (MPI) 169; pension system 186, 191; population distributions of GDP per capita groups 194; poverty, manifestation of new sources of 161; poverty, NPM and 168–70; poverty assessment (UNDP) 168–9; professional training, improvements in 158–9; provincial HDI results (2008) 154–8; provincial inequalities of income and opportunities 166–8; public health, improvements in 159; rebalancing of Chinese society 178–97; rebalancing of Chinese society, evaluation of results of 192–7; reform acceleration, effects on poverty and inequalities 161; regional disparity in health 176; registered unemployment rates in urban areas 162–3; Rejuvenation of Old Industrial Bases in Northeastern China (2004) 193; renewable energy generation 181–2; Rise of Central China Strategy (2006) 193; rural cooperative medical scheme 191–2; Russia, position of China in purchasing power parity *vis-à-vis* 148; services, employment and GDP changes in 146; Sino-Singapore Tianjin Eco-city 182; social imbalances, priority of reduction of 154; social insurances 185–6; social perspective 159–78; social relief in rural areas 192; social relief in urban areas 189; social security developments 185–92; social welfare, investment in 180; state-owned enterprises (SOEs), income gaps in 164–5; support for unemployed workers 163–4; UNDP *Human Development Reports*, results for China 152–8, 164, 168–9; unemployment, NPM and 161–4; unemployment insurance in urban areas 188; United States, position of China in purchasing power parity *vis-à-vis* 148–9; urban per capita disposable income 151–2; wealth distribution in, inequality of 165–6; West Regions Strategy (2001) 193; work-related injury insurance in urban areas 188–9; World Bank, policy initiatives statement 178; World Bank, poverty assessment by 168–9; World Bank, regional disparity in health 176–7; World Watch Institute 181

Chinese New Public Management (NPM), foundation of 91–105; capitalism in West 97; Cardinal Principles of Party leadership 99–100; Central Party School in Beijing 103, 253n44; Centre for Economic Research at Peking University 102; Chinese characteristics, importance of 100–1; Communist Party, restoration of world power as fundamental goal of 94–5; context in decision-making, importance of 98; decision-making knowledge, training and 103; decision-making process, opening up of 101–5; definition of strategies 96–9; economic sphere, opening up of 100; environmental protection 104; foreign-educated returnees (*haigui*) 102; implementation of NPM, fundamentals of strategy for 99–100; international organizations, cooperation with 102–3; learning organization, Party as 104–5; legal system, organization of 98; liberal democracy in West 97; liberalization 102, 104; market mechanisms, choice of 91, 98–9; market mechanisms, introduction of 97; Marxism–Leninism 99, 101; modelling, use of 97–8; modernization, process of 95; modernization, restoratory domains

99–100; National Development and Reform Commission (NDRC) 103; non-governmental organizations (NGOs), emergence of 104, 254n47; opium wars 93; Party leadership of reform process 98–9, 99–100; People's Republic, restoration of world power as fundamental goal of 94–5; privatization 102; public policy choices 98; scientific evidence, decision-making based on 103–4; socialism, importance of reference to 100–1; state-owned enterprises (SOEs) 98; strategic thinking 96–9; superpower, emergence of China as 95–6; theory of the 'two whatevers' 99; Tiananmen Square, events (1989) in 100, 262–3n25; wealth and strength, importance of 94–6; Western superiority 93; world power, restoration of China to status of 92–6; World Trade Organization (WTO), membership of 98; Yuanmingyuan, Garden of Perfect Splendour 93

Chinese People's Political Consultative Conference (CPPCC) 235–6n102

Chongqing experimental zone 39–40, 182–5

Chow, Gregory C. 260n2

Christensen, Tom 241n6

Chun-Chien Kuo 264n38

Cicero review 271–2n19

Cinalli, Manlio 238n121

citizenship, workers and 78

Civil Affairs, Ministry of 190–1, 268n103, 268n105

clean energy, production of 181

Coase, Ronald H. 221n4, 249n81

Communist Party, restoration of world power as fundamental goal of 94–5

comparison of NPM in China and West 26–63; Australia 44, 53, 54, 57; Austria 52, 53, 54; Belgium 52, 53, 54, 57; bourgeois socialism 38; Canada 44, 52, 53, 54, 57; capital, freedom and dominance of 34; capital markets 50; capitalism 26, 27, 28–31, 32–3, 34, 36, 37–8, 39; capitalism, development after Great Depression 34; capitalism, international dimension of 47, 49; capitalism, Li Minqi's view on 36–7; capitalism, long-term trends and emergence of 29; capitalism, monopolistic nature of 30, 202; capitalism, neo-Marxist view 36–7; capitalism, strength of 37; capitalism, types of 54–5; capitalism, Welfare States and public management in West 51–2, 53, 54–5; capitalist states, typologies of 53–4; China, implementation of NPM in 49–50; China, perspective on 'Chinese market' and democratic model 35–47; Chongqing experimental zone 39–40; competition, capitalism and 30; consequences of NPM on economies 31; conservative corporatist-statist regime 52; coordinated market economies 53; crime rate data 56, 62; crisis of 2008–11, consequences of 63; crisis of 2008–11, neoliberalism and 35; data collection, problems of 56–7; democracy for China, Wang Shaoguang on 44; democracy in West, factors in decline of 41–2; Denmark 53, 54; development stages, dealing with difference in 63; development strategy for China 26–7; development strategy for China, Cui's ideas 39–40; development strategy for China, Hu's pragmatic approach 42–3; development strategy for China, Wang Hui's paradox 41; development strategy for China, Wang Hui's perspective 40–2; development strategy for China, Wang Shaoguang's perspective 43–5; economic activity, Braudel on 29–30; 'embedded market', Polanyi's idea of 44–6; empirical (or real) typology 51; employment data 56, 58; fairness, promotion of 38; financial markets 50; Finland 53, 54; France 53, 54, 57, 58; free market economy 28; free markets 26; Gender Inequality Index (GII) 62; Germany 53, 54, 57; globalization, global convergence of economic management 49; Good Governance, umbrella of 57–8; Greece 44, 53, 54; historical perspective, Braudel on 28–9; Human Development Index (HDI) 60, 61–2, 261n11, 261n12; human rights, poverty measurement and 60–1; impacts of, measurement of 55–; income distribution and inequality data 56, 58–9; institutional innovation in China 38–9; intelligentsia in 36; international regulatory mechanisms 41; international relations 46–7; Ireland 53, 54, 57; Italy 48, 53, 54, 57; Japan 53, 54; joint-stock cooperative system 38; land reform in China 40–1; liberal analysis 33; liberal countries, polarization between 52; liberal democracy, implementation of 48; liberal market economies 53;

Luxembourg Income Study (LIS) data 56; market and capitalism, Braudel on 28–30; market and capitalism in China, Braudel on 30–2; market characteristics, Chinese introduction of 31; market economy, Chinese experimentation with 27–8; market mechanisms 26, 27, 28, 30–1, 32, 33, 45, 47, 49, 50; market mechanisms, use of term 28, 31; marketization in China 38; markets 26, 29, 30, 31, 50, 51; Marxist analysis 33; material life 29; material life, partial character of market economy and 30–1; 'Mediterranean' capitalism 53, 54; monopolistic nature of capitalism 30, 202; multidimensional poverty index (MPI) 60; neoliberal analysis 33; neoliberal democracy, functioning of 34–5; neoliberalism, NPM and, link between 47–50; neoliberalism, orthodoxy of 50; neoliberalism, 'Washington consensus' and NPM, link between 50, 201, 204; neoliberals in China 46–7; Netherlands 53, 54; neutral state, role and essence of 41; 'New Left' in China 36, 37, 38, 40, 42, 43, 44–5, 46–7, 49; 'New Left' in China, influence of 45–6; New Public Management (NPM), essence of 48; New Zealand 52, 53, 54, 57, 62; Norway 53; Oxford Poverty and Human Development Initiative (OPHI) 60, 61; partnerships between workers and capitalists 38; Party in China, changes in role of 42; Party-State, monopolistic control of 31–2; petty bourgeois socialism 38; political mechanisms of liberal democracy 33–4; political system in West, rightward displacement of 34–5; Portugal 53, 54; poverty and inequality data 56, 59–62; poverty measurement, problems of 59–60; poverty or income distribution, causal links between NPM and 55–6; privatization in China 38; problems with 26; production, property of 33; production and consumption, organization of 33–4; public health data 56, 63; public management, empirical typologies in West of 51–5; public–private partnerships (PPPs) 58; Scandinavian countries 52, 54; scientific innovations in China 27–8; self-reliance in China 42; social-democratic model 52; social-democratic Scandinavian countries, polarization between 52; social policies, liberal system and 34; socialism 26, 27, 28, 36, 37, 38, 39, 52; socialist market economy in China 31–2; socialist market economy in China, progressive implementation of 32; South Korea 54; Spain 53, 54, 57; Sweden 53, 54; Switzerland 48, 52, 53, 54, 57, 62; transition for China, Wang Shaoguang on 44–5; transparency, capitalism and 30; Turkey 53; UN Development Programme (UNDP) 60, 61–2; United Kingdom 44, 52, 53, 54, 57, 58, 62; United States 44, 52, 53, 54, 57, 62; vested private interests in China 47; 'Washington consensus' 47, 49, 50; Weberian ideal-type 51; Welfare State, institution of 51–2, 54; Welfare States in West 35, 51–2, 54, 56; West, perspective on 'Chinese market' and democratic model 32–5; Western public management, types of 54; World Trade Organization (WTO) 41

competition, capitalism and 30

competitive tendering 86, 111, 248n68

Congress of the Chinese Communist Party 19; death of Deng, reform process and 19; reform, acceleration of 20; World Trade Organization membership 20

Conrad, Douglas et al. 247n65

Conservatism 24, 224n30, 237n113, 241n4, 243n24

conservative corporatist-statist regime 52

contracting out 72, 83, 89, 254n3; generalization of 90; policy of 247n65

control bodies, implementation of 89

convergence (consensus?) on NPM implementation 70–1

'Coordinated Human Development', aim of 166

coordinated market economies 53

Il Corriere della Sera 270n9

Couchepin, Pascal 244n35

Cox, David 249n81

Crettaz, Eric 238n124

crime rate data 56, 62

crisis of 2008–11: consequences of 63; EU impositions on countries as result of 201–2; market fundamentalism and 203; neoliberalism and reactions to 35, 205; opportunity for China in reaction to 205; Rachman's view of causes of 72–3; unemployment and 112–14

criticism of NPM 14, 15, 16–17, 242–3n21; intolerance of NPM advocates to 68–9

Crozier, Michel 78, 83, 245n45, 246n58

Cui Zhiyuan 38–40, 182–4, 231n56, 232n59, 232n63, 232n66, 235n95, 252n33, 267n79
Cultural Revolution 23, 44, 92, 95, 204, 207, 232n62
customer, citizen and NPM 77–8
customer satisfaction, orientation of state activity towards 86–7
Czech Republic: Gini indexes of disposable and market income in 120; inequality patterns in 121

Daily Telegraph 270n10
Danziger, S. 257n43
data collection, problems of 56–7
D'Avanzo, Barbara 259n64
debureaucratization, questions concerning 80–2
decentralization: NPM type 73, 75; principle of 86; questions concerning 83–4
Delamothe, Tony 258n57, 270n7
delegation of public tasks to private organizations 83
Delley, Jean-Daniel 70–1, 77, 242n16
democracy: for China, Wang Shaoguang on 44; NPM and democratic values 75–7; responsibilities of, problems for NPM of 89; in West, factors in decline of 41–2
Deng Xiaoping 8, 19, 38, 43, 92, 96, 99–100, 101, 104, 105, 145, 177, 179, 250n5
Denmark 53, 54; anti-poverty effect of government spending in 125, 127; child poverty in 128; Gini indexes of disposable and market income in 120; HDI ranking of 130–3; health expenditures in 139–40; health indicators in 138; income inequality in 115, 116, 118; inequality patterns in 121; unemployment in 112, 113
deregulation, questions about 82
Desia, Meghnad 273n36
development strategies: for China 26–7; Cui's ideas 39–40; Hu's pragmatic approach 42–3; Wang Hui's paradox 41; Wang Hui's perspective 40–2; Wang Shaoguang's perspective 43–5
Dickson, Bruce J. 227n20, 228n22, 253n36, 273–4n37
diffusion, beginnings of 13–14
Dilulio, Jr., John J. 246n55, 248–9n78
Dirlik, Arif 36, 230n42, 240n147
Domberger, Simon 239n135
Domenighetti, Gian-Franco 259n64

Domenighetti, Gian-Franco *et al.* 141
Dorn, James A. 263n26
Dowding, Keith 241n10
downsizing type of NPM 73, 75
Draghi, Mario 201
Durlauf, Steven N. 242n12
Dyer, Geoff 273n33

Ebrey, Patricia Buckley 94, 251n10
economic activity, Braudel on 29–30
economic efficiency 72; principle of 85–6, 250n2
economic globalization, NPM and 78–9
Economic Policy Institute 256n28, 256n34
effectiveness and efficiency of state actions, questions of 69–70
efficiency drive type of NPM 73, 74–5, 77–8
elasticity in definitions of NPM 71
Elder, Neil 248n71
'embedded liberalism' 16
'embedded market', Polanyi's idea of 44–6
Emery, Yves 222n16, 275n1
empirical (or real) typology 1–2, 51
Engels, Friedrich 231n48
entrepreneurship, service and 16
Esping-Anderson, Gosta 51–2, 54, 225n9, 230n39, 238n121, 238n124
Estonia, inequality patterns in 121
Eucken Walter 221n4
European Central Bank (ECB) 201–2
European Union (EU) 239n135, 257n39; composition of 261n7; creation of 4; crisis of 2008–11, impositions on countries as result of 201–2; decision-making process 4; indexation of wages, call for elimination of 202; labour market reforms, call for 202; neoliberal orthodoxy in 50; position of China in purchasing power parity *vis-à-vis* 147–9; structural reforms, call for substantial and comprehensive 202; wage flexibility, call for enhancement of 202
excellence, type of NPM in search of 73, 75
exclusivity, requirement for 72–3

Factbook 2009 (CIA) 149, 152
Factbook 2010 (CIA) 117, 118, 148, 162, 164, 261n8, 261n10, 262n17
Fairbank, John King 94, 251n13
fairness, promotion of 38
Fan Gang 36
Farrell, Diana 264n49
Fayol, H. 241n5
Fenby, Jonathan 251n18

Ferlie, Ewan 241n6
Ferlie, Ewan et al. 73, 74, 75, 243n22, 247n63
Ferrie, Jane E. 259n61
Fewsmith, Joseph 230n41, 231n46, 235n99, 253n39
financial and economic crisis (2008) 4, 8–9, 12; *see also* crisis of 2008–11
financial control, primacy of 87
financial markets 50, 78, 79, 84, 108, 239n133, 271–2n19
Financial Times 49, 72–3, 228n25, 262–3n25
Finkelstein, David M. 235n99, 253n39
Finland 53, 54; anti-poverty effect of government spending in 125, 126, 127; child poverty in 128; Gini indexes of disposable and market income in 120; HDI ranking of 130–3; health expenditures in 139–40; health indicators in 138; income inequality in 115, 116; inequality patterns in 121; unemployment in 113
Flora, Peter 238n121
Flückiger, Yves 242n13
Forbes Magazine International 244n40
Foreign Policy 36
Foster, John Bellamy 229–30n37, 231n53, 249n80, 254n1, 273n36
France 53, 54, 57, 58; child poverty in 128; Ecole Nationale d'Administration (ENA) 20; Gini indexes of disposable and market income in 120; HDI ranking of 130–3; health expenditures in 139–40; health indicators in 138; income inequality in 115, 116, 118; inequality patterns in 121; unemployment in 113
Francis, John 246n55
free markets: concept of 8; economy based on 26, 28
Freeman, Richard B. 257n48
Frenkiel, Emilie 44, 232n66, 235n91, 267n79
Friedman, Milton 15, 16, 46, 74, 76, 85, 98, 221n4, 221n8, 241n8, 243n27, 244n36, 247n64, 252n28
Fukuyama, Francis 244n34

Gaebler, Ted 240n2, 242n15, 249n85, 275n4
Galbraith, James K. 244n41, 248n76
Galimberti, Umberto 6–7, 220n12, 220n13
Garnaut, Ross 260n2
Gender Inequality Index (GII) 62
Geneva Graduate Institute of Developmental Studies 17
Geneva Graduate Institute of International Studies 18
George, Henry 38, 267n79
Germany 53, 54, 57; anti-poverty effect of government spending in 125, 126, 127; child poverty in 128; Gini indexes of disposable and market income in 120; HDI ranking of 130–3; health expenditures in 139–40; health indicators in 138; income inequality in 115, 116, 118; inequality patterns in 121; unemployment in 113
Gernet, Jacques 250n6
Gersch, Ulrich A. 264n49
Giddens, Anthony 33, 229n32
Gilley, Bruce 230n41
Gilmour, Robert S. 241n6, 249n83
Gini index 255–6n20, 255n19, 256n21, 263n35, 269n2; income inequality changes in West 117–20; of income inequality in China 164, 193
Girling, John 250n87
Giugni, Marco 238n121
Glasshouse Forum, Paris 234n89, 274n42
Glattfelder, James B. 271n13
globalization 24; global aggregate demand and 199; global convergence of economic management 49; rationalization and 84
Godlee, Fiona 258n57, 270n7
Goldman, Merle 94, 251n13
Good Governance, umbrella of 57–8
Goodin, Robert E. et al. 225n9
Goodman, Alyssa 255n14
Gore, Al 221n3, 243n29, 248n72
Gouldner, Alwin A. 223n23, 245n44
Grabel, Ilene 223n19
Gramsci, Antonio 267n79
Greece 44, 53, 54, 270n8; HDI ranking of 130–3; income inequality in 118; inequality patterns in 121; unemployment in 112, 113
Gregg, Paul 257n44, 257n45, 257n47
Gu Xin 235–6n102
Guidotti, Matteo 239n134
Guttmacher Institute 259n59; teenage pregnancy study 139

Haibing Ma 266n74
Hall, P., Soskice, D., and Amable, B. 113, 131
Hall, Peter A. 51, 53, 54, 225, 238n121, 238n124, 257n41
Halper, Stefan 237n112
Hammer, Michael 244n42

Hana Brixi 265n57
Harries, Stephen 258n57
Harvey, David 221n2, 221n6, 240n147, 254n1
Hayami, Yujiro 222n18, 237n112, 246n52
Hayek, Friedrich A. von 15, 46, 56, 76, 221n4, 239n132
Hayek, Nicolas G. 271–2n19
He Li 36, 45, 230n41, 230n43, 231n45, 231n46, 235n98, 235n100, 251n18
He Ping 95, 251n17
Health Effects of Job Insecurity (Domenighetti, G.-F. *et al.*) 141
Hellgren, Johnny 259n61
Henry, Nicholas 90, 246n57, 250n87
Hipgrave, David 265n57
Hobsbawm, Eric 273n36
Hobson, John M. 224n4
Hoff, Karla 242n12
Holbig, Heike 230n41
Hood, Christopher 219n2, 241n6
Horber-Papazian, Katia 214
Hsiao, William 264–5n52
Hsü, Immanuel C.Y. 94–5, 251n15
Hsu, S. Philip 274n42
Hu Angang 25, 42–3, 43–4, 45, 95–6, 146, 148, 149, 150, 154, 159, 163, 165–6, 170, 173–4, 175–6, 179, 193–5, 197, 228n26, 230n44, 233–4n82, 234n83, 234n84, 234n86, 235n96, 251n19, 257n37, 260n2, 261–2n16, 261n6, 261n15, 262n19, 262n23, 264–5n52, 264n38, 264n41, 264n50, 265n62, 265n63, 268–9n106, 268n92, 272n28
Hu Jintao 17, 22, 23, 45, 47, 101, 174, 180, 187, 197, 230n41
Hu Sheng 251n16
Hu Xudong 266n68
Huang, Philip C.C. 267n79
Huang Ping 233n80, 237n112
Huang Zhouhui 268n94
Hui Pokeung 40
hukou system in rural areas of China 184, 267n87, 268n98, 273n29
Human Development Index (HDI) 60, 61–2, 261n11, 261n12
Human Resources and Social Security, Ministry of 164, 189, 191
human rights, poverty measurement and 60–1
Hungary, inequality patterns in 121
Husson, Michel 259n65, 269n2
hypotheses 8, 19–20, 21, 25, 51, 136, 245n48; bureaucracy can disappear only with the disappearance of the society it supports 80; differences in implementation of NPM will produce different outcomes 1–2, 12, 48–9, 55, 142, 177–8, 200–1; differences in political system structures and economic relationships impact on capacity to deal with negative impacts of NPM implementation 3, 12, 142, 177–8, 200; market expansion will impact of social equity unless counterbalancing social policies are implemented 3, 11–12, 105, 142–3, 177, 178, 200, 201; poverty and inequality exhibit a positive correlation 59–62, 114, 131–4; similar public management strategies produce similar outcomes 3, 11, 12, 50, 105, 142, 177, 200

ideal-type New Public Management (NPM) 84–7
ideologies: ideological foundations of NPM 15, 68–9; policy options and 22; pragmatism and 22; timing of appearance of 24
implementation of NPM in United Kingdom 74–5
Index of Health and Social Problems (IHSP) 143
India, position of China in purchasing power parity *vis-à-vis* 148
inequalities: development of 110–42, 159–78; Gender Inequality Index (GII) 62; Gini index, income inequality changes in China 164, 193; Gini index, income inequality changes in West 117–20; health problems, link between inequalities and 143–4; income distribution, inequality data and 56, 58–9; income distribution and inequality, NPM and 114–22, 134, 164–8; income inequalities 165–6, 204; income inequalities and NPM in West 199; poverty and inequality, data on 56, 59–62; poverty and inequality, positive correlation between 59–62, 114, 131–4; provincial inequalities of income and opportunities in China 166–8; reform acceleration, effects on poverty and inequalities 161; social problems, link between inequalities and 143–4; wealth distribution in China, inequality of 165–6
Inglehart, Ronald 240n147
Institut de Hautes Etudes en Administration Publique (IDHEAP), 17–18

institutional innovation in China 38–9
intellectual support for NPM 14
intelligentsia in China 36
International Monetary Fund (IMF) 49, 50, 78, 81, 260n3, 270–1n11
international regulatory mechanisms 41
international relations 46–7, 94–5
Interpol 257n50
Ireland 53, 54, 57; anti-poverty effect of government spending in 126; child poverty in 128; HDI ranking of 130–3; health expenditures in 139–40; health indicators in 138; income inequality in 115, 116, 118; inequality patterns in 121; unemployment in 112, 113
Irvine, I. and Xu, K. 136, 257n48, 258n55
Israel: Gini indexes of disposable and market income in 120; inequality patterns in 121
Italy 48, 53, 54, 57; anti-poverty effect of government spending in 125, 126, 127; HDI ranking of 130–3; health expenditures in 139–40; health indicators in 138; income inequality in 115, 116, 118; inequality patterns in 121; unemployment in 112, 113
Iversen, Torben 238n124

Jäntti, M. 257n43
Jäntti, M. and Danziger, S. 131
Japan 53, 54; inequality patterns in 121; position of China in purchasing power parity *vis-à-vis* 148
Jiahua Pan 266n74
Jian Gao 228n25
Jiang Zemin 101, 145, 179
Jing Jin 228n25
joint-stock cooperative system 38
Joshua, Isaac 249n80, 254n1
Le Journal de Genève 14–15, 211, 274n1
Journal of Economics Perspectives 123, 126, 256n29
Journal of European Economic History 150
Jouvenel, Bertrand de 221n4
Joyce, Robert *et al.* 116, 255n18
Jr-Tsung Huang 264n38
Jullien, François 23, 224n27, 251n22, 274n44

Kangxi, Emperor of China 92–3
Kay, John 246n55
Keidel, Albert 261n9, 263n26, 269n107
Kelsey, Jane 125, 240n3, 254–5n9, 256n31, 258n53

Kennedy, Scott 233n73, 236n110, 237n112
Kernen, Antoine 268n92
Kester, I.-H. *et al.* 249n81
Kester, Isaac-Henry 247n63, 254n6
Kettl, Donald F. 247n63, 248–9n78, 249n79
Keynes, John Maynard (and Keynesianism) 15–16, 75, 207, 221n6, 229–30n37, 271n12
King David 249n79
Kivimäki, Mika *et al.* 259n61
Kivlehan, Marianne 235n99, 253n39
Korean Journal of Policy Studies 219n4
Krugman, Paul 15, 59, 88, 114, 212, 239n138, 241n6, 248n76, 255n12, 273n36, 274n2, 275n10
Kuijs, Louis 261n5
Kuo Ming-Cheng 268n92
Kynge, James 262–3n25

labour market 25, 52, 56, 73, 75, 85, 97, 108, 124, 152, 160, 180, 202, 204; competition in 169, 177; deregulation of 58, 87, 104, 111, 113–14, 139, 142, 162–3, 201, 269–70n6
Laegreid, Per 241n6
Lagarde, Christine 229n36
Lamy, Pascal 229n36
Lan Peijing 250–1n9
land reform in China 40–1
Landes, David S. 225–6n9
Lane, Jan-Erik 245n43
Lardy, Nicholas R. 260n2
Lempert, David 216–17, 222n15, 275n7
Lenin, Vladimir I. 231n48
The Leopard (Lampedusa, G. di) 205, 272n21
Leuba, Jean-François 77, 244n35
Leys, Colin 247n65, 258n57
Li Hongzhang 94
Li Keqiang 232n65
Li Minqi 36–7, 230n40, 231–2n57, 231n48, 231n50, 231n51
Li Xiguang 267–8n90, 267n89
liberal analysis 33
liberal countries, polarization between 52
liberal democracy, implementation of 48, 97
liberal market economies 53
liberalism 24, 224n29; departure from 'traditional' liberalism, NPM as 15–16; 'embedded liberalism' 16
liberalization 274n41; foundation of NPM in China and 102, 104
Lieberthal, Kenneth 94, 251n12, 251n14
Ligang Song 260n2

Light, Paul C. 248–9n78
Lim Tin Seng 268n92
Lin Yi-Min 260n2
Littré French dictionary 4–5
Liu Jingjing 264–5n52
logic of NPM: continued influence of 74–5, 81; implementational diversity of 75
Luo, Xubei 164, 262n18, 262n24, 264n44
Luxembourg, inequality patterns in 121
Luxembourg Income Study (LIS) data 56
Lynn, Jr., Laurence E. 219n2, 237n119, 241n6, 248–9n78

Ma Jun 2, 219n4, 219n5
Machin, Stephen 257n44, 257n45, 257n47
Machlup, Fritz 221n4
McIntyre, Robert S. *et al.* 271n13
McKinsey Quarterly 74, 243n26, 254n49
Madariaga, Salvador de 221n4
Maddison, Angus 148, 149
Magdoff, Fred 229–30n37, 249n80, 254n1, 273n36
Magri, Silvia 239n141
Majone, Giandomenico 246n55
Major, John (and government of) 115
management tools, adoption of 21–2
managerial power, transfers towards 87
Mao Zedong (and era of) 22, 23, 32, 33, 36, 45, 47, 63, 161, 177, 207, 231n48, 232n62; economic and social development 27–8, 39, 93–4, 95, 99, 152, 159–60, 171–2
market economy, Chinese experimentation with 27–8
market failures 88
market fundamentalism 85, 203, 204, 248n76, 274n41; avoidance of 208
market-like experiments 72
market mechanisms 8, 26, 27, 28, 30–1, 32, 33, 45, 47, 49, 50, 221–2n11; choice in China of 91, 98–9; implementation in China of 23; international economic organizations' faith in 50; introduction in China of 97; management in China of 207–8; quasi-market 69, 72, 137, 216, 219; use of term 28, 31
market-mindedness 72
marketing in public management, NPM and 79–84
marketization in China 38; positive outcomes of 145–59
markets 26, 29, 30, 31, 50, 51; and capitalism, Braudel on 28–30; and capitalism in China, Braudel on 30–2; characteristics of 242n18; characteristics of, Chinese introduction of 31; concept of 8; state and market, reinterpretation of relationship between 67–8
Marriott, Neil 258n57
Marx, Karl 231–2n57, 231n48
Marxism 32–3, 36
Marxism–Leninism 99, 101
material life 29; partial character of market economy and 30–1
Maxwell, Robert 258n57
Mayer, Colin 246n55
Meade, James E. 39, 267n79
'Mediterranean' capitalism 53, 54
Meiskins Wood, Ellen 225n9
Mellett, Howard 258n57
Meneguzzo, Marco *et al.* 242–3n21
Merckx, Véronique 242n14
Merrien, François-Xavier 268n92
Merton, Robert 223n23, 245n44
Mexico, inequality patterns in 121
Mierzejewski, Dominik 230n43
Mihn, Stephen 229–30n37
Milanovic, Branko 259n65
Mill, John Stuart 38, 232n58
Miller, Alice 236n104
Mises, Ludwig von 221n4
Mishel, Lawrence 255n10
Mishra, Pankaj 232n67
models of NPM (Ferlie and colleagues) 71–4
modernization 23, 96; economic modernization 63, 145; Four Modernizations 95; of law system 98; process in China of 95, 173, 175, 189–90; radical modernization 12; restoratory domains of 99–100; socialist modernization 43
Moe, Ronald C. 89, 241n6, 249n83
Mokyr, Joel 225–6n9
Le Monde 37, 203, 271n16
Le Monde Diplomatique 240n3
Mönks, Joost 242n19, 243n31
monopolistic nature of capitalism 30, 202
Montebourg, Arnaud 274n41
Mount Pèlerin Society 221n4
multidimensional poverty index (MPI) 60, 169, 264n47
Multilateral Agreement on Investment (MAI) 240n3, 246n53
multinational companies, interconnections between 271n13
myths and mythic status: characteristics of 4–6, 7, 204; Galimberti's view of myths

302 *Index*

of our time 6–7; justice and good faith in politics, myth of 5; rationale for mythic status of NPM 4–6

Näswall, Katharina 259n61
National Bureau of Statistics (NBSC) 150, 151, 167, 193, 260n3, 268n104, 274n38
National Development and Reform Commission (NDRC) 103, 253n42, 254n46
National Health Service (NHS) 137, 258n57
National Performance Review (NPR) 243n29
National Population and Family Planning Commission 196, 266n68, 269n111
Naughton, Barry J. 228n25, 228n29, 252n30, 260n2, 273n30
Needham, Joseph 224n5
neoliberal analysis 33
neoliberal austerity policies, effects of 202–3
neoliberal democracy, functioning of 34–5
neoliberal imposition of will of private sector 71
neoliberal project, untouchable status of 203–4
neoliberalism: consequences of 204–5; fraudulent nature of 204; irrationality of 204; link between NPM and 47–50; neoliberals in China 46–7; orthodoxy of 50; 'Washington consensus' and NPM, link between 50, 201, 204
neoliberalism, NPM and the 'Washington consensus' 6, 7, 15–17, 67–90; absolute truth 68, 69; administrative inflation 84–5; Asian crisis (1997) 79; audits, generalization of 87; bureaucracies, radical challenging of 80–1; bureaucratization, process of 81–2; centralization, need for 83; China, adaptation to international finance 79; citizenship, workers and 78; contracting out 72, 83, 89; contracting out, generalization of 90; control bodies, implementation of 89; convergence (consensus?) on NPM implementation 70–1; crisis of 2008–11, Rachman's view of causes of 72–3; criticism, intolerance of NPM advocates to 68–9; customer, citizen and NPM 77–8; customer satisfaction, orientation of state activity towards 86–7; debureaucratization, questions concerning 80–2; decentralization, NPM type 73, 75; decentralization, principle of 86; decentralization, questions concerning 83–4; delegation of public tasks to private organizations 83; democratic responsibilities, problems for NPM of 89; democratic values, NPM and 75–7; deregulation, questions about 82; downsizing type of NPM 73, 75; economic efficiency 72; economic efficiency, principle of 85–6; economic globalization, NPM and 78–9; effectiveness and efficiency of state actions, questions of 69–70; efficiency drive type of NPM 73, 74–5, 77–8; elasticity in definitions of NPM 71; excellence, type of NPM in search of 73, 75; exclusivity, requirement for 72–3; financial control, primacy of 87; globalization, rationalization and 84; ideal-type New Public Management (NPM) 84–7; ideological foundations of NPM 68–9; implementation of NPM in United Kingdom 74–5; labour market deregulation 87; logic of NPM, continued influence of 74–5, 81; logic of NPM, implementational diversity of 75; managerial power, transfers towards 87; market failures 88; market-like experiments 72; market-mindedness 72; marketing in public management, NPM and 79–84; models of NPM (Ferlie and colleagues) 71–4; neoliberal imposition of will of private sector 71; New Zealand 81; organizational functioning, necessity for evaluation of 69; performance evaluations, generalization of 87; political foundations of NPM 68–9; power transfers towards managers 87; private bureaucracies 81; privatization 83; procedures, orientation of state activity away from respect for 86–7; public debt, deficits and 87; 'public management at the service of the market' 67; public management principles of NPM, global application of 78–9; public service orientation type of NPM 73, 75; quasi-market 72; regulatory excess 84–5; savings, systematic policy of 87; service agreements within public sector 83; state and market, reinterpretation of relationship between 67–8; strategic and operational decisions, principle of separation of 86, 88; Switzerland, introduction of NPM in 70–1; Switzerland, political liberalism in 77; taxation 85; technical difficulties of

NPM 88–90; trade union marginalization 87; United Kingdom, negative consequences of implementation of NPM in 90; variants of NPM, typology of 71–5; vested interests 68; 'Washington consensus' 69; Weberian–Keynesian approach 68; Welfare State immoderation 84–5; World Bank, call to service markets 67

Netherlands 53, 54; anti-poverty effect of government spending in 125, 126, 127; child poverty in 128; Gini indexes of disposable and market income in 120; HDI ranking of 130–3; health expenditures in 139–40; health indicators in 138; income inequality in 115, 116, 118; inequality patterns in 121; unemployment in 112, 113

neutral state, role and essence of 41

'New Left' in China 36, 37, 38, 40, 42, 43, 44–5, 46–7, 49; influence of 45–6

The New Public Management in Action (Ferlie, Ewan *et al.*) 73

New Public Management (NPM): 'Administration in All Its Moods: Realizations and Consequences' 18; beneficiaries of 15; China as country embracing 2–3; criticism of 14, 15, 16–17, 242–3n21; departure from 'traditional' liberalism 15–16; diffusion, beginnings of 13–14; 'embedded liberalism' 16; empirical (or real) typology 1–2; entrepreneurship, service and 16; essence of 48; ideological basis, lack of 15; intellectual support for 14; negative consequences of implementation of 3, 17; neoliberalism and 6, 7, 15–17; and poverty or income distribution, causal links 55–6; practical weaknesses of 15; privatization, opening for 16; 'Public Management at the Service of the Market' 17; rationale for mythic status of 4–6; 'self-proclaimed new paradigm' 14; supporters of, attitudes of 14–15; Weberian ideal-type 1–2, 245n28; *see also* China; hypotheses; West

New Zealand 52, 53, 54, 57, 62, 81, 254–5n9, 258n53; child poverty in 128; HDI ranking of 130–3; health and disability system 258n58; health expenditures in 139–40; health indicators in 138; income inequality in 115, 116, 118; poverty levels in 125; unemployment in 112, 113

New Zealand Institute 256n23

Newsweek 225n8

Nolan, Peter 260n2

non-governmental organizations (NGOs) in China, emergence of 104, 254n47

Nong Zhu 164

Norway 53; anti-poverty effect of government spending in 125, 127; child poverty in 128; Gini indexes of disposable and market income in 120; HDI ranking of 130–3; health expenditures in 139–40; health indicators in 138; income inequality in 115, 116, 118; inequality patterns in 121; unemployment in 112, 113

Obama, Barack (and administration of) 225n8

Ocampo, José Antonio 237–8n120, 237n119

Ohmae, Kenichi 246n53

opium wars 93

Organisation for Economic Co-operation and Development (OECD) 50, 53, 54, 57, 168, 199, 237–8n120, 264n45; imbalances report 178; poverty assessment 168–9, 169–70; *Rural Policy Reviews: China* 264n48, 265n60; Western experiment with NPM 118, 142

Organization, Department of 21

organizational functioning, necessity for evaluation of 69

Ormerod, Paul 244n41

Osborne, David 215, 240n2, 242n15, 249n85, 275n4

Oxford Poverty & Human Development Initiative (OPHI) 61, 239n142; multidimensional poverty index (MPI) 60, 169, 264n47

Page, Edward 248n71
Painter, Chris 247n63, 254n6
Palonka, Krystyna 267n79
Parchet, Raphaël 268n92
Parkin, Michael 249n79
partnerships between workers and capitalists 38
Party in China: changes in role of 42; monopolistic control of 31–2
Paton, Calum 258n57
Peerenboom, Randal 98
performance evaluations, generalization of 87
Petrella, Riccardo 240n2
petty bourgeois socialism 38
Pickett, Kate 55, 143, 144, 238n131, 259n66

Picquier, Philippe 224n27
Pinsent Masons LLP 181, 267n76
Pirazzoli-T'Serstevens, Michèle 250n6, 250n7
Plastrik, Peter 275n4
Player, Stewart 247n65, 258n57
Poland: Gini indexes of disposable and market income in 120; inequality patterns in 121
Polanyi, Karl 44–5, 221n4, 235n93
political foundations of NPM 68–9
political mechanisms of liberal democracy 33–4
Political Science Quarterly 241–2n11
political system in West, rightward displacement of 34–5
Pollit, Christopher 214, 215, 218, 275n2
Pollock, Allyson M. 247n65, 249n82, 257n49, 258n57
Pope Clement XI 92
Popper, Karl 221n4
Portugal 53, 54; HDI ranking of 130–3; income inequality in 118; inequality patterns in 121; unemployment in 112, 113
poverty: anti-poverty effect of government spending in 125, 126, 127; child poverty 128; human rights, poverty measurement and 60–1; income distribution and poverty in West, NPM and 131–4; inequality data and 56, 59–62; multidimensional poverty index (MPI) 60, 169, 264n47; NPM and poverty or income distribution, causal links 55–6; Oxford Poverty & Human Development Initiative (OPHI) 60, 61, 169, 239n142, 264n47; poverty assessment in China (OECD) 168–9, 169–70; poverty assessment in China (UNDP) 168–9; problems of measurement of 59–60; reform acceleration in China, effects on poverty and inequalities 161; social expenditures and child poverty in West 129–30; vulnerable groups in West, poverty of 126–7; of working people in West 112; World Bank, poverty assessment in China by 168–9
Powell, G.B. 223n25
power transfers towards managers 87
Principles of Political Economy (Mill, J.S.) 38
Prins, Nomi 272n25
private bureaucracies 81
Private Finance Initiative (PFI) 248n69

privatization 83; in China 38; foundation of NPM in China and 102; opening for NPM in 16
procedures, orientation of state activity away from respect for 86–7
production: and consumption, organization of 33–4; property of 33
Proudhon, Pierre Joseph 38
Public Administration Review 18, 216
Public Body Review Programme 249–50n86
public debt, deficits and 87
public health data 56, 63
public management, empirical typologies in West of 51–5
'Public Management at the Service of the Market' 17, 67
public management principles of NPM, global application of 78–9
public–private partnerships (PPPs) 58, 209
public service orientation type of NPM 73, 75
Pye, Lucian W. 223n25

Qianlong, Emperor of China 93
Qing dynasty 27, 92, 94, 148, 156
quasi-market 69, 72, 137, 216, 219

Rachman, Gideon 49, 72–3, 224n30, 237n113, 241n4, 243n24
Ramo, Joshua Cooper 237n112, 246n52
Ran Yan 254n47
Rao, P.K. 241n4
Rappard, William 221n4
Reagan, Ronald (and administration of) 13, 90, 238n130, 246n51, 250n87
regulational excess 84–5
Rejuvenation of Old Industrial Bases in Northeastern China (2004) 193
Ren Bo 264–5n52
Report on China's State Capacity (Wang S. and Hu, A.,1993) 44
Rey, Jean-Noël 229n33
Ricardo, David 224n29
Riedel, James 228n25
Rise of Central China Strategy (2006) 193
Röber, Manfred 249n85
Robinson, K.G. 224n5
Rocard, Michel 203
Romania: Gini indexes of disposable and market income in 120; inequality patterns in 121
Roosevelt, Franklin D. 34
Röpke, Wilhelm 221n4

Rosanvallon, Pierre 225n9
Rosembloom, David H. 249n79
Roubini, Nouriel 229–30n37, 249n80, 273n36
Russia: inequality patterns in 121; position of China in purchasing power parity vis-à-vis 148; prisoners per 100,000 population in 136

Santos, Maria Emma 264n47
savings, systematic policy of 87
Scandinavian countries 52, 54; *see also* Denmark; Finland; Norway; Sweden
Schedler, Kuno 244n33
Schmitt, John 255n10
scientific innovations in China 27–8
scientist, role in strategies of reform 18
self-reliance in China 42
Selznick, Philip 223n23, 245n44
Sen, Amartya 225–6n9
Senarclens, Pierre de 78, 244n37
Sender, Henry 228n25
service agreements within public sector 83
Shanghai Daily 35
Sherman, Arlock 255n13
Sigurdson, Jon 267n79
Simon, Herbert 86, 223n24, 241n5
Sino-Singapore Tianjin Eco-city 182
Slovak Republic, inequality patterns in 121
Slovenia, inequality patterns in 121
Smeeding, Timothy M. 56, 115, 116, 122, 123, 124, 125, 126, 127, 239n141, 255n17, 256n27, 256n29, 256n33, 257n42
Smith, Adam 224n29
SNCF (French Railways) 20
social-democratic model 52
social-democratic Scandinavian countries, polarization between 52
social market economy 221n4
social policies, liberal system and 34
socialism 8, 24, 26, 27, 28, 36, 37, 38, 39, 52; importance in China of reference to 100–1
socialist market economy in China 31–2; progressive implementation of 32
Sorman, Guy 35, 230n38, 230n39, 247n60
Soskice, David 51, 53, 54, 225n9, 238n121, 238n124, 257n41
South China Morning Post 158–9, 262n21
South Korea 54
Soviet Union 38, 46, 100
Spain 53, 54, 57; anti-poverty effect of government spending in 125, 127; HDI ranking of 130–3; health expenditures in 139–40; health indicators in 138; income inequality in 118; inequality patterns in 121; unemployment in 113
Spiegel, Shari 237–8n120
Stacey, Blake 271n13
state and market, reinterpretation of relationship between 67–8
State Assets Supervision and Administration Commission (SASAC) 227n19, 252n31
The State of Working America (Economic Policy Institute) 121–2, 128, 129
state-owned enterprises (SOEs) 98; efficiency of 209; income gaps in 164–5
Statistical Communiqué for Social Security (Ministry of Labour and Social Security) 185
Stephens, John D. 238n124
Stephenson, Elisabeth 264n49
Stigler, George 221n4
Stiglitz, Joseph E. 50, 199, 203, 204, 205, 221n6, 222n18, 223n19, 225n9, 227n21, 229n36, 236n110, 237–8n120, 237n112, 237n119, 239n136, 241n4, 246n59, 248n76, 249n80, 269n3, 271n12, 271n15, 272n23, 274n40
Stone, Chad 255n13
strategic and operational decisions, principle of separation of 86, 88
strategic public management 1, 11–12, 47–9
Strauss-Kahn, Dominique 229n36
Su Nanhai 164
Suleiman, Ezra 229n35, 237n119, 265n58
Sun Tzu 91, 97, 224n27, 250n4, 251n23
Sverke, Magnus 259n61
Sweden 53, 54; anti-poverty effect of government spending in 125, 126, 127; child poverty in 128; Gini indexes of disposable and market income in 120; HDI ranking of 130–3; health expenditures in 139–40; health indicators in 138; income inequality in 115, 116; inequality patterns in 121; unemployment in 113
Sweezy, Paul 231n48
Switzerland 48, 52, 53, 54, 57, 62; adoption of NPM in 258n51, 258n52; child poverty in 128; Federal Statistical Office 255n11; Gini indexes of disposable and market income in 120; HDI ranking of 130–3; health expenditures in 139–40; health indicators in 138; income inequality in 116, 118; inequality patterns in 121; introduction of NPM

in 70–1; political liberalism in 77; self-perceived health status in 141; services and taxation in, example of 24; Swiss Federal Polytechnics, Zurich 271n13; unemployment in 112, 113

Taiwan: Gini indexes of disposable and market income in 120; inequality patterns in 121
Talbot-Smith, Alison 258n57
Tanquerel, Thierry 248n70
Targa, Beatrice 265n57
Tax Justice Network 271n13
taxation 24, 36, 55, 69, 74, 77, 85, 87, 108, 125, 127, 139, 183, 201, 212, 258n58
Taylor, W.T. 241n5
technical difficulties of NPM 88–90
Temple, Robert 224n4
Thatcher, Margaret (and government of) 13, 115, 134, 137, 246n51, 248n68
Three Represents, theory of 45, 101, 253n35
Tian Yu Cao 231–2n57
Tiananmen Square, events (1989) in 40, 100, 160, 162, 179, 205, 231n48, 262–3n25
Times of London 112, 212, 274n3
Timmins, Nicholas 270n7
Todd, Emmanuel 274n41
trade unions: marginalization of 87; rights of 248n74
Trans-Pacific Partnership (TPP) Agreement 240n3
transition for China, Wang Shaoguang on 44–5
transparency, capitalism and 30
Trichet, Jean-Claude 201–2, 270n10
Tsao, K.K. 219n4
Turkey 53

Ugrin, Krisztina 272n25
underemployment 141, 163, 200, 269–70n6
unemployment: crisis of 2008–11 and 112–14; insurance in Chinese urban areas 188; NPM in China and 161–4; NPM in West and 111–14; registered unemployment rates in Chinese urban areas 162–3
Unger, Roberto Mangabeira 225n9, 247n61
United Kingdom 44, 52, 53, 54, 57, 58, 62, 81; anti-poverty effect of government spending in 125, 126, 127; child poverty in 128; Gini indexes of disposable and market income in 120; HDI ranking of 130–3; health expenditures in 139–40; health indicators in 138; income inequality in 115, 116, 118; inequality patterns in 121; National Health Service (NHS) 270n7; negative consequences of implementation of NPM in 90; non-elderly poor in 122–3; public health arrangements 270n7; revenue distribution in 115; savings, reports of 254n4; unemployment and invalidity benefits in 112, 113
United Nations (UN): Development Programme (UNDP) 60, 61–2, 152, 153–4, 156–7, 239–40n145, 254n2, 256n24, 257n38, 261n10, 261n13, 262n20, 263n26; Human Development Index (HDI) status in West and non-Western countries 109–10, 122, 129–33; *Human Development Reports*, results for China 152–8, 164, 168–9
United States 44, 52, 53, 54, 57, 62, 81, 239n136, 248–9n78, 259n67; anti-poverty effect of government spending in 125, 126, 127; child poverty in 128; Gini indexes of disposable and market income in 120; HDI ranking of 130–3; health expenditures in 139–40; health indicators in 138; health reform in 259n60; income distribution in 114; income inequality in 115, 116, 118; inequality patterns in 121; National Performance Review (NPR) 255–6n20; neoliberal orthodoxy in 50; non-elderly poor in 122–3; position of China in purchasing power parity *vis-à-vis* 148–9; prisoners per 100,000 population in 136; Troubled Asset Relief Program 272n25; unemployment in 113
University of Geneva 13, 222, 239n134, 254n47
Urio, Paolo 137n117, 220n1, 220n7, 223n22, 223n27, 224n1, 228n24, 229n36, 230n43, 237n114, 240n1, 242n14, 244n41, 248n70, 248n77, 250n1, 253n37, 260n1, 265n55, 272n20, 274n1, 275n1, 275n8

Vahtera, Jussi *et al.* 259n61
variants of NPM, typology of 71–5
Verba, Sidney 223n25
vested interests 68; private interests in China 47
Vietnam: international training programme in 18; National Academy of Public Administration in Hanoi 18

Vitali, Stefania 271n13
Vogel, Steven K. 246n55

Wallerstein, Immanuel 37, 225–6n9, 226n10, 226n11, 231n48, 231n54
Walmsley, Roy 136, 258n55
Walsh, Kieron 254n4
Walsh, Kieron *et al.* 247n65
Wan Gang 103
Wang Hui 36, 40–2, 43–4, 205, 232n67, 232n68, 232n69, 233n70, 233n74, 233n80, 235n99, 262n23, 272n27
Wang Ming 254n47
Wang Shaoguang 43–5, 193, 197, 233–4n82, 234n87, 234n88, 234n89, 235n94, 235n97, 253n37, 262n23, 264n38, 265n62, 266n64, 268–9n106, 269n108
Wang Xiaolu 165, 264n40
Wang Yahua 260n2
Wang Yi 265n63
'Washington consensus' 6, 8, 47, 49, 50, 69, 204, 222n18, 236n108; Chinese rejection of 19
wealth: neoliberal redistribution of 204; and strength, importance for China of 94–6
Webb, Steven 255n14
Weber, Max 2, 29, 48, 51, 71–2, 80, 81, 88, 215, 219n3, 236n105, 237n119, 243n22, 243n23, 245n46, 275n11; Weberian ideal-type management 1–2, 51, 245n28; Weberian–Keynesian public sector management 68–9, 109
Webster, Charles 258n57
Weeks, John 118, 256n22
Welfare State 16; immoderation of 84–5; institution of 51–2, 54; in West 35, 51–2, 54, 56
Wen Jiabao 45, 47, 174, 228n25
West: analysis of NPM in 11–12; China and, differences in development stages 63, 200, 206; crisis of 2008–11, convergence towards NPM in dealing with 200; foundation of NPM in 8, 67–90; income inequality and NPM in 199; models and reality in 22–3; neoliberalism, effects of 199; perspective on 'Chinese market' and democratic model 32–5; public management in, types of 54; public management reforms, results of 4, 7, 8–9, 12; reform process in, markets and 25; reforms in, major dimensions of (1978–2011) 108; state role in, NPM and reduction of 24; superiority of, Chinese perspective on 93; 'Washington consensus' 199; *see also* comparison of NPM in China and West; neoliberalism, NPM and the 'Washington consensus'; Western experiment with NPM
West Regions Strategy (2001) 193
Western experiment with NPM 109–44; crime rates, NPM and 134–7; crisis of 2008–11, unemployment and 112–14; development of economic power 109–10; economic perspective 109–10; Gini index, income inequality changes in West 117–20; Guttmacher Institute, teenage pregnancy study 139; health, NPM and 137–42; health problems, link between inequalities and 143–4; income distribution and inequality, NPM and 114–22, 134; income distribution and poverty, NPM and 131–4; inequalities, development of 110–42; intergenerational mobility, NPM and 131–4; labour market deregulation 111–12; National Health Service (NHS) 137; non-elderly poor 122–3; OECD 118, 142; part-time working 111; poverty, NPM and 122–33, 134; poverty of working people 112; social expenditures and child poverty 129–30; social perspective 110–42; social policies, impact of 123–4; social problems, link between inequalities and 143–4; *The State of Working America* (Economic Policy Institute) 121–2, 128, 129; UNDP, Human Development Index (HDI) status in West and non-Western countries 109–10, 122, 129–33; unemployment, NPM and 111–14; vulnerable groups, poverty in 126–7; World Health Organization (WHO) 137
White, Martin King 262n23
Wilkinson, Richard 55, 143, 144, 238n131, 259n66
Williamson, John 222n18, 236n108, 236n110, 246n52
Williamson, Oliver E. 249n81
Wilson, Woodrow 86, 241–2n11, 247n66
Woodward, David 60–1, 239n143
'working poor' 35, 70, 141, 242n12
World Bank 17, 49, 50, 78, 81, 143, 253n42, 260n2, 260n3, 260n4, 261n5, 263n32, 263n34, 264–5n52, 264n46, 264n51, 265n61, 267n77, 270–1n11; call to service markets 67; *China 2020: Development Challenges in the New*

Century 221n10, 240n3, 260n2, 269n1; *China 2020: Development Challenges in the New Century* (1997) 240n3; 'Empowering China's green growth' (2011) 266n75; *Mid-Term Evaluation of China's 11th 5 Year Plan* (2009) 180–2, 266n70; policy initiatives statement 178; poverty assessment in China by 168–9; regional disparity in Chinese health 176–7

World Development Indicators 2009 (World Bank) 149

World Development Indicators 2011 (World Bank) 150

The World Economy: A Millennial Perspective (Maddison, A.) 148, 149

World Health Organization (WHO) 137; *World Health Statistics* (2010) 140

World Prison Population List (Walmsley, R.) 136

World Trade Organization (WTO) 41, 50, 78, 270–1n11; Chinese membership of 98

World Watch Institute 181, 266n71, 266n72

Worthley, J.A. 219n4

Wu Jinglian 260n2

Wu Xiaoying 148, 149

Xingua News Agency 267n80

Xu Youyu 230n41

Yan Mu 265n57

Yang Yansui 186, 268n94

Yang Yongheng 165–6, 264n41

Yangzheng, Emperor of China 93

Ying Zhang 266n74

Yip, Winnie 264–5n52

Yiyi Lu 254n47

Yu-Shan Wu 274n42

Yuanmingyuan, Garden of Perfect Splendour 93; plunder of 250–1n9

Zacher, Hans F. 268n92

Zakaria, Fareed 225n7

Zeng Peiyan 253n39

Zhang Xudong 240n147

Zhang Yongle 233n80

Zhang Yongnian 46

Zhang Zhibin 2, 219n4, 219n5, 252n30

Zhao, Li 228n26

Zhao Litao 268n92

Zhao Suisheng 274n42

Zheng Yongnian 231n46, 232n60, 232n62, 233–4n82, 235n100, 235n101, 236n103

Zhu Jie 250–1n9

Zhu Nong 262n18, 262n24, 264n44

Zhu Rongji 98

Zhu Suli 98, 252n25

Zizek, Slavoj 273n36

Zou Ping 265n63

Zufferey, Nicolas 252n29

Routledge International Handbooks is an outstanding, award-winning series that provides cutting-edge overviews of classic research, current research and future trends in Social Science, Humanities and STM.

Each *Handbook*:

- is introduced and contextualised by leading figures in the field
- features specially commissioned original essays
- draws upon an international team of expert contributors
- provides a comprehensive overview of a sub-discipline.

Routledge International Handbooks aim to address new developments in the sphere, while at the same time providing an authoritative guide to theory and method, the key sub-disciplines and the primary debates of today.

If you would like more information on our on-going *Handbooks* publishing programme, please contact us.

**Tel: +44 (0)20 701 76566
Email: reference@routledge.com**

www.routledge.com/reference

ROUTLEDGE Revivals

Are there some elusive titles you've been searching for but thought you'd never be able to find?

Well this may be the end of your quest. We now offer a fantastic opportunity to discover past brilliance and purchase previously out of print and unavailable titles by some of the greatest academic scholars of the last 120 years.

Routledge Revivals is an exciting new programme whereby key titles from the distinguished and extensive backlists of the many acclaimed imprints associated with Routledge are re-issued.

The programme draws upon the backlists of Kegan Paul, Trench & Trubner, Routledge & Kegan Paul, Methuen, Allen & Unwin and Routledge itself.

Routledge Revivals spans the whole of the Humanities and Social Sciences, and includes works by scholars such as Emile Durkheim, Max Weber, Simone Weil and Martin Buber.

FOR MORE INFORMATION

Please email us at **reference@routledge.com** or visit: **www.routledge.com/books/series/Routledge_Revivals**

www.routledge.com